MINOR PROPHETS FOR LIVING

MINOR PROPHETS FOR LIVING
Daily Prayers, Wisdom, and Guidance

Mark Lanier

1845BOOKS

Book Design by Baylor University Press

Cover Design by *the*BookDesigners
Cover image © Shutterstock/ArtMari

Hardcover ISBN: 978-1-4813-2098-6
Paperback ISBN: 978-1-4813-2099-3

Library of Congress Control Number: 2023917236

Dedicated to my sweet wife, Becky, a student of the Word, and my mom, Mimi, who taught me to love the Word

ACKNOWLEDGMENTS

Few people produce a daily devotional and teaching on the twelve pro-phetic books that, owing to their smaller size, are often called the "Minor Prophets." These prophets lived over several centuries of Israel and Judah's history. Their messages spoke the word of the Lord to their day and still reverberate with the student who studies them today.

This effort is to bring those books to a larger audience, seeking to find not only teaching in their chapters and verses but also inspiration. My pre-scription for this devotional book is simple: take one a day!

Special thanks to the many who made this book far better than it would have been otherwise. The eagle-eye edits of Harvey Brown and Skip McBride were critical to the final product. Michelle and Gary Rendsburg found much to change, reading it aloud together and bringing their superb knowledge and love to this project. My class at Champion Forest Baptist Church served as my sounding board as I taught through the Minor Proph-ets. The support of Pastor Jarrett Stephens and Pastor David Fleming was deeply appreciated. The insights of Dr. David Capes aided me in my writing as well. I am always indebted to my Hebrew professors, Theo Klein, Rodney Cloud, and Clyde Miller.

My family inspires me to write, and I want my work to speak into the lives of my mother, Carolyn ("Mimi"); my wife, Becky; and our chil-dren, Will and Nora Danielson-Lanier, Gracie and JT Thee, Rachel and Lee Cirsch, Rebecca and Daniel Navid, and Sarah Lanier, along with her fiancée Jack Sparks. Our grandchildren were constantly in my mind in prayer as I wrote, and I hope this book is a blessing to each of them in life: Ebba and Francis Danielson-Lanier; John Henry, Lydia, Abigail, and Zoey Thee; and Cloe, Mia, Violet, and Caleb Cirsch.

Thanks also to the amazing people at Baylor University Press (Dave Nelson, Jenny Hunt, Cade Jarrell) as well as the strong editorial and pro-duction staff at Scribe Inc. I appreciate all your hard work and support.

Pronunciation note: In writing Hebrew words into their English sounds, I have used the conventional /ḥ/ for the Hebrew letter ח. This sound is guttural, where one sounds a bit like they are clearing their throat while pronouncing an *h* sound.

May God use this effort to his glory.

JANUARY 1

The word of the Lord *that came to Joel, the son of Pethuel.* (Joel 1:1)

One day long ago, when I was in middle school, my mom won a turntable! She had attended the grand opening of a store, and the store had a drawing for various gifts. I was so excited. We didn't have a sound system, and a first-class record player seemed super. She brought it home, we plugged it in, and it produced zippo! No sound. None at all. My great records were useless. I read the instructions and realized that the turntable didn't have any speakers! Without speakers, the system was useless.

Speakers don't create the songs. But without them, you can't hear the music. Speakers take recorded sound from others and turn it into audible sound for our benefit and pleasure. We want and need good speakers, but only so we can hear the beautiful music.

In high-fidelity terms, Joel was a speaker. He didn't write the songs; he was merely the mouthpiece through which God delivered his message. As we read the message of Joel, as with the other prophets, we are reading the message of God.

It should surprise no one that God speaks. God is not an absent parent. He didn't set this world into motion only to ignore it. He loves his creation, each one of us. His eyes observe our comings and goings, and he wants to help us in our lives. He knows that we need language to grow and thrive. People use words to talk, read, and even think. So for God to speak to us, we can rightly expect he would use words.

This devotional is written for January 1. It is the start of a new year. What can we expect this year? It will certainly include an interested God seeking to communicate his messages to listening ears. I want and need to be a listening ear. Listening takes hard work because of the distractions of life. I need to focus on God and his word as he expresses it through speakers like Joel.

The sweetest song is useless without speakers to make it heard. God has spoken. He has produced and secured his word. My goal this year is to hear it and let it infuse my life with meaning, direction, and blessing.

Lord, as you speak to me, please give me ears to listen carefully! I pray in your name, amen.

JANUARY 2

The word of the LORD *that came to Joel, the son of Pethuel.* (Joel 1:1)

My parents named me William Mark Lanier, in part after my father, William Howard Lanier. They didn't give me Dad's full name because they weren't too fond of *Howard*. To keep me distinct from Dad, they called me by my middle name: Mark. I like Mark. It is easy to say and easy to spell. Mark is a biblical name, but at its root, it seems to come from Mars, the Roman god of war.

I don't want to change my name, but if I were looking for a new one, the name *Joel* wouldn't be a bad one to earn. I say "to earn" because simply having a name might not be much more than having a melodic sound or syllable with some element of coolness. No. To me, the beauty of the name *Joel* is its meaning. The Hebrew *yoel* (יוֹאֵל) means "whose God is Jehovah (or 'YHWH')." That is a name to earn. This is why I spend a second day on the same verse as yesterday.

Different people have different gods, but as Bob Dylan sang in his song "Gotta Serve Somebody," "You're gonna have to serve somebody." I know people who worship fame. It was said of a friend of mine, "The easiest way to get hurt is to get between him and a reporter." I know people who worship money. Another friend made it his goal in life to accumulate the greatest net worth possible. I know others who worship popularity, bending their ethics and behaviors to be liked and even adored by a group.

Joel's God was the God of Scripture. He is the Creator and Sustainer of the universe. As we saw yesterday, he speaks to us. He reveals himself in creation, history, and Scripture so that people will come to him and walk in a relationship with him. He consoles the brokenhearted and gives direction to the lost, purpose to the aimless, joy to those weeping, comfort to those mourning, and life to those dying. In Christian understanding, he willingly gave of himself to offer eternal life to humanity. Joel worshiped the real God, not some useless idol.

Joel likely came by his character and name because of a deep family commitment to God. This same passage tells that Joel's father—who, following ancient customs, would have picked Joel's name—was Pethuel. *Pethuel* (פְּתוּאֵל) likely means "the open-heartedness or sincerity of God." Joel's dad, who knew the sincerity of God, picked Joel's name with the hope and promise that his son would worship Jehovah God. That's my hope for me and my children too!

Lord, may I worship you alone. May I follow you faithfully. In your name, amen.

JANUARY 3

Hear this, you elders; give ear, all inhabitants of the land! Has such a thing happened in your days, or in the days of your fathers? (Joel 1:2)

As a young man beginning my adult journey, I found myself fairly fresh out of law school, getting established in a new city and a new job. I joined a new church, began teaching a class there, and became part of the preaching rotation. I desperately wanted to help people, blessing them in my teachings as well as by plugging into their lives. I found one older lady to be particularly difficult. We seemed to be on totally different wavelengths. It was as if we used the same words but different languages. In truth, while I had tried to connect with her, I got to a point where I tried harder just to avoid her.

One day, I heard of a death in her family. I saw her in church and told her, "I heard about your loved one. I know how you must feel, and I am praying for you all." She snapped at me in response and said, "You have no idea how I feel! Everyone feels differently. Until you are me, with my life experiences, going through what I am going through, you will never know how I feel!" I apologized.

Today's passage reminds me of that encounter almost forty years ago. Joel is delivering the prophetic word of the Lord, and he begins by affirming that no one has ever faced what the people were about to go through. Their life events would soon be unlike anything anyone had experienced or heard.

Life is that way. While in one sense, we all go through life with a common set of experiences—events that produce joy, grief, excitement, tedium, companionship, loneliness, satisfaction, frustration, peace, fear, and more—we also experience each uniquely. Joel needed to teach the people (and us!) that God is at work in all of life.

In the uniqueness of life experiences, God is the constant. God is always present and plugged in. No one experiences anything without the involvement of God. As I go through today, I can affirm that I don't walk in anyone else's exact path, yet no one walks alone. Wherever we are, God is there. God knows what we are going through.

Lord, thank you that you are with me today. Please give me awareness of your presence. In your name, amen.

JANUARY 4

Tell your children of it, and let your children tell their children, and their children to another generation. (Joel 1:3)

God blessed us with five children (four more if we count their spouses) and, as of this writing, ten grandchildren. They live throughout the United States, and it is rare that Becky and I get to be with all eighteen of them at once. One year, we had planned a family vacation, and it seemed almost all the children, spouses, and grandchildren would get to join. (Our newlywed daughter and son-in-law couldn't make it, as he was in his second year of medical school and would already be in class.)

We were all disappointed at who wouldn't be there but still delighted that the rest of us would have family time. One late afternoon, we walked into our vacation home and found our newlywed couple standing with their arms in the air, shouting, "Surprise!" The joy was beyond description.

We want to share good times with our families. That is natural. It gives us delight in the moment and great memories in the future. We find ourselves reflecting back on rich family times with gratitude and joy. How we spend those rare times together is important. Some families can't get together without fussing and fighting. For some, family encounters are painful.

Joel makes an important point about families early in his prophetic book. Joel is speaking about some experiences that are about to unfold in the lives of God's people. The coming events were not chance. They were coming under the eyes of a watchful God.

Joel wants his listeners to share God's work with their families. He tells them to speak about the hand of God to their children. Joel wants the grandchildren to hear God's message. Even the great-grandchildren. What God does in our lives should never happen in a vacuum. We should never fail to see God at work, and we should intentionally speak of his work to those we love. I write my devotional with Joel's words in my ears. I heard the message from my parents, now speak it to my family, and hope they will speak it to future generations.

No family event is complete without recognizing the presence of God. See God, speak of God, and make him known—to each generation.

Lord, may I always proclaim your mighty hand to all. By your grace, amen.

JANUARY 5

What the cutting locust left, the swarming locust has eaten. What the swarming locust left, the hopping locust has eaten, and what the hopping locust left, the destroying locust has eaten. (Joel 1:4)

Judge Ted Poe told of the time he had to determine whether a five-year-old child was competent to testify in his court. The key for a judge is to determine whether the child understands the difference between a lie and the truth as well as the consequences of perjury. With a court reporter in tow, Judge Poe took the young girl into chambers. After sitting with her, he explained why he had to talk with her before deciding if she could testify. Then he asked her, "Do you know the difference between a lie and the truth?" The girl answered, "The truth is real; a lie is made up." Satisfied, the judge asked the appropriate follow-up question, "Do you know what would happen if you told a lie?" She said, "I would go to hell!" Swallowing his laugh, the judge then asked, "But do you know what would happen if you told a lie in my court?" The child looked at him sincerely and asked, "What is worse than going to hell?" Judge Poe let her testify.

Some things are so bad that it seems nothing could be worse. So it was with today's passage. One set of locusts swept the crops and cut them, ruining them for the people. Could it be any worse? Yes! A second swarm of locusts came through, eating anything that survived the cutting locusts. Could it get worse? Yes! Then the hopping locusts came through, snatching anything left. Could it get worse? Yes! Finally, a fourth type of locust (Joel uses a different word for each kind) came through, destroying any shred of crop remaining.

We might believe we are on the cusp of things being so bad they can get no worse. But we are wrong. I was complaining once to my older sister, "It can't get any worse!" Kathryn gave me a stern look, shook her finger at me adamantly, and said, *"Never challenge worse!"*

I knew an alcoholic who was forced into treatment. After over a month in inpatient care, he got out. He went a day before turning back to alcohol. It wasn't until he "hit rock bottom" that he found the way out. I don't want to be that way. I don't want God to have to send swarm after swarm of locusts into my life to get my attention. I want to pay attention today. I want to get serious about my faith and my service to God and find his strength to grow in holiness *today*!

Lord, give me strength and wisdom to grow before you today. In your name, amen.

JANUARY 6

Awake, you drunkards, and weep, and wail, all you drinkers of wine, because of the sweet wine, for it is cut off from your mouth. For a nation has come up against my land, powerful and beyond number. (Joel 1:5–6)

I found myself one thousand miles from home in a stressful six-week trial. The case was pending in the Midwest, and I was living in Houston. The lawyers for the other side were specialists flown in from New York City to defend a major international company. Each day was spent in the courtroom, and each night I would huddle with my team and work late into the night in preparation for the next day.

I knew the lawyers on the other side. They were good lawyers who had earned their reputations as some of the nation's best. One of their lead lawyers, it seemed, had a problem. He arrived each morning to trial a bit off his game. Perhaps it was the stress of a complex trial. But my team had another possible explanation. One of them saw him one night at his hotel bar, drinking when we were in the middle of a trial. Maybe, my team member said, he was drinking a bit too much to reduce the trial stress.

Pay attention! That is today's phrase for life; it is also the impact of today's passage. The nation of Judah was about to encounter great difficulties. Judgment was coming on the nation. But the people were numb to the events. They were drunk, at least in a metaphorical sense. They were so busy satisfying their own pleasures that they were missing what was happening and why it was happening.

Centuries later, people said, "Nero fiddled while Rome burned." The idea is the same. All too often, while life is happening, people are focused on matters that ultimately are trivial, like their favorite TV shows or sports teams. Sometimes, anesthetized to the true significance of events, we get distracted by life. Other times, the diversion from attentiveness arises from business, or we become so busy that we become insensitive. Some people are simply too selfish to care about other's troubles. And yes, some are too drunk to be sensitive to the moment.

My buddy thought he was winning his case, and until the jury returned its verdict, he never saw his ship sinking. But sink it did. His experience was a twenty-first-century one found in Joel's instruction: Wake up! Sober up! God is at work. The world is happening around you. See it, understand it, experience it, and work for good!

Lord, open my eyes to see this world. Tune my heart to respond. In you, amen.

JANUARY 7

Lament like a virgin wearing sackcloth for the bridegroom of her youth. (Joel 1:8)

We were on a family vacation, and one of our family was holding our two-month-old grandson while his mother (our daughter) took a much-needed shower! The sweet little boy was wailing. This was not a low-volume cry but the wail of an infant who wanted his mother and wasn't going to be satisfied with anyone else. I took the boy from the arms of his aunt and got a pacifier. I adjusted him, gave him the pacifier, jiggled him, sang to him, and voilà: he kept wailing! OK, after another five minutes, I finally got him to quit, proclaiming myself the baby whisperer, but he had quite the persistent ear-piercing cry for a while.

"Wail" is a good way to translate the first word in today's passage. It is the Hebrew *eli* (אֵלִי), which sounds like "ey-lee"—kind of a wailing sound. Translated "lament" above, it is in the imperative form of the verb, meaning that it is a command. Unlike my grandson, whose wailing we were trying to stop, this verse instructs the people TO wail!

There is a time and place for lamenting. There are tragedies in life that unfold around us. We should not be dismissive of our own misfortunes and setbacks, nor those of others. Some confront tragedy with chemical aids, seeking to drown sorrows in alcohol or to find an opiate to dull the pain. But Joel is instructing his listeners to do something quite different. He instructs them to wail away.

Lamenting the tragedies that unfold in life is part of the human experience. But it is more than that. It recognizes the true hurt experienced in this fallen and sinful world. Our world can be a world of pain. We should never be happy with the pain, nor should we be dismissive of it. We should see it for what it is, lament it, wail about it, and search for ways to address it.

For Christians, this is exemplified by Jesus, who knew the human power of lamenting. When Mary and Martha's brother Lazarus was dead, and Mary and Martha were wailing over his death, Jesus also wept. This was the Jesus who would shortly resurrect Lazarus, yet the wailing was still important. Wailing was a necessary part of the healing process. It is the proper human response to the devastation and hurt of sin.

Lord, never let me run from pain. Help me to find comfort in you in my lamentation. In your name, amen.

JANUARY 8

The grain offering and the drink offering are cut off from the house of the LORD. *The priests mourn, the ministers of the* LORD. *The fields are destroyed, the ground mourns, because the grain is destroyed, the wine dries up, the oil languishes.* (Joel 1:9-10)

I hate sin. It is sneaky, it seduces, and it appears tasty. But in the end, it's always destructive. As a lawyer, I have seen this firsthand. I've watched people joyfully get inebriated. I've also seen lives destroyed by a drunk driver blowing through a red light. I know of people who have pursued infidelity. I've also seen families deal with the wreckage of broken marriages and homes. I've seen people lie to others and to themselves. Like falling dominoes, the consequences and ravages of sin go on and on.

The effects of sin take front and center in today's passage. Joel has prophesied that an upcoming ecological disaster is going to take Judah by storm—a locust storm! This storm would destroy crops so severely that the people won't have the necessary supplies to sacrifice to the Lord. The people mourn, the priests mourn, and even the ground mourns the devastation.

How one sees the locust plague depends on whether one looks upon it through human eyes or through eyes of faith. From a human perspective, the locusts that have multiplied and matured without adequate natural predators produce a ravenous army that devours all crops and vegetation. But through the eyes of faith, this devastation is a result of sin.

God didn't make the world for locusts to rule the day. God designed humanity to live in paradise. Rebellion against God is a rebellion against his blessings. Like a cancerous cell that alters DNA in ways that destroy the body, so humanity's sin alters the earth's DNA (metaphorically speaking) such that it turns on itself. Sin assuredly brings devastation, just as putting one's finger in fire produces a burn.

My question is simple: Why, when I know the consequences of sin, am I so beguiled by it? Why don't I flee from sin? The same goes for us. Oh, maybe we avoid the "big" sins, but what about worrying (i.e., lacking faith)? Gossiping? Judging others? Expressing anger? What about . . . ?

Lord, I repent of my sin. Give me eyes to see through the enticement of sin and the strength to live more holy for you. In your name, amen.

JANUARY 9

The vine dries up; the fig tree languishes. Pomegranate, palm, and apple, all the trees of the field are dried up, and gladness dries up from the children of man. (Joel 1:12)

One of my earliest memories is going to Vacation Bible School (VBS) at church. That summer week was undoubtedly a time of rest for Mom, but it was also a time of learning and fun for me as a kid. I believe it was at VBS that I first learned the song "I've got the joy, joy, joy, joy down in my heart. Down in my heart. Down in my heart. I've got the joy, joy, joy, joy down in my heart. Down in my heart to stay."

That joy—gladness—was missing among the children of Joel's prophecy. Their joy was going to dry up as the land lay barren, devoured by the locust swarm. Instead of feeling joy, the children would be crying in hunger, experiencing the homelife of frustrated and worried parents who had no solutions to life's urgent need to eat. All their food came locally, so they couldn't go to the grocery store to buy food shipped in from overseas, where there was no drought.

Joel's prophecy is rooted in the realization of sin producing judgment—a judgment that destroys normalcy in life. As noted in yesterday's passage, the consequences of sin affected the people, even the priests. Today, we see it affects even the children.

Sin is that strong. It wreaks havoc on even the youngest and most defenseless. One day, I was entertaining questions from college students at Wheaton, a Christian campus in the upper Midwest. One student asked me why a good God would allow an opioid addict who sells her body to feed her habit to bring a child into this world. I explained that God didn't create a computer program that runs this world. You and I aren't software with each move determined. Humans get to make real choices that have real consequences. God isn't the celestial birth-control device.

God mourns sin. Sin isn't a good or even neutral thing. It produces death, as he warns the people through Joel, just as he warned Adam and Eve earlier. Yet we exercise our free will to pick sin over and over. It hurts us and robs even children of the joy in life. True joy in life comes only from victory over sin. That is a joy to stay.

Lord, please work out your victory over the sin in my life. I pray joyfully in your name, amen.

JANUARY 10

Consecrate a fast; call a solemn assembly. Gather the elders and all the inhabitants of the land to the house of the LORD your God, and cry out to the LORD. (Joel 1:14)

The day turned bad before I had breakfast. I found out some really troubling news. It leaked into my inbox first but was followed by phone calls from a variety of sources. With each revelation, the news didn't get better; it got worse. The horrible pit in my stomach grew. I was ready to crawl into a hole and let the world go by while I disappeared.

I'm not a medical doctor, but I know to take aspirin or ibuprofen to reduce a fever. Similarly, I know the "religious prescription" for dealing with bad problems. "Take it to God" is the pious prescription. Yet "take it to God" always sounds easy until the problems are deep. Then it can border on a platitude.

So what do we make of today's passage? Joel has shown the spotlight on serious life-changing trouble coming down the road as a consequence of the nation's sin. Severe suffering is right around the corner. In response, Joel doesn't give a religious platitude. He gives detailed instructions.

Joel tells the people to fast and to consecrate that fast. This instruction isn't simply to skip eating; it's to sacrifice time, energy, and personal desire in order to vigilantly pray and seek God's counsel. He then urges the people to gather with others who know God. People of common faith and communal love can share one another's burdens. They can also give greater insights. Joel then tells the people to "cry out to the LORD" (emphasis mine). This is a cry for help. This is a cry of repentance. This is a cry of faith. One can fast. One can get counsel and human help. But the final step is to lay before God all one's thoughts, feelings, worries, and concerns and let the God of power and mercy extend his compassion. God will not leave the penitent alone.

My day's problems didn't resolve in an hour. That happens only on television. The troubles continued through the week, through the month, and over the next year. But God never abandoned me. With my wife and friends in tow, through prayer and constant outpouring to God, resolution came. Healing came. God came through.

Lord, help me place my trust and focus in you as times are tough. Give me godly friends to stand with me in trouble. Keep me close. In your name, amen.

JANUARY 11

Alas for the day! For the day of the LORD is near, and as destruction from the Almighty it comes. (Joel 1:15)

I don't like messes, even though I frequently make them! But I still don't like them. One year, we had an overseas vacation with twenty-one people in the family coming, some for several weeks. Because so much was hard to pack, almost everyone ordered a number of items online for delivery to the vacation house. By the time we arrived, the place was loaded with boxes. A number of our family are quite ecologically minded, so merely throwing away the trash would never do. There were piles and piles of various types of recycling. It gave me a rash—an emotional rash, not a real physical one. I wanted the trash all destroyed, not lying around taunting me.

Trash should be destroyed. It can be recycled, buried, or burned, but it should be destroyed. It has no place in a beautiful, well-kept house. Which brings me to today's passage.

Joel speaks of the "day of the LORD" (emphasis mine). This is an important idea in the prophets, but it is also a metanarrative of the entire Bible. The "day of the LORD" is the judgment that God will bring upon all creation. It is trash day, when God takes out the garbage. The prophets describe it as a day of devastation. Ungodliness is destroyed. God sits in judgment over evil and terminates it finally and irreversibly. God burns up anything and everything that usurped his rightful place in the lives of people and on earth.

This universal destruction is a divine appointment. It's coming most assuredly. The key for me, and for you, is where we stand on that day. I know that my life is riddled with bad choices and times of outright rebellion, selfishness, envy, and self-focus that result in times of self-pity, self-centeredness, and even self-aggrandizement. My life is full of the dirty garbage, and the day of the Lord is a day of dread *but for the mercy and forgiveness of God.*

As a Christian, I believe God manifests his mercy and forgiveness by taking on my garbage, much like an insurance company takes on responsibility for a wreck. I receive coverage from God, and he graciously provides me with cleanliness and righteousness so I don't fear the day of the Lord. Whew!!!

Lord, I confess I need your loving forgiveness. Please save me in your name, amen.

JANUARY 12

*To you, O L*ORD*, I call. For fire has devoured the pastures of the wilderness, and flame has burned all the trees of the field. Even the beasts of the field pant for you because the water brooks are dried up, and fire has devoured the pastures of the wilderness.* (Joel 1:19–20)

I'm a citizen of the United States, but I get to travel outside the country quite a bit. Once when I was in England, I was washing a glass that broke and gashed my ring finger, nicking a blood vessel and producing enough blood to make the kitchen look like a slaughterhouse. England has national health care, and the system is truly foreign to me. I didn't know who to call or where to go for help. So wrapping my finger with paper towels, I tried to stop the blood from baptizing my keyboard as I searched the internet for medical care late on a Saturday night in the Cotswold countryside of England. I found a hospital fifteen minutes away and was able to get some help.

It worked out surprisingly well. But things aren't always so simple. Today's passage gives an illustration from the mouth of Joel, a prophet who lived 2,700 years ago.

Catastrophe is falling on the country. The destruction is so complete that even animals are perplexed. (It's a metaphorical illustration of deep grief and misery.) The prophet doesn't need to check the internet for the right place to go. The prophet knows the answer. Call on the Lord!

God is the right place to go when times are tough. We might understand why the crisis exists, or it might perplex us. It may challenge our sensibility of what is right or fair. Yet God rises above the understanding and comprehension of our three-pound brains. The all-seeing God has a plan for the universe and a plan for you and me. His plans are intricate, finer than the beating of a butterfly's wings. In the midst of these plans, you and I live. The world lives around us.

We can live trusting that God sees, God cares, and God doesn't forget us. So when we find ourselves gashed on the broken glass of life, we might not understand, but we don't need the internet for instructions. We can call on God, who is ready to listen and help, twenty-four hours a day, every day of the year.

Lord, be my help in the struggles of life. Please come to my aid. In your name, amen.

JANUARY 13

Blow a trumpet in Zion; sound an alarm on my holy mountain! (Joel 2:1)

I grew up a child of the Cold War. We were taught that nuclear annihilation might be right around the corner. Even in elementary school, I can remember "nuclear drills." An alarm would sound, and the teacher would stop teaching immediately, instructing all students to get under their desks and remain there until the drill was over. Once I grew up, I realized the absurdity of thinking that hiding under my desk at Vollmer Elementary would save me from the nuclear fallout of a world war!

Sounding alarms wasn't a twentieth-century invention. Alarms have signaled important events throughout the history of the world. At the time of the prophet Joel, the alarm was generally a *shofar*, or a ram's horn. The horn had the marrow removed, and holes were made at both ends. Blowing into the small end could produce a loud sound. In today's passage, *shofar* is translated as "trumpet."

The shofar was sounded often, from New Year's services (Rosh Hashanah) to times of battle as well as in parts of various temple services. Joel instructs the priests to blow the shofar from the temple grounds at the top of Mount Zion. The temple was also called the "house of the LORD," although Israel understood that no human house could truly contain God. But the prophet wants us to understand that the trumpet is a proclamation of God. God is having the trumpet sounded as an alarm. It's God's battle cry. It's a shout into the people's lives. Listen carefully! This is important!

God sounds the trumpet to warn that decisions come with consequences. We're naïve to think that we know all the consequences of our actions. God's instructions to us are for *our* good, to maximize our benefits and blessings. Over 750 years later, the Apostle Paul would write it this way: "Do not be deceived: God is not mocked, for whatever one sows, that will he also reap" (Gal. 6:7). This should cause us to tremble. Especially people of faith should realize that even though God is merciful and forgiving, life is still full of consequences. If someone puts their finger in fire, it will burn. As I focus on my actions today, in faith, I am going to try to make righteous decisions, trusting in the warning of God.

Lord, give me focus and presence of mind and heart to make righteous decisions today, in large things and small things. May my choices in life reflect my appreciation of your warnings and instructions. In your name, amen.

JANUARY 14

Let all the inhabitants of the land tremble, for the day of the LORD is coming; it is near.
(Joel 2:1)

I have a friend, Manuel, who once helped me build an arbor over our garden. Although now a U.S. citizen, Manuel lived into his teenage years in Mexico, and Spanish is his first language. The arbor project was pretty intense. We had to sink twelve massive ten-foot-long 8″×8″ posts into the ground. We put up smaller boards around the top. I estimated the project would take us a good week to finish. The first day, we dug the holes and began sinking the posts. We were hot and tired, and I suggested we quit for the day. Manuel said, "We will finish mañana." I was skeptical: "You really think so?" Manuel then chuckled, "Yes, Mr. Mark, even tomorrow I will tell you, we will finish mañana. It is always safe to say, 'Mañana.'"

In much the same way, the prophet writes about the "day of the LORD." There will be a cataclysmic day, but in the meantime, the day of the Lord should be seen as "near." It is close by. It is at hand, even as it was when Joel wrote over 2,500 years ago. One routinely gets glimpses of God's judgment before the final day.

The day of the Lord is both a fearsome and reassuring thing. Fearsome, as God executes judgment on that which is evil. God uproots the unhealthy plants. God heats the silver and gold to their melting points to skim off the impurities. Just as God washed the world with floodwaters, removing those who were beyond help and hope, so God purifies his kingdom.

Yet this day is reassuring because God is always looking out for those who turn to him. Just as he gave a prophet's warning in the time of Joel, so Scripture warns people today that history is not a train hurtling uncontrolled down the tracks of time. Those tracks were laid by God himself. Furthermore, God is at the controls of the locomotive, and the train runs on his time for his purposes. God is seeking those to ride his train and escape the judgment. To carry the analogy further, one can see God calling "All aboard" as he brings his deliverance to his people.

Manuel was right about tomorrow, and Joel was right about the day of the Lord being near. I live today mindful that I need to get ready for tomorrow!

Lord, give me presence of mind to live deliberately for you today. In you I pray, amen.

JANUARY 15

A day of darkness and gloom, a day of clouds and thick darkness! Like blackness there is spread upon the mountains. . . . The land is like the garden of Eden before them, but behind them a desolate wilderness. (Joel 2:2–3)

I spent my high school years living in Lubbock, Texas. Lubbock (a.k.a. "the hub of the plains") sits atop a long and wide mesa. The land is flat for hundreds of miles. As a result, the storms and cloud formations are spectacular. One Saturday, I was at a friend's house, which had a living room with windows that faced north and south. Out of the north windows, it seemed almost pitch black. Out of the south windows, it was bright as noon. We went outside. A front was blowing in from the north, and it had almost reached the house. It was a solid line of deep, dark clouds that enveloped the sky as far east and west as one could see. Yet to the south of that wall of stormy clouds was a cloudless sky, as blue as could be. The storm marched on and eventually turned the entire sky dark as hail, rain, and wind pelted my town.

The contrast between light and dark made an impression on me. That memory is etched into my brain in graphic color. I can even smell the ozone in the air decades later.

Joel uses an image similar to the one I remember in ways that evoke a metaphor for life as well as a warning of God's judgment. The metaphor is worth chewing on.

We all experience easy days—the sun is out, the wind is behind you, and you feel you can sail through life. But there are also days of darkness and gloom. Days when no light seeps in. Days when you don't want to get out of bed. Days when you fear what is to come. Days that are a wilderness compared to the garden of Eden where you "used to live."

God isn't missing in the storms of life. God is present. God will see you and me through those days. They won't be easy. They may not pass as quickly as we would like. They may shake us to our core. They may scare us to death. But as we cling tightly to God, we can be sure of riding out the storm and finding him and life on the other side. Whether our days are bright, dark, or a mixture of both, we need to cling to God in wonderment and trust.

Lord, hold me tightly, please. I need you today and every day. In your name, amen.

JANUARY 16

Their appearance is like the appearance of horses, and like war horses they run. As with the rumbling of chariots, they leap on the tops of the mountains, like the crackling of a flame of fire devouring the stubble, like a powerful army drawn up for battle. (Joel 2:4–5)

The king of Aram was furious. Somewhere, there must have been an informant. He had carefully drawn up his plans for battle and expected a resounding victory. But everything he tried against Israel failed. Surely someone was leaking his information to the Israelites. The king called in his best advisers. One of them explained that it wasn't a leak. Rather, Israel's king was listening to a prophet named Elisha who knew everything that was going to happen *before* it happened. This prophet of the Lord was the reason the king's plans were repeatedly thwarted. The king instructed the servant to go to Dothan, where Elisha lived, and seize him. The king sent his great army under cover of night and surrounded the city.

Elisha's helper arose early the next morning and saw the city surrounded by the enemy king's army. The helper panicked and said to Elisha, "What shall we do?" Elisha said, "Don't be afraid. Those who are with us are more than those against us!" Then Elisha prayed that God would open the helper's eyes to the truth. God did, and the servant saw that the army of God had filled the mountains with horses and chariots of fire! The story can be read in 2 Kings 6, but needless to say, things worked out well for Elisha and God's people. God's army is a game changer. His army is undefeated. His army always achieves its purpose.

With this background, consider today's passage from Joel. Here, the coming locust devastation is seen as a metaphor for God's army. Like running horses and rolling chariots, crackling and rumbling over the countryside, God's army—the locust swarm—was out to achieve its purposes. People without God's vision might have thought that the locusts were a natural devastation. But they were God's doing. (Even today, insurance policies use the phrase "act of God" for such occurrences.) The locusts were God's army sent out for God's purpose.

I want God's army fighting for me. When my problems and difficulties feel like an enemy arrayed against me, I want my eyes of faith to see and trust that God's army is more powerful and he will protect me.

Lord, help me align myself with your good causes and your will. I want to be a part of your army, in service to you. Help me in your name, amen.

JANUARY 17

Before them peoples are in anguish; all faces grow pale. (Joel 2:6)

Being a man, I have never been pregnant. I can't remotely describe what it feels like to give birth, having never endured the process personally. That said, I do have five children (and ten grandchildren, as of this writing!). Attending those five births, I have seen my wife in labor. She appreciated her epidural, and so did I.

Labor pains start slowly, but they build, getting more intense and more frequent. They can reach a point where they are almost unbearable. They may be occurring in the abdominal area, but they can affect the whole person physically, emotionally, and even psychologically.

In ancient Hebrew, the verb used for a woman in labor was *ḥ-y-l* (חיל). Joel uses that word in today's passage, where it is translated as "anguish." Joel is describing not a woman in labor but people who are writhing in pain. The pain the people were about to experience was terrifying. It would affect them physically, emotionally, and psychologically. It would affect their families and their jobs and even shorten their lives. There would be no epidural. No wonder it left people pale.

Certain things in this world rightly leave people in deep anguish. There are times and events that leave any sane person hurting profoundly. But there are also events and circumstances that cause us to worry and feel anguish, *even though they shouldn't*. Sometimes we overreact. Sometimes we panic. Often, the key is discerning the difference between what is worthy of anguish and what isn't.

When faced with anguishing labor pains (or even false labor pains that aren't the real deal), we have an epidural available, something that can keep debilitating anguish at bay. We have available a sort of "spiritual epidural," which is nothing less than the presence of Almighty God. This is the assurance of Psalm 23: when walking through a dark valley, God is by our side as a shepherd, with his protecting rod and staff.

God doesn't abandon those experiencing anguish; he comes to their rescue. It doesn't always mean that he solves their problems with a wave of his hands. Often, it means he holds our hand as he walks with us through the travail. But our answer is to seek his presence.

Lord, be with me. Take my burden. Help me now, please. In your name, amen.

JANUARY 18

The earth quakes before them; the heavens tremble. The sun and the moon are darkened, and the stars withdraw their shining. The LORD *utters his voice before his army, for his camp is exceedingly great; he who executes his word is powerful. For the day of the* LORD *is great and very awesome; who can endure it?* (Joel 2:10–11)

Three of us sat at counsel table in a St. Louis court. My buddy Eric, my daughter Rachel, and I, along with our two small firms, represented twenty-two women suffering from ovarian cancer in what some would deem a Don Quixote moment. We set out to prove that one of the world's largest corporations, represented by a stable of thoroughbreds from the world's largest law firms, had ruined the lives of these women and countless others by selling talcum powder products—including the most famous baby powder—laced with asbestos. The company had the money, the political power, the reputation, the massive legal teams, and over one hundred years of goodwill. Before the opening statement in the trial, I was asked whether I was nervous. I said, "No. If I'm doing what God wants of me, should I be nervous?"

Joel put it this way: The earth quakes. The heavens tremble. The sun, moon, and stars go into hiding. God is at work. God's army is exceedingly great! Then Joel inserts an important nugget: Whoever is doing ("executing") God's word is a powerful part of God's army! Not because of one's own strength but because the day belongs to the Lord! God makes the one doing his word powerful.

This passage is especially notable because in the overall context of Joel, God's army is a swarm of bugs! They are a bunch of locusts—a kind of grasshopper! So a grasshopper has the earth and heavens trembling? A grasshopper shuts down the sun, moon, and stars? Yes! When grasshoppers are doing the word and work of God, they can be very powerful. It is God who makes that army come together and become powerful, not the lowly grasshopper.

I am writing this four years out from that courtroom excursion. The jury found the powders contained asbestos, and the appellate courts upheld their record-setting verdict. Importantly, the company quit selling the talcum powder version of the product worldwide. I was asked how I felt when our small team accomplished so much. My reply? The day of the Lord is great and awesome! God is amazing. Do his work today. You will be powerful!

Lord, put me to work, imbued with your power for your tasks. In you, amen.

JANUARY 19

"Yet even now," declares the Lord, *"return to me with all your heart, with fasting, with weeping, and with mourning; and rend your hearts and not your garments."* (Joel 2:12–13)

I was driving down the highway in a desolate area of West Texas, thinking about my relationship with God. I wasn't as close to him as I had been earlier in my life. The fire that had burned so brightly seemed dim. The ardor I experienced, where God was so vividly real, where my excitement over his work was sky-high, where he was my reason to awaken and my peace for sleep each night—those days seemed only a memory.

What had happened? Was the mere passage of time the reason for the ebbing of fervor? I didn't think so. As I looked at my life and thought through it, I realized that my focus had blurred. Somehow I had wandered from the path I had been walking with God. The departures had been small at first, but sin had crept in the door and then expanded its grasp. The instructions of God hadn't been the guardrails of my life for some time.

I was living in a personal way what Joel was addressing in a national way. While I wasn't God's country, I was no less one of God's people. As I had lost my way, I had drifted from the moorings of my faith.

In the car, at that moment, I knew the prescription. It was given by Joel in today's passage, but it is an instruction found throughout God's word. I needed to turn around and return to the Lord. I needed to repent. I needed to change my attitude. As Joel put it, I needed to "return to" the Lord "with all my heart" and "rend my heart"—that is, approach God with a broken, torn heart full of remorse for my sin.

In some ways, a relationship with God is no different from a relationship with anyone else. Relationships require time, energy, and focus. Yet in some ways, my relationship with God is quite different. With God, how I live deeply impacts my relationship with him. It is a bit more like a marriage, another analogy God uses in Scripture. Following God and his ways is like being faithful in a marriage. It is a prerequisite to being close to him.

This lesson needs repeating. Return to God with your heart. Walk in his ways.

Lord, I repent. I want to be yours. I want to walk with you. In your name, amen.

JANUARY 20

Return to the LORD your God, for he is gracious and merciful, slow to anger, and abounding in steadfast love; and he relents over disaster. (Joel 2:13)

Our law firm had headed to the mountains for a retreat. Our goal was to become a more coherent and better firm. We wanted our lawyers to work together better, so we brought in an expert to help us. One of the expert's exercises was a personality test. He wanted each person to identify his or her personality traits that affected not only their dispositions but the how and why of what they did. Many social studies have indicated that people act consistently with their personality traits.

This principle wasn't discovered just in the twenty-first century. It is a truism as old as time. Not surprisingly, then, the prophet Joel pointed his listeners toward understanding the traits and attributes of God. God acts consistently with his character.

Joel spoke of God as "gracious"—*ḥannun* (חַנּוּן) in Hebrew. This word conveys kindness in one's treatment of others. It is similar to the next trait: "merciful." In Hebrew, this word (*ra ḥum*—רַחוּם) fits well with "gracious." They even sound good together in Hebrew (*ḥannun va-raḥum*). Translated as "merciful," *raḥum* is a tender word of love. It is used to describe a mother protecting the life in her womb. The word has the same root as the Hebrew word for "womb."

Joel then adds that God is "slow to anger." God doesn't fly off the handle at the slightest matter. Instead, he is "abounding in steadfast love." This is one of Hebrew's most important words—*ḥesed* (חֶסֶד). Translators struggle to put it into one English word. It refers to loyalty to a covenant, faithfulness to a promise, and goodness and graciousness toward another in a relationship. One translation says God is "boundless in loyal love" (New English Translation [NET]). His love is steadfast and abounding.

These exact same four traits for God are used not only by Joel but by David in Psalm 145:8. These are amazing traits of God that should change my world. As I reflect on God's character as one who is kind and merciful, one who is amazingly patient and cares for me as a mother cares for the child in her womb, I can face today! Knowing that God will be gracious, compassionate, patient, and full of a loyal, forgiving love for me gives me confidence and a kick in my step. Come what may, I walk with a God who treats me consistently with his amazing character!

Lord, I lean on you to be YOU! With you, I will face my day with a smile. In your name, amen!

JANUARY 21

Blow the trumpet in Zion; consecrate a fast; call a solemn assembly; gather the people.
Consecrate the congregation; assemble the elders; gather the children, even nursing infants.
Let the bridegroom leave his room, and the bride her chamber. (Joel 2:15–16)

I moved from Rochester, New York, to Lubbock, Texas, in the middle of seventh grade. Among the many unusual features of my new school was the South Plains Fair in September. The entire school shut down early one day each year so the school kids could go to the fair. Kids being kids, they would go in groups or set up places to meet up at the fairgrounds. Meeting up wasn't easy, however, because there was a slew of people there: young people, old people, elementary schoolers, middle schoolers, high schoolers, college kids, young adults, and old adults. It illustrated the barker's call, "Come one, come all!"

I knew my wife when she was in middle school, but we were never among those who met up at the fair. It seemed wrong to me, and we were well into our forties when I surprised her with a date to the South Plains Fair. We flew from Houston to Lubbock just for the evening, and I secretly took a massive amount of quarters and one-dollar bills, determined to play as long as it took to win her the jumbo-sized teddy bear.

In a similar and yet very different way, Joel in today's passage calls everyone to meet up. Young and old, leaders and followers, even the newly-weds are to come together. It's a "come one, come all" moment. But these people aren't coming together to experience a fair. They're coming to experience a fast. No corn dogs and lemonade, but a solemn affair addressing the people's attitudes.

The people were distracted. Their hearts were swept up by the pleasures of the age, not the joys of the Lord. They needed to rededicate and consecrate themselves to God. They needed to meet up with God in a serious way. They needed to hear God's message—the message of devotion to God.

I went to a lot of trouble to take my wife to the fair. I worked hard and prepared fully to win her that big bear. It leaves me wondering how hard I am willing to work to meet up with God.

Dear Lord, I want to meet with you; I dedicate my life and heart to you. In your name, amen.

JANUARY 22

Between the vestibule and the altar let the priests, the ministers of the LORD, *weep and say, "Spare your people, O* LORD, *and make not your heritage a reproach, a byword among the nations. Why should they say among the peoples, 'Where is their God?'"* (Joel 2:17)

One of my daughters called me, distressed. She had something on her mind and didn't ease into her concern. Rather, as is typical of this daughter, she dove in headlong. She had read some news reports about what some notable people were doing and saying "in the name of Christianity." "Dad," she said, "I don't believe that way, and it angers me that they act and say those things. No wonder some of my friends don't want to have anything to do with Christianity. They think we are all angry racists who are more concerned with earthly kingdoms than the kingdom of God."

My daughter rightly recognized that God has a reputation in the world, and his reputation is impacted by what his people do and say. Most people will not know God, at least initially, in any way other than the reflection emanating from God's people. The prophet Joel alludes to this in today's passage. Joel was fearful of God's reputation, but in a different sense. God was meting out judgment on his people to help them rediscover an appropriate focus on him. Joel knew that God's people were suffering, and his fear was that God's reputation would be severely tainted. Those watching "God's people" could have a few choices: (1) God wasn't powerful enough to take care of his people, (2) God didn't care enough to care for his people, or (3) God had the power but was a malicious and trickster God, not unlike the Norse god Loki.

Under any of those scenarios, God's reputation was on the line. Joel instructed the priests to intercede for the people, seeking God's help. Part of what the priests were to say to God included the reminder, "God, the nations are thinking that you don't care! They think you've left the scene. They think you aren't reliable and trustworthy. Please God, for your own reputation, act!"

Like it or not, people will decide who and what God is by looking at his people. We are his "image" in the sense that when people see us, they attribute our character traits to what it means to follow God. My daughter was right to be concerned.

Lord, I don't always reflect you as I should. Forgive me, and make me conscious of doing better! In your name, amen.

JANUARY 23

Then the LORD became jealous for his land and had pity on his people. (Joel 2:18).

When our son was getting his doctorate in philosophy at Oxford University, he wrote a 153-page dissertation on "intentional identity." He told me about it, and I struggled to understand the material. While I have read a good bit of classical philosophy, this was vastly different. This involved "dynamic," "guise," and "exotica" theories to resolve logical semantic problems. I told Will that I wanted a copy of the final product, and I set myself a goal: I wanted to read it from A to Z and see if I could claim to have fully understood two consecutive paragraphs. I failed.

The field of study where my son excelled was so particular that one needs a great deal of background to understand certain complexities of the subject. It is no less true when one speaks of God. While most Scriptures are readily available for a child to grasp, there are some Scriptures that take careful study to comprehend.

In today's passage, Joel says the Lord became "jealous" for his land and his people. To speak of God as "jealous" is a bit hard to understand. Jealousy is not a virtue in the world and can often carry an idea of teenage drama, immature passion, or an insecure spouse. More background on the Hebrew word translated as "jealous" helps. The Hebrew root (*qana'*—קנא) denotes a very strong feeling tied to desire. It can be a negative idea, like *envy*, or a positive one, like *zeal* or *ardor*. With God, the reference is positive; God seeks a relationship with us and wants us to stop anyone or anything from impeding that relationship.

God has an intense desire for his people. By growing in our relationship with him, he will help us become our very best. Joel makes this point about God's intense desire even in the midst of a book about suffering and tragedy. The word Joel uses reminds me a bit of what my father would tell me as a child when I was getting punished. Dad would say, "This hurts me worse than it hurts you."

God doesn't delight in our misery. God fervently desires his children to have joy and blessings. We have that assurance, even when things aren't bright and happy. God will bring things to a good conclusion.

Lord, give me faith in the midst of life's difficulties. Help me to follow you without needing you to send me "alerts" that grab my attention. In your name, amen.

JANUARY 24

The LORD answered and said to his people, "Behold, I am sending to you grain, wine, and oil, and you will be satisfied." (Joel 2:19)

I was five years old when I heard a cool song on the radio. It wasn't the words that caught my ear; I wasn't old enough to have a clue what they meant. But the hook, sound, melody, and phrasing combined to produce a memorable line that I would walk around the house singing. So I, as a five-year-old, was entranced by Mick Jagger and the Rolling Stones' "(I Can't Get No) Satisfaction." I still think the intro guitar lick is one of rock's most iconic introductions.

Mick was missing out on the prophecy of Joel, a short book of just three chapters, with only two main sections. The first section was of judgment and devastation that was befalling the nation of Judah. The second section begins here in Joel 2:18–19, and it speaks of God's promises to bless and restore his people.

Joel's people experienced a massive locust plague with an accompanying unrelenting heat wave. It was the dawning of God's day of judgment that would culminate in the future. Yet as the people repented, Joel promised that blessings would follow. God had a zeal and ardor for his people. God wanted to bless them.

God promised something greater than a good day, a good meal, or money in the bank. God promised satisfaction.

The Hebrew translation of *satisfied* here, *sava'* (שָׂבַע), means not just eating but eating to the point of satisfaction. It's drinking one's fill. It's having enough of whatever is being referenced. It gives one satisfaction.

I want satisfaction in life. I don't want to be the one who eats, drinks, exercises, or works to excess because I can't get satisfied. I don't want to be someone who goes for excess in *any area* because my hunger can't be satiated. I want to experience peace and contentment rather than a constant hungering for more.

If I ever get to visit with Mick, I think I might talk to him about Joel 2:19. It might not make another hit song for him, but it would be the answer to his longing!

Lord, may I find satisfaction in you and you alone. In your name, I pray, amen.

JANUARY 25

I will remove the northerner far from you, and drive him into a parched and desolate land, his vanguard into the eastern sea, and his rear guard into the western sea; the stench and foul smell of him will rise. (Joel 2:20)

I knew a young man who was very predictable. He loved personal competition and he loved watching any sporting competition. While he supported his local teams, his general support was fairly thin. He hated to lose so much that it seemed that on a game-to-game basis, he rooted for whoever was ahead or seemed likely to win. In many games, I remember him switching his allegiance several times during the game because one team or another would go ahead.

Supporting the underdog has a certain appeal, but with the hope that the underdog can pull off the big upset. In the end, people always hope to support a winner. They never like their team or player to lose.

This idea of winners and losers is underscored in today's passage. Joel prophesied to God's people in Judah that God was going to rout the opposing enemy (the northerner was either the locust swarm that devastated the land or a prophecy for an opposing army invader from the north). God was going to destroy those that were against him.

Many like to think of God as always happy, thinking of nothing but the best for everyone. But that isn't what Scripture reveals of God. God always finds the best for his people. There are those, however, who fight against God. Those who are set against God's people. But they aren't going to be victors; they will be defeated. God will destroy those who set themselves against him and his work.

Some might say, "But I've seen many who are set against God and yet seem to prosper." To this I say, "It's not over yet. Don't count the score in a game and declare a winner until the game is over." For I am confident that God will bring down those against him. In the end, they will end.

So if you want to root for the winner, or more importantly, if you want to be on the victor's side, declare yourself on God's team. Seek him. Do his will. Let him give you direction. In the end, you will win even while others don't.

Lord, I pledge myself to you. Use me as you will. Help me to do my part in your plans. Bring the enemy to naught, as you are lifted up. In you I pray, amen.

JANUARY 26

Fear not, O land; be glad and rejoice, for the LORD has done great things! Fear not, you beasts of the field, for the pastures of the wilderness are green; the tree bears its fruit; the fig tree and vine give their full yield. (Joel 2:21–22)

When I was young, I was unusually afraid of certain things. I remember, around age eight or nine, having a dream about a fire truck screaming its siren as it went down our street. As people went to their doors to see what was going on, the firemen had machine guns and were shooting the families at their doorsteps. I awoke petrified. My parents worked hard to convince me a dream was nothing to be frightened about. Yet I was. Several nights later, I had the dream again. But this time, in my dream I remembered my earlier dream. I knew we shouldn't open the door to see the fire truck. That was how people were getting shot. Yet Mom and Dad, in my second dream, explained that my earlier dream was nothing to be afraid of, and to show me, they opened the door. Of course, the firemen had machine guns and again fired at everyone.

Some of our fears are based in reality; some are irrational. That fear of mine was irrational. Yet a large number of fears *are* rational, including the fear in today's passage. Joel is speaking at a time when a life-altering national catastrophe has befallen. It has destroyed not just people's lives but much of the life of the land. Crops were eaten down to the roots. Even the grazing land for livestock was spent. Fear was a rational recognition that the land and its people had reached a breaking point. If things didn't turn abruptly around, there was no future.

But although this fear was rational, God, speaking through his prophet, pointedly and directly says, "Fear not!" That isn't surprising. With God fighting your battles, who needs to fear? Yet what is surprising is that the admonition against fear is directed toward the land and the beasts! This echoes God's earlier statement that he is "jealous" or deeply caring about his land. But here, Joel uses a different word for land than he has been using. Here (and in Joel 1:10) Joel uses the word *adamah* (אֲדָמָה). It is the word for the arable land or ground yet also the root for Adam, which means "man." God's instruction to the earth not to fear is surely an instruction to you and me.

God is not beaten by the powers of this world. We have nothing to fear. Not even renegade firemen. We have the Almighty fighting our battles.

Lord, please remove my fears and replace them with faith in your name. Amen.

JANUARY 27

You shall know that I am in the midst of Israel, and that I am the LORD *your God and there is none else. And my people shall never again be put to shame.* (Joel 2:27)

I love my grandkids, all ten of them. Regretfully, none of them live in the same town as Becky and me. When we get pictures and videos, we watch them over and over. We get FaceTime calls, which are priceless. But something really special happens when we are with them. Being with them brings joy and opportunity on a level unequaled by even the best video. Live presence, full interaction, holding, laughing, going on walks, talking, and playing games—so much can be done when in their presence.

This is why today's passage stands out so much to me. God speaks of a day when his people will know that he is in their midst. God won't be something people read about. He won't be simply the subject of a sermon. God won't be a debatable concept. God will actually be in the present, in the middle of the people, interacting, with all that that entails. Who wouldn't yearn for that?

I long for the presence of God, even though it is something I have already found and experienced. Having an actual awareness of God's presence is hard to describe. It isn't visible, but then neither is oxygen. It brings joy, but not like joy found anywhere else. The Apostle Paul described God's indwelling presence in contrast to being intoxicated with alcohol (Eph. 5:18), yet God's presence has an effect far beyond intoxication.

Most often, I have found God's presence during times of worship. Gathering with others in the name of God and singing songs of praise and worship before his throne have shown his presence in my life to be a reality. Times of communion in prayer and study have placed me in his presence. Even walking in life during difficult times, I have felt the blessing of his presence and comfort.

I hope you, the reader, have experienced God in your midst. If you have, you know what I mean. If you haven't, seek him. Find times of prayer and study, times of genuine communion through worship and praise. God in your midst is the greatest blessing.

Lord, be real to me. Bring me into your presence. In your name, amen.

JANUARY 28

And it shall come to pass afterward, that I will pour out my Spirit on all flesh; your sons and your daughters shall prophesy, your old men shall dream dreams, and your young men shall see visions. Even on the male and female servants in those days I will pour out my Spirit. (Joel 2:28–29)

A recent article in the *Jerusalem Post* asked if God was punishing the United States of America. The first listed reason particularly caught my eye. The author asserted that in 2022, the United States was "in the midst of a civil war." This wasn't a war where either side had taken up arms against the other, but it was a war between "us" and "them." Politics, policies, and personages divided the country without a common nationalism overcoming the differences.

Whether or not one agrees with the article, it is apparent that many in the United States and elsewhere readily identify with their own group, to the exclusion of other groups. The "us" and "them" mentality is common. I suspect it has often been that way. It is one of the jolting aspects of today's passage.

Joel prophesies about a unique time coming to God's people. It would be a time where God's Spirit would be poured out (i.e., be given in abundance) to *all kinds of people*. This would not be only to one gender, one age group, or even one social status. The sons and daughters, the old and young, and even the servants would receive this Spirit outpouring.

This was a monumental promise, one that Moses had sought for the people (Num. 11:29). But the time hadn't arrived yet when Joel penned these words. God's Spirit came selectively in Old Testament days, indwelling and speaking through prophets, certain priests and kings, and a select few others. But the future would be different.

Why? His Spirit would come to indwell every individual who has a relationship with God. Peter referenced this passage in his explanation of Pentecost, saying the time had arrived (Acts 2). God isn't picking out his favorites. Everyone is invited to his banquet. God wants everyone to have a relationship with him. There is no "us" and "them" among the children of God. No civil war there, only peace, love, harmony, and common purpose!

Lord, please indwell me richly with your Spirit to your praise and glory. In your name, amen.

JANUARY 29

And it shall come to pass that everyone who calls on the name of the LORD shall be saved.
(Joel 2:32)

Almost all our kids are frugal with money, but one stands out for having had a "savings account" for as long as she has known what that is. Once as I was driving a country road in the middle of nowhere, I saw a little kitten abandoned on the side of the road. I stopped and "saved" him, although we did name him Roadkill. I love Premier League football (a.k.a. "soccer"). My team has a great goalkeeper who had four "saves" on the day I type this. I just paused to watch him while typing and "saved" this document.

Save, save, save—the word has diverse meanings in English. So too in the Hebrew of Joel's day. Lot was told to flee to the hills to "escape" (Gen. 19:17). Over and over, King Saul tried to kill David, but David "escaped" with his life (1 Sam. 19:17, etc.). Once king, David "saved" the Israelites from the hand of the Philistines (2 Sam. 19:10). King Josiah saved the bones of a dead man from being moved (2 Ki. 23:18). Isaiah says God will "rescue" Jerusalem (Isa. 31:5). When the owl lies in her nest, she saves her young (Isa. 34:15). Burdens too heavy to carry easily can't be "saved" (Isa. 46:2). When one rescues captives, one "saves" them (Isa. 49:24-25). All of these passages use the same word translated as "saved" in today's passage by Joel: "Everyone who calls on the name of the LORD shall be saved."

In contemporary Christian culture, the word *saved* is most often associated with eternal life. That causes many to read passages like today's with a mind-set simply of eternity. Yet the Hebrew is laden with many more layers of thought.

Devastation happens in this life. God rescues or saves his people who call on him. Sometimes that salvation comes only in eternity, but often it is also found in this life. God saves his people from maladies of sin in this life as well as in eternal life.

With that in mind, I am ready to "call on the name of the Lord." I want to call on his character, his power, his saving desire, and his faithfulness. I need him to save me today and every day. I need him to save me from tragedy, disappointment, and so much more.

Lord, I call on you. Save me in your name and by your power. Amen.

JANUARY 30

Beat your plowshares into swords, and your pruning hooks into spears; let the weak say, "I am a warrior." (Joel 3:10)

Standing outside a courtroom in Dallas, Texas, the company lawyer told me, "There is no way we will ever pay you a dime! You will have to try every case against us. You will have to beat us every time. You will then need to win in every appellate court all the way to the U.S. Supreme Court before we will pay you."

I was livid. This massive multinational company owed my clients and thousands of others for a defective hip product that had crippled and hurt many patients. The fight was on. I declared to the lawyer and anyone listening that I would spend my legal career trying to make that company rue that day and that decision.

I accepted every case I could find that implicated this company. From one coast to the other, with all points in between, I began prosecuting cases against it. Some wins did indeed go all the way to the U.S. Supreme Court before being paid. I galvanized my lawyers, my legal assistants, and others and put us all on a warpath.

Years later, the company came back to me and said, "Enough. We want peace." The company stepped up and paid all my clients and many more of those who had the implant placed in their bodies. The company also settled my other cases that were unrelated to the hips. They wanted to end the conflict. My legal team—many of whom had spent ten years pursuing this company—and I turned to other tasks.

Joel speaks of war. He says the mighty men are to take their metal plows and use the metal to fashion swords. Their pruning hooks are to become spears. There is a time to battle evil. If you doubt this, think of Hitler and the Nazi regime. It was godly to shut them down.

In an interesting turn of phrase, another prophet, Isaiah, spoke of a time of peace, when swords would be refashioned into plowshares and spears into pruning hooks (Isa. 2:4). The point of war is always to find peace. War is a last resort. God knows this, but he always works toward peace. I need to be a peacemaker first and a warrior only when absolutely necessary.

Lord, make me an instrument of your peace. In your name, amen.

JANUARY 31

Multitudes, multitudes, in the valley of decision! For the day of the Lord *is near in the valley of decision. The sun and the moon are darkened, and the stars withdraw their shining.* (Joel 3:14–15)

My buddy Kevin introduced me to fantasy books early in high school. His favorite was Tolkien's *Lord of the Rings,* and rightly so. We read that and so many others. Another high on our list was the *Earthsea* trilogy by Ursula Le Guin. Those books produced strong characters who always faced daunting challenges wrapped in choices. Frodo Baggins had to decide whether to keep the ring himself or carry it to Mordor for destruction. Sparrowhawk had to decide whether to fulfill his destiny and become the greatest wizard of his time.

Life is filled with making decisions, and those decisions become more difficult and carry greater consequences as you grow into adulthood. As a lawyer, I have seen decisions affect not only individuals but whole families and even communities. In one of my cases, company employees decided not to alert government authorities when water aquifers became polluted with cancer-causing benzene. In another set of cases, employees decided to falsify test results to allow the selling of a product that would go on to kill untold numbers of people.

In today's passage, decisions are closely linked to the day of the Lord, a day of God's judgment. Consider the somewhat bizarre affirmation of "multitudes, multitudes, in the valley of decision!" Joel uses the word *multitudes* twice. It is functionally equivalent to saying in English, "Lots and lots of people in the valley of decision." Then Joel adds that the day of the Lord is "near," or at hand, in the valley of decision.

From several verses earlier, it is clear that this is the valley where God is going to judge the nations. Why is this the valley of decisions? Everyone gets to choose their destiny. Everyone chooses whether to relate to God as friend or foe or whether to ignore him altogether. Those decisions are the basis for God's judgment. God isn't blind to our choices. God cares for his people deeply, and God will make his decisions based on how people make their decisions.

This makes me want to be careful. It also makes me pray for those who are lost. This is no fantasy; it is real life.

Lord, help me help others to make good decisions about you. In your name, amen.

FEBRUARY 1

The LORD roars from Zion, and utters his voice from Jerusalem, and the heavens and the earth quake. But the LORD is a refuge to his people, a stronghold to the people of Israel.
(Joel 3:16)

Law school teaches precision regarding citation form. For some, that sentence might not make sense, so please allow me to explain. Whenever a lawyer cites a case, statute, or reference work, the lawyer is required to follow detailed rules on how that citation should be given, including precise commas and the correct uses of abbreviations and italics. (The rule book is over three hundred pages long!!) This is important because source material confers a degree of authority. It is also important because copyright laws preclude people from taking the work of another and passing it off as their own.

Citation form was a bit different 2,700 years ago. In fact, it was relatively, though not totally, unknown. This arises because in today's Joel passage, depending on who wrote first, Joel quotes the prophet Amos, or Amos quotes Joel using the exact same words but without any citation! Amos and Joel also share words in Joel 3:18. For that matter, Joel 1:15 shares a sentence with Isaiah 13:6.

Amos and Isaiah do so because this prophecy in Joel is both important and memorable. Amos quotes Joel, saying, "The LORD roars from Zion and utters his voice from Jerusalem" (Amos 1:2). Joel then says that as a result, the heavens and earth quake. In Amos, the roar results in the shepherds of the pasture mourning.

Both Joel and Amos understand the awesome effect of God's word. When the Holy God speaks, even the elements shake. I have been through earthquakes before, and it's a scary thing. You quickly wonder where you can go for protection. No one wants a building collapsing on them.

Joel tells the people where to go. When God's word comes forth, when the earth and heavens shake, run *to* the Lord! He's the refuge spot. He's the stronghold that can't be shaken.

These words magnify the weight and importance of God's word. It's right and good not only that we study and respect God's revelation but also that we let it drive us to God! That's its purpose.

Lord, may I find you as my refuge today and always. In your name, amen.

FEBRUARY 2

Now the word of the LORD came to Jonah the son of Amittai, saying, "Arise, go to Nineveh." (Jonah 1:1–2)

When I was just starting out as a lawyer, I worked in an old-line, extremely large firm. It was a bit scary to me because most of the lawyers had graduated from well-heeled national-caliber law schools, while I had come from a regional school. I had many concerns over how to do my job. I had been there for only a few days when my supervising attorney explained to me the philosophy of the firm: "There are partners and there is every-body else. The partners reign supreme. When they say, 'Jump!' you say, 'How high?'" There was no question to the rule: partners were to be obeyed.

It makes sense. The partners owned the law firm. I worked for the firm, so I worked for the partners. They were paying me to do what they wanted me to do. The fact that there were hundreds of partners in no way changed the truth that *I worked for them*. So I was to do what they told me to do or find another job.

That experience makes these first two verses in Jonah stand out to me. The word of the Lord came to Jonah the prophet. This wasn't a first. Jonah the son of Amittai was a prophet from Gath-hepher who, 2 Kings 14:25 tells us, spoke the word of the Lord during the reign of Jeroboam II in Israel. I would think Jonah would feel intense honor at being chosen by the Lord to speak and act on God's behalf. Yet as the story unfolds, we see that wasn't the case.

The second thing that stands out is that God gave Jonah a job to do. Again, this would seem a no-brainer. God is not only Jonah's "boss," but he is also the *Lord of the Universe who reigns supreme over all of creation*. That seems more than sufficient reason to do exactly as God instructed. Yet here also, bizarrely, Jonah chose not to obey.

I can dismiss Jonah as a fool, or I can look at myself critically. The word of the Lord has come to me in the form of Scripture. For centuries, many didn't have a Bible to read in their own language, and some still don't. I have many copies, yet so often the text sits unread! Furthermore, God gives me many clear instructions, yet so often I don't follow them. I can't judge Jonah. I have too much work to do myself!

Lord, forgive me as you inspire and strengthen me to do better. In you, amen.

FEBRUARY 3

"Arise, go to Nineveh, that great city, and call out against it, for their evil has come up before me." (Jonah 1:2)

My daughter got "cold-called" on her first day in "Evidence" class in law school. This means that the professor called on her to answer questions in front of the whole class. This is rarely pleasurable. The professors seek to challenge and cross-examine you and your thinking in front of everyone. Sarah recounted the experience and told me, "Dad, I purposely sat in the area of class where he doesn't really see you to call on you. Yet somehow, he saw me, pointed at me, and called on me to answer his questions."

Trying to be invisible doesn't usually work. Spies get sent to spy school to learn how to be invisible, and at times even that fails! Whether we like it or not, none of us are invisible to God. The evil of Nineveh arose before him. Now, to most in Israel, Nineveh is not where you'd expect to find God's gaze.

Nineveh was one of several great cities in the Assyrian Empire. For centuries, Assyria had been the major world power to the northeast of Israel, even though it was suffering a bit of decline at the time of Jonah. Even though Nineveh wasn't one of "God's cities" in that God's chosen people didn't live in Nineveh, Nineveh wasn't invisible to God. Similarly, Jonah wasn't invisible when he foolishly tried to flee from God.

The psalmist understood this, writing, "O LORD, you have searched me and known me! You know when I sit down and when I rise up; you discern my thoughts from afar. You search out my path . . . and are acquainted with all my ways" (Ps. 139:1–3). As the old saying goes, "You can run, but you can't hide." So with God, no one disappears from his radar screen. We might ignore him, but he never ignores us. No one is invisible to God. God knows you, me, and everyone else. He knows our hearts and minds. He is tuned in to our needs.

Moreover, God wants us to be aware of his interest in us. He's always seeking to bring us into a direct relationship with him. I like this about God. I don't want to run from him; I want to run to him. I'm not trying to find the law school seat away from his gaze! I want to sit front and center in close fellowship with him!

Lord, I am in awe at your interest in me. I want to know you better daily. I offer this prayer in your name, amen.

FEBRUARY 4

He went down to Joppa and found a ship going to Tarshish. (Jonah 1:3)

We were on a recent family vacation. My mom, who our children call "Mimi," was there, along with our five children, their four spouses, and (at that time) all nine grandchildren. At one point, among a group of us, one of my daughters made an announcement with deep and genuine grandiosity, as if she was announcing the birth of a child. She said, "*Y'all! Mimi reads books by reading the last chapter first!*" My mom was calm as she replied, "Then I know what I am reading up to."

Now, not many people I know use Mom's model of reading the last chapter first. But in today's passage, it might help. Christian history becomes very relevant in today's passage if you read the Bible back to front. The key is the port city of Joppa (modern Jaffa). This city will take on an important role in the spread of Christianity. The two roles of Joppa stand in stark contrast, illuminating the significance of both and teaching an important lesson.

For Jonah, Joppa was the dropping-off place. Jonah fled Galilee to go to non-Israelite Joppa, where he would catch a ship to avoid preaching to the pagans in Nineveh. But centuries later, the Apostle Peter was in Joppa when the non-Israelite Cornelius sent for him (Acts 10). Peter was not expecting this call from Cornelius, who would soon become the first Gentile convert to the church. Peter ultimately preached to the Gentile—who was considered unclean by Peter and Jewish society—only because God sent a vision to Peter while Peter was in Joppa. In the vision, Peter saw a sheet descending from heaven with all sorts of unclean animals. Peter was told to eat, and he recoiled, explaining he has never eaten unkosher food. In the vision, Peter was reprimanded, being told, "What God has made clean, do not call common" (Acts 10:15).

As well versed as Peter was in Scripture, he must have chuckled when realizing that God called Peter to preach Jesus' message to Gentiles at a time when Peter was in the very port city where Jonah fled God's instruction to preach to Gentiles. It explains why when Peter recounted the story, he was always quick to relate that it happened in Joppa (Acts 11:5, 13)! Here, reading backward helps! It illustrates the importance of God's universal truth as well as the importance of obedience in sharing that truth.

Lord, give me opportunities to share your truth, even with those who aren't just like me. In your name, amen.

FEBRUARY 5

So he paid the fare and went down into it, to go with them to Tarshish, away from the presence of the LORD. (Jonah 1:3)

My dad bled burnt orange, the color of the University of Texas. He despised the Oklahoma Sooners. For my dad, there were few things worse than Texas high school football players choosing to leave Texas and play football for Oklahoma. He would get on his soapbox and rant about it annually during the fall season. The "ours" and "theirs" mentality was strong with Dad.

There is something comforting in thinking of God as "ours" rather than "theirs." The idea that we might have some special connection with the Almighty that ensures us special status in his eyes gives us confidence and security. Have you ever heard someone pray for victory before a sporting event? It's as if God will hear one side's prayer over against the other side's prayer.

Jonah was an Israelite. God had defined the nation, removing them from Egypt and giving them Canaan. God had "chosen" Israel to be "his people." God entered into a special covenant with Israel, revealing himself in ways he hadn't revealed himself to other nations. Israel was God's "treasured possession, out of all the peoples who are on the face of the earth" (Deut. 7:6; 14:2; etc.). But Jonah took these promises too far. He adopted a "mine versus them" mentality, and therefore, he walked in deep hypocrisy. Israel was chosen by God to be a light to the nations, not to try to keep God to itself. Wrongly, then, when God told Jonah to be a light himself to the people of Nineveh, he rebelled. Jonah's attitude was no different from that of other Israelites who scorned Gentiles.

In Jonah's day, the Israelites were evil. Bizarrely, God was still blessing Israel. Jeroboam was king, and "he did what was evil in the sight of the LORD." Yet God "restored the border of Israel from Lebo-hamath as far as the Sea of the Arabah, according to the word of the LORD, the God of Israel, which he spoke by his servant Jonah the son of Amittai, the prophet, who was from Gath-hepher" (2 Ki. 14:23-25).

Jonah had prophesied that God would execute mercy on Israel in his days rather than the judgment deserved. Yet the idea of God extending such mercy to other nations really galled Jonah, and he wanted no part of it. Jonah would sooner disobey God than see God's mercy set out on those outside his group!

Lord, help me remember and see that you are God of all. In your name, amen.

FEBRUARY 6

But Jonah rose to flee to Tarshish from the presence of the LORD. . . . The men knew that he was fleeing from the presence of the LORD, because he had told them. (Jonah 1:3, 10)

Over one hundred lawyers were headed to a courtroom in New York City. We knew there would be a fight for certain seats in the courtroom. We wanted to be in direct eyesight of the judge. One fellow joined the throngs early in front of the metal detector line, ensuring he would be close to the courtroom doors once they were unlocked. He went further than others, however. With seeming graciousness, as the elevator doors opened, he held the doors with his hand and ushered in others with a polite "You first." Some were stunned at his willingness to do this, and they scampered on, delighted to get that early position. What my friend understood that the others didn't was that once the elevator arrived on the right floor, by being last on the elevator, my friend would be first off! He was first in the courtroom.

There is something strategic about where we spend our time. Twice in this early part of Jonah, one reads that Jonah was fleeing the "presence" of God. The Hebrew for *presence* (*paneh*—פָּנֶה) references the face of God. For example, it is used when God tells Moses to bless Aaron with the following blessing: "The Lord bless and keep you; the Lord make his face [a.k.a. 'presence'; emphasis mine] to shine upon you" (Num. 6:24-25). (That's a worthy prayer for those you love!)

Everyone should pursue the presence or face of God, not flee it. Psalm 95:2 says, "Let us come into his *presence* [lit. his 'face'; emphasis mine] with thanksgiving; let us make a joyful noise to him with songs of praise!" Psalm 100:2 adds, "Serve the LORD with gladness! Come into his *presence* with singing!" (emphasis mine). David feared his sin would drive him from the presence of God, and he prayed, "Cast me not away from your presence, and take not your Holy Spirit from me" (Ps. 51:11).

Jonah knew he was disobeying God. He thought he could hide from him. But he was wrong; God always sees us. The futility of Jonah trying to flee God's presence is illuminated by Psalm 139, which asks, "Where shall I flee from your presence?" (v. 7). The answer? Nowhere! It is futile to even try.

I want the intimacy of the face of God shining on me and my life. Heaven forbid I seek distance from the Almighty.

Lord, help me remember and see that you are God of all. In your name, amen.

FEBRUARY 7

But the LORD hurled a great wind upon the sea, and there was a mighty tempest on the sea, so that the ship threatened to break up. (Jonah 1:4)

Once I was asked to represent a fellow who always seemed to be in trouble. His troubles would snowball because he refused to deal with them. He had a situation where he owed another person ("Person B") some money. The amount was in dispute, but the case could have been resolved by paying Person B the sum of $2-3 million. But this potential client didn't settle the matter. Instead of addressing the issue, he went radio silent. He left Person B no option but to sue him. I didn't take the case, but another lawyer did. It wound up costing the man over $20 million at the end of the day. Wounds that aren't addressed can fester and get worse. It is true in medicine, in law, and in life. Jonah and today's passage are Exhibit One.

God told Jonah to go to Nineveh. Jonah decided instead to disobey and flee. He got in a boat headed as far from Nineveh as possible. Those of us reading the story might chuckle at the absurdity, yet I suspect we are all guilty of trying to hide from God at various times in life. When it is our behavior and choices under the microscope, our clarity of vision becomes blurry. We don't realize what we are doing.

Let me strip this down to the basics. God gave Jonah instructions. Jonah disobeyed, ignoring God. God then showed a simple truth: God will NOT be ignored. Not by Jonah, not by you, and not by me.

Recently, I watched one of my daughters parenting her two-year-old son. He was doing something he shouldn't. She asked him to quit. He continued doing it. She called him by name and said, "Look at me." He looked away, thinking he could ignore his mother and not get in trouble. Without going into unnecessary details, I ask you this: Do you think my grandson's ploy worked? No, it didn't. My daughter, who is an amazing mom, certainly got her son's attention!

God is no less going to get our attention when we ignore him. It bears repeating: God will *not* be ignored.

Lord, forgive me when I foolishly ignore your instructions. May my attention always be on you. In your name, I pray, amen.

FEBRUARY 8

Then the mariners were afraid, and each cried out to his god. . . . Then the men feared the LORD exceedingly, and they offered a sacrifice to the LORD and made vows. (Jonah 1:5, 16)

Prereqs was the common term used back in my day for college courses you needed before taking another college course. For example, if you wanted to take an advanced economics course, you first had to take Economics 101. Similarly, if you hadn't learned basic algebra, you wouldn't be taking statistics!

Sometimes, the School of Hard Knocks has some prereqs as well. These are on display in today's passage. The pagan mariners weren't atheists as they began their journey. While the story doesn't record their level of religious fervor, it is clear they believed in gods of various sorts. Surveys indicate that by far the majority of people in the world even today have some religious belief in one or more gods. God has planted eternity in the hearts of people, and a longing for the divine can be found in almost everyone.

The mariners' gods are unnamed in Jonah, but typical Mesopotamian gods of the day wore names like Marduk, who was the king of the gods, or Ishtar, who was the queen of the universe. The sailors likely had some collection of gods from the pantheon. But Israel didn't create gods from their own thinking. Israel received a divine revelation. God spoke to Moses. Moses was even able to ask God his name, and God answered, "YHWH" (יהוה; Ex. 3:15). This name of God is translated in our texts as either "Jehovah" or LORD.

The sailors began their harrowing time praying to their own deities. As they feared they were about to die, they heard from Jonah that the only real God was (and is!) the God of heaven, who also made the sea as well as land. Their gods were totally useless, but as they cried out for rescue to the LORD out of their new revelation, they found immediate relief. The true God then became the sailors' God.

The sailors needed the prereqs of life's experiences to teach them both (a) the ineptitude of seeking help in places other than YHWH and (b) that YHWH judged Jonah's disobedience. Knowing that, the sailors could understand that God is real, his power is without limits, and he cares about humanity. With those prereqs, the sailors were ready to seek God. I have the prereqs; I need to seek God!

Lord, be my God. Be my focus. Be my strength. In your powerful name, amen.

FEBRUARY 9

Then the mariners were afraid, and each cried out to his god. And they hurled the cargo that was in the ship into the sea to lighten it for them. But Jonah had gone down into the inner part of the ship and had lain down and was fast asleep. (Jonah 1:5)

Crisis reveals character. When the heat is on, when the world comes crashing down, and when the pressures of life intensify, the crisis reveals our deepest character and makeup. It did for Jonah, and it wasn't a nice picture.

Running from God, Jonah imperiled the lives of the sailors on his getaway boat. God's judgment was flashing with lightning (literally) and thunder, announcing God's displeasure to Jonah as well as those with him. Jonah should have been crying out for mercy, but I think he figured his life was over. He just went below deck and went to sleep, letting the boat, the men, and everything go down with him.

The text conveys this profoundly when reading it in its original Hebrew. The Hebrew is written to emphasize that Jonah was in a deep sleep, hence the translation "fast asleep." The Jewish translators of this text into Greek (in the centuries right before Jesus) emphasized this point by saying Jonah was snoring! Jonah knew the solution to the storm was to throw himself overboard (Jonah 1:11–12), but he seemed content to sleep and let them all die with him!

Jonah may have been a prophet of God, but Jonah certainly didn't share God's heart for others! In the midst of a crisis, Jonah's self-centeredness and disdain for non-Jews is on full display. He didn't seem to give a whit for the pagan crew.

This part of the story is unsettling to me. Whenever I find myself disgusted by the actions of others, a warning bell goes off in my head. I wonder where I may also be blindly guilty of something similar. Where are the places in my heart where I have lost compassion while instead focusing only on myself or my people?

As a final note, not only does Jonah's heart and character show in this time of crisis, but so does God's. God could have sunk the boat and rescued Jonah alone. But instead, God showed his compassion and concern for the lost Gentiles, in spite of Jonah. I'm glad God is bigger than I am.

Lord, forgive my callousness and times of self-centeredness. Help me to find my heart knitted to yours. I pray amen in you and your love.

FEBRUARY 10

The LORD hurled a great wind upon the sea. . . . Then the mariners were afraid, and each cried out to his god. . . . But Jonah . . . was fast asleep. So the captain came and said to him, "What do you mean, you sleeper? Arise, call out to your god! Perhaps the god will give a thought to us, that we may not perish." (Jonah 1:4–6)

My wife's name is Becky. I call Becky by a number of nicknames, some given by our grandchildren, but many of my own creation. I can write of Becky, or I can write of my wife. There are plenty of wives in the world, but I only have one.

Some people are shocked to find out that Scripture has a "name" that is given to God. That is the "name" God gave to Moses at the burning bush. It is the four Hebrew letters that take the English form of Y-H-V-H (or YHWH). From this word, first William Tyndale, followed by the King James Version of the Bible, developed the name *Jehovah* (see Ex. 6:3). When one reads *Jehovah* in the Bible, it is a translation of the Hebrew name *YHWH*. Most modern Bible translations translate God's name as LORD, using all capitals but a smaller font for the letters ORD (LORD). This is to distinguish the name of God from the general title of *Lord*, a translation of a different Hebrew word often referring to a human superior. While YHWH is God's "name," Hebrew also has the common word *god*, much like how *Becky* is the name of my spouse, while *wife* is who she is to me.

The book of Jonah includes a variety of Hebrew words for different gods. Consider the selected verses today. YHWH hurled the great wind. The sailors cried out to their gods (the common word for deities). The captain awakens Jonah, telling him to cry out to his "god," meaning whatever deity he worshiped. The captain adds that maybe *the* god of Jonah might help.

Later, Jonah will tell the sailors that his god is YHWH, the God who made heaven, earth, and the sea. Reluctantly, the soldiers throw Jonah overboard, and YHWH saves them all, stilling the sea. Then the sailors fear YHWH and sacrifice to him.

There is only one God. All the other places we look for help in the storms of life are useless unless they are used by the true God, YHWH. I may think the doctor will cure me, but he won't without the help of YHWH. I may think that my resources will provide me with food, but without the blessings of YHWH, I will starve. I need to recognize that all good things come from the one God, YHWH.

LORD, thank you for your love. May I live in your reality. In your name, amen.

FEBRUARY 11

And they said to one another, "Come, let us cast lots, that we may know on whose account this evil has come upon us." So they cast lots, and the lot fell on Jonah. (Jonah 1:7)

For most of my life, I have been a trial lawyer. Some weeks I work one hundred hours, some weeks just forty. I love my job, but it always seems to have me on call 24-7. Recently, I decided to take a rather long vacation with my family. While I couldn't shut work off, I consciously tried to shut it down, or at least restrict it to small time blocks. I wasn't being irresponsible. I decided that God wanted me to spend this time investing in my family. When God wants us to do something, we should make it a top priority. Yet even with all this, I struggled to detach. When I go five hours without checking emails because I am in court, I don't have a second thought. But when I go that same five hours because I am investing in family, I feel guilty and out of place for not being "at work."

Work is strange in that way, and it brings me to today's passage. Jonah had a paying job. The king paid Jonah to be a prophet and ostensibly wanted Jonah's support (2 Ki. 14:45). It was a good job, and it allowed him to go home each night. Intruding on Jonah's comfortable, rewarding world, God assigned him a new job. Jonah was to travel to the far-away enemy country of Assyria and find the great city of Nineveh. He would be a stranger there without any support from family or friends. There, he was to preach God's message of repentance. Jonah liked his current job and had no desire to go do his new calling. Jonah could be the originator of the phrase "I'd rather die than do that!"

So Jonah rebelled. He said "no!" to God. But he didn't just say "no," he headed the opposite way. Jonah went to great lengths to find a life outside of what God had instructed him. Jonah was willing to sacrifice home, family, and more to be out from under God's calling. Wow.

I need to get over my discomfort where God is involved. If God wants me to invest my time in my family, or in a ministry, or in a community, or in . . . (fill in the blank), I need to do so even if the task at hand is outside my comfort zone. My worries never need to be about myself or my abilities when I am out on God's business. My worry should be failing to do God's business!

Lord, give me direction for my steps today. Embolden me in faith to walk in your will. In your name, amen.

FEBRUARY 12

And he said to them, "I am a Hebrew, and I fear the LORD, *the God of heaven, who made the sea and the dry land." Then the men were exceedingly afraid and said to him, "What is this that you have done!" For the men knew that he was fleeing from the presence of the* LORD, *because he had told them.* (Jonah 1:9–10)

Gédéon Tallemant des Réaux (1619–1692) was a French lawyer turned writer who published a French history in the form of short biographies. He completed his *Historiettes* around 1659. In his stories about the reign of King Henry IV, Gédéon wrote, "Henry IV understood very well that to destroy Paris was, as they say, to cut off his nose to spite his face." This is one of the first modern uses of an expression that goes back several hundred years or more. Although it can't be found earlier than the 1100s, it certainly belongs in the life of Jonah!

In today's passage, Jonah spoke to the crew of a ship that was imperiled. Despite their considerable skills and efforts, the ship was going down. The crew sought divine help by casting lots and learned that the problem was Jonah. In response to their questions, Jonah told the crew that YHWH (a.k.a. "Jehovah" or "the LORD") was the one who made the sea. He was the God over the sea and everything else. It was YHWH who was responsible for the storm and would cause the deaths of all on the boat. The men were petrified over this because Jonah had previously confessed that he was on the run from YHWH.

I can excuse the crew. They had no clue that they were helping an outlaw run from the Judge of all judges. But Jonah? He's the epitome of cutting off his nose to spite his face.

Jonah would rather die than do what God had asked him to do. How did Jonah justify his decision in his head? "Oh, I'll show God! I'll refuse to go where he tells me to, and I'll go the opposite way!" Nothing good was going to come from that disobedience, and Jonah had to know that he would pay the price.

Sin is that way. It may seem marvelous in the moment, but it always bites in the end with a viciousness that far outweighs its benefits. I may not see the consequences immediately, and sometimes those consequences are missed opportunities for blessing, but they are always present!

Lord, forgive my foolish sin. Give me a mind to decide rightly in you. Amen.

FEBRUARY 13

He said to them, "Pick me up and hurl me into the sea; then the sea will quiet down for you, for I know it is because of me that this great tempest has come upon you." Nevertheless, the men rowed hard to get back to dry land, but they could not, for the sea grew more and more tempestuous against them. Therefore they called out to the LORD, "O LORD, let us not perish for this man's life, and lay not on us innocent blood, for you, O LORD, have done as it pleased you." So they picked up Jonah and hurled him into the sea, and the sea ceased from its raging. (Jonah 1:12–15)

In 1939, John Steinbeck published his iconic novel *The Grapes of Wrath*. Showing the harsh living of the Great Depression, Steinbeck follows families fleeing the desolate dust bowl in Oklahoma to migrant life in California. The two families at the core of the journey are the Joads and Casys. Midway through the story, Uncle John (Joad) is trying to figure out what to do, carrying the burden of feeling that he cost his wife her life by failing to get her medical care for a stomachache. Uncle John seeks the advice of ex-preacher Jim Casy. Casy tells Uncle John, "I know this—a man's got to do what he got to do." His lesson: sometimes people have to do things that they deem necessary, even if they don't want to.

That might be the adage spoken by the sailors in today's passage. Jonah's rebellion before God had put all their lives at risk. Jonah didn't voluntarily jump overboard, but he did tell the crew that they should throw him overboard. The crew tried everything, even rowing against the storm, to try to get to the safety of land. When nothing else worked, the crew prayed to Jonah's God (the LORD) for mercy and dumped Jonah overboard. Of course, killing another person by throwing him into the middle of a stormy ocean (a.k.a. "murder," or at least "negligent manslaughter") is not generally at the top of what one should be doing. But in the sense of Casy, "a man's got to do what he got to do."

If I had to defend these sailors for attempted murder, I would argue that their actions fall under the category of not getting in the way of what God is doing. How often we as parents step in to rescue our children from consequences that should follow from their behavior. I don't mean to imply there is no such thing as mercy, but sometimes people need to learn the hard lessons of life. Ultimately, there is no bright-line test; rather, on a case-by-case basis, wisdom is needed to know when or if to intervene to alleviate those consequences.

Lord, give me discernment to know proper mercy even as I let you have your way in this world. In your name, amen.

FEBRUARY 14

Then the men feared the LORD exceedingly, and they offered a sacrifice to the LORD and made vows. (Jonah 1:16)

I had a fellow driving me in a car in New York City. A somewhat gruff fellow, with Italian heritage, he softened noticeably when he found out I was serious about my Christian faith. Calling God "the Man Upstairs," he told me something he considered mildly offensive. He said, "I respect people who are serious about their faith, but I'm bothered by people who spend their life ignoring the Man Upstairs, and then when a crisis happens, they suddenly seek him to bail them out. I mean," he continued, "where were they talking to him for decades before the crisis? And now he's supposed to drop everything like they are best friends?"

I may not agree with his theology, but I find his point thought-provoking. In today's passage, the crew—whose lives were in danger, as their boat could not cope with the horrendous storm—suddenly found themselves in a peaceful sea. They had thrown Jonah overboard because of the wrath of YHWH, the God of Israel (called "the LORD" by our English translators). Then and only then, YHWH stilled the storm. Before throwing Jonah into the sea, the men had been praying each to their own god. Those prayers were totally ineffective. Only YHWH had the power to still the storm. Their ineffectual prayers to their own gods and YHWH's provision of a peaceful sea taught them that lesson. They didn't thank or sacrifice to their ineffective gods. They feared YHWH and sacrificed to him.

Sometimes we find YHWH in peaceful times of life. Sometimes we find him in times of difficulty. It is a fascinating irony in the story that the one who knew YHWH, Jonah, didn't sacrifice to YHWH; he fled from YHWH in disobedience. Meanwhile, the pagan sailors who didn't know YHWH properly feared God, sacrificed to him, and committed their lives through vows to him.

I think my NYC driver had a point. But I'm also concerned about those of us who have known the Lord for a long time and may have become complacent in following him, may have lost a bit of fear for him, and may not be concerned enough about what he has to say to us. If people come to God afresh because of an emergency in their lives, the critical question isn't where they were before but where they will be after the emergency. We all need to embrace our Lord.

Lord, may I fear you, follow you, and serve you. In your name, amen.

FEBRUARY 15

Then the mariners were afraid, and each cried out to his god . . . Then the men were exceedingly afraid and said to him, "What is this that you have done!" For the men knew that he was fleeing from the presence of the LORD, because he had told them. . . . Then the men feared the LORD exceedingly, and they offered a sacrifice to the LORD and made vows. (Jonah 1:5, 10, 16)

Mrs. Kingston made us read *The Scarlet Letter* our junior year of high school. I loved to read, but not stuff like that. I dreaded the book, thinking it tedious. Mrs. Kingston did make it a bit more interesting as she taught us about motifs. Motifs are recurring words, structures, or other literary devices that further the themes of the book. In *The Scarlet Letter*, for example, the author's use of the forest in contrast to the city highlights the distinction between natural authority and human authority.

Motifs are not new. Jonah had motifs as well. One word in constant repetition in the early story of the sailors is the Hebrew word for "fear" (*yir'ah* יִרְאָה). It is used six times in just eleven verses. By focusing on this word, we see a remarkable story within the story or a development of the story's overriding themes through the literary device of *motif*.

Consider the fear of the sailors. These were pagans with their own sets of gods. Verse five says that when the storm raged out of control, the mariners were "afraid." The storm continued unabated as the men figured out that Jonah was to blame. When Jonah explained he was on the run from YHWH, the Creator of heaven, earth, and the sea, the English reads that the sailors were "exceedingly afraid" (v. 10). Then finally, after heaving Jonah overboard followed by the restoration of peace to the sea, the men "feared the LORD exceedingly" (v. 16).

The Hebrew uses the word *fear*, but it's modified to show that its intensity grows during these events. Initially, the sailors simply "were *afraid*" (v. 5). Then the literal Hebrew says the men were "*afraid* with a great *fear*," using the word twice (v. 10). Finally, the men "*feared* with a great *fear*" in the Hebrew (v. 16). Notice the explosive shift! Early on, the men feared the storm, but in the end, when everything was peaceful, they feared the God of the storm. They feared God the most at a time when he was on their side and had rescued them!

I have fears, but it is God alone I should fear. Other fears are wasted.

Lord, teach me to fear as well as love you. In your name, amen.

FEBRUARY 16

And the Lord appointed a great fish to swallow up Jonah. (Jonah 1:17)

In 1980, George Lakoff and Mark Johnson published the landmark book *Metaphors We Live By*. In it, they discuss how humanity thinks in metaphors. Metaphors lace our language, often without us noticing. An example is the metaphorical concept "time is money." That common metaphor finds its way into our everyday speech as we say, "Don't *waste* my time." "The computer will *save* you hours." "How do you *spend* your day?" "I've *invested* a lot of time in parenting." Or one of my favorites, "He's living on *borrowed* time."

While I'm not sure I concur with all of Lakoff and Johnson's conclusions, they are certainly on target that people think metaphorically. Metaphor not only permeates our language, but it also infiltrates our literature. Grand sagas like *The Lord of the Rings* and *The Chronicles of Narnia* are metaphors on a large scale, laced with other metaphors on a small scale.

This surfaces as a point when anyone poses the question about Jonah, "Was it real?" People debate whether the story is a factual account of a large fish gobbling and then regurgitating Jonah or whether it is more akin to a C. S. Lewis story that teaches important lessons through a narrative, as in *The Chronicles of Narnia* and *The Great Divorce*. To me, that subject is moot. God certainly has the ability to appoint a fish grand enough to accomplish the task. He similarly has the ability to sustain life for three days and nights underwater with no breathing apparatus, which is the real miracle in a literal reading of Jonah. He is God. But we also know that he has chosen to communicate his truth in a wide variety of ways, both through symbolism—using stories and parables—and through illustrations.

Regardless of the actual events that occurred, almost everyone can agree that the story of Jonah is not a lesson in ichthyology (the study of fish). As with all biblical passages, my goal needs to be to understand the narrative for *its purposes*. Among the clear purposes of Jonah is that the sea obeys God. Even the fish of the sea obey God. Yet for some reason, we often struggle in that department. I am no different. I must never get so caught up in arguing how God is communicating his message that I fail to see his message. He is calling me to obedience. I need to answer that call.

Lord, I am so often at a loss to walk in obedience. I tend to do so with the easy stuff, but I get a bit lost when times are tough. Help me, please. In your name, amen.

FEBRUARY 17

And Jonah was in the belly of the fish three days and three nights. (Jonah 1:17)

On a recent family vacation, one of our grandchildren was acting up. In fairness to him, he was short on sleep and quite hungry as well. He was a bit out of control playing in the ball pit alongside his younger sisters. Our daughter corrected him about how to behave, but he ignored her, continuing to do some things that could hurt his younger sisters. So our daughter removed him from the ball pit and placed him in "time-out" to give him time to think about what he was doing and to discipline him for not obeying her. He quickly adjusted his mind-set and was released to be the brilliant, marvelous boy he is.

This parenting moment reminded me of Jonah's story. God basically put Jonah in time-out—a long, obscure time-out! Jonah had failed to obey God. Jonah had somewhat lost his senses. This prophet of God became a renegade, and rather than let him continue in reckless disobedience, God placed him in time-out.

This gave Jonah time to think. It removed him from the life of this world, with its pleasures and opportunities, and placed him face-to-face with death. (More on that tomorrow.) This disciplined Jonah in the best way that discipline can work. It gave Jonah the negative consequences of fleeing God and did so in a way that would encourage his obedience in the future.

God has placed me in time-out before. As I have walked in areas of disobedience, God has removed me from fun blessings and opportunities. He has let me experience some of the fear and negative consequences of my sin. He has also given me chances to repent and has graciously accepted me back into his mission for me and my life.

I don't hold this discipline against God. I thank him for it. In some ways, I am not that much different from my nearly three-year-old grandson. I get distracted, hungry, tired, and so on, and my behavior can be less than it should be. God hasn't had to send me into the belly of a fish, but he's still placed me in my own time-out. God's discipline still has me thinking. . . . It's a challenge to live right before God.

Lord, I repent over my disobedience in this life. I thank you for your forgiveness and mercy. I seek to serve you. In your name, amen.

FEBRUARY 18

Then Jonah prayed to the LORD his God from the belly of the fish, saying, "I called out to the LORD, out of my distress, and he answered me." (Jonah 2:1–2)

As a young boy, about age fifteen, I had a chance to attend a set of meetings in New Mexico taught by a Nashville preacher, Don Finto. To say I was impressed would be a major understatement. I was blown away. God used those several days to teach me, inspire me, motivate me, and set me down a road that still affects me today. The daylight hours were spent knocking on doors and walking through the community to invite people to attend a nightly service. Then for three consecutive nights, Don preached and taught and answered audience questions.

Many of his sermon points remain in my memory. One in particular came out of the Q and A time. Someone had submitted a question along the lines of "I know God had a plan for my life, but I have blown it. I didn't follow his will, and I made a mess of my life. What hope is there for me now?"

Don replied with a core biblical teaching. He explained that nobody was on God's Plan A for her or his life. Everyone has blown Plan A. Don then added that he was likely on Plan triple Z. Yet God was still using him. God still had a plan for him. The important thing is for people—wherever they are in life and with whatever mess they have made—to turn their hearts to God in repentance and to call on his power and character (a.k.a. his "name") to deliver them.

Don didn't use Jonah as an example that night, but he could have. When Jonah disobeyed, God still used him. God told him to go to Nineveh, and he could have done so, but he didn't, at least not immediately. Jonah went to the harbor and could have changed his mind, turning inland for the northeastern journey to Nineveh, but he didn't. He went the opposite direction. Jonah could have had the boat turn around, but he didn't. He had it sail into the storm. Jonah could have repented while in the boat, but he didn't. He was thrown overboard. Jonah could have cried out from the waves for God's mercy, but he didn't. He was swallowed by a fish. Even then, he was three days into his burial in the fish's guts before he finally cried out to God.

God heard Jonah. God forgave him and rescued him. God still had a plan. That's the kind of God we serve.

Lord, forgive me for my misses. I pray for mercy and purpose in you, amen.

FEBRUARY 19

"Out of the belly of Sheol . . ." (Jonah 2:2)

I played racquetball yesterday and got killed. OK, not literally. In fact, I won the match, but I was dead afterward. OK, still not literally. But I was shot for the rest of the day!

Over and over, Jonah uses the metaphor of "death." It is found in the Hebrew, although it isn't so readily recognizable in English. English expressions of death include *passed away* or *kicked the bucket*. Phrases like *bite the dust, rest in peace, breathe your last,* and *give up the ghost* pepper our language. We know what is meant when we hear that someone has gone to "meet their maker."

One common Hebrew word that references death is *Sheol. Sheol* is a Hebrew word that has a broad meaning; it can refer to the underworld, the grave, or death. (Hence the Apostle Paul used the word provocatively, asking, "O death, where is your sting?" in 1 Cor. 15:55, where he quotes Hos. 13:14 but replaces the Hebrew word *Sheol* with a common Greek word for death [*thanatos*].)

Over and over, Jonah uses the language and images of death:

- Jonah 2:3—"You cast me into the deep . . . the flood surrounded me."
- Jonah 2:5—"The waters closed in over me to take my life; the deep surrounded me."
- Jonah 2:5–6—"Weeds were wrapped about my head at the roots of the mountains. I went down to the land whose bars closed upon me forever."
- Jonah 2:6–7—"Yet you brought up my life from the pit . . . when my life was fainting away."

Jonah thought himself dead during the three days and nights in the belly of the fish. In his rebellious flight from God's face, he found himself as far away as might be found. He was as good as dead and considered himself beyond the land of the living. He had sought to flee from God by venturing to a foreign land, and he went further than even he planned! It was as far as the point of death. There is a lesson for me here: Why would I ever be so foolish as to ignore or flee my God?

Lord, please give me life in your presence today and every day. In you I pray, amen!

FEBRUARY 20

"I called . . . he answered . . . I cried, and you heard my voice." (Jonah 2:2)

The passage harkens to a song melody in my head. "Came to My Rescue" is a 2008 Hillsong recording that moves me. The song has a chorus that says, "I called, you answered, and you came to my rescue, and I wanna be where you are." In the song, we both praise God but also offer our devotion to God. The song begins with worship: "Falling on my knees in worship . . ." and moves quickly to devotion: "Giving all I am to seek your face, Lord all I am is yours. My whole life I place in your hands."

It is apparent to me that Jonah didn't know this song. Since the song came out in 2008, I can cut him some slack, but looking at his life, it is clear Jonah didn't live what the lyrics teach.

Jonah might have understood this part: "I called, you answered, and you came to my rescue." But the parts about worship? The devotion? Somehow Jonah would have missed those concepts. To be sure, Jonah did wind up going to Nineveh as God commanded, and he even ended his prayer with a promise of devotion, but his motives were never quite right. The story line shows Jonah never knitted his heart to God's purpose. Jonah follows God but ends up quite bitter over what God "made" him do.

I don't want to miss *all* the lyrics to the song. I don't want my dedication to God to be one of deed only. I also want to mean that part of the song that focuses on my heart: my worship and devotion. God has intervened in my life over and over. I have cried out to him in distress, and he has heard my voice; he has rescued me. His faithful love should move me to a humble dedication. I should strive to be consecrated and committed not only to God's directives but to his heart. God rightly deserves my fidelity, attentiveness, and support. I need to get these song lyrics right in my life.

The song concludes with the plea "In my life, be lifted high; in our world, be lifted high; in our love, be lifted high." May God be praised in what I do, in the world beyond my life, and in the attitude that moves me.

God of Mercy, humbled, I bow down in your presence at your throne. Be glorified in my life. In your name, amen.

FEBRUARY 21

"For you cast me into the deep, into the heart of the seas, and the flood surrounded me; all your waves and your billows passed over me." (Jonah 2:3)

One summer as a young man, I had the amazing opportunity to work for a church south of Houston, Texas. Part of my responsibilities that summer included preaching on alternating Sunday nights. I remember well the Sunday I decided to preach on Jonah. I had prepared by carefully and repeatedly reading the book, both in English and at least partially in Hebrew. (At the time, I had taken only two years of Hebrew, so my reading was less than thorough!) I had also read through a few commentaries on the book. I had written a good three-point sermon with what I had hoped was an attention-getting introduction as well as a poignant, thought-provoking conclusion. I thought, "I am ready to go!"

After some singing and a prayer, I stood up to deliver my thirty-minute sermon. I began by telling the story. "The word of the Lord came to Jonah . . ." The story was already known by almost everyone. After telling it, I moved on to the next sermon points, discussing and then applying the lessons from the story. Afterward, the "encouragers" of the congregation came up to make sure I felt good about my efforts. As I visited with people, I basically heard the same comment over and over: "You did really good except for one thing—*you never said 'Jonah.' The whole sermon, you called him Noah! You just preached on Noah and the big fish!*"

There's a big difference between Jonah and Noah. In some ways, about all they had in common was a lot of water! Noah was a righteous man who heeded God's instructions; Jonah ignored God. Noah rose above the floodwaters; as noted in today's passage, the flood surrounded Jonah. Noah is a biblical hero, an example of what to do; Jonah is a biblical example of what not to do.

I still confuse the two in my brain. In fact, in writing this devotional, I twice mistakenly typed *Noah* instead of *Jonah*! Yet I should never confuse the actions of the two. I want and need to be a Noah, by hearing the word of God and obeying in faith. I want to avoid being a Jonah, by hearing the word of God but deciding I just don't care.

Lord, make me sensitive to your word. May I have a heart for your mission, trust in your strength, and faith that moves me to obedience. In you I pray, amen.

FEBRUARY 22

"At the roots of the mountains. I went down to the land whose bars closed upon me forever; yet you brought up my life from the pit, O LORD my God." (Jonah 2:6)

In 1993, I lost one of the most devastating cases in my career. I represented a widow with ten children whose husband had died in a helicopter crash, and the jury decided that the company and pilot had not committed any errors, awarding zero to the family. That same year, I won one of the most significant cases in my career, when a jury decided that a large oil company had defrauded my client, awarding him substantial damages. I have always looked back on that year as one of notable highs and lows.

"Highs and lows" in life are not new ideas or expressions. In Jonah, the writer uses those ideas to great effect, although in Jonah, they are "ups and downs" rather than highs and lows. This contrast starts early, in Jonah 1:2-3. God calls Jonah to go to Nineveh because the "evil has *come up* before" God. Instead, Jonah *"went down* to Joppa" and then *"went down* into" the ship (emphasis mine). The image is clear: Jonah got the command of God to raise himself up to travel to Nineveh because its evil had risen before God. Jonah was called to stand with God against the evil arising before God's face. Instead, Jonah rebelled. He didn't stand with God. Instead, Jonah went down away from God.

Jonah's downward spiral continues, as he had *"gone down"* into the inner part of the ship (1:5). Then Jonah is tossed overboard, and one pictures him going down into the sea, gobbled by a fish that then swims even deeper (1:15, 17). This picture continues in chapter 2 as the "deep" surrounds him (2:5). Then a pivot is found in today's passage. As Jonah says, he *"went down* to the land whose bars closed upon" him, and God *"brought [him] up"* from the pit (2:6; emphasis mine)!

I love the metaphor of up and down. We use it today. My friend Richard is fond of saying, "Do the right thing. Take the *high* road; there's less traffic on it!" Why is it often said, "I didn't turn around until I hit rock bottom"? What is it about us that numbly refuses to be humble and obedient servants to the King? I suspect one reason is that we often have more faith in ourselves than in the Lord. We are more confident that we will navigate a good course for our lives than God will. It's often not until we reach the deep pit of despair that we finally relent and we find the saving Lord.

Lord, lift me from my sin. Teach me to walk your high road of life. In you, amen.

FEBRUARY 23

And the LORD *spoke to the fish, and it vomited Jonah out upon the dry land. Then the word of the* LORD *came to Jonah the second time, saying* . . . (Jonah 2:10–3:1)

My friend Kevin is a punny guy. No, that isn't a typo. Kevin can and will make a pun of almost anything. Usually they're funny; sometimes they're simple punishment. But Kevin's puns could easily roll off his tongue with Jonah.

At this point in Jonah's life, having tried to flee from God, Jonah found himself washed up. He'd made a wreck of his life. His plans were fishy at best. Not even a fish could stomach Jonah. Jonah got in over his head. When it came time to sink or swim, Jonah did neither. Jonah at his best was still all wet. Yet with all the puns, and with all the problems, something rings clear: God was not letting Jonah go.

In 1893, Francis Thompson published a famous poem entitled "The Hound of Heaven." In it, God seeks out the author, even as the author flees from God day and night for years, trying to get lost in the maze of his own mind. Though he hid, tried to laugh away God, chased hopes, and lived through fears, the author couldn't get away from God. For God sought him deliberately, with God's timing and with majesty. As the poem draws to an end, the author realizes that God is not his gloom but the very answer to all that he has been seeking in life.

So it was with Jonah. Jonah sought to be done with God, but God wasn't done with Jonah. All was well and good for Jonah as he prophesied the good things from God's hand. But when God set Jonah to a chore that Jonah didn't want to do, Jonah sought release from his master. But the master said, "No!" God brought Jonah back, even though Jonah was unhappy about it, pouting like a baby! God even gave Jonah time to get his act together before getting to Nineveh, since Nineveh was over four hundred miles from where the fish regurgitated Jonah. God didn't punt on Jonah. He continued to work on Jonah until Jonah fulfilled his mission.

I am glad God doesn't give up easily. I don't want to become the subject of puns. I want to be God's servant the first time, every time, and I am thankful we worship a God of second chances.

Lord, may serving you be my highest desire. In your name, amen.

FEBRUARY 24

Then the word of the LORD came to Jonah the second time, saying, "Arise, go to Nineveh, that great city, and call out against it the message that I tell you." (Jonah 3:1–2)

Among the many changes initiated in society from the pandemic of 2020 was the increased commonness of paperless payments. Instead of handing over potentially germ-laden money from one possible infectee to another, people began paying retailers by tapping or inserting credit cards or using their smartphones to transmit banking data. I have been in a number of locations post-pandemic lockdown where no cash is allowed; all payments have to be electronic.

But be it in cash or in an electronic medium, money is still money. If I pay in cash, my available money dwindles. If I pay electronically, my money dwindles. Money is money.

The "word" of God can be viewed similarly. The word of God is God's message whether it is transmitted by one source or another. I can have a paper copy of God's word or an electronic copy. But either way, it is still the word of God.

Look carefully at today's passage. The "word" of the Lord comes to Jonah. The word tells Jonah to deliver God's message or word to Nineveh. God sends his word directly to Jonah, but that word is an instruction to carry God's word for Nineveh to Nineveh. This is God's word moving from a message to Jonah to a message to Nineveh. But in both messages was the word of the Lord.

This affects the way I read Scripture. I want to read in context, understanding the word of the Lord as it came originally to the prophets who put it in written form so people could read it for ages to come. But I also want to read it in application, seeking to understand what it says to me. The prophets didn't just speak God's word; they *wrote* it at God's instruction because that word *does* have something to say to future generations.

I may wish that God would speak directly to me in the sense he did to Jonah or Moses. But sometimes God isn't using the communication methods I would like. Nevertheless, just as money is money, so the word of God is the word of God.

Lord, give me ears to hear your word for me today. In your name, amen.

FEBRUARY 25

So Jonah arose and went to Nineveh, according to the word of the LORD. Now Nineveh was an exceedingly great city, three days' journey in breadth. (Jonah 3:3)

One of the most difficult things I had to learn as a lawyer was eliminating impersonal pronouns in speech. Words like *her, him, his, hers,* or *its* are often ambiguous. When I use these pronouns, I'm never in doubt of who or what they reference, but the listener may easily take them the wrong way. Two of my mentor lawyers were consistently correcting my speech. When I would say, "He did thus and so," they would interject, "He who?" Soon I broke the habit!

I am reminded of this because of potential ambiguity in today's passage. Nineveh is described here as "an exceedingly great city." The literal Hebrew reading, given by the English Standard Version in its footnotes, is that Nineveh was "a great city to God." I really like chewing on this passage in Hebrew. My main source of meditation is the Hebrew word for "great" (*gadol*—גָדוֹל).

In Hebrew, *great* can refer to a vast reservoir of ideas. Great can mean large in size, which Nineveh certainly was. Great can mean tall in height, and Nineveh certainly had some tall buildings for that region. Great can refer to a population, as in a large number of inhabitants, again something true of Nineveh. Great can also refer to significance. Some of the smallest things are still great in significance. Nineveh was certainly a significant city in the Assyrian Empire. Great can refer to age, power, influence, and so much more. In the world's eyes, Nineveh merited the adjective *great* in almost every way.

Yet the Hebrew says that Nineveh was great *to God.* Why? I don't think God was impressed with Nineveh's size, the height of its buildings, its significance to the region or the empire, the age of the city, or many of the things that could be referenced by "great." But the people of Nineveh were significant to God. As God makes clear to Jonah at the end of the story, Nineveh had over 120,000 people in need of knowing God. That was God's care. Those people made the city "great" to God.

You and I are "great" to God too. He cares about people. God wants us to know him, and he works to that end. I am glad we have this caring God.

Lord, thank you for your love and caring. I find peace in it. In your name, amen.

FEBRUARY 26

Jonah began to go into the city, going a day's journey. And he called out, "Yet forty days, and Nineveh shall be overthrown!" And the people of Nineveh believed God. They called for a fast and put on sackcloth, from the greatest of them to the least of them. (Jonah 3:4–5)

Modern songwriter and singer Dua Lipa's song "Be the One" is about how differently she sees the world than her boyfriend. She sees the moon, while he looks at the sun. She sees in blue, while he sees everything in red. Despite those differences, she believes he could be the one! Different people see the world differently, especially in matters of faith. Yet I am convinced that even as the world can be seen through different lenses, we can find truth in more than one lens. That is what I see in today's passage.

Today's passage is a stunner, at least if one doesn't know the story! I am reminded of how many people hear the word of God and ignore it, fight or argue against it, or simply reject it. Not so the Ninevites. Why? What was it that brought them to respond so readily and quickly to this word of a foreign God? The answer depends in part on through which lens you look.

As to Nineveh, we have volumes of historical information from written sources recovered by archaeologists and explorers. Nineveh was one of several great cities in the Assyrian Empire. The empire had reached great strength under earlier kings, but at this time, Assyria was rather weak. Furthermore, a very rare occurrence in Nineveh happened during the time of Jonah. On June 15, 763 BC, a near total eclipse of the sun occurred from 9:33 a.m. to 12:19 p.m. The record of this eclipse has been found in excavated texts of Nineveh. No doubt, it was highly disturbing to the people! A final note on this time in Assyrian history concerns an external threat by the nation of Urartu. Urartu, a nation to the north of Assyria, had been threatening to invade Assyria. These events already had the people on edge when Jonah came preaching, "In forty days Nineveh will be overturned!"

While history gives reasons the people would be sensitive to God's message, the eyes of faith see that God chose the right time for Jonah to preach. The moment was propitious. It was no accident. Reading this, I wonder why I ever question God's timing. He sees it right, even when I don't!

Lord, you are the One, and I want to see things as you do. In your name, amen.

FEBRUARY 27

The word reached the king of Nineveh, and he arose from his throne, removed his robe, covered himself with sackcloth, and sat in ashes. (Jonah 3:6)

In high school, I went on a two-week trip in a van with a bunch of other students and several adult sponsors. At one point, an adult sponsor was talking to several other students about Izod shirts. I had no clue what they were talking about. They explained that Izod shirts had alligators on them and that we should all wear our alligator shirts on the same day. I told them I didn't have an Izod shirt. Looking back, I not only didn't have the clothing of status; I didn't even know what it was!

Status clothing didn't begin in the twentieth century. It predates the time of Jesus. In the days of Jonah, the king of Nineveh wore regal robes as a status sign (as we know from Assyrian artwork). Those robes marked him off as accountable to no one. No one else could wear such robes. They set him apart as the sovereign ruler of the empire. But there came a day when he was told God had taken notice of him and his kingdom. God was going to bring judgment.

The king removed his clothes of status because he saw that his status had changed. No longer was he the determiner of the destiny of his people. No longer was he defender of his people. Like everyone else, the king was under the judging sword of the Lord God Almighty. The king needed to repent.

Removing his clothes of status, the king put on sackcloth, which was a course, rough burlap used for hauling grain. The sackcloth was a symbol of repentance, mourning, and submission. All three purposes reflected the changed status of the king. He was repenting of his sin, mourning his sin, and submitting to the mercy of the judging God.

Today, people talk about "wearing" an air of superiority. Some will wear their persona. Some wear tattoos, piercings, or other body art. Some still wear clothing to denote a position or job (judge's robes, police uniforms, etc.). But everyone, regardless of job or position, needs to remember that there comes a call from God for genuine change in one's life. At that point, we need to change our status. We don't need to fit into some prescribed role in this world. We need to fit into the role God has for us. Changing into that role requires genuine repentance and submission—a change in status.

Lord, I repent of my sins. Help me walk in your ways. In your name, amen.

FEBRUARY 28

And he issued a proclamation and published through Nineveh, "By the decree of the king and his nobles: . . . Let everyone turn from his evil way and from the violence that is in his hands. Who knows? God may turn and relent and turn from his fierce anger, so that we may not perish." (Jonah 3:7–9)

Authentic, genuine, real—these are important traits for people. I want to be an authentic person, where what you see is what you get. Yet I find that wanting that and achieving that are not the same! Consider parenting. I once took a test to determine what kind of parent I was. In the cool, calm testing room, with time to think, I considered test questions with various fact patterns: "When you are in the middle of a phone call, and your child comes up to you and interrupts, how do you respond?" The answers of A–E included ignoring your child, giving your child a bad look, being rough in your language, or calmly explaining to your child that you are on the phone, and unless it is an emergency, your child needs to wait until you are done.

Those test questions were easy to answer. I found I could give the "right" answer because in that calm testing environment, I knew exactly how I wanted to parent. Yet when the events really happen, it's much harder! The interruption comes during an important call that is taxing your emotional and mental energies already. Or you are in the middle of an intense problem, and your child has been "difficult" for much of the last hour. Or you are pressed for time to deal with the phone matter, and you're also "hangry" (a term our daughter taught us expressing the anger that occurs when you are hungry). Suddenly, you aren't the perfect parent that you want to be under test conditions.

In today's passage, the king of Nineveh declared a state of mourning and repentance for all his subjects. But it started with his own repentance. He had already removed his robes and put on sackcloth before having his subjects do the same. His call to his subjects came out of genuine authenticity, not some "you do this, but I will do that" hypocritical attitude. He was practicing what he preached.

I admire the king's authenticity. I'm not surprised that it caused God to relent in his judgment. It also challenges me to grow in my own life. *I* want to practice the things I write in this book urging others to do. Authenticity doesn't happen overnight, but it should be an all-day-every-day pursuit.

Lord, help me to live in authentic, genuine ways. In your name, I pray, amen.

MARCH 1

When God saw what they did, how they turned from their evil way, God relented of the disaster that he had said he would do to them, and he did not do it. (Jonah 3:10)

Scenario 1: A teacher at the local high school gave a student a failing grade. That student was a nice fellow, came from a good family, and was really pretty smart. It didn't matter. The teacher failed the student anyway.

Scenario 2: A teacher at the local high school told the class that everyone had to turn in a term paper. Failure to turn in the term paper would result in an automatic failure in the class. The students were given plenty of time, the teacher was available for any questions or help the students needed, and the teacher sent out frequent calendar reminders of when the paper was due. The class included a student who was a nice fellow, came from a good family, and was really pretty smart. It didn't matter when the student failed to write and turn in his paper. The teacher failed the student anyway, and the student was unable to graduate.

These two scenarios are the same. Scenario 2 simply gives more details than scenario 1. These scenarios bring to mind today's passage.

God has hardwired people to understand right from wrong. God made the world where right leads to better circumstances and results, while wrong leads to poorer ones. The adverse consequences may not be immediately evident, but this principle is inevitable in the long-term. So when people are going haywire in their lives, when sin is counted as a virtue rather than something to avoid, then society will suffer, as will people in society. That was the road of the Ninevites before Jonah. They needed someone to remind them that without a behavioral change, they would fail. But if they turned from their sin, God would ensure that they would not fail.

Sin begets pain, misery, and heartache. It's as sure a fact as two plus two is four. God has made that clear. It's in the fabric of the world and cosmos. People might wish it otherwise, but wishes aren't reality. People might imagine life differently, but life isn't found in our imaginations. Fortunately, God has also incorporated mercy into the world. God wants joy, happiness, and a rich life for everyone. But that rich life comes from walking in his truth and not the ways of the world. We need to do our term paper.

Lord, forgive me for my sin. May I walk purely in you and your name, amen.

MARCH 2

But it displeased Jonah exceedingly, and he was angry. . . . [And he said,] "Therefore now, O LORD, please take my life from me, for it is better for me to die than to live." (Jonah 4:1, 3)

I try hard to like Jonah. After all, he is a memorable Bible character. Here is a fellow who gets swallowed by a fish and is then spat out. He goes to a foreign land and preaches repentance to a receptive people who repent. He gets the satisfaction of fulfilling his calling before God and seeing it bear fruit. But then he broods and feels angry because God showed mercy on these penitent foreigners. It leaves me struggling to like him.

I want to cross-examine Jonah. I have more than a few questions to ask him: What's your problem? Don't you care about people? Are you a racist? Do you only care about yourself and your relatives? Do you mind if the world falls apart on others? Aren't you supposed to be on God's team? Aren't you supposed to have the heart of God? Don't you rejoice when people come to have faith in God? Don't you feel satisfaction when God uses you to reach an unreached people? Don't you celebrate when God's plans work and come to fruition?

Jonah doesn't seem to have good answers to these questions. Jonah says he would sooner die than live, perhaps feeling God wasted his time. This strikes me as incredibly selfish, narcissistic, offensive, and sinful behavior. It almost makes me wish God would have said, "OK, sounds good. I will take your life now!"

But the same God who had mercy on the Ninevites also had mercy on Jonah. So God goes to work teaching Jonah a better perspective. God's patience amazes me in this story.

I can be appalled at Jonah, but in truth, I know that my behavior isn't much better. In some ways, I am likely worse. God gives me opportunities to share his love and mercy with the world, and many times I shy away from the moment. There are times when God shows mercy to others, and I think it's fairer if they get what's coming to them. I'm not any better than Jonah, and yet the patient God still has mercy on me. He's still working on me to develop me into a godlier person. I'm eternally grateful for our God.

Lord, forgive my judgmentalism, and have mercy on me in your name, amen.

MARCH 3

And he prayed to the LORD and said, "O LORD, is not this what I said when I was yet in my country? That is why I made haste to flee to Tarshish; for I knew that you are a gracious God and merciful, slow to anger and abounding in steadfast love, and relenting from disaster." (Jonah 4:2)

I had been on a diet for several months. It was going really well. I had lost a good bit of weight, my clothes fit much better, and I was feeling lighter on my feet. Then Becky and I took our grandson for ice cream. I decided I could afford a day off my strict regime and I ordered an ice cream cone. The vendor asked how many scoops, and I said, "One. . . . No, two! . . . Let's just make it three scoops!" Then I ate all three, and I felt both great and horrible at the same time.

So it is with today's passage. Certain messages jump out at me, and they make me feel both great and horrible at the same time. First, I find Jonah's prayer life fascinating. He has no problem saying outright to God, "I told you so." This prophet of God wasn't praying saintly prayers of praise and adoration. His were dialogue prayers like he might have with his neighbors. They are loaded with familiarity and even challenge.

Second, I find today's passage sets up questions of Jonah's motives, none of which shine as "prophet worthy" in my mind. John Calvin thought Jonah was angry because God's actions denigrated the name of God by letting the scoffing heathen find life. Luther was likely more accurate in that Jonah was biased against the city of Nineveh and the Assyrians in general and didn't want them to experience God's forgiveness. Others believe that Jonah was upset because he thought that God wasted Jonah's time. Jonah figured God was merciful and therefore was going to have mercy on the Assyrians, even if they were merely temporarily repentant.

Even though tired, the prophet Jonah accurately describes the character of God. God is gracious. God is merciful. While God's anger builds slowly, his love never ceases. His love overflows and abounds. God looks for ways to save people from the catastrophes of life as well as the consequences of eternity.

Like my triple-scoop cone, this passage leaves me feeling both up and down. I like God in the story, not so much Jonah. Jonah's cavalier attitude and poor motivations, all with good insight into God, frustrate me.

Lord, I need your steadfast love and mercy; may I want it for others too. Amen.

MARCH 4

"Therefore now, O LORD, please take my life from me, for it is better for me to die than to live." And the LORD said, "Do you do well to be angry?" (Jonah 4:3–4)

Star Trek was never a show; it was an enterprise. Set three hundred years in the future, the original series spawned sequels and prequels. Regardless of the show or the season, however, certain things remained constant. One constant was the ability of a starship to self-destruct. On all the shows, it was "Starfleet Order two-zero-zero-five." However, the show's writers could have called it "Jonah four-three-four-four."

Jonah's prayer above is so extreme that it seems like hyperbole. As a reminder, the backstory is relatively simple: God tells Jonah to go to a foreign people in Nineveh and preach repentance. Jonah doesn't want the people to repent, doesn't want them to find God's mercy, and tries to opt out of God's job. Jonah heads west—the opposite direction. God intervenes in Jonah's flight as only God can, and Jonah is again instructed to go preach repentance to Nineveh. Jonah goes, Nineveh repents, and that brings us to today's passage.

Jonah asks God to take his life because, he claims, "it is better to die than to live." Even after all he has seen God do, Jonah still has no interest in walking in God's purposes for his life. But death is only better than life when God is done with our lives. As long as God has work for us to do, we properly stay alive.

I like the way the Apostle Paul saw this issue. Paul was steeped in Judaism, having been a top student of Rabban Gamliel, one of the most prestigious teachers of Judaism in the first century. Paul knew the story of Jonah like the back of his hand. Paul wrote from a Roman prison to a church in Macedonia (modern northern Greece) and explained that for Paul, death would be a "gain" so he could "be with Christ." Yet Paul had a mission from God, and hence his life was necessary. So he gladly lived for Jesus even though dying was a personal gain (Phil. 1:21-26).

Jonah had a very narcissistic focus. He had a vital mission from God, but for Jonah, his faith walk seemed only important when it coincided with what he already wanted for his own life. When God's desires and directions conflicted with Jonah's wants, Jonah wanted nothing to do with them. I have a lesson here.

Lord, I don't want to be a Jonah. I want to align my desires in life with your desires for me. Help me, Lord, to have your heart and mind. In you, I pray, amen.

MARCH 5

Jonah went out of the city and sat to the east of the city and made a booth for himself there. He sat under it in the shade, till he should see what would become of the city. (Jonah 4:5)

In 1876, Samuel Clemens (a.k.a. Mark Twain) published the classic novel *The Adventures of Tom Sawyer*. One of the iconic scenes occurred when Aunt Polly punished Tom by making him whitewash the fence. As Tom was painting the fence, a neighbor boy, Ben Rogers, began teasing him. Tom's response was to make painting the fence seem like an honor, not an order. Tom explained not many boys got to do such a task. Ben begged to get to paint. By setting out painting as a privilege, not an obligation, Tom manipulated enough boys to paint the fence, some even paying for the chance to do so, while Tom watched and played.

Can you manipulate God? Is he a genie that, if you rub the right way, will grant three wishes? Is there some secret formula to get him to do what we want instead of doing his will? Does God respond to our pouting or passive-aggressive behavior? Is the Creator of the universe a bellhop who will come get our luggage if we ask him to? Jonah seemed to have fallen into the trap of thinking so. I fear we often do as well, albeit not necessarily wanting the same thing Jonah wanted.

Jonah was ready either for God to destroy Nineveh—a sight for which he had found a front-row seat—or for God to take Jonah's life. Jonah has already told God as much in the preceding verses (see yesterday's devotional). Having thrown a hissy fit in the prior verses, Jonah sat to see if God would do as Jonah wanted.

It didn't work. God was no more manipulated by Jonah than by you or me. One of the most difficult challenges for everyone is to get on God's page. Most people try to get God on their own page. Prayer can often evolve into a list of things one wants rather than a time of seeking and then submitting to God's will.

The Almighty God has a plan for the universe. He has given me and you roles to play in that plan. Our goal in life should never be to get God to twist his plan to fit our particular wants or perceived needs. Our goal should be to find his plan for our lives and seek his help in living as he wants us to live.

Lord, I confess too often I make this life about me rather than you. Forgive me and give me direction and strength to walk in your ways. In you, amen.

MARCH 6

Now the LORD God appointed a plant and made it come up over Jonah, that it might be a shade over his head, to save him from his discomfort. So Jonah was exceedingly glad because of the plant. But when dawn came up the next day, God appointed a worm that attacked the plant, so that it withered. (Jonah 4:6–7)

Looking back in life, almost everyone can identify a teacher that had a profound influence in his or her life. Mrs. Kingston drove students to love literature and learning. She was stringent, yet kind. She worked us hard, yet did so with humor and fun. She insisted we get things right, yet taught us step-by-step how to do so.

Some of life's effective teachers aren't in a typical classroom. Joe Stapleton taught me the value of hard work, whether mopping floors or stocking shelves in his corner store. My parents taught me the importance of family, as they always sacrificed for the good of their children. At one point, my dad told his employer that he needed to be transferred back to Texas, or he would find another job because he and my mom decided we kids needed to be in Texas at that stage of life. Technically, most of my courtroom work involves teaching. I teach a jury the facts along with any applicable science or medicine.

God is the consummate teacher. He doesn't simply wag a finger in the general direction of the world and see that his tasks are completed. God constantly seeks those moments to teach, instruct, clarify, explain, and educate his people. He is at work trying to renew and rewire minds to think the way he does.

In today's passage, Jonah has continued his poor attitude that has been on display throughout the book that bears his name. Jonah doesn't want God's salvation for the Ninevites. Jonah wants them destroyed under God's righteous judgment. When Jonah won't snap out of it, God uses Jonah's stubbornness and anger as a teachable moment. God has a plant grow up miraculously overnight to provide shade for Jonah's vigil. (Jonah has declared he will sit and wait for God's destruction.) Jonah was thankful for the shade, but God caused the plant to wither the next day. God then turned the weather to a blazing sun and scorching heat, causing Jonah to wish for death. God then taught this lesson: callous Jonah cared more for the plant than he did the city of 120,000 people (see Jonah 4:11 and the devotional for tomorrow). Jonah needed to heed the lesson of God. What is God teaching you today?

Lord, thank you for teaching me. Give me the patience and presence to learn from you as you transform my thinking and life. In your name, I pray, amen.

MARCH 7

And the LORD said, "You pity the plant, for which you did not labor, nor did you make it grow, which came into being in a night and perished in a night. And should not I pity Nineveh, that great city, in which there are more than 120,000 persons who do not know their right hand from their left, and also much cattle?" (Jonah 4:10–11)

Today's passage ends the book of Jonah. The book began with the word of the LORD coming to Jonah, instructing him on his mission. The mission repulsed Jonah, and he refused. Finally, Jonah does as God instructed, but Jonah's heart never got in line with God until *perhaps* the end. The reader doesn't know for sure, because while the last verses show the reasoning behind God's mercy and grace, Jonah has not yet responded properly to God's lesson as the book closes.

Yet Jonah was a prophet. Jonah "worked" for God. Jonah's job was to be God's voice in the world. Somewhere, however, Jonah mixed up his role. Jonah began taking on the role that belonged to God. Rather than simply giving God's message to the people, Jonah wanted to give his own message. Jonah wanted God's words and actions to reflect Jonah's will, not God's.

When people substitute their own desires for God's desires, religious faith becomes hypocrisy. Evil people are easy to see, but when people disguise their desires in religious clothing, the deceit makes the evil harder to see. In his classic song "Slow Train Coming," Bob Dylan sings as follows:

Big-time negotiators, false healers and woman haters
Masters of the bluff and masters of the proposition
But the enemy I see
Wears a cloak of decency
All nonbelievers and men-stealers talkin' in the name of religion.

The readers of Jonah are left hanging at the end. Did Jonah simply talk religion while his heart was far from it? Did Jonah continue to do only what God forced him to rather than what God wanted him to? These and similar questions are left hanging because they are questions still to be determined in the life of the reader. Will I live my life by God's wishes or my own? Will I seek his will or my own? Will I live in authentic faith or merely talk in the name of religion?

Lord, I want to serve only you. Purify my desires in your name, amen.

MARCH 8

The vision of Obadiah. (Obad. 1:1)

I am staying in a hotel room in New York City. Having been on the road for the better part of the week, I am weary. Thinking about it as I type, I realize I have been on the road for the better part of the last six weeks. I get to go home tonight, but I leave again in two days. My alarm was set for later in the morning, but an hour before I needed to get up, I awoke with a song coursing through my head. The song? Amy Grant's "1974."

The song is about her conversion: 1974 was the year Amy found the transformation in life that comes from yielding yourself to God. The lyric coursing through my head sang, "Purer than the sky behind the rain, falling down all around us, calling out from a boundless love, love had lit a fire. We were the flame burning into the darkness shining out from inside us." This was the experience of the change that happened when Amy gave her life to God. It was also my story.

Forgetting my fatigue, I was excited to get out of bed and went straight to my computer to write this devotional on Obadiah 1:1. Obadiah would have liked Amy's song. His name tells us a good bit about him. *Obadiah* combines two Hebrew words that give his name as "little servant of the Lord." (*Obad* is a slightly different form of the standard word for servant—*eved* / עָבֵד—and *iah* is an abbreviation for YHWH, the name of God.) Obadiah had achieved what Amy Grant's song proclaims. He had given his life irrevocably to the Holy One.

This little servant of God had a "vision." This Hebrew idea isn't something that might happen while dozing off or by taking hallucinogenic drugs. A vision (*chazon*—חָזוֹן) was receiving God's message. It's in the promise that God will put a message into the hearts of all his children in the days of his Spirit coming upon all people (Joel 2:28). It's found in the deep-seated recognition that God will change his children who follow him. Without a vision of the future, people live uncontrolled, without restraint (Prov. 29:18). But with it, people are changed.

Amy's year, 1974, happens to have been mine as well. That change wakes you up fresh, even in the midst of fatigue. It puts a song in your head and dances your fingers across the keyboard.

Lord, I am yours. Period. Keep me ever fresh and new by your power, amen.

MARCH 9

*Thus says the Lord G*OD *. . .* (Obad. 1:1)

My Hebrew degree came from a religious college, and unsurprisingly, the other students taking classes with me were devout and pursuing degrees that aligned with ministry. We all wanted to be able to read the Old Testament in its original language. However, things were different in my first-year Hebrew class. I took that at a secular university, and the students in the course included a few who simply needed a foreign language requirement. Our professor had grown up in an Orthodox Jewish family, and an early rule he taught us was that when we came upon the "name" of God (Y-H-W-H), we were never to pronounce the name. Instead, we could substitute the generic Hebrew word for "Lord," (*adonay*) or we could simply say the Hebrew for "the name" (*ha-shem*).

One day when we were reading, a young lady who had either not heard or learned that rule was reading a passage aloud and she began to try to pronounce the name of God. Our professor broke out in a cold sweat to get her to stop. She insistently kept trying, and finally he proclaimed, "No! It is considered blasphemy to say the Holy Name of God!" This holy name is one that the Bible translators typically translate as "Jehovah" (King James Version) or "LORD" with large and small capital letters in most modern English translations.

Writing today's devotional, I begin by reading the Hebrew, and something immediately jumped out at me. The Hebrew has an additional word that gives a slightly more specific meaning than we typically pick up on in English. The Hebrew reads, "Thus says *my* Lord, YHWH." Since this is using the common Hebrew for "Lord," rather than repeat it as "Lord LORD," which a modern version would do to indicate the name of God, the translation uses "GOD" for the name of God, just reducing the font size of the last two capitalized letters. That is notable, but more notable for me was the addition that says "*my*" Lord, per the usage *adonay* (though not reflected in an English translation). Obadiah writes of YHWH as *his* Lord. It is personal.

I'm not sure if the young lady in my Hebrew class knew God as her personal Lord, but when you do, it changes everything. Whenever *my* Lord speaks, I will try to listen. Whatever *my* Lord has to say is important to me. This needs to be my attitude every day as I read his word.

My Lord, may I listen intently to your words for me today. In your name, amen.

MARCH 10

*Thus says the Lord G*OD *concerning Edom: We have heard a report from the L*ORD*, and a messenger has been sent among the nations: "Rise up! Let us rise against her for battle!"* (Obad. 1:1)

One summer as a college student, I was asked to housesit for a family from church. I was only needed for a week, and my main job was to feed their dog each day. One evening, I went out to his doghouse and reached down to place the bowl with food. No sooner had my hand put the food down than the dog bit me. Hard. The dog literally bit the hand that fed him! Some would term him a "territorial, aggressive dog." I just called him mean.

Territorially aggressive dogs have areas that they define as their own. As bizarre as it might sound now, in the ancient world, many people thought of the gods as territorial in much the same way. The gods had lands (or water in the case of the sea god [Yam, Poseidon, etc.]) that were their territories. In their territories, the gods reigned supreme. If one nation went to war against another, it was often thought that each nation's gods were going to war as well. If one nation conquered another, the god of the triumphant nation was newly worshiped in the conquered territory. The god's territory was expanded, and the god was viewed as more powerful than the defeated god.

This primitive and pagan view of the gods was *contrary* to Old Testament teachings. Israel's God was the sole true God, and his reach wasn't limited to the territory of Israel or Judah. God reigned everywhere. He was the God of heaven and earth—that is, the entire cosmos.

Knowing God was unlimited in his "territory" makes a passage like today's extra significant. God had a word about Edom, a neighboring nation. Edom had often been a thorn in the side of God's people. God sent out a rallying cry to respond to the thorn, but God doesn't send the battle cry to his own people. God sent the command to go against Edom to nations other than Israel and Judah. God could do this because he wasn't a territorial God. The nations might not have worshiped Israel's God, but he was still God. He still moved among all the nations, weaving his will into the fabric of history.

There is no area where God's territory ends. I have no corner in my life where God isn't present. God reigns supreme, and I find comfort in that.

Lord, I need you to reign over all of my life. I pray in your power and name, amen.

MARCH 11

Behold, I will make you small among the nations; you shall be utterly despised. (Obad. 1:2)

A cowboy turned lawyer was one of the toughest lawyers I have ever encountered. I got to know him when I was young and impressionable. He had a case where another lawyer, not much older than me, had irked him in a proceeding. The young lawyer showed disrespect to the older fellow as well as the older fellow's client. The crusty old cowboy told the young lawyer he would rue the day he had done so. The cowboy returned to his office and called the partner over the young lawyer to complain about him. The cowboy said, "You better get that boy to apologize, or I will destroy you, your client, and your law firm." I was scared just listening in on it all!

Now that cowboy lawyer was tremendously talented and doggedly determined. He was not one with whom to be trifled. But as strong and calculating as the lawyer could be, he holds no candle to God.

Today, many like to paint a picture of God as a happy or jolly fellow who can look beyond the bad circumstances of one situation or another and smile. It's as if God understands poor behavior and it rolls off his back, like water off a duck. This is not, however, the biblical view of God. Yes, God is patient. God is slow to anger. God has steadfast love. God wants and seeks the best. God is a forgiving God. But today's passage gives a glimpse into God that is just as much a part of his character. God does not flirt with or approve of evil. God works to destroy evil.

Edom was an ancient foreign nation that was a consistent thorn in Israel's side. One moment it was refusing safe passage for the Israelites as they marched through the wilderness to access the Promised Land; another moment it was raiding Israel and Judah to pillage and plunder before returning home. To this nation, God announced judgment. God was going to make Edom small. We will see tomorrow that God turned the nations against Edom.

I take a deep breath reading this passage. I never want to take God for granted. I don't want my knowledge of his mercies to cause me to ignore his judgment.

Lord, may I take you and your holiness seriously. May I follow you and not set myself against you. In your name, amen.

MARCH 12

The pride of your heart has deceived you, you who live in the clefts of the rock, in your lofty dwelling, who say in your heart, "Who will bring me down to the ground?" Though you soar aloft like the eagle, though your nest is set among the stars, from there I will bring you down, declares the LORD. (Obad. 1:3–4)

If you ever make it to Jordan, go to Petra. If you don't think you'll ever make it to Jordan, Google Petra. Or better yet, watch *Indiana Jones and the Last Crusade*, as several scenes were filmed there. The ancient ruins dug into the red limestone mountains were created by the Nabataean Empire a few hundred years after Obadiah's prophecies and after the destruction of the Edomite kingdom. During Obadiah's time, these red mountains and canyons were part of the land of the Edomites. These people of Edom (which derives from the word for "red" in Hebrew) are the subject of Obadiah's prophecy.

Archaeological excavations have shown that during the eighth through sixth centuries, Edom had a large number of fortified cities. In their arrogance, the Edomites thought themselves almost invincible. Their hilly fortresses gave a physical protection that translated into a spiritual arrogance. God was not amused.

I have never met an Edomite. They were a people and nation that dissolved long ago into the pages of history. They were succeeded by an empire that built jaw-dropping structures into the very rocks that sourced their arrogance. These grand structures will make the movies, bring about articles in *National Geographic*, and make for many tourist photos and souvenirs. Yet no one much knows or cares about the Edomites.

God brought the Edomites to their end. God left an explanation in today's passage. God doesn't countenance arrogance. Human vanity is an affront to the glory of God. Isaiah said it this way: "For the LORD of hosts has a day against all that is proud and lofty" (Isa. 2:12). James said, "God opposes the proud but gives grace to the humble" (Jam. 4:6).

I have seen the ruins at Petra, and they are stunning. But more important than a vacation visit to the ancient land of Edom is the journey I need to make regularly into my heart. I don't want the souvenirs of Edomite arrogance to infiltrate my life. I want to find humility before God.

Lord, forgive my pride, and help me walk humbly before you. In your name, amen.

MARCH 13

If thieves came to you, if plunderers came by night—how you have been destroyed!—would they not steal only enough for themselves? If grape gatherers came to you, would they not leave gleanings? How Esau has been pillaged, his treasures sought out! (Obad. 1:5–6)

When I was young, I spent a good bit of summertime with my maternal grandparents. My grandfather Tommy would occasionally give me chores, including work in his garden. He wanted me to learn the lessons of life from dirt rather than television cartoons. Once he had me weed the tomatoes. I did a half-baked job. He examined my work and then had a sit-down with me. He explained that if I left the job as I'd done it, the grass and weeds would just regrow with stronger and deeper roots. If I was going to do something, he explained, I needed to do it completely.

God does his work completely. When God sets himself to a purpose, he accomplishes his purpose—100 percent. Today's passage sets out this truth through historical analogies. Thieves, especially in Obadiah's day, might sneak in at night, but they didn't take everything. They took what they could haul off. Similarly, when workers picked grapes or any other crop, they would not haul off every single grape but leave droppings and gleanings for others to come scavenge. Not so, however, with God and his judgment.

God was coming against Edom. (Edom in today's passage is called "Esau." This works in Hebrew because Esau was born "ruddy," from the same root as "Edom" in Hebrew; Gen. 25:25.) God was going to do his job completely. He would not leave a remnant. God wouldn't do a half-slop job.

God reliably accomplishes his judgment. But that doesn't scare me. Because God also reliably accomplishes his other promises. This means that God will not do a half-baked job at bringing me into his righteousness. God won't have partial mercy on me. God doesn't forgive some of the sins of the repentant. God's work is done right and fully.

I don't want a half-attentive God. I can trust God to be there, to be reliable in his love and attentive to his work in me and the world. We serve a 100 percent God.

Dear Lord, please continue to work in me for your righteous ends. Smooth my rough edges, soften my hard heart, and purify my love for you. In your name, amen.

MARCH 14

All your allies have driven you to your border; those at peace with you have deceived you; they have prevailed against you; those who eat your bread have set a trap beneath you—you have no understanding. (Obad. 1:7)

We knew the evidence was there; we just needed to find it. The pharmaceutical company had deliberately decided to move forward with selling its product even though testing indicated it might cause heart attacks. The best picture one could paint was a belief that millions might get relief from arthritis, even if a few more died from heart attacks. Our team worked hard to find the evidence that would betray the true motives and reveal the calloused decisions.

We did find the evidence. It brought the company to the table, and before long, the product was off the market and the victims had been compensated. Early on, a younger lawyer asked me how I was certain the evidence was there even though we hadn't found it all. My response was "You can't practice vice virtuously."

I have found this to be true. It is a truth that is also borne out in today's passage. The prophet is speaking God's words to the nation of Edom, which was situated to the south and east of Judah, and Israel and was historically its enemy. God's promise is that the very allies of Edom would be its destruction.

For lack of a better way to say it, Edom had practiced vice against Judah. Edom had made raids on Judah, grabbing crops at harvest time and capturing and enslaving Israelites in the process. Edom itself, however, was a relatively weak country. To accomplish this vice, it had turned to more powerful neighbors, aligning themselves as allies. This was Edom's undoing.

Obadiah predicted that the allies would turn against Edom to its ultimate destruction. History shows that God is true to his word. Edom was itself invaded and captured (multiple times), and ultimately, its people were lost to the pages of history.

One cannot practice vice virtuously. Vice and sin leave behind a trail that will earn ruthless and devastating consequences. On a national scale, it was true with Edom. On a corporate level, I have seen it's true over and over. On a personal level, it's no less true. There is a challenge here for living authentic and good lives untainted by evil or ulterior motives.

Lord, give me the presence to make right decisions in life. In your name, amen.

MARCH 15

Will I not on that day, declares the LORD, destroy the wise men out of Edom, and under-standing out of Mount Esau? And your mighty men shall be dismayed, O Teman, so that every man from Mount Esau will be cut off by slaughter. (Obad. 1:8–9)

Superhero movies drive box office returns for a reason. Most people, albeit not all, love a movie where there are incredibly gifted or empowered people who are able to combat evil and bring about a happy ending. The plotlines don't vary much beyond that. Whether in comic books, TV shows, or full-length movies, the bad guys create a crisis, and through cunning, strength, and superpowers, the heroes rescue the day.

But what if the bad guys had the cunning minds and the superpowers? What if the superheroes turned out to be supervillains? If God is on the scene, then the ending will still work out. That is what Edom found out in today's passage.

Edom had its share of "wise men." These were people in charge of making decisions that would further Edom's causes—causes that were det-rimental to God and his people. These weren't nimble minds seeking to do good. They were devising strategies to pillage and plunder, ruining lives and families in the process. The modern civilized world often forgets the law-lessness of a time when one group of people would invade with incursions, killing those who stood in their way and capturing and enslaving women and children.

These schemes were enacted by cunning men who had strong and mighty men at their disposal to execute their plan to destroy the security and future of God's people in Judah. Judah had no superhero of its own to rescue people. At least not among its populace.

But Judah had something stronger than a superhero. Judah had the LORD God. YHWH, the Holy One of Israel, was going to destroy the wise and cunning leaders of Edom. God would see that the mighty men lost their own lives as they sought to destroy God's people. God is not to be trifled with. He is to be trusted. If God is on our side, nothing can stand against him and his purposes.

We can pray, trust, and act, knowing God will be victorious.

Lord, be my wisdom and strength this day and every day. In your name, amen.

MARCH 16

Because of the violence done to your brother Jacob, shame shall cover you, and you shall be cut off forever. (Obad. 1:10)

Domestic violence is a plague that haunts too many families. Sometimes the violence happens in private and never surfaces. Sometimes allegations of abuse take center stage, like in the public trial of Johnny Depp and Amber Heard.

The prophet Obadiah couched today's passage as a tale of family violence. The Edomites were considered descendants of Esau, the twin of Jacob. In a certain sense, at least going back over five centuries, the people were related. Hence the prophet calls the Edomites the "brother" to Jacob.

This violence was vicious and mean, and God planned to put an end to it. That is the thrust of Obadiah's prophecy. People reading this aren't likely to be slugging it out with their brothers or distant relatives. But that doesn't mean the prophet's lesson should go unheeded.

Not all violence is hand-to-hand combat. Some of the most damaging violence comes from words and other deeds. Words said in anger can burn into another's brain, leaving lasting damage with mental and emotional scars that are every bit as hurtful as physical scars. Passive-aggressive schemes can also leave their victims bludgeoned psychologically.

God says that those who do violence like this should be ashamed. Physical and verbal abuse will hurt not only their victims but ultimately the abuser as well.

We can't just brush this off as a problem for others. Each of us should ask ourselves how we interact with our fellow humans, especially with family and close friends, when they hurt us or hurt other loved ones. God's people need to be known for kindness, gentleness, and self-control. Some might say, "Well, fine! But not when people deserve it!" Those are the times when God's people need to be rich in mercy. Does that mean God's people should be doormats? No. Sometimes, the best course of action is simply to remove oneself from a bad situation. But God's people shouldn't perpetuate violence, even of the verbal variety!

God, please help my patience and self-control. In you I pray, amen.

MARCH 17

On the day that you stood aloof, on the day that strangers carried off his wealth and foreigners entered his gates and cast lots for Jerusalem, you were like one of them. But do not gloat over the day of your brother in the day of his misfortune; do not rejoice over the people of Judah in the day of their ruin; do not boast in the day of distress. (Obad. 1:11–12)

Growing up in Lubbock, Texas—the home of Texas Tech University—made college football both fun and frustrating. The fun was college football! The frustration was that in Texas, it seemed the A and A-plus athletes went to the University of Texas, while Texas Tech attracted those whose star was not as illustrious. For many Lubbockites, that meant every Saturday, you rooted for two teams—Texas Tech and whoever was playing the University of Texas.

It is one thing to root against a college football rival. It is something altogether different to wish ill on a person, be they friend or foe. Edom and Judah (the southern kingdom of Israel) were not always friends. Their existence next to each other often had them at odds. Manifesting this antagonism, Edom's reaction when foreign invaders came up against Jerusalem and Judah was appalling. Edom offered no assistance, which in itself wasn't right. But beyond that, Edom celebrated Judah's defeat. As Judahites were plundered; as their men, women, and children were murdered; as their young women were raped and taken captive, Edom rejoiced and gloated. God wasn't going to leave Edom alone over this.

Often, two things are at work in the soul who rejoices in another's downfall. For some, the rejoicing comes from an attitude of "Well, they finally got what they deserved." For others, an inner envy wells up, as they covet what another person has and are unable to obtain it themselves. People who covet feel satisfaction when another loses the coveted item.

The Bible teaches the people of God to be different. From a Christian perspective, Jesus taught people to pray for their enemies (Matt. 5:43–44). Paul explained that vengeance belongs to the Lord, not God's followers (Rom. 12:19). But these are also concepts found in the Old Testament. Paul is quoting from Moses (Deut. 32:35). I'm not going to start rooting for the University of Texas, but beyond Saturday game day, I will work to wish the best for others, even my enemies.

Lord, I will need your help in this, please. It isn't natural or easy for me. In your strength, amen.

MARCH 18

For the day of the LORD is near upon all the nations. As you have done, it shall be done to you; your deeds shall return on your own head. (Obad. 1:15)

In 2015, Sean O'Brien, a forty-eight-year-old Brit, went viral. He had been dancing at a pub, and someone recorded a video of him. Sean, who was overweight, was enjoying his evening of dance without concern for appearances. The video was posted with cyberbullying comments making fun of him, his weight, and his dancing. The mocking video was seen by millions, including an amazing woman in Los Angeles who reached out to find the unknown Sean. Once Sean was identified, money was donated, and Sean was brought to America and given a hero's treatment. He threw out the first pitch at a Dodgers baseball game. He was on national TV and went to parties held in his honor, where he danced with elite A-list celebrities while world-famous DJ Moby played.

Call that "good karma." See it as "what goes around comes around." People have slogans for this because it's seen constantly in the world. Paul would later write, "You reap what you sow" (see Gal. 6:7; Prov. 22:8). My buddy John Gilbert says, "It's a short road that doesn't have a turn in it."

This well-recognized dynamic is the basis of today's passage. Obadiah says it as, "As you have done, it shall be done to you." This fits into the prophetic promise that God wasn't going to leave Edom alone for the way it behaved toward God's people.

This is the way of God, and it applies both for good and for evil. As people do good things or *mitzvot* (Hebrew for "commandments," but commonly used to signify notably good deeds), as they live righteously and help others, God will see that goodness follows. As people mistreat, abuse, and run roughshod over others, misery will follow the perpetrator. Often the consequences are instantaneous. Sometimes it takes a day, a week, a month, a year, or a lifetime. But the consequences come. The balance on the account might not be paid each night, but ultimately, the bills become due, and the balance is righted.

This should change how we behave not simply because we will come out ahead if we do. More importantly, we should be shaping our minds to do right. It is also what God desires.

Lord, give me a heart and desire for what is right and good. In you I pray, amen.

MARCH 19

For as you have drunk on my holy mountain, so all the nations shall drink continually; they shall drink and swallow, and shall be as though they had never been. But in Mount Zion there shall be those who escape, and it shall be holy, and the house of Jacob shall possess their own possessions. (Obad. 1:16–17)

I have a good friend named David. David is smart, compassionate, well read, and thoughtful. While David is culturally and genetically Jewish, he is an avowed atheist by faith. David's family had been deeply affected by the Holocaust (his dad was incarcerated at a concentration camp), and combined with other tragedies in life, David decided no good God could possibly exist.

I get David, but then I don't get David. I have published extensively on reasons to believe, and I won't rehash them now, but one word alone should cause all people to reflect on faith. That word is *Israel*.

The Old Testament Scriptures note God's promises to Abraham and his offspring, promises that have their genesis in history as early as four thousand years ago. God promised over and over to sustain these people until the end of time. Contrast today's passage, where this same God says that the Edomites and other nations or people groups would "be as though they had never been." Ask yourself, have you ever met an Edomite? How about a Midianite? Have you met a Horite or an Amorite? An Amalekite?

These people groups and nations that were contemporaries of ancient Israel have vanished, dissolved into the pages of history. But not the Jews. There have been many, many rigorous campaigns to consume or destroy the Jews, including those by the Egyptians, Edomites and other neighbors, Assyrians, Babylonians, Romans, and many groups during the Middle Ages; the Russian pogroms and Stalinist purges of Jews; Hitler's efforts during the Third Reich; and current antisemitic groups in the Middle East. Yet the Jews are still here, even as the other people groups vanished.

God is faithful to his word to protect his people. History shows this truth. It causes me to read Scripture with an eye toward God's promises. I know that when history is finished, God's promises will shine fully accomplished. His love and mercy, his purpose and work, his restoration of the broken—these promises and more I will experience in the fullness of God's time.

Lord, thank you for your faithfulness. I rest in your promises and name, amen.

MARCH 20

The house of Jacob shall be a fire, and the house of Joseph a flame, and the house of Esau stubble. (Obad. 1:18)

For a good while, our law office in Houston, Texas, resided in two different buildings. It made for good sport among personnel, particularly on the basketball court. We were fairly evenly matched and played hard for bragging rights. One day, an ex-pro basketball player came to me for some help. I suggested I would be honored to help him if, in return, would he "work" for me one afternoon. He agreed, and I told him to bring his basketball shoes and some shorts. Then I sent out a challenge to the neighboring office. Before we went over to play, I had our ex-pro make a copy of a legal document. Then we went to play.

The opposing office showed up and saw immediately that we had a new player. They asked who he was, and I told them that he had done some copy work for us. He was a new guy. It was his first day. We annihilated the other team. It wasn't close. They left with their tails between their legs, and it took them fifteen minutes on their cell phones to identify our ringer. They were not happy.

Everyone likes to be on the winning side. Nobody wants to be a loser. It's true on the basketball court, and it is true in life. This brings today's passage into focus. God isn't a passive watcher of history. The Bible doesn't teach the deist view that God set up the world and then sat back and watched it unfold. The idea that God binge-watches the earth is out of place. God has an agenda. He is orchestrating history toward his will and his promised conclusion. Sometimes that makes our lives happy and easy. Sometimes our lives are a struggle and hard. Life takes on all shapes for God's history to culminate as he plans.

The passage says that the houses of Jacob and Joseph will be a flame or fire. Edom? It will be stubble. The biblical record notes that at this time, the Edomites were invading Judah and taking Hebrews back as slaves (2 Chron. 28:16–17). As a result, God made Edom fuel for his burning fire.

In an eternal and yet present sense, teams exist in this world. We often get to choose our teams. As Pete Seeger sang many decades ago, we get to answer the question, "Which side are you on?" I want to be on God's side—the victor's side!

Lord, I choose you! Put me in! Let me play for you! In your name, amen.

MARCH 21

The words of Amos, who was among the shepherds of Tekoa, which he saw concerning Israel in the days of Uzziah king of Judah and in the days of Jeroboam the son of Joash, king of Israel, two years before the earthquake. (Amos 1:1)

People enjoy a good vacation. Even if just for a day, a break from the daily grind is refreshing and enjoyable. Some find their vacation spot near home. I like mine on the road. My idea of a vacation is traveling to a great location where I can see sights as well as relax, eat good food, and bond with family. My dream vacation should never be confused with the events set forward in the book of Amos.

The prophet Amos went on a road trip, taking a break from his job. But his was no ordinary vacation. Today's passage sets the scene. Amos, who was a breeder of sheep and cattle, hailed from a village about six miles south of Jerusalem, in the kingdom of Judah. (Although, some argue Amos hailed from the Tekoa in Galilee rather than Judah.) Amos wasn't a full-time prophet who derived income from contributions or reigning kings. The background of Abraham's descendants is important in understanding Amos' trip.

Amos lived in the time when the Israelites had a divided kingdom. The northern kingdom was called *Israel* or sometimes *Samaria*. The southern kingdom was named *Judah* after the largest tribe that had settled in that region.

Judah and Israel were the offspring of Abraham and therefore were relatives. But they frequently warred against each other, and they were rarely chummy. While there were exceptions, all too often, the Bible relates that the kings of Israel did evil in the eyes of the Lord, while a larger number of the kings of Judah seemed to live godlier lives. Certainly, that was the case during Amos' time of prophecy. King Jeroboam II of Israel did evil in the eyes of God, while King Uzziah (a.k.a. Azariah) of Judah "did what was right in the eyes of the Lord" (2 Ki. 14:24; 15:3).

God called Amos out on his road trip as he instructed him to take a break from his sheep breeding to deliver the divine word to an ungodly king. This wasn't a fun or relaxing vacation, not the way most would spend a trip away from work. It was potentially perilous. God doesn't always call us to the easy journey, but we can be confident that God gives us what we need for *his* journey.

Lord, please fortify and empower me for your journey! In your name, amen.

MARCH 22

And he said: "The LORD roars from Zion and utters his voice from Jerusalem; the pastures of the shepherds mourn, and the top of Carmel withers." (Amos 1:2)

C. S. Lewis. Just reading his name causes many to sharpen their focus and tune in. Lewis was one of Christianity's leading writers of the mid-twentieth century. He wrote on understanding Christianity, the validity of Christianity, practicing Christianity, and more. Perhaps his best-known works, however, were allegories. The seven-volume set of *The Chronicles of Narnia* enthralled me as a young man and is still enjoyable and fruitful for me to read today.

In the allegorical land of Narnia, Lewis paints God as a lion named Aslan. Frequently, the reader finds the statement "Aslan is not a tame lion." While Aslan's ferocity is a good thing when Aslan is on your side, he was quite a fright to those who were enemies of the good.

I don't know all the influences that went into Lewis choosing to use a lion for God. But I suspect that today's passage might have played a role. God sent Amos to deliver his message to the northern kingdom of Israel. With punch, Amos began his message by saying, "The LORD roars from Zion." The Hebrew word translated as "roars" means just that (*sha'ag*—אַשׁ)! It's a lion's roar.

God's message is one that should be heard. This was an important message, not a secret to be hidden away. God wanted people to not only hear his word but fear his word. God doesn't speak idly. He isn't someone who constantly dribbles out words like a leaky faucet. God doesn't meander with his words, moving from one point to another with no purpose.

Amos reflects a profound truth. The Maker of the Universe, who has made everything from intergalactic space and distant suns to particles smaller than an atom, speaks to humans on a small out-of-the-way planet. This should give everyone pause. The ready availability of the Bible in print and online can cause us to take God's word for granted. Furthermore, our own desires, wants, opinions, positions, and so on can cause us to disregard Scriptures that seem disagreeable. We should not lightly ignore the roar of the Lord. God, like Aslan, is no tame lion.

Father, as I study your word and work through these devotionals, soften my heart, clean out my ears, open my eyes. May I hear and see you in your power, amen.

MARCH 23

I will send a fire upon the house of Hazael. . . . I will break the gate-bar of Damascus, and cut off the inhabitants from the Valley of Aven. . . . And the people of Syria shall go into exile. . . . I will send a fire upon the wall of Gaza. . . . I will cut off the inhabitants from Ashdod. . . . I will turn my hand against Ekron. . . . I will send a fire upon the wall of Tyre . . . upon Teman . . . in the wall of Rabbah . . . upon Moab . . . (Amos 1:3–2:2)

Everyone has a tendency toward self-centeredness. We think in our own brains, and so what we think about tends to tie back to ourselves in some way. In writing these devotionals, my tendency in each one is to start with the word *I*. I have to fight this tendency. My initial thought today was "I have a tendency toward self-centeredness," for indeed I do. But I don't want to make this "about me," so I wrote from the recognition that we all tend to see things in terms of ourselves.

That is what makes today's passage remarkable to me. For the reading, I selected phrases from a number of verses where God is announcing his judgment. His judgment isn't against the nations of Judah or Israel (yet). God will get to them shortly. On today's list are foreign nations. God wanted Israel to see that God's concerns stretched far beyond their national boundaries. God's concerns extend in all directions to all people and all situations. What is more, God *acts* in regard to all people in all situations.

So what does this mean to me? Well, that question is self-centered, but as I said in the beginning, this is part of who we are as humans. The irony is that one of its lessons for me is that God has concerns with others that are *not* me. God has a grand plan for the cosmos, and I'm but one among billions in that plan. If I lose sight of that, I run the risk of my self-centeredness turning into full-blown narcissism!

Yet even recognizing that God's full reach extends into every recess of existence, I must never forget that I'm important to God. God knows me by name and cares for me with an unconditional love. He knows my tendency toward self-centered thinking and seeks to change it. I don't exist in isolation from the all-knowing and all-caring God. I exist within his eyesight and care. He knows my day today, even before it happens. He goes along before me and also goes with me. I have peace in that.

Lord, I praise your grandeur. May I find my place before you. In your name, amen.

MARCH 24

Thus says the LORD: "For three transgressions of Damascus, and for four, I will not revoke the punishment." (Amos 1:3)

When our son was young, I would frequently entertain him with mental math problems. By the time Will was seven, I could give him fairly difficult problems. On one car trip, I asked him, "Will, if you had six apples, and I gave you two more, then you had to share them equally between you and three friends, how many would you each get?" After a moment, he said, "Two!" I said, "Correct!" At this point, his three-year-old sister wanted a stab at it: "Ask me! Ask me, Daddy! I want to do math!" So I simplified the process for her, asking, "Gracie, if you had one apple, and I gave you one more, how many would you have?" She proudly answered, "Three!" Then she added, "Daddy, if you had an apple and I gave you a banana, how many would you have?" I said, "You tell me!" She proclaimed, "You would have a fruit salad!" Alas, I decided math might not be her future.

Numbers don't always mean the same thing to different people or cultures. Today's passage is a marvelous illustration of this in antiquity. The cultures of the ancient Near East, including the Israelites, found numbers useful for the same reason we use numbers today, much like my son in the story above. But those cultures also had symbolic meanings for numbers, a bit more akin to my daughter's fruit salad. The number three, for example, could mean three distinct items. But it was also considered a symbol for heavenly expressions. This is seen in many Bible passages that work in threes, like "Holy, holy, holy [three times] is the LORD of hosts" (Isa. 6:3). A similar example is "Holy, holy, holy [three times] is the Lord God Almighty [three labels], who was and is and is to come [three time periods]" (Rev. 4:8). These examples of three successive uses of three items are heavenly expressions par excellence. The number four symbolized earthly matters. There were four corners of the earth, four directions for the winds, and four elements (fire, earth, wind, water), to name just a few examples.

Amos isn't concerned with the actual numbers three or four in today's passage. Amos notes that the sins of Damascus offend both heaven (three) and earth (four). Amos is right. Sin isn't only an offense against a holy God. Sin has earthly ramifications as well. Sin may seem innocuous or even fun, but its consequences—both in heaven and on earth—are damaging. I need to be conscious of that today.

Lord, give me strength to walk holy before you in thought and deed. In you, amen.

MARCH 25

Thus says the LORD: *"For three transgressions of Gaza, and for four, I will not revoke the punishment . . ."* (Amos 1:6)

In law school, a few Latin phrases are still used. One phrase everyone learns early in criminal law is *mens rea*. The Latin translates into "guilty mind." In the law, it references the state of mind that is required to convict someone of a crime. Different crimes require different states of mind, but if you don't intend to commit a crime, the basis for holding you accountable isn't there.

The classic example of the role "intent" plays in a crime is often quoted from an 1882 publication by Oliver Wendell Holmes, who would later serve on the U.S. Supreme Court. He wrote, "Even a dog distinguishes between being stumbled over and being kicked." Mental intent means that one either acted purposefully, or knew the conduct would likely cause the result, or disregarded a substantial risk, or while not aware of the risk, reasonably should have been aware. Without this intent, the crime isn't technically "committed."

"Intent" is relevant in today's passage, as Amos spoke of God's concern over the "transgressions" of Gaza and others in the first set of oracles in Amos. The word *transgressions* (*pesha'*—פֶּשַׁע) is rooted in the Hebrew idea of "rebellion." A rebellion against the government is against the law, and hence this word is sometimes used about a crime. But here, when the Lord speaks of their transgressions or rebellion, he is speaking not of criminal acts but of a rebellion against God's moral code. The Scriptures frequently use *transgressions* in conjunction with *sins* (e.g., Ex. 34:7; Lev. 16:16; Josh. 24:19; etc.). Sins are departures from God's code, and this Hebrew idea involves one's mental state, as *transgressions* illustrates the rebellious nature of sin.

In my daily life, I face choices—choices in what I do and choices in what I think. I can do things right, or I can choose sin. But sin isn't something I simply stumble into. It's deep within my heart. Sin is a rebellion against God. If I judge my actions (in court or out of court) by what I feel is justifiable, I have set up my rebellion. I have become my own God who dictates my own morality even when I'm in rebellion against the true moral God. Transgression and rebellion begin in my mind!

Lord, I confess my rebellious sin. Over and over, I tend to define my own right and wrong. Forgive me. May I live more purely by your power, amen.

MARCH 26

"Because they carried into exile a whole people to deliver them up to Edom." (Amos 1:6)

A lawyer from New York approached me and said, "We are getting into human trafficking cases, and we want you to get into them as well." I was a bit taken aback. In my seemingly sheltered life, I didn't realize how significant the human trafficking problem was in modern America. Yet it turns out to be a massive problem. Most human trafficking in the United States stems from either forced labor or forced prostitution. The trafficked might not be U.S. citizens, but many are, especially in the prostitution arena.

While I was ignorant of the extent of the modern problem, I knew it to be a massive problem in antiquity, including in ancient Israel. People traded human flesh like they traded any other object. As Amos set it out, God was going to judge the Philistines (noted by their major city "Gaza" in this passage) because they were marauding into Israel, taking individual Israelites, and selling them to the nation of Edom, many for prostitution. They weren't taking the old people, who wouldn't command a high price. They took young people of productive ages, many of whom could be sexually exploited and therefore sold at a higher price.

Reading passages like today's gets me thinking. First, I need to be aware of human trafficking. Whether I'm at a truck stop filling up with gas, at a hotel watching as people file in and out, or on an airplane noticing unusual pairings of people (something airlines are now training their flight attendants to do), I need to be alert. I also need to be prayerful in general about those being exploited.

There is something else notable about this passage. Everyone knows that slave labor and forced sexual conduct are heinous crimes and sins, exploitations of humans on a horrendous level. Yet as we interact with people all day long, we need to be careful that we aren't taking advantage of people, albeit in a lesser way. For most, we interact with our family daily. For some, there are regular interactions at school or the workplace. For some, there are routine social interactions with friends. In all these interactions, any action that fails to take into account the true value of a human is wrong. I want to do the opposite of exploiting people. Instead, I want to enhance the lives of others. How much better would this world be, and what better example of God could I be, if I approached every relationship seeking to help the other person be the best that person can be.

Lord, help me to make the lives of those around me better. In your name, amen.

MARCH 27

Thus says the LORD: "For three transgressions of Tyre, and for four, I will not revoke the punishment, because they delivered up a whole people to Edom, and did not remember the covenant of brotherhood." (Amos 1:9–10)

In cases where I have caught a company doing something wrong, occasionally the defense offered amounts to "Well, we may have made *that* mistake, but other people have done worse!" In the opioid litigation, I was trying a case against certain pharmacies that failed to write and enforce policies to stop the reckless dispensing of opioids. One of the pharmacies defended itself by saying, "Well, maybe we put X number of doses onto the streets wrongfully, but this other pharmacy put 2X doses onto the streets wrongly!" That argument doesn't work, generally. Just because someone is number *two* on the FBI's Top Ten Most Wanted list doesn't excuse their behavior.

God was speaking of this same concept in today's passage. Phoenicia ("Tyre" being one of its major cities) was judged by God because it "delivered up" Israelites as slaves to Edom. The judgment in yesterday's devotion that God declared against the Philistines was based on more than selling Israelites. The Philistines had actually been marauders and invaders who captured the Israelites, carted them off, and sold them to Edom and others. Phoenicia didn't do the marauding but limited its abuse to buying and selling Israelites. This "lesser" sin was no "lesser sin" in God's eyes.

Today's passage causes me to reflect on my own shortcomings. No, I'm not buying and selling slaves. But my sin of mistreating or disrespecting others is still repugnant to God and his absolute purity and holiness. I may not be number one or two on the FBI's list, but I am under indictment nonetheless.

Even if my sin seems lesser in human eyes, who can say what effect it might or might not have? When I gossip, who can say what the full fallout is? When I'm greedy, how does it affect my influence? When I'm gruff, easily angered, or brash with others, what chances to change people's hearts have I missed? When I'm critical, how have I disturbed the growth of others? When I'm bitter toward or judgmental of others, how can I know the fruits of my bad attitude? When I let my worries stifle my actions, who can determine what God was going to do if I had exercised my faith? I have some serious work to do!

Lord, give me the presence of mind to walk in your grace and goodness. In you, amen.

MARCH 28

Thus says the LORD: "For three transgressions of Edom, and for four, I will not revoke the punishment, because he pursued his brother with the sword and cast off all pity, and his anger tore perpetually, and he kept his wrath forever." (Amos 1:11)

When we married, my wife was a practicing lawyer. We had five kids, and she soon quit the legal world to stay at home with the children. People would ask her if she still practiced law. Often she would respond, "No, unless you count mediating disputes with our kids." Becky was gifted at mediation, but part of her success was our children's readiness to apologize for their mistakes in a genuine and sincere way. The apologies were always accepted with forgiveness, and now decades later, our children have grown into adults who may live thousands of miles from each other but are still tightly bound together in fellowship and love.

Living peacefully with one another doesn't mean there aren't times of anger, frustration, and hurt. But it does mean those are dealt with responsibly. Problems arise when anger is unresolved, when bitterness festers, when sincere regret and apologies don't come forth, and when walls of hatred get built. This is true in individual relationships, and exemplified by the larger-scale problems experienced in Amos' day.

In today's passage, God seeks to punish Edom for "keeping his wrath" forever against its enemies. There was no pity, only anger. That is a tough way to live. God's judgment on Edom is a lesson for everyone. Living in constant anger and wrath will produce sour fruit that harms both the person who's angry as well as the person who's the target of the anger.

Today's passage implies that there are virtues people should pursue as well as dangerous traits to avoid or grow out of. Forgiveness should be learned over anger and wrath. As we learn to understand and forgive others, we can begin to soothe the anger in our hearts. Wrath can melt away in the face of forgiveness. For some, forgiveness comes easy; for some, it is hard. For all, however, it is critical. Forgiveness is a worthy pursuit. Don't be like the scorpion whose anger leads to self-destruction!

Lord, I need to learn better forgiveness. Melt my anger and take away my bitterness. Help me learn to live for others' good. In your forgiving name, amen.

MARCH 29

Thus says the LORD: *"For three transgressions of Moab, and for four, I will not revoke the punishment, because he burned to lime the bones of the king of Edom. So I will send a fire upon Moab." (Amos 2:1–2)*

Look at today's passage. Does it strike you as odd? God is going to send a consuming fire upon the Moabites because they took the bones of a dead king of Edom and burned them into a lime powder. Was this an ancient cremation? This is the only action identified by the prophet to explain God's judgment against Moab. But what does this have to do with Israel? The king of Edom was generally an enemy of Israel. So what if his bones were burned to powder?

Before writing this story off as one of those "reasons" not to spend much time studying the Minor Prophets, let me divert this discussion briefly. As I studied to be a minister, one of the classes required was called "Practical Aspects of Preaching." The point of the class was to teach certain tasks like conducting weddings and funerals as well as making hospital visits. For funerals, we were taught two goals. First, tell stories about and the biography of the deceased to honor his or her memory and permit the surviving loved ones to grieve. The second goal is to reinforce the idea that death is not the end of things.

I have now attended and conducted more funerals than I can count, always focusing on these two goals taught to me eons ago. When these goals are met, people respond positively. They are touched that people remember and honor their deceased loved ones.

Honoring the dead isn't something that only people care about. According to today's passage, God cares about this as well. Honoring the dead helps those who live aspire to do better. It inspires people to pursue the best as was done by those preceding them. People find their heroes and motivation in those who lived honorably. In this sense, it is logical and even expected that God would want the dead to be honored, not dishonored. God is always looking for people to grow into their best. Dishonoring the dead will bring pain, hatred, and bitterness into the hearts of the deceased's loved ones. God seeks to comfort the hurting, not grind their noses in the pain.

This has me thinking about God on a whole new level. He cares more than I realized. I need to thank him, and I need to learn to care more.

Lord, thank you for caring. Teach me to be like you. In your name, amen.

MARCH 30

Thus says the LORD: "For three transgressions of Judah, and for four, I will not revoke the punishment, because they have rejected the law of the LORD, and have not kept his statutes, but their lies have led them astray, those after which their fathers walked." (Amos 2:4)

Academics use the term *confirmation bias* to label a mental phenomenon that exists in almost everyone. I first came across the term in a study of those who were struggling to determine which of two cars to buy. Both cars met their criteria, and they shifted back and forth trying to choose. Ultimately, they chose and bought a car. The testers let three months go by and then quizzed the people on whether they bought the right car. Almost everyone confirmed they had made the right choice, and they gave affirmative reasons reinforcing their decisions.

Confirmation bias describes how once a person has made up his or her mind, that person will tend to listen to and accept evidence that *reinforces* the decision, as people generally reject evidence and arguments that might indicate that they made the wrong decision. This likely lies behind the actions of Judah described in today's passage.

As a reminder, Judah was the southern portion of the nation of Israel, after its civil war had split it in two. Jerusalem and the temple were in Judah, and the Judahite kings descended from King David. Judah had the law of Moses (the "Torah"), the system of priests, and the attendant sacrifices of the temple. Yet Judah was going to be judged by God. The judgment was coming because the people had "rejected" the Torah, the "law of the LORD," even as they claimed to be godly. Instead of following the law, they followed lies. They deceived themselves into thinking that they were better than they really were and that God would forgive them regardless because they were his "special" people. They thought the law passé and that they had grown beyond it, understood God better, or knew better what was right or wrong. Confirmation bias set in, and they would interpret events, attitudes, and opportunities in ways that confirmed their views of religion and God. God said a big jolt was coming to their confirmation bias.

Everyone tends to believe what reinforces what they already believe and want to be true. This can be a dangerous trait. It can lead one astray from what is godly and right. I don't want to miss God because I like where I am.

Lord, jolt me. Teach me aright. Let me truly follow you. In your name, amen.

MARCH 31

Thus says the LORD: "For three transgressions of Israel, and for four, I will not revoke the punishment, because . . ." (Amos 2:6)

King David had it all. But he wanted more. While his troops were off fighting, he decided to stay home even though he was their king and leader. One evening, while in his home high on the hill, he saw, on another rooftop below his, the striking Bathsheba bathing. Bathsheba was alone, as her husband was in the army fighting David's battles. Entranced by her beauty, David had her brought to the palace, where he seduced her and got her pregnant. David went into damage control and tried to get her husband, Uriah, to return home and sleep with his wife, hoping everyone would believe Uriah had impregnated her. But Uriah refused to sleep with his wife, as his fellow soldiers were allowed no such reprieve from war. Ultimately, David sent a note to his general to orchestrate an attack in such a way that Uriah would be killed. David then took Bathsheba and added her to his stable of wives. Not David's finest moment.

God sent his prophet Nathan in to confront David. Nathan didn't arrive saying, "God told me to tell you he saw, he knows, and you are in trouble!" Instead, Nathan came in with a story, a parable. He told David about a subject who had only one sheep, a family pet. A neighbor with hundreds of sheep needed one to slaughter to feed a visitor. Rather than slaughter one of his flock, the neighbor stole the fellow's family pet, his one sheep, and killed it to feed the guest. David was irate. He wanted to know who this neighbor was, for this neighbor was deserving of death! Then Nathan sprung the news: "The neighbor is you. The sheep was Bathsheba." Scales fell from David's eyes, and David fell in repentance.

Amos the prophet came to Israel and pronounced God's coming judgments on the nations. Starting from the Southwest and going clockwise around Israel, Amos finally zooms in on Israel. Doubtless, Israel was applauding God's coming judgment on others, but once the geographic circle was completed, Amos zeroed in on Israel's judgment. Using the same common poetic formula of "three and for four," Israel was no better than the rest.

I see sin in others more readily than I do in myself. I need to be more careful about this. I need to address the log in my eye, not the speck in another's.

Lord, forgive my sin, open my eyes, help me focus rightly by your power, amen.

APRIL 1

"For three transgressions of Israel, and for four, I will not revoke the punishment, because they sell the righteous for silver, and the needy for a pair of sandals—those who trample the head of the poor into the dust of the earth and turn aside the way of the afflicted." (Amos 2:6–7)

His mom named him John, but shortly after his birth, his father changed the infant's name to Francis. Francis grew up among the privileged and wealthy. His dad was a successful cloth merchant, and Francis was set to step into the family business. After serving in the military, having some medical issues, and seeking spiritual fulfillment, Francis started selling his dad's inventory to rebuild a church. His dad was furious and brought the young man to account in front of the church bishop. Francis stripped all his clothes off and, standing naked, declared that henceforth, his father would be his heavenly Father. Francis spent the rest of his life in purposeful poverty, spending all he had on those in need.

Saint Francis of Assisi, as he is known today, famously set poverty front and center as a virtue. He also started nativity scenes, befriended animals and all people groups, and began an ecclesiastical order still present today.

Francis' deep concern for the poor sits in contrast to many Israelites of Amos' day. (He sits in contrast to many people of today!) Israel didn't share God's concern for the downtrodden and oppressed. The rich weren't just looking away from those hurting; they were affirmatively abusing and taking advantage of them.

Mistreatment and exploitation of people without the resources to stand up for themselves should be offensive to everyone. When people enrich themselves off the backs of others, it affects both the poor and the abusers. God sees to that.

Capitalism is a marvelous way to move society and its citizens forward. But capitalism without restraint runs amuck, and many get hurt. The old adage "The rich get richer, and the poor get poorer" should be an alarm to a problem. The people of God need to have a heart for the poor. Regrettably, many think that tending to the poor is the job of government, but that isn't biblical. God's people have a responsibility to love and care for the poor. Homeless shelters, food banks, educational programs, and skill opportunities are not just afterthoughts. They need to be part of everyone's concern for those in need. God cares; so should I.

Lord, give me a heart for the poor and a mind for helping. In your name, amen.

APRIL 2

"My holy name is profaned; they lay themselves down beside every altar on garments taken in pledge, and in the house of their God they drink the wine of those who have been fined." (Amos 2:7b-8)

Interstate 10 is one of the major highways in Houston, Texas. I have driven it more times than I can count. If I were to drive down to it right now, when I finish typing this, and if I were to turn right, I would head toward Los Angeles, California. If instead I turned left, I would head toward Jacksonville, Florida—2,460 miles and a coast away from Los Angeles. Same driver, same highway, just a difference in how I use it.

Interstate 10 serves as a good metaphor for Amos' indictment of the Israelites in today's passage. The Israelites were going to worship. In modern parlance, we would say they were going to church or synagogue. They were religious people. But their worship was a stench to God because they were trampling on the rights of the impoverished and down-on-their-luck folks. When Amos says the worshipers would "lay themselves down beside every altar on garments taken in pledge," he was saying that these seemingly religious people would loan someone money and then take their outer cloak as collateral. This was a direct violation of God's law that stated if you took someone's cloak as collateral, it should be returned in the evening so the borrower could use it for sleeping (Ex. 22:25-27). Further, the self-professed religious people had turned worship into a chance to drink wine that was taken from those who were "fined," or whose debt service was being enforced by collecting more than the principal amount of the loan by confiscating their wine.

In churches today, we don't see worshipers sleeping on borrowers' coats. Nor has worship become a place for me to soak up the goods of the poor. But I can't deny that there are two different directions my worship can take. One is centered on me and my life; the other is centered on God.

When I come to God focused primarily on myself, his "holy name is profaned" or desecrated. I have taken a time when my focus should be on God, who he is, and what he has done—a time that should be of worshipful praise—and I have turned it into a selfish or self-centered activity. Hence my Interstate 10 analogy. I am on the highway, but I am headed in the wrong direction. I won't remotely end up where I should.

Lord, teach me to focus on you and not my own wants and desires. In you, amen.

APRIL 3

"Yet it was I who destroyed the Amorite before them. . . . Also it was I who brought you up out of the land of Egypt and led you. . . . And I raised up some of your sons for prophets, and some of your young men for Nazirites." (Amos 2:9–11)

Our team was in Indiana getting ready to take depositions (a legal proceeding where witnesses are put under oath and examined by attorneys while a court reporter and videographer record the proceeding to play it later in court). I was going to be taking one witness, and my buddy Larry from another firm was taking another. We had agreed to meet for breakfast before going to the offices for the depositions. At breakfast, Larry appeared disheveled. I asked about his sleep, and he told me he really hadn't slept well. He was his usual jovial self, but it soon became apparent that he had no clue why we were in Indiana or if we even were in Indiana. We canceled Larry's deposition, and a friend flew with Larry back to his home. We came to find out that Larry was suffering from early onset Alzheimer's or some similar memory-impairing disease.

Memory is a funny thing. When it works, it can recall events, dialogue, and even feelings and thoughts. When it doesn't, it can be a recipe for disaster. Larry had a legitimate and sad reason that impaired his memory. Not so the Israelites in Amos' day. They had forgotten what God had done in their midst and had no one to blame for that but themselves.

God had taken the Israelites out of slavery in Egypt, leading them through the wilderness into the land of the Amorites and Canaanites— two groups with mighty warriors. Yet when faced by Israel under God's divine hand, the story was different. Those that fled lived, but those that remained to fight met defeat. Then once the Jews were established in the land God promised to Abraham for his progeny, God sent prophets to guide them.

Yet the people turned against the prophets and forgot what God had done. They turned their religion into something that fed their own desires, and they spurned any genuine praise for what God had done in their lives.

I confess that God has done incredible wonders in my life, and I too often fail to remember them and praise him for them. It isn't that I have a disease like Larry. Mine is self-inflicted. I need to do better.

God, you have worked wonders in my life. Praise you for who you are! Amen!

APRIL 4

"Flight shall perish from the swift, and the strong shall not retain his strength, nor shall the mighty save his life; he who handles the bow shall not stand, and he who is swift of foot shall not save himself, nor shall he who rides the horse save his life; and he who is stout of heart among the mighty shall flee away naked in that day," declares the LORD. (Amos 2:14–16)

A sure formula for a successful movie is when an underdog finds victory over the powerful favorite. Sylvester Stallone made the *Rocky* franchise out of this plot. Consider *Rocky III*: Clubber Lane, played by Mr. T, is an arrogant and vicious bruiser who whips Rocky early in the movie, showing Clubber's greater strength and power as a boxer. Rocky's old nemesis Apollo Creed steps in to teach Rocky how to box, as opposed to simply slugging his opponent in the ring. Rocky learns and, in the end, defeats the stronger Clubber Lane.

This plotline isn't far off from today's passage. Amos declares that God is going to step into Israel's timeline and make some changes. The Israelites have been abusing the poor and downtrodden, and God is coming into the fight to make a difference. God is going to strip the speed of the swift and weaken the strong and mighty. Even the "stout of heart" will fall apart before God and his judging hand.

Many people don't like reading passages like today's. We want God to intervene in our world when we are in trouble. When life's storms threaten to destroy us, when life's pain drives us to tears, when the fears of life paralyze us into inaction, we are thankful for God's intervention. God becomes a refuge from the storm. He gives strength to the weary and soothes and supports those in life's fiery furnace.

Yet this same God who lifts up the lowly also brings down the haughty. This is what perturbs many about today's passage. God doesn't support the proud. God doesn't seek to uphold those who have their own might and strength. Those who lean on their own accomplishments, their own might, and their own brains or brawn will never have the true success that comes to those who are dependent on God. The proud may seem to win at one moment in time, but before the movie is over, God will bring down the proud and lift up the humble.

Lord, give me a humble heart that relies on you in big and small ways. In you, amen.

APRIL 5

Hear this word that the LORD has spoken against you, O people of Israel, against the whole family that I brought up out of the land of Egypt. (Amos 3:1)

In *Fiddler on the Roof*, the rabbi is fond of saying there is a blessing for everyone. One of the Jews asks him, "Rabbi, is there a blessing for the tsar?" The rabbi thinks reflectively and then pronounces, finger lifted in the air, "May God bless and keep the tsar . . . *far away from us!*" Everyone laughs and cheers.

God speaks over everyone. The voice of God goes to the ends of the earth. God's words might be words of blessing or words of judgment. Here God is speaking over Israel, the "family" he brought out of Egypt. The Hebrew word translated twice in the passage as "against" is the Hebrew for "on," "upon," "over," "in front of," or "above" (*al*—עַל). The usage means that God is speaking over the Israelites, but whether he is speaking for them or against them is understood by the context. Here the context is clear: God is speaking *against* the Israelites.

I want God speaking over me, my family, my friends, and my loved ones, but I want God speaking blessing and favor. I want his delight to be expressed in his words. I want to hear his pleasure, not his judgment. Which brings me to ask this question: How do I find God's pleasure and blessing in his words rather than his judgment?

The answer isn't hard or surprising. It's rooted in God having a will for this world and for humanity. God seeks to bring his kingdom into full fruition, defeating and ending evil and sin and their consequences. People are key actors who God uses to achieve his good ends. But at the same time, people have choices in this world. We can choose to do A or B, and both have consequences. This isn't a predetermined world where people are puppets and God pulls the strings. God values people so incredibly that he gives us free will. As beings made in God's image, people decide how to live.

When we choose to live in God's will, seeking to pull this world into his directives, then God speaks over us with his blessings. When we decide to go against God and his will, then he will still speak, but he will speak in judgment. We have free choices, but God and his plans will not be thwarted by how we choose. His kingdom will come.

Lord, may I walk in your will. Speak your blessings over me in your name, amen.

APRIL 6

"Do two walk together, unless they have agreed to meet? Does a lion roar in the forest, when he has no prey? Does a young lion cry out from his den, if he has taken nothing? . . . Does a snare spring up from the ground, when it has taken nothing? Is a trumpet blown in a city, and the people are not afraid? Does disaster come to a city, unless the LORD has done it? For the Lord GOD does nothing without revealing his secret to his servants the prophets. The lion has roared; who will not fear? The Lord GOD has spoken; who can but prophesy?" (Amos 3:3–8)

In the early autumn of 2022, Hurricane Ian blew into Ft. Myers, Florida, utterly destroying much of the town and leaving a trail of death and destruction. Katrina devasted New Orleans and the Louisiana coastline in 2005, and the list goes on. A preacher friend of mine believed that Katrina was an Amos-type judgment of God upon the sins of New Orleans. After all, he reasoned, Amos 3:6 says that disaster doesn't come to a city unless the Lord has done it. I disagreed. I believed he was taking Amos 3:6 out of context.

The prophet in this passage uses similes to make a devastating point about God and Israel. Walk through it carefully. First, he asks if two walk together unless they agreed to meet. In Amos, the two are God and the prophet Amos. God sent Amos with his message of Israel's coming destruction; Amos (unlike Jonah!) agreed to go! The lion who roars in the forest or in his den with prey in sight is God, and the prey are those upon whom his judgment is coming, as already set out in the prophecies. This is made clear by the ending of the passage, where Amos writes, "The lion has roared . . . ; The Lord God has spoken." They are one and the same. The bird who will fall in a snare is Israel. As for the trumpet that people are to fear, it is the prophet's warning of what is to come.

This is the context of "The destruction of the city is coming from God." Interpretating Scripture without its context is nonsense! Amos is *not* lapsing out of his simile string to articulate a principle that applies to all people for all time and circumstances. He is in a flow of saying that what he has proclaimed will surely happen, and it will be from God's hand.

I don't want to suggest that God can't or won't use nature and every other tool to bring about his purposes. He does. But we must be cautious about blaming God for tragedies. He can easily be maligned by Scripture taken out of context.

Lord, give me trust in your love and care. In our world, be glorified. Amen.

APRIL 7

Proclaim to the strongholds in Ashdod and to the strongholds in the land of Egypt, and say, "Assemble yourselves on the mountains of Samaria, and see the great tumults within her, and the oppressed in her midst." "They do not know how to do right," declares the LORD, "those who store up violence and robbery in their strongholds." (Amos 3:9–10)

In Anthony Trollope's 1867 novel *The Last Chronicle of Barset*, set in Victorian England, Adolphus Crosbie seeks to borrow from Mr. Butterwell a large sum of money (£500 then, so about $75,000 as this is written). Before Crosbie asks for the money, Trollope, as the narrator, discusses all the different ways people can ask to borrow money. The "slow and deliberate" way seeks to walk someone through the needed loan by force of logic. The "piteous manner" seeks another's pity through either a lie or the truth. There are more approaches, but the "piteous manner" through truth is the approach used by Crosbie. Butterwell is stunned by the request and asks why it is needed. Crosbie gives an explanation, but not without first saying, "There is nothing, I think, so bad as washing one's dirty linen in public."

Trollope's is the first reference in English to the idiom that has become "Don't wash your dirty laundry in public." The phrase is used to say, "Keep private matters private." That phrase was not going to work for Israel in the days of Amos. God told Amos to get the nations of Ashdod and Egypt ready to see Israel exposed in all its sin.

There is a lesson here for us today. Like Crosbie in Trollope's novel, people don't like to air their dirty laundry in public. No laundry is as dirty as one's sin. No one likes to put their sin on full display for others to see. Sin is best locked up in a closet, secreted away in the hopes that no one, perhaps even God, sees it.

Yet God always sees sin, and furthermore, he doesn't leave it alone. Sin is a cancer to the character of God, and God seeks to cut out and destroy sin. So we as sinners have a choice. We can deal with our sin, letting God work with us to grow. Or we can continue to feed our sin, let it thrive, and try to keep it secret. But there will come a time, as there did for Israel, when God will reveal the sin to others. The dirty laundry will be hung for the world to see. Thank God for the chance to repent and deal with things early, before the laundry is hung!

Lord, I confess my sins. Help me grow out of sinful patterns. In your name, amen.

APRIL 8

"Hear, and testify against the house of Jacob," declares the Lord GOD, *the God of hosts, "that on the day I punish Israel for his transgressions, I will punish the altars of Bethel, and the horns of the altar shall be cut off and fall to the ground." (Amos 3:13–14)*

Our grandson was having his "I'm turning three!" birthday party, and Becky and I were more excited than he was. Our daughter tasked us with getting the balloons and picking up the cake. We weren't sweating it. We had the time, we had the directions, we had the money, and we were enjoying each moment of it. We had it under control! Contrast those events with our friend who was in a real difficult medical situation. He didn't know what to do and was desperate for help. "Under control" was the last way he would have described his situation.

While those situations may seem to be in contrast, in reality, they have much in common. Becky and I were relying on other things for what we needed. My friend was too. We were relying on our car to work. We trusted there wouldn't be a wreck that set us back from our goal. We trusted that the retailers would accept our plastic cards for payment and the credit card company would approve the purchase. We trusted that our health would hold up until we got to the party. We were trusting in much; it's just that Becky and I have relied so often on those things we didn't give them a second thought. My friend, in contrast, was in new territory, having to rely on doctors and nurses (and medicines) that he had never needed or used before.

Our friend prayed for divine help during his medical woes. We had general prayers for God to be glorified but didn't pray specifically for the party prep beyond that. It never occurred to us to do so. In truth, we trusted in things.

Today's passage speaks to Israel trusting in things other than the Lord God. Israel had constructed altars to idols seeking the help of those gods. This idolatry was not only an affront to God; it harmed the worshipers. They put their trust in things other than God.

People are often guilty of that today. Maybe my birthday example isn't the best, but trusting in things other than the Lord God is a recurring problem. Next time our grandson has a birthday, we will help. But we will thank God for the resources *he* has provided each step along the way.

Lord, thank you for your provisions. May I trust only in you. In your name, amen.

APRIL 9

"Hear this word, you cows of Bashan, who are on the mountain of Samaria, who oppress the poor, who crush the needy, who say to your husbands, 'Bring, that we may drink!'" (Amos 4:1)

Most parents teach their kids the mantra "Sticks and stones may break my bones, but words will never hurt me." I know my parents taught me that around third grade, when name-calling became fashionable for us kids.

In today's passage, God, through the prophet, isn't engaged in third-grade antics of name-calling. God is using name-calling to teach a lesson. He's singling out certain rich women of Israel who have lost sight of their mission among the poor. God calls them "cows of Bashan" or, in some translations, "fat cows of Bashan." Bashan was a highland plateau rich in pastures and well known for producing fat livestock. These cows were the perfect metaphor for the Israelite women.

The women, like the cows, were consumers. They ate and ate from the riches of the land, giving no thought to those less fortunate. The "poor" have always been those not only without money but whose needs were unmet. Every society has those who are in a tough place and are depending on the kindness and generosity of others. Not to be missed, however, in this passage, is that the women were not simply ignoring the poor and needy; they were also abusing and oppressing them. The women wrongfully used the needy to meet their own desires.

A final condemnation of these thoughtless Israelite women were their callous and bossy attitudes toward their own families. In a society where women were supposed to be tending to the house and its needs, these women were demanding that their husbands fill that role.

God wasn't name-calling by terming these women "fat cows of Bashan." God was accurately describing them. I'm blessed to worship at a church with a vibrant community outreach. As a fellowship, we work to feed thousands each year. I know law firms with bake sales and challenges to raise money for food banks. Many other groups help the poor. Passages like today's should challenge everyone to work to be part of the solution for those in need and hurting. It is God's mission. No one is called to be a fat cow only concerned with feeding in the meadow. We are called to prioritize serving others.

Lord, help me see where and how I can serve the needy in your name, amen.

APRIL 10

"The Lord GOD has sworn by his holiness that, behold, the days are coming upon you, when they shall take you away with hooks, even the last of you with fishhooks. And you shall go out through the breaches, each one straight ahead; and you shall be cast out into Harmon," declares the LORD. (Amos 4:2–3)

Have you ever had a really great vacation? Years ago, we had one where all five of our adult children, their spouses, and all of our grandchildren were able to join. One of our daughters, who thrives on planning and organization, was working toward that vacation for months, making lists of things to do, things to pack, and so much more. The vacation came, and it was amazing. Afterward, we all talked about it incessantly. What a trip!

Today's passage brings that vacation to mind. Not because Israel was in for a treat. No, the Lord wasn't announcing a vacation. Israel had the opposite on the horizon. Misery and difficulty were around the corner. Israel had been living steeped in sin, and the bill was coming due. God gave Israel time to get ready, but the future was set.

This passage reminds me of the vacation because I can see both in three phases: the preparation phase, the experience itself, and the reflection phase. Those three phases exist in life for times of delight and times of gloom. Because we all experience both happiness and sadness in this life, we should reflect on both.

Life will unfold with times of sorrow and trouble, and we should take time now to prepare. The best preparation comes from finding a profound, abiding relationship with God, which includes daily prayer, a deep understanding of God through Scripture, and a fellowship of brothers and sisters who also know and love the Lord. Then when a difficult experience unfolds, we're able to walk through it, holding on to God tightly, with the prayers and support of other believers. And after we have walked through the fires, the time of reflection comes—a time to rejoice and praise the God who sustained us through the trials of life.

The Israelites brought much of their misery on themselves, but whether we are the reason or simply a victim, at times, life brings misery. If we are ready and endure, we will praise God on the other side.

Lord, prepare me, help me, and let me praise you in the trials of life. In you, amen.

APRIL 11

"Come to Bethel, and transgress; to Gilgal, and multiply transgression; bring your sacrifices every morning, your tithes every three days; offer a sacrifice of thanksgiving of that which is leavened, and proclaim freewill offerings, publish them; for so you love to do, O people of Israel!" declares the Lord GOD. (Amos 4:4–5)

When I was young and fresh out of law school, I took a job at a big, prestigious law firm. Among the hundreds of lawyers at the firm was one who played the role of my friend. After a tough year of learning how to be a lawyer, getting to know the partners and my colleagues, and adjusting to my first professional job, my "friend" came to me with a sheet of paper. He told me that it was my annual job review that had been done by one of the firm's partners. The review suggested that I be terminated. I was devastated. I had a wife, a baby, and a mortgage. My heart sank. I asked my friend for any suggestions, and he said not to worry. He said he had removed the review from the file and held the original in his hand. He had secured my job for another year, and all I had to do was work extra hard and, of course, be appropriately appreciative to him.

I told this fellow that my faith wouldn't let me benefit from him stealing my review from my file and that he had to return it. He replied that he knew I would say that, but he had done what he had done. Sometime later, I found out from others that the whole thing was a poorly constructed joke. There was no review. There was no recommendation I be fired. I also realized that he was not a close friend.

I don't want fake friends, and God doesn't want fake worship. Today's passage speaks of people who were worshiping God with the same lack of authenticity that my coworker displayed. The people sacrificed. The people tithed. Yet they were doing so because of selfish motives, not because of adoration and respect for God. As a result, God declared through the prophet that not only were the religious acts transgressions but they were multiplying, with transgression upon transgression piling up.

God wants real worship. Our faith should never be a tool focused on us, our preferences, our politics, our power, our tastes, our desires, or our anything! Worship should be based on God and his awesomeness. No more, and no less.

Lord, purify my heart in worship to you. In your name, I pray, amen.

APRIL 12

"I gave you cleanness of teeth in all your cities, and lack of bread in all your places, yet you did not return to me," declares the LORD. (Amos 4:6)

Our daughter Sarah was about three or four years old when she went through a stage of making up songs. The songs had no repeatable melodies but always featured a crescendo at the end. The lyrics were understandably simple, typically about how she loved one family member or another. On one memorable trip, Sarah was in the backseat singing, and as she neared the crescendo at the end of her song, she sang, "I love my mommy"—pause and crescendo—"but *not the dentist*!!!"

Dentists often get a bad rap, but I am rather fond of mine. He's great! One of our daughters has a dentist for her father-in-law, and he is also a prince of a man. Into our experiences with dentists intrudes today's passage. God declares that he gave the people of Israel "cleanness of teeth"! Is God staking a claim to work as a dentist or dental hygienist? Is he commending their work? While it may seem that way, we would be misreading this passage if we thought so.

This passage features the common Hebrew poetic tool called *parallelism*. It's where two clauses marry up to each other to help explain each other. Most often, the second clause repeats the same idea as the first clause. But sometimes, the second illuminates the first through a contrasting clause. Here, the "cleanness of teeth" is explained by the "lack of bread." This is saying that God took from the people of Israel their food—that is, he brought famine into their midst. Their teeth were clean because they had nothing to eat.

God's actions didn't come out of nowhere. Centuries before, God had warned the people that blessings would follow their obedience and curses would follow their disobedience (see, e.g., Deut. 30). That principle wasn't because God was harsh. God produced the curses to drive the people back to their faith. As Moses explained, "When you are in tribulation, and all these things come upon you in the latter days, you will return to the LORD your God and obey his voice. For the LORD your God is a merciful God. He will not leave you or destroy you" (Deut. 4:30–31).

God doesn't inflict pain without purpose. In that sense, he might be a dentist after all! That said, I want to walk in his blessings without his correcting stick.

Lord, I come to you and want to stay in your presence. In your name, amen.

APRIL 13

"I also withheld the rain from you when there were yet three months to the harvest; I would send rain on one city, and send no rain on another city; one field would have rain, and the field on which it did not rain would wither; so two or three cities would wander to another city to drink water, and would not be satisfied; yet you did not return to me," declares the LORD. (Amos 4:7–8)

Recently, I was in a car with an amazing man of faith. We were discussing obstacles to faith, and he told me the biggest shake-up he had experienced was when his brother became an atheist. He and his brother were third-generation devoted believers, with both grandfathers in the clergy as well as their dad and several of their generation. I asked why his brother had left the faith. He explained that it was a gradual process that wasn't rooted in any academic or intellectual objection. It started with a desire to live a life contrary to biblical morality and then expanded from there.

Very few people just up and decide one day that they are not going to walk with God. For most, it is a gradual move away from God—a step here, a subtle shift there, a few bad decisions that don't align with faith. Then one day, people find themselves far away from the faith they had embraced earlier. God isn't a bystander when this occurs. As well as in Scripture, God sends messages through people, through nature, and through life events to stir people to acknowledge and lean on him.

In today's passage, this moving hand of God is apparent. God used the weather to induce people to faith. No one can control the weather, and an agrarian society like ancient Israel was very weather dependent. When the rains were withheld, the economy was wrecked, people went hungry, and the nation weakened. This drought should have reminded people about their reliance on God, but it didn't. They blithely continued down the path away from God.

God called on the people to "return." This Hebrew word (*shuv*—שׁוּב) is an important biblical concept. It denotes "turning." The people had turned away from God and gone their own way, likely little by little. God was telling them to do a U-turn. He wanted their hearts. He was trying to guide them back. Yet they stubbornly refused. Ugh. I want to be different.

Lord, I want my path in life to be with you—no turning away. When I lose that path, give me eyes to see your call for me to do a U-turn. By your power, I pray, amen.

APRIL 14

"I struck you with blight and mildew . . . yet you did not return to me," declares the LORD. "I sent among you a pestilence . . . and I made the stench of your camp go up into your nostrils; yet you did not return to me," declares the LORD. "I overthrew some of you . . . yet you did not return to me," declares the LORD. "Therefore thus I will do to you, O Israel; because I will do this to you, prepare to meet your God, O Israel!" (Amos 4:9–12)

Rearing five children became a master class in parenting. Just about the time we were done, we finally had a clue about how to do it! Of course, it was a bit too late, but by God's grace, our children turned into marvelous adults anyway! One issue all parents face with their children concerns discipline. We decided early on that any discipline would be the least strident tactic that would work. So if a gentle hand could coax the child, we used a gentle hand. If something sterner was required, we used something sterner, but always the least measure needed for results. For some of our children, a dour look was all that was needed. Others needed a time-out. We got our children to the necessary result; it was just a question of how easy the road was for all.

In today's passage, I see God as a parent with some extremely wayward children. God tried one approach after the other, yet the Israelites continued their life voyage away from God. Each successive effort by God to entice their return failed. But after all these efforts proved futile, the Israelites were not dismissed and allowed to get away with their disregard for God and his message and will. God told them that their failure to return to him meant they better prepare to meet him anyway. God was coming, and they could not avoid him.

Today's passage reminds me a bit of the Jonah story. Jonah sought to distance himself from God and God's call on his life. God said, "Go east," and Jonah said, "No!" and went west. God told Jonah to go inland, and Jonah took to the sea. God told Jonah to preach repentance to pagans, and Jonah went down into a boat, shut his mouth, and went to sleep. But Jonah wasn't successful in fleeing God and God's calling. Jonah had to meet God anyway, even if it was in the depths of the sea from the belly of a fish.

I don't want to wander from God and his purposes, and when I do, I want to return on my own. I know I will meet him one way or the other.

Lord, I want to follow your will for my life. Period. Full stop. In your name, amen.

APRIL 15

For behold, he who forms the mountains and creates the wind, and declares to man what is his thought, who makes the morning darkness, and treads on the heights of the earth— the LORD, the God of hosts, is his name! (Amos 4:13)

Steve Matthews was reputed to be the toughest guy in our high school. None of us were 1,000 percent certain of that because everyone was too afraid to test him. Steve had muscles most of us never dreamed of. He seemed chiseled out of stone. No one was going to fight with Steve, lest they not live to tell the tale. If there were going to be a tug-of-war, however, I can say Steve would have been my first pick for my team. The other side wouldn't have stood a chance!

For all his Goliath-type strength, however, Steve wasn't even a drop of water in the ocean compared to God's strength. Somehow, it had escaped Israel's attention that God was who God was. Today's passage gives just a glimpse into God's résumé.

God formed huge mountains the way a child plays with modeling clay. God created the hurricane wind and the tornadoes as well as the gentle breeze. God knows the thoughts of every person. God is the author of consciousness. But for God, humanity would have no more ability to "think" consciously than a mosquito. God makes the morning. God makes the darkness. God uses the highest places on the earth, places where people would struggle to climb, as places for his feet to stroll. What a résumé! What a God!

The point of Amos isn't to give a scientific dissertation about creation. Nor is it to give God human features, as if he is a giant who walks upon mountains. Amos uses powerful imagery to explain the omnipotence of God. God is stronger than the elements. He is stronger than our minds can conceive. God's strength was his calling card at a time when Israel doubted him.

God's strength hasn't diminished with time. He's still the all-powerful God today. You and I don't have a problem that's beyond God's ability to solve. You and I don't have a worry that's beyond God's care. You and I don't have a thought that isn't known to our Father in heaven. This can be a blessing when we turn to him in need. It can also be trouble when we turn away from him and disregard him. We choose what we do with our hearts. God will be God either way.

Almighty God, I place my life and cares in your powerful hands. In you, amen.

APRIL 16

Hear this word that I take up over you in lamentation, O house of Israel: "Fallen, no more to rise, is the virgin Israel; forsaken on her land, with none to raise her up." (Amos 5:1–2)

There once were people of promise. Moms and dads, grandparents, kids, aunts, uncles, neighbors, and friends. They'd had really hard lives with no hope for a future. Then God entered the picture. He offered them an incredible adventure. He would work all the necessary miracles to see them live the best lives they could—prosperous, safe, enjoyable—lives with futures. God gave the people some instructions. These instructions not only were for the people's good but also served God's larger plans for the world and its people. The key was that the people teach successive generations the truth of who God is, what God had done, and their agreement to follow God daily. The promise was made: If the people would do so, God would be faithful and provide them with secure and prosperous lives. God also made it clear, however, that if the people should fail to walk the path God set out, then he would no longer provide for their security and success.

Initially, the people followed God, although they had occasions of failure. Then over time, the people grew cold toward God, eventually using God as an excuse to do as they chose, consistently defying God's instructions. The people didn't understand how precarious a position they maintained among the nations. The people didn't grasp that but for the intervention of God's strong hand, the nation would crumble. The safe and prosperous people would return to the hard life with no discernible future. God warned them—over and over—but the people didn't listen. They didn't believe God. And so they fell. The nation that had not previously been conquered—the nation that was metaphorically a virgin among the nations—was consumed and taken. They lost all the benefits and potential and became as nothing.

This is the sad story in today's passage. It is a story worthy of a lament or a sad song appropriate for a funeral dirge. All the opportunities lost, all the blessings frittered away, and all the joy and peace evaporated because the people didn't believe and follow God. This story should be instructive to everyone who reads it. When we follow God, his blessings follow. When we abandon God, it's to our own detriment. Yes, even followers of God have difficult times, but we can endure those with God. But being without God—that is worthy of lament.

Lord, I want to walk in your blessings. Help me, please. In your name, amen.

APRIL 17

For thus says the Lord GOD: "The city that went out a thousand shall have a hundred left, and that which went out a hundred shall have ten left to the house of Israel." (Amos 5:3)

The funny thing about God is he never leaves things as they were.

I handled thousands of cases involving defective artificial hips. A British surgeon who used the hips was the first to sound the alarm over their defects. His surgery statistics showed the hips were defective. The manufacturing company said his high numbers indicated he was a poor surgeon. We said, no, he was simply "the tip of the spear." The failures were mounting for other surgeons as well.

The expression "tip of the spear" is good. The tip is followed by the full spear. Where the tip goes, things are about to radically change. I think of that expression as I look at today's passage.

God is telling Amos and the people that he was about to radically change things. He was depopulating the cities. Under God's control, the city of a thousand would be reduced to one hundred. The town of one hundred was going to shrink to ten people.

This is the way of God. Things are not the same when the tip of the spear passes. This can be a good thing or a bad thing, depending on whether we are aligned with God. Today's passage shows God's judgment on those set against him. The Bible's wisdom book of Ecclesiastes says the positive side of this truth: "Cast your bread upon the waters, for you will find it after many days" (Eccl. 11:1). Jesus spoke similarly: "Give, and it will be given to you. Good measure, pressed down, shaken together, running over, will be put into your lap" (Lk. 6:38).

I need God to be the tip of the spear and change things in and around me. I need the difference he makes. He has changed things in the past, and I am confident he will do so in the future. My goal is to be aligned with him so that his touch will be a blessing and I will be useful to him.

Lord, touch my life and make it useful in your kingdom. In your name, amen.

APRIL 18

For thus says the LORD to the house of Israel: "Seek me and live; but do not seek Bethel, and do not enter into Gilgal or cross over to Beersheba; for Gilgal shall surely go into exile, and Bethel shall come to nothing." (Amos 5:4–5)

I have been hunting twice, not counting Easter eggs. When alligator hunting, we had whole chickens from the grocery store put onto big hooks that hung from thirty to forty feet of chain, which was draped over a tree limb and dangled out over a Louisiana bayou. Hung in the evening, the bait was left out overnight. The next day, we got on skiffs and made our way down the bayou, knowing that where the chickens were gone, we had an alligator at the end of a forty-foot chain somewhere. As the helper on shore grabbed the end of the chain tied off on the tree, the gators would surface and meet their demise.

While I found the hunt fascinating, it didn't captivate me to the point where I became an avid hunter. I might add, I found it humorous that the fried alligator tasted like chicken. But I realized that, intriguing as it was, my days were not going to be spent hunting alligators.

I do want to spend my days on a different hunt. I want the hunt discussed in today's passage. I want to hunt for God. "Seek me and live" is a great promise and reward.

The hunt for God is a bit different from the hunt for alligators. I don't need bait to draw God out into the open. I don't need a tracker to seek out God's hiding place. God is in the open. God is calling out to me. God is seeking me before I ever seek him! God wants to be found.

Yet despite God seeking us, many people ignore him. Many overlook him their entire lives, never acknowledging his existence. Others snub him temporarily, disregarding him in certain situations. This is my problem. As the minutes of each day go by, I'm continuously making decisions. God calls on me to seek him in those minutes. In those decisions that come and go routinely, God promises if I seek him, I will find life. By promising life, God promises that he will work in and through me for the best results in my life as I hunt for him in the moment.

God isn't hiding. He's in the open. I just need to seek him with a willing heart.

Lord, may I seek you minute by minute today in your glory. In your name, amen.

APRIL 19

Seek the LORD and live, lest he break out like fire in the house of Joseph, and it devour, with none to quench it for Bethel, O you who turn justice to wormwood and cast down righteousness to the earth! (Amos 5:6–7)

In the middle of World War II, C. S. Lewis published a book dedicated to his friend J. R. R. Tolkien of *The Hobbit* and *The Lord of the Rings* fame. The book, *The Screwtape Letters*, is a fictional novel of satire. In it, a senior demon named Screwtape writes thirty-one letters to his nephew, a novice demon named Wormwood. While I have never conversed with Lewis (he died when I was three), I am fairly confident that Amos was one of his sources for naming the nephew Wormwood.

The Hebrew for "wormwood" (*la'anah*—לַעֲנָה) refers to absinthium, a plant yielding a bitter oil that was often added to wine in ancient times. This word gets used occasionally in the Old Testament as a metaphor for bitter or bitterness. Amos uses it twice. Here he speaks of those who turn justice from something that should be holy and sweet into a bitter and harsh injustice. In Amos 6:12, the prophet writes of those who turn righteousness into wormwood, or bitter immorality.

What is Amos speaking to? People in the ancient world, like people today, sought selfish gain. Everyone has to fight selfish tendencies. Our self-seeking inclination must be set against the greater good of seeking success and fairness for everyone.

Often, my courtroom wins (side point: I have had losses too!) involve cases where companies sacrificed integrity and the common good for selfish gain and accomplishment. In one case, a drug company pushed a drug onto the market before proper testing to make over $200 million by being first on the market with a new class of drugs. But this was no lifesaving drug. It was a pain reliever that diminished pain no better than Advil. Subsequent testing—testing that was started and should have been finished much earlier—led to removing the drug from the market, as it was deemed to have caused many unnecessary heart attacks. Stories of greed uncovered in litigation are unfortunately quite common.

As Lewis understood, the temptation to deviate from righteousness and justice is strong. Using the name *Wormwood* for the demon was itself a powerful message. The temptation to abdicate fairness and righteousness for self-gain is great!

Lord, may I live for what is right and fair. Forgive my selfishness. In you, amen.

APRIL 20

He who made the Pleiades and Orion, and turns deep darkness into the morning and darkens the day into night, who calls for the waters of the sea and pours them out on the surface of the earth, the LORD is his name. (Amos 5:8)

Mom had great creativity. Once when she was my "den mother" (the volunteer leader for a Cub Scout troop), she took us to the basement during our weekly meeting. There, she gave each of us an empty can along with a hammer and nails. She passed out various star constellations on pieces of paper that we placed over the ends of the cans, and we nailed holes at the position of each star. Afterward, she turned out the lights, and we put flashlights into the open ends of the cans opposite the nail holes and pointed them toward the ceiling to get the constellations shining in our basement. From there, it was a short step outside to gaze up and find our constellations in the heavens.

That was my introduction to Orion, the constellation I nailed into that can. But Orion had been a constellation for millennia before that. That collection of stars was known in the times of Amos the prophet. He proclaims that the constellations of Pleiades (or "Seven Sisters") and Orion were made by God. He adds that the same God brings on day and night, moves water and rain, and oversees life. God's name is the "LORD," the English given to the four Hebrew letters *YHWH*. In Exodus 3:14, God revealed the meaning of his name YHWH to Moses, explaining it to mean "I am." God is the unchanging, self-existent God. He's eternal. He is the I am—present tense. In other words, God is the same today as yesterday, and he will be the same tomorrow.

Sometimes, in my intimacy with God as my father and friend who gives me day-to-day guidance, love, and support, I forget his awesomeness. I tend to see him in the immediacy of my life and needs, overlooking that he always has been and always will be. God was God before human life existed. God isn't dependent on me, and his universe doesn't revolve around me. He has a plan, an agenda, that graciously includes me but is much bigger than what I can conceive.

I get to be in God's plans. He has made me part of his kingdom. For that, I rejoice. I am grateful, and it fills each day with meaning. But I must never lose sight of the awesome wonder that is God, with or without me.

Lord, I pause in wonder at your grandeur. I praise you as God Almighty, and I thank you for the honor and privilege of being your child. In your name, amen.

APRIL 21

They hate him who reproves in the gate, and they abhor him who speaks the truth. Therefore because you trample on the poor and you exact taxes of grain from him, you have built houses of hewn stone, but you shall not dwell in them; you have planted pleasant vineyards, but you shall not drink their wine. (Amos 5:10–11)

Go to any county in the United States, and you will find a courthouse. Courts are a—if not the—fundamental institution to ensure a fair and just society. In law school, we were taught that fairness in the courts could be thought of in analogies or metaphors. If one were having a race, then neither side should get a head start. Likewise, in courts, both sides of litigation start even. Using scales as a metaphor, the scales should start at zero (or at even weight if those scales are two-sided). This fairness requires everyone to be treated as innocent until proven guilty in criminal cases. In civil lawsuits, it means that the poor and powerless stand toe-to-toe and even with the richest and most influential. Without that justice, the United States as an idea would be undermined.

This idea of fairness in American courts can be traced back through England and the Western roots of history. But ultimately, one will find that the British system, since at least Alfred the Great (848–889 CE), is based on the Bible. Amos was a bedrock basis for the court system being fair to everyone—those who could afford it and those who couldn't.

Today's passage sets forth an important principle of which Israel had lost sight. The "gate" was where the courts of ancient Israel sat. The judges, generally village elders, would hear cases in the gates and assess the poor with extra charges, claiming to mete out justice, which the passage calls "taxes of grain," and becoming rich off those proceeds. God, however, was watching, and God was not pleased. God was going to put a stop to this. God is a God of justice and fairness, and this important aspect of God was being blasphemed by a people to whom God's character had been revealed. God wasn't tolerating that.

This passage should speak to us beyond our county courthouses. It applies to how we treat one another every day, in court or out. We should be recognizing everyone as worthy of fair treatment. In what we say and what we do, we should treat others as we would like to be treated. That is right before a holy, fair, and just God.

Lord, give me wisdom and insight to see where I am not fair to others in day-to-day living. I pray to do better by your power and in your name, amen.

APRIL 22

Therefore because you trample on the poor and you exact taxes of grain from him, you have built houses of hewn stone, but you shall not dwell in them; you have planted pleasant vineyards, but you shall not drink their wine. (Amos 5:11)

A common concept circulates in many adages and sayings. In high school, I heard it as "What goes around comes around." Or how about the phrase "cosmic karma"? Maybe you've heard, "If you're gonna dance, you gotta pay the band." The old television cop Baretta was fond of "Don't do the crime if you can't do the time." Paul wrote, "Whatever a person sows is what they will assuredly reap" (Gal. 6:7; my translation). "You get what you deserve" is akin to another: "Be careful what you ask for; you might get it."

These phrases and concepts are not new. Similar phrases have been around forever because the concept is embedded into life. It was certainly present in Amos' day, as attested to by this passage.

Amos was writing in the context of his society's failure to maintain a fair judicial system. The judges were exacting payments from legitimate claimants before those claimants could get their rights. But they apparently only charged those who could do little to object: the poor and disenfranchised among the community. The judges didn't call these payments "bribery"; they called them "taxes," or what might be called costs of court. This dishonesty was not going to thrive, and God was going to see to it.

At the root of God's character is the concept of "fair and just." We as people made in God's image are hardwired to appreciate that truth. Hence we come out of the womb almost ready to complain, "That's not fair!" But God didn't simply hardwire humans to the importance of justice and fairness. He also made society a place where justice and fairness bring about good and injustice brings bad consequences. This is why the sayings set out above have taken root. This is why Amos can confidently proclaim that the enriched abusers will not ultimately thrive.

Everyone has choices every day about how they treat others. We can treat others fairly or not. If we really want to pursue the heart of God, we will, at a minimum, treat people fairly and, even better, treat them with generosity and mercy. For God demonstrates generosity and mercy to us over what we justly deserve, over and over. I want to pursue God. I want to be fair, generous, and merciful.

Lord, give me a heart and the eyes to be fair and merciful. In your name, amen.

APRIL 23

For I know how many are your transgressions and how great are your sins—you who afflict the righteous, who take a bribe, and turn aside the needy in the gate. (Amos 5:12)

The scene happens often in movies and books, echoing what many experience in life. As an example, I was reading a popular spy novel in which a British MI-5 agent was asked by the widow of her recently deceased coworker to have lunch. The agent was concerned about the lunch because the agent had an improper relationship with the deceased coworker. The agent didn't know whether the widow knew about it, and she spent much of the lunch trying to determine this. Many of us live out that same scene, where we try to hide our sins from God.

In today's passage, a fact is set out immediately in the sentence. This fact takes two words in Hebrew, and they are the first two words to give them emphasis: *ki yada'ti "Because I know!"* God knows.

The verse goes on to describe what God knows, but it could also give a full stop. God knows. Period. It really doesn't matter what the sin is. The actions done in private are seen by God. God knows the thoughts in the deepest recesses of the mind. God knows and understands all people amid all cultures and throughout all time. This omniscient God isn't simply a theological concept. God is a practical reality.

Sometimes, people are like horses that are given blinders on their eyes to stop them from being distracted. Our brains and hearts commit us to courses of sin (don't think merely the "big" stuff like murder and adultery, but everyday sins like gossip, envy, pride, and anger!), yet we wear blinders that keep us from realizing in the moment that God knows. God is watching. God cares.

If we were constantly aware of the immediate presence and knowledge of God, our behavior would modify tremendously. After all, what child doesn't behave better when watched by a parent as opposed to when acting in apparent secrecy? Amos made it clear: "God knows . . ." We can fill in the blank from there, assured that the sentence is 100 percent correct.

Lord, I confess my sin. Help me regularly to be aware of your presence. In your name, I ask, amen.

APRIL 24

Therefore he who is prudent will keep silent in such a time, for it is an evil time.
(Amos 5:13)

On May 17, 1961, President John F. Kennedy addressed the Canadian Parliament. In his speech, President Kennedy said, "Evil triumphs when good men do nothing." One can find that speech on the internet, but in classic internet fashion, one will also often see that the phrase is from the eighteenth-century Irish philosopher and statesman Edmund Burke. It isn't. No one knows where the phrase comes from, but it does resonate in today's passage.

That phrase echoes in my ear when studying today's passage from Amos. The passage arises in a lamentation that God pronounces over the evil judges who were selling their decisions, ruling for the powerful and popular over the needy and destitute, and ultimately cascading Israel toward God's judgment and exile. If there were ever a time for the righteous to speak up, it was in Amos' day. Yet Amos proclaimed that the "prudent will keep silent" in the face of that evil time.

What shall be done with this instruction from Amos? Does it mean that in the face of evil, God's people should be silent? Does it encourage some complicity in the evil by failing to speak out? Upon careful reflection, I don't think the passage means that at all. Time travel back to Amos' day and think it through.

Injustice is rampant. The powerful are the perpetrators of this sin. If one speaks out against the perpetrators, it isn't going to change anything. Hence Amos is careful to say that the "prudent" are silent. The word *prudent* (*sakhal*—שׂכל) refers to one who is going to have success. Amos notes that the times are so evil that those who want to succeed are silent about the evil. Those are evil times indeed!

It is worth noting that in the very next verses, which are in the next few devotionals, Amos himself doesn't keep silent. Amos continues to exhort the people—both those who are abusing the needy as well as those who aren't. Amos wasn't silent, but neither was he successful! At least in his day. Let's speak out against evil when God gives us a chance, knowing it won't always lead to success.

Lord, give me a voice in the face of evil and injustice. For your cause, amen.

APRIL 25

Seek good, and not evil, that you may live; and so the Lord, the God of hosts, will be with you, as you have said. (Amos 5:14)

"My wallet was stolen!" I exclaimed to my wife, with natural frustration in my voice. She wasn't convinced. "Are you sure you haven't just misplaced it?" she inquired. I replied, "Absolutely sure! I've searched everywhere. It isn't here!" We then went through the arduous task of canceling credit cards, ordering replacement cards, and most difficult of all, ordering a new driver's license. The next day, I found my wallet in my shoe in my closet. I vaguely remember placing it there when changing clothes, but I told my wife that clearly whoever stole it felt guilty and must have placed it in my shoe. The standard joke now when anything is lost is to say it was stolen.

Seeking my wallet was an all-hands-on-deck moment. I searched high and low for it, everywhere except inside my shoes. I wonder what my life would be like if I searched equally hard for "good."

Today's passage urges the listener to "seek good, and not evil." The Hebrew word for "seek" (*darash*—דרשׁ) is laden with connotations that enrich this instruction. The word can mean "to seek," like one seeks that which is lost—for example, my wallet. It can also mean to care for, inquire about, investigate, search, be intent on, and similar ideas. The fullness of this meaning significantly broadens Amos' instructions.

My life will be better if my energies are spent in the positive ways of seeking that which is good. This isn't an instruction to simply avoid evil. That would be the equivalent of if my wallet is missing, I just go about life without one. No, the instruction is affirmative. My time should be spent in the search for good. This means I look for good to do each and every day. I search for good in others. I seek good results. Goodness is a treasure that I investigate, that I am intent on, that I invest in and care for. Goodness is my focus.

I want to do as the prophet teaches. I want my thoughts to be driven by a search for good. This instruction comes with a promise that life is found in goodness and God will be with me in that search. I couldn't ask for anything more than the presence of God in my life. I need to search for good, even inside my shoes!

Lord, I seek goodness. Help me keep that my priority today, in both active times and idle times. Be ever present with me in that search. In your name, I pray, amen.

APRIL 26

Therefore thus says the LORD, *the God of hosts, the Lord: "In all the squares there shall be wailing, and in all the streets they shall say, 'Alas! Alas!' They shall call the farmers to mourning and to wailing those who are skilled in lamentation, and in all vineyards there shall be wailing, for I will pass through your midst," says the* LORD. (Amos 5:16–17)

I love those talent shows where the performer takes the stage and the judges moan. The performer's act looks to be utterly dismal, or the singer's appearance indicates a lack of effort. As the performance begins, everyone is stunned. Out of the mouth of the least likely comes the most special voice. I love to watch everyone, from the judges to the audience, move in stunned appreciation over the unexpected.

Those shows come to my mind when studying today's passage. Look carefully at the end of the passage. It says God is going to be passing through Israel's midst. Isn't that great? Isn't that marvelous? Wouldn't everyone treasure having God come into their midst? No. Be stunned. This isn't what it seems.

I liken evil to a cancer, a proliferation of aberrant cells that, left unchecked, breed incessantly. Evil is a cancer that Israel had let grow to massive proportions in its culture. This cancer needed to be excised. God was coming in—but as a surgeon, coming to cut. The evil included fake worship, rotten justice, selfish living, ignoring and even exploiting the poor, and more. No antibiotic was going to work on this level of evil. The time had come for surgery.

Anyone who has experienced surgery knows the pain involved. One can't cut into a body without the body knowing it. Major surgery equates to major damage, and the body takes a great deal of time to recover.

Israel needed to know that God's holy presence was not a minor procedure. God was going to see that those responsible for the evil and the society that they had constructed were ended. This happened in 722 BCE, when the Assyrians swooped down into the northern kingdom of Israel, bringing destruction. This destruction is described in 2 Kings 17. It was horrid, and it was complete. The northern tribes were gone, and only the southern kingdom of Judah remained. Their vapid belief of "God in our midst" didn't have the results they might have expected—quite the contrary.

Lord, I want you walking with me in peace, not judgment. Help me in your name, amen.

APRIL 27

"I hate, I despise your feasts, and I take no delight in your solemn assemblies. Even though you offer me your burnt offerings and grain offerings, I will not accept them; and the peace offerings of your fattened animals, I will not look upon them." (Amos 5:21–22)

As a young lawyer, I was trying to figure out how to fit into a new job and workplace. In my first job out of law school, I was amazed to find a few folks who might say one thing when the bosses were present but, once the bosses were out of earshot, would challenge or even mock the bosses. I suspect that the disingenuousness of my compatriots didn't completely fool our supervisors. I know for sure that disingenuity doesn't fool God.

In today's passage, God expresses his disdain for the Israelites keeping the feasts that God had instructed them to keep. The required assemblies where burnt offerings and grain offerings were made were unacceptable to God. Importantly, all of these things God despised were rituals that God instituted for the people to do. Yet the people did them in ways that God rejected. Why?

The book of Amos places this stunning comment into context. The people were playing religion. They would follow certain rituals, assuming that what they did the rest of the time didn't matter. They were ticking boxes off the to-do list rather than authentically seeking and living for God. The evidence of the people's true motives was on daily display. They would ignore those who were needy. They would abuse those unable to fend for themselves. They kept values that were ungodly. To God, the periodic displays of religiosity were offensive.

I am reminded of a judge who once called all counsel into chambers. The case was important, and the judge was upset. With anger, the judge told my opposing counsel that his brief was riddled with inaccuracies. The judge said that the brief implied one of two things: either the lawyers thought the judge too stupid to know the truth, or they thought him too lazy to do the work. Either way, he was chunking the brief out. So it is with God and the fake religious people. Did they think God was too stupid to know their hearts? Or that God just didn't care?

Authenticity is a buzzword for the generation coming of age in the 2010s and 2020s in the United States. Authenticity has always been a concern of God's.

Lord, may my heart be open and honest to you. In your service, amen.

APRIL 28

"Take away from me the noise of your songs; to the melody of your harps I will not listen. But let justice roll down like waters, and righteousness like an ever-flowing stream." (Amos 5:23–24)

In August 1963, Martin Luther King Jr. ascended the steps of the Lincoln Memorial and delivered one of the most powerful speeches of the twentieth century. His "I Have a Dream" speech railed against the inequities and unfairness of racial treatment in America. At the midpoint of that speech, King quotes today's passage. The context is the inadequacy of America's progress in the one hundred years since the abolition of slavery. King said, "No, no, we are not satisfied and will not be satisfied until—justice rolls down like water and righteousness like a mighty stream."

In response to King's pleas, a number of religious people argued that God doesn't promote social issues. This view is belied by not only today's passage but all of Amos—indeed, all of Scripture. An important part of the message of the Old Testament is the fair treatment of others. The Christian New Testament writings include similar admonitions. Jesus spoke over and over of social justice, taking the rabbinic golden rule and teaching people to treat others as they would like to be treated.

Why would God care about social issues and the treatment of others? It's inherent in God's character. God made all people, and he wishes for all people to thrive in a relationship with him.

Look carefully at what God says of people who perpetuate injustice. Their songs to God are nothing but noise. God doesn't listen to their most skillful or dedicated works. I might try my best to serve and praise God, but when I slight those that he cares about, I am not truly serving him. Nor am I truly praising him.

If I want my relationship with God to be solid and meaningful, I need my relationships with others to be based on righteousness and justice. I need to care for those who cannot care for themselves. I need to reflect the mind and heart of God to others and not simply bask in the glow of his love for me. This is deliberate living, and it is important, godly living.

Lord, please give me eyes for injustice and a deep motivation to work for righteousness. May I do this in your name and to your glory, amen.

APRIL 29

"You shall take up Sikkuth your king, and Kiyyun your star-god—your images that you made for yourselves, and I will send you into exile beyond Damascus," says the LORD, *whose name is the God of hosts.* (Amos 5:26–27)

Jackson Browne put out an amazing album entitled *Saturate before Using*. In its feature song, "Doctor My Eyes," he sings, "As I have wandered through this world, and as each moment has unfurled, I've been waiting to awaken from these dreams. People go just where they will; I never noticed them until I got this feeling that it's later than it seems." I don't pretend to understand the depth of Browne's concern and message, but I've seen the reality that most people tend to believe in whatever they invest their time and effort in. Objective truth is an illusion for most. Whatever we are experiencing becomes our truth.

Today's passage is relevant here. The passage names idols that Israel worshiped. These idols were fictional gods, man-made efforts to find meaning. The passage names Sikkuth and Kiyyun as gods to Israel, idols they added to their worship of the LORD.

Today, people don't worship Sikkuth and Kiyyun—at least, not anyone I know. But idols are anything or anyone that we place over God as the primary recipient of our worship. Importantly, worship should never be equated just with songs or ceremonies done in a church, mosque, or synagogue. Worship might occur there, but worship is ascribing worth and value to something to such a degree that one pursues and submits to that object. We worship idols when we place our trust, hopes, or dreams in anything that isn't centered first and foremost in God.

Idolatry is a fraud. It's a self-perpetuating dream from which one needs to awaken. Idolatry introduces into life a scam or a deception. It alleviates the need for true ethics and morality, excusing and justifying all sorts of exploitation of situations and people for our own gain. This comes about when we pursue that which isn't worth our devotion, be it money, popularity, physical sensation, worldly security, attention, or any other vice.

God sends idolators into exile. He sent the idolatrous Israelites into exile, and he will do the same today. While exile today may not be a physical relocation, God will see that idol worshipers are never satisfied, always wandering in their hearts.

Lord, open my eyes to what is real and true. Reveal my idols. In your name, amen.

APRIL 30

"Woe to those who are at ease in Zion, and to those who feel secure on the mountain of Samaria, the notable men of the first of the nations, to whom the house of Israel comes!" (Amos 6:1)

Jesus told the story of a foolish rich farmer. The farmer's land had produced a record-setting bumper crop. There was so much that the barns couldn't store it all. Instead of reducing his price to sell it all or giving the extra away to the poor, the man built larger barns, storing his grain for sale at higher prices to ensure his future prosperity. You can see the man kicking off his sandals and relaxing in a comfortable chair, saying, "Relax, eat, drink, and be merry." Jesus said the man was a fool, because unknown to him, he would be dying that night (Lk. 12:13–21).

Something scares me about worldly security. Feeling that you have it made or that you're in good shape without recognizing God in the calculus is akin to the Israelites in today's passage. The wealthy were comfortable in their possessions. They saw no need to worry and felt secure. After all, their place in the world was set. Or so they thought.

God knew better, and he said so through the prophet in today's passage. God knew that he would be sending judgment on the people, and their so-called security had all the strength of a sheet of paper.

This world might seem to offer all we need, but that is an illusion. We may think that if we have enough in the bank, our worries are gone. But we are deluded. Those who trust in anything to deliver joy, happiness, or success in life are deceived, unless those things are brought under the umbrella of God and his will.

I was taught at an early age that if I were to speak of the future, I should add the comment "If God wills." I might say it quietly or out loud. I might even say it internally or under my breath. But it's right to recognize that unless God is behind what I trust, my trust is misplaced. This is ultimately a question of faith. Do I trust God or something else? That trust extends beyond security to all of life. If God is the trustworthy one, then I can rely on him in every way.

Lord, I confess I seek security in the world at times, apart from you. Forgive me and redirect my confidence. May I look to you as my sureness in an insecure world. In your name, amen.

MAY 1

"Woe to those who lie on beds of ivory and stretch themselves out on their couches, and eat lambs from the flock and calves from the midst of the stall, who sing idle songs to the sound of the harp and like David invent for themselves instruments of music, who drink wine in bowls and anoint themselves with the finest oils, but are not grieved over the ruin of Joseph! Therefore they shall now be the first of those who go into exile." (Amos 6:4–7)

What do you live for? What thrills you or at least pleases you in life each day? What motivates you in life? What are you working toward or looking forward to? For many, these questions are answered with some variation of a cushy lifestyle or some fun experience. That would make sense if life were nothing more than experiences. But life is more, and that calls into question one's purpose.

In today's passage, Amos singles out people who were living for the pleasure of the moment. In ancient speak, this included lying on luxurious beds and couches while eating rich food, drinking exquisite wine, and listening to melodious music, all while smelling really good. These people thought they had the good life. They thought their days were well spent. Life had dealt them a winning hand, and they were enjoying its fruits. To these people, Amos issued a severe wake-up call.

Amos scolded and rebuked these pleasure seekers for their selfish lives. They had no grief "over the ruin of Joseph!" God was coming in judgment over the people who had thumbed their noses at God and his instructions. The people's ruin had been assured by God in Leviticus 26. The prophets had declared that the time was near. But the audience was tuned out. They continued on blithely enjoying the moment's excess when they should have been mourning and grieving.

Today's passage causes me to reflect on my life—not just the long-term perspective of living but the daily grind. What am I doing *today*? What matters to me *today*? A well-lived life can all too easily fall into the habits of a diet or exercise routine—something better started tomorrow. Of course, tomorrow never comes.

I need to care about what matters. Where there is sin in my life or others', I need to grieve. Where there is selfishness, I need to reform. This is not something to put off. It needs to start afresh each day.

Lord, give me a heart for truth and righteousness. In your name, amen.

MAY 2

The Lord GOD has sworn by himself, declares the LORD, the God of hosts: "I abhor the pride of Jacob and hate his strongholds, and I will deliver up the city and all that is in it." (Amos 6:8)

What kid isn't asked by his or her folks to clean up their room? It was a regular feature in my home growing up. Sometimes I did it straight-away; sometimes I didn't. I do remember once when my dad discovered that I hadn't done as I was asked. He responded with his famous phrase "Don't make me ask you twice!" That was generally all it took to get me in there cleaning! I wonder if God ever wants to use my dad's line. Because there are many things that God has to say over and over in the Bible. It seems folks never got it! Of course, the same can be said of us today. Consider today's passage.

God affirms his hatred of pride in this verse. He doesn't just say he hates "Jacob's pride" (Jacob being a forefather of Israel), but he emphasizes it by swearing to it! After invoking this solemn oath, he further empha-sizes his hatred of pride by invoking his name, title, and character. It isn't obvious in English, but God uses his name *twice* (the four Hebrew letters that constitute the name of God being YHWH—יהוה), then he adds his title as "Lord," and finally he adds his deity as the "God of hosts." In English, this becomes "The Lord GOD . . . declares the LORD, the God of hosts."

This oath isn't the one *to* God used in a courtroom: "Do you swear to tell the truth, the whole truth, and nothing but the truth, so help you God?" It is an oath *by* God himself, YHWH (twice), the Lord, the God of all the Hosts. So what is so great that God swears and affirms it so boldly? It's simple: God hates pride.

Dad would say, "Don't make me say it twice; God repeats his condem-nation of pride more than that!" Isaiah the prophet wrote that God would put an end to the pomp (pride) of the arrogant (Isa. 13:11). Similarly, the prophet Jeremiah said God would spoil the pride of Judah (Jer. 13:9). Eze-kiel affirmed that God would put an end to the pride of the strong (Ezek. 7:24). In the law of Moses, God had spoken of "breaking" the pride of the powerful (Lev. 26:19).

What is it about pride that God so detests? Pride is the root of most sin. It places us in a position of self-accomplishment, robbing God of his glory, his work, and his placement in this world.

Lord, forgive me my pride. May I see only you as great. In your name, amen.

MAY 3

And when one's relative, the one who anoints him for burial, shall take him up to bring the bones out of the house, and shall say to him who is in the innermost parts of the house, "Is there still anyone with you?" he shall say, "No"; and he shall say, "Silence! We must not mention the name of the LORD." (Amos 6:10)

I had a friend in high school who was close to God. He was a spiritual leader among his peers. When my friend got to college, he found the distractions that many do. He never "left" his faith, but God took a backseat to indulging in worldly opportunities. My friend's relationship with God was strained, and for a period of time, he didn't want to talk about God or acknowledge God. This lasted about two years until my friend turned back to a life with God.

My friend's experience reminds me of today's passage. The passage speaks of the aftermath of God's judgment on Israel. God brought judgment on the unholiness of the people, and the consequences were profound. The unholiness of the people destroyed their way of life and their relationship with and desire to commune with God.

This passage speaks of relatives taking the dead out of their homes. In one home, the relative finds someone hiding, still scared of the invaders and the terror they brought. The relative tells the one in hiding to stay silent and then adds, "We must not mention the name of the LORD"! This is profound. The relative who had sinned so readily against God didn't turn to him in repentance as judgment fell. Instead, he (and the people he represents) were avoiding even saying God's name. God was no longer friend, but foe.

This is how far gone the people were. This is a depressing cost of sin. Willful sinning against God causes the sinner to become numb to God. It can reach a point where people want to avoid God, avoid invoking his name, avoid seeking his help, and avoid even talking about him.

I want to be careful here. Of course, I never want my sin to so alienate me from God that I want nothing to do with God. Yet this isn't a threshold that is clearly marked in front of us. It is gradually reached. So I need to always be mindful, avoiding willful sin and its negative effect on my walk with God.

Lord, I confess myself a sinner. I ask you for forgiveness. I want to be in a close fellowship with you each day. In your name, amen!

MAY 4

Do horses run on rocks? Does one plow there with oxen? But you have turned justice into poison and the fruit of righteousness into wormwood. (Amos 6:12)

I was trying a case about a defective ladder. The ladder was made outside of code, and my client fell, tearing up his back. The defendant called a professional witness to the stand as an "expert." At one point as I was cross-examining him, the judge hit his frustration limit over the witness playing word games and denying reality. The judge ordered the jury back to the jury room. Once the jurors were out of earshot, the judge lit into the witness: "Stop it! Stop your lying! This is a court of law, not *Alice in Wonderland*, where little is big and big is little. I know you're lying. The jury knows you're lying. And that won't be tolerated in my court. Do you understand?" The judge then had the jury brought back, and we finished.

The judge's no-nonsense admonition would have fit in back in Amos' day. In this passage, Amos laments those who were playing *Alice in Wonderland*-type games, denying the reality of justice and righteousness. No one would run horses on rocks. No one would plow up rocks with oxen. It just didn't happen. That's not reality. But the people had taken justice—something that should taste sweet, something that should be nutritious, something that should be pleasant—and turned it into poison. They took righteousness, which should be a marvelous fruit, and turned it into wormwood, a bitter and fruitless timber.

Do you think the people were purposely doing something stupid? Maybe, but I suspect not. I think they probably justified their sin. The heart and mind have a great ability to convince us that it's OK to do something that we want to do when the reality is that it isn't. I know this from what I eat, if nowhere else!

What we need are eyes to see what we are really doing. We need discernment to identify good and bad and avoid hypocrisy. Where are these found? Not in Wonderland but in God's presence. This should draw me to my knees each day, seeking God and his input into my life. This will transform my mind and heart. This is a reason for these daily devotionals. I am seeking God on his terms, expressed through his prophets, not through my own desires.

Lord, please hear my prayers for growth in purity. Help me to properly see the world, repent of my sins, and find life in your mercy. In your name, amen.

MAY 5

You who rejoice in Lo-debar, who say, "Have we not by our own strength captured Karnaim for ourselves?" "For behold, I will raise up against you a nation, O house of Israel," declares the LORD, *the God of hosts; "and they shall oppress you."* (Amos 6:13-14)

Israel was always in a precarious position, geographically speaking. The Mesopotamian cultures to the north—first Assyria and later Babylon—were always a threat. Similarly, Egypt to the south had been a threat as well. As the two superpowers of the day, Assyria and Egypt challenged each other frequently through the land of Israel. Israel was caught in the middle between two superpowers.

God had warned the Israelites about this dangerous position, assuring them that if they would be his light shining in the surrounding cultures, he would make them prosperous. However, God warned Israel that if they became no different from the idolatrous nations, they would lose his protection and would suffer at the hands of the various superpowers.

Israel grew callous, idolatrous, and apathetic to God. Yet at the time of Amos, Israel seemed to be thriving. Assyria was in a downturn with many internal struggles, and Israel, with its wicked king Jeroboam II, was expanding its territories. Israel was for a season prosperous, even as it pursued other gods and disregarded God's word.

But it wouldn't last. Amos spoke to God's coming judgment. The people were rejoicing in "Lo-debar," a town that means in Hebrew "nothing." Israel claimed to have conquered Karnaim by themselves, a town that means "horns," a symbol of strength. Yet God was raising up a nation, and within a couple of decades, Assyria would conquer the northern kingdom of Israel once and for all.

Today's passage gives me pause. I don't want to be like Israel, rejoicing in "nothingness," which is any strength or accomplishment that I claim to achieve on my own. I don't want to walk outside of God's will or morality. I don't want to substitute other idols in God's place. I want to cling to him, his teachings, and his will for me. In that, I will find his blessing, regardless of how things look for the next few years!

Lord, forgive my shortsightedness. Hone my focus on you and your name, amen.

MAY 6

*This is what the Lord G*OD* showed me: behold, he was forming locusts when the latter growth was just beginning to sprout, and behold, it was the latter growth after the king's mowings. When they had finished eating the grass of the land, I said, "O Lord G*OD*, please forgive! How can Jacob stand? He is so small!" The L*ORD* relented concerning this: "It shall not be," said the L*ORD*. (Amos 7:1-3)*

I've listened to a lot of debates over whether humanity has dignity. These debates don't often frame themselves that way, but that is how I see them. Usually, the debate is framed as one centering on whether people can truly choose one thing or another or whether the die is cast by virtue of some combination of genetics and environment. If every decision is made based on genetic coding and the effects life has had on that coding, thereby removing human choice and responsibility, then the dignity of a human disappears.

Yet the biblical picture is starkly different. Having already declared that people have dignity because they are made in God's image (Gen. 1:26), Scripture sets up an incredible dynamic. In the first chapter of Genesis, God created light and darkness, calling the light *day* and darkness *night.* God made the expanse and named it *heaven.* Having made humanity in his image, God then assigns to humanity naming rights over the animals, affirming that the animals will bear the names given by people. This shows God assigning to humanity the job that was rightly God's. People are in God's image, so they can do that.

Furthermore, God then gives Adam and Eve the instructions to tend and care for the garden of Eden. This is another attestation to humanity's value. Then sin enters the picture, and fallen humanity must leave paradise for a hard life. Yet God never revoked people's value. Similarly, God never revoked the instructions given to people to tend and care for the earth. He merely said it would be much tougher.

This value of humanity extends into today's passage. God is about to destroy the land of Israel with a locust infestation. Amos intercedes for Israel, and God relents from his actions. Amos—a mere human—caused God to alter history on the planet. Wow!

Theologies that consider God inflexible aren't biblical. Humanity has value, and God recognizes that. We should take seriously what we can *choose* to do.

Lord, may I make choices that honor you today and every day. In your name, amen.

MAY 7

This is what he showed me: behold, the Lord was standing beside a wall built with a plumb line, with a plumb line in his hand. And the LORD *said to me, "Amos, what do you see?"* (Amos 7:7–8)

I went to a large church from middle school through high school. Our middle school and high school programs each had several hundred kids in them. I moved to this church (and city) midway through the first middle school year, so I didn't know many people at the church. Because the church was so large, it had several staff members whose sole job was to work with the youth. One of them was Carl Cope. He was in his twenties, drove a Porsche, and was *cool*. I watched him from afar. One evening as I was walking across the parking lot, Carl was headed the other way. He saw me and said, "Hi, Mark." I was stunned! I couldn't believe it. The cool Carl Cope knew my name! I remember that almost fifty years later.

Today's passage reminds me of that day. I have spent a considerable amount of time with the Hebrew of today's passage because it has a bizarre Hebrew word that stumps many translators. The word is translated as "plumb line" typically, but out of the whole Bible, it only appears in these two verses. A really good case can be made that the word means "tin," as in the metal. I wrestled with this translation and passage and, reading one last time through the Hebrew, realized the most stupefying aspect of this verse for me devotionally. It isn't what God meant by building and standing by a tin wall or a plumb line. It is the phrase "Amos, what do you see?" Or as it is ordered in the Hebrew, "And the LORD said to me, what do *you* see, Amos?"

God calls Amos by name in this dialogue. That is stunning. The book contains God's message to Israel, a nation, speaking into their culture and practices. God discusses their destiny and coming judgment. Yet here, God pauses in that divine communication to the people to have a one-on-one dialogue with Amos, and God actually uses Amos' name!

This speaks profoundly of God. God has national or, more accurately, international concerns. God cares about people, cultures, and history. But God is also concerned with individuals. He knows my name and your name. He speaks into our lives, calling us by name. If Carl Cope knowing my name made my day, what should it mean that the God of the cosmos calls me by name? It should rock my world!

Lord, may I listen intently as you speak to me. You amaze me. In your name, amen.

MAY 8

Then Amaziah the priest of Bethel sent to Jeroboam king of Israel, saying, "Amos has conspired against you in the midst of the house of Israel. The land is not able to bear all his words." (Amos 7:10)

Rats running on wheels fascinate me. I guess they are getting exercise, but mainly I see them running and running and running but going nowhere. The frenetic activities of people remind me of rats running on wheels. Many people seem to go through life trying to get through the day. They work for food on the table, a place to live, and clothes to wear and spend time with their family. But at the end of a day, a year, or a life, they find that they lived without a greater purpose.

Today's passage challenges a purposeless approach to life. Amaziah had a job. The Hebrew indicates he was not simply a priest but the high priest of Bethel, a place where Israel had placed a golden calf idol for idolatrous worship. This idolatry was part of the reason for Amos' prophecies. God was coming to judge Israel, in part, because Israel had created a golden calf to represent God (or perhaps another god). Amaziah's position kept him tight with an idolatrous king, but not with God.

Amaziah spent his time overseeing blasphemous worship. But this wasn't just a here-and-there waste of time; this was a destructive life's work. He had reached the pinnacle of his profession. He had tremendous influence over not only the people of Israel but also the king. Amaziah was able to bend the king's ear and alert the king to the troublesome prophecies of Amos.

Amaziah hypes up his report to the king, accusing Amos of conspiring with others, something akin to political treason. The story line doesn't indicate that the king did anything about it, but my focus isn't on the king; it is on Amaziah. Amaziah used his time, his life, and his influence to a bad end. He was just awakening each day, climbing on his wheel, and running to go nowhere. Yet he should have done something different. He should have examined his life and made changes. He should have listened to Amos and used his high-priestly influence for good.

I want to live life with purpose. I want my time, my life, and my influence to account for something more than a rat running on a wheel.

Lord, show me your purposes, and guide me in them. To your glory, amen.

MAY 9

For thus Amos has said, "Jeroboam shall die by the sword, and Israel must go into exile away from his land." (Amos 7:11)

Ancient Roman historians reported that when Julius Caesar returned to Rome after conquering Gaul in what is now France, he proclaimed, *Veni vidi vici*: "I came, I saw, I conquered." Some of the beauty of this line is its simple threefold declaration that knits together three independent actions as if they were one. Caesar came to France. Caesar saw the enemy. Caesar beat the enemy. One-two-three goes the flow.

Bruce Springsteen has a similar line. In "Prove It All Night" he sings, "You want it, you take it, you pay the price." Short and succinct, this line in triplet form ties three actions. If you want something, you can take it, but you assuredly will pay the price. King Jeroboam II should have listened to Bruce Springsteen!

In today's passage, Israel's high priest Amaziah has gone to wicked King Jeroboam II to report Amos' prophetic ministry. Amaziah was not a proper priest for the LORD God but was high priest at Bethel, leading idolatrous worship to a golden calf. This idolatry was a cause of Amos' prophetic pronouncement of God's coming judgment. Amaziah reported that Amos was announcing God's judgment on King Jeroboam, his household, and all of Israel. The king (and his lineage) was going to be extinguished. Israel was going to be captured and carted off to a foreign land. Amaziah wanted Amos arrested for such treasonous comments.

Jeroboam ignored Amaziah's report and Amos' prophecies. The king had options. He could have repented before God. He could have arrested Amos. He could have sent a team to investigate. But history shows that the times were good for Jeroboam and Israel. He had found success by expanding his borders. He wasn't worried about some kook delivering prophecies of doom. With such great times, the king easily could write Amos off.

The problem for the king and Israel was that Amos was speaking the truth. God was on the march, and God was bringing judgment. The people and their king-leader were living in rebellion against God, and that was not going to fare well. Anyone can hear the truth, but if they don't accept it and act on it, they will face the consequences. It's so certain Bruce Springsteen put it into song.

Lord, I want to hear your truth and act on it. Help me, please. In your name, amen.

MAY 10

And Amaziah said to Amos, "O seer, go, flee away to the land of Judah, and eat bread there, and prophesy there." (Amos 7:12)

In 1994, the movie *Forrest Gump*, starring Tom Hanks, hit the theaters to rave reviews. In the movie, when Forrest is asked whether he is stupid, he replies, "Stupid is as stupid does," popularizing a saying that people should be judged on their actions, not their appearance. Actions speak loudly. They come from core beliefs, prejudices, and biases. When we examine our actions, we can learn about our minds. Today's passage highlights that.

Here is the scene: Amos is a livestock breeder who most think is from the southern kingdom of Judah. God takes him away from work and sends him to the northern kingdom of Israel to deliver prophecies of condemnation and doom. These weren't mean prophecies; they were true statements of what was coming to a nation that had rebelled against God and his instructions. The northern kingdom was making a mockery of God and hurting many people in the process. Amos declares as much, and a priest of the northern kingdom hears Amos and tries to get him arrested. His attempts to have Amos arrested fail, so the priest Amaziah then tries to get Amos to return to the southern kingdom of Judah. "Leave!" he says. "Ply your trade somewhere else!"

Amos doesn't leave yet because he isn't done with God's job. But the interesting focus for me in today's passage is what the priest Amaziah was doing. Amos was a hotline to the thinking and plans of God. The LORD God himself was speaking through Amos. So in very real terms, Amaziah, an alleged holy man, was telling God to take his thoughts, words, and plans and leave! Amaziah wanted to have nothing to do with God.

Why is it that at times, we so loath hearing and honoring the word of God? Oh, when things are going well, we're great at accommodating what God has to say, but when times are tough? When God's ways don't seem to fit with what the situation requires? Why is it so easy to send God packing?

Stupid is as stupid does. Rejecting God's message and instructions proceeds from a heart and mind that ultimately don't have the faith to hold on to God's words. I don't want to be that person.

God, help me to listen to you, to trust you, and to obey you. In your name, amen.

MAY 11

"But never again prophesy at Bethel, for it is the king's sanctuary, and it is a temple of the kingdom." (Amos 7:13)

Two of our granddaughters are identical twins. When they were fifteen months old, I was watching them play. All children are fun to watch, but identical twins add a new element. They were getting to the age of individuality, at least when it came to toys. As I watched, they both began to want the same toy. One had the toy, and the other tried to take it. They were equal in size, so the fight over who got it was fairly matched. It was the fifteen-month-old equivalent of "Mine!" "No! Mine!" "No! Mine!" being played out between two children who looked exactly alike. I could smile at them being fifteen months old.

Their story comes to mind reading today's passage. The passage is buried in the narrative of Amos 7, exposing the high priest of Bethel, where he led the wayward nation of Israel (the northern of the split kingdoms of God's people in the 700s BCE) to worship an idolatrous golden calf. These were people who claimed to be worshiping the LORD God who rescued them from Egypt while they simultaneously worshiped other gods. This idolatry was repeatedly condemned by the prophet Amos. Amos wasn't a professional prophet, but God had sent Amos to prophesy his coming judgment on the northern kingdom. The high priest reported Amos to the king for conspiracy to treason, but the king took no action. So the high priest told Amos to leave and stop prophesying.

Look carefully at the words used by the high priest, a man set apart to serve God who should have known differently. The idolatrous temple is called "the king's sanctuary" (i.e., the king's "holy place") as well as the "temple of the kingdom." See the problem? A temple should be God's holy place, not the king's. The high priest not only was leading idol worship but asserted in his speech that the king—not God—owned the temple. In a sense, he was betraying that the idol was made by human hands and wasn't real.

We should recognize reality. All things belong to God, not just houses of worship. We should not be fifteen-month-old children, thinking each toy we touch is our own. That behavior is cute in toddlers; it's pathetic in adults. I need to examine how I treat my possessions. Do I think of them as "mine," or are they God's things that he has given me stewardship over?

Lord, all I have is yours. Let me know that and live that. In your power, amen.

MAY 12

Then Amos answered and said to Amaziah, "I was no prophet, nor a prophet's son, but I was a herdsman and a dresser of sycamore figs. But the LORD took me from following the flock, and the LORD said to me, 'Go, prophesy to my people Israel.'" (Amos 7:14–15)

In middle school, we were required to take a career aptitude test. The goal of the test was to identify which careers made the most sense with each student's talents and to help students select their high school electives. I scored highest in the careers of trial lawyer, preacher, and politician. So in high school, I began my studies in public speaking and debate along with Latin, which was the closest my school had to a biblical language. In life, I became both a lawyer and a preacher—two of the three.

Amos lived in a different era. In his day, many careers involved working with livestock. Amos worked with livestock, but not as a common shepherd. The Hebrew indicates that Amos was a breeder of sheep. He also traveled and worked to ripen figs on plantations. Some scholars describe Amos as an "agribusiness specialist." In his day, some people were professional prophets who earned income by giving divine insights, like today's fortune-tellers. Amos was no professional prophet, no ordinary fortune-teller. He had an occupation, and God had removed him from that job for a time to deliver God's warning to a wayward nation.

Amos carried the divine message of the one true God. It was a critical message to the people. It wasn't filled with joy and excitement; it warned of doom and destruction. It drove the obedient Amos from his prosperous agribusiness that produced offspring of animals and fruit to one that seemed to produce no fruit. Yet even though his prophecies failed to bear fruit, Amos didn't let them deter him. He was a man on a mission, and God defined the mission. His mission was to proclaim God's word. That was a mission in itself.

Today's passage calls on us to examine why we do what we do. Are our lives simply reflections of our aptitude? Or are we trying to find and follow God's will for us? If we live each day seeking God in what we do, we will be on a mission and be like Amos.

Lord, put me on a mission for you today and every day. In your name, amen.

MAY 13

Now therefore hear the word of the LORD. "You say, 'Do not prophesy against Israel, and do not preach against the house of Isaac.' Therefore thus says the LORD: 'Your wife shall be a prostitute in the city, and your sons and your daughters shall fall by the sword, and your land shall be divided up with a measuring line; you yourself shall die in an unclean land, and Israel shall surely go into exile away from its land.'" (Amos 7:16–17)

In college, I took a course where I had to translate Amos from the Hebrew. The book of Amos is nine chapters long. Most of those nine chapters are prophetic pronouncements that are challenging to translate. Once you get to chapter 7, however, you get a break. Much of chapter 7 is basic Hebrew biography or history, which is much easier to translate. It is also fascinating. Today's passage brings the easy section to an end, and what an end it is.

Amaziah held the position of high priest at the exalted yet idolatrous site of worship at Bethel. His worship included sacrifices to a golden calf, in direct violation of the law of Moses given after God miraculously brought Israel out of Egyptian bondage. Amos was a true worshiper of the LORD God, who had both revealed himself to Moses and had entered into a covenant with the people of Israel. Compare the two objects of worship: a bull made by metal craftsmen versus the God who created the heavens and the earth. Or an object with no reality beyond its material substance versus a God who is the ultimate reality. Or a muted, silent chunk of gold with no capability or consciousness versus the God of unlimited power and awareness.

The comparison is no comparison! Amaziah the priest worshiped nothing real. Amos the agribusiness specialist worshiped the one and only God. Seeing that distinction makes today's passage stand out for the audacity of the foolish priest Amaziah. He insisted that Amos refuse to obey the commands of God and instead obey the priest of the chunk of metal.

Amos had harsh words for Amaziah. Amos pronounced God's coming judgment on Amaziah and his family. It would not be pretty. Somewhere in this passage, the message shouts out, "Be careful with whom you pick a fight!" No one should be fighting God. It is foolish. No one will beat him. It simply isn't possible. To think otherwise is to live a delusion. I want to live God's reality, not a delusion.

Lord, forgive me for living by my desires rather than yours. In your mercy, amen.

MAY 14

This is what the Lord God showed me: behold, a basket of summer fruit. (Amos 8:1)

This is my fourth devotional book. Having written ones on the Psalms, the Torah (Genesis through Deuteronomy), and the life/teachings of Jesus, I am still finding great joy in writing this one. These devotionals flow out of my private study time with God. I have a host of dear friends reading them to give me insights, fix my grammar, correct my typos, and let me know if these have any merit in the lives of others. One of the comments my friends have made to me concerns the stories and illustrations I try to include in each devotion. One friend said, "I would run out of stories by May!" I doubt that.

Each day, God communicates to us through common and ordinary things. These are the stories of life. In today's passage, God is going to give a metaphor for his coming actions upon Israel. But before getting to that metaphor (which I will do tomorrow), I find it worth pausing to note the setup.

God showed a basket of "summer fruit" to Amos. Amos knew summer fruit. Amos spent part of his life as a "dresser of sycamore figs" (Amos 7:14). This was someone who knew how and when to make a small slice in the fruit of the sycamore fig tree to allow it to ripen more quickly and in the most flavorful way. These figs in Israel begin to ripen in July and continue throughout the end of summer. Figs are "summer fruit" and were well known to Amos.

God is able to take what is normal and everyday and speak into our lives. Becky and I have five great children and ten wonderful grandchildren (as of now), and we can both attest to the many ways God has spoken to us through our children. I don't mean simply that our children encourage us in the Lord, which they have certainly done. But lessons from God on compassion, forgiveness, steadfastness, patience, love, joy, peace, discipline, faith, and so much more have come to us from God through our children, grandchildren, and many ordinary things in life.

I think one of the keys to finding God in our midst is *looking* for God in these times and moments. Look for his lessons, and look for his opportunities to learn. These surround us all the time! There are enough for hundreds of devotional books yet to be written!

Lord, open my eyes to see your message. Open my ears to hear your message. Soften my heart to receive your message. With gratitude in your name, amen.

MAY 15

And he said, "Amos, what do you see?" And I said, "A basket of summer fruit." Then the LORD said to me, "The end has come upon my people Israel; I will never again pass by them." (Amos 8:2)

Almost everyone loves a good book. For those who don't read, I suspect they enjoy a good show. We like to experience a measure of life beyond ourselves, and good books or shows allow us to do that. We can enter a fictional world and be that detective or spy. We can be enthralled by the documentary of a great athlete and wonder if that could be us. We can live the thrill of someone's tryout on a talent show and imagine what life would be like if we had that skill or voice. It seems a natural human thing to do to place ourselves in alternate shoes, going on vacation from our reality, even if for just a bit. Yet there is a danger lurking here.

The danger becomes clear if we begin to let our imagination alter our reality—if we start thinking that the fiction we read, see, or imagine is what the world and life could be. Many people think that relationships should be like what they see on some show or YouTube clip. Many might succumb to thinking that their life should be like those portrayed by others in a fictional world, and they struggle to understand why the perfection of others isn't present in the imperfection of their own life.

Today's passage brings this truth to mind, as Amos was shown a basket of summer fruit. This basket was loaded with fruit in season: fruit that had ripened and was ready for feasting. Back in an era before prepackaged foods and processed ingredients for fancy desserts, it was hard to beat ripe summer fruit for an amazing epicurean treat!

But looks can be deceiving. For this fruit was serving as an indicator of God's message. The fruit was ripe, and so was the time. God's judgment had ripened over the people who were not only ignoring him but twisting his instructions to hurt those under God's protection. God was hearing the outcry of the poor, downtrodden, and abused. God was coming to their rescue.

The difference between real life and the illusion of life is living in the reality and true presence of God. When we focus on who he is and let that be our guide for each day and decision, we are in the real world, not some fiction. Reality is good.

Lord, be my focus today and every day. May I find my truth in you, amen.

MAY 16

"The songs of the temple shall become wailings in that day," declares the Lord God. *"So many dead bodies!"* (Amos 8:3)

Each day is full of decisions—what to do, how to do it, what to think, what to plan. The list of decisions occurs on a nearly moment-by-moment basis. I have a good buddy Richard with whom I have spent a lot of time trying cases. As we face various decision points, Richard is fond of saying, "Let's take the high road; there's less traffic!" Inherent in Richard's statement is the core truth that decisions have consequences. Going left or right won't always get you to the same place.

This truth of life is well illustrated in today's passage. This passage ends a series of four visions had by Amos about God's judgment coming on the actions of the people of Israel. This last vision draws out God's judgment and its effect on the people's religious practices. The religious practices of the people, as sanctioned by the government, were a mix of apparent devotion but without morality, without worship of God apart from idols, and without caring about truth.

Israel was going to find out that peace and harmony without justice and truth is a false illusion. Their bubble was going to pop, and it was going to pop hard. Their religion was going to be zero help. Their songs of piety would become wailings of woe. The trappings of religious fervor are useless if one is not in true fellowship with the living God.

Religion is not a game. It isn't a formality that "should be in" one's life. True religion is a devotion to and relationship with the one true God. This type of faith is based on the truth of who God is and the desire of his people to meld their hearts to him. It is evident in how people live. Israel's religion was a cold formality, a process based on illusion. Their religious practice had zero to do with their day-to-day relationships with others.

I want a faith that is real. I want to find and know God as he is. I want to sing songs of praise to him on my good and bad days. If I am wailing and moaning, I want it to be in the caring arms of a consoling God, not in a cold world without the true God. This will be seen in my choices in life. The high road may have less traffic, but because I can trust God is there, it is important that I find it and live it.

Lord, may my life reflect a vibrant faith in you and your truth. In your name, amen.

MAY 17

Hear this, you who trample on the needy and bring the poor of the land to an end . . .
(Amos 8:4)

I was born into a middle-class home. Mom and Dad weren't rolling in dough, but neither were we wondering if we would eat our next meal. Mom and Dad worked hard to make ends meet and to be sure my sisters and I received a good education and had opportunities to pursue our dreams. But nearby, both at church and at school, I knew kids born into what I considered luxury. Their houses were akin to mansions in my eyes. They got cars when they turned sixteen. They always had spending money. They had the latest clothes and shoes and went on great vacations. I loved my life and upbringing, for Mom and Dad taught us to love God and others. But I used to wonder what it would be like to be born into a family with wealth.

There is a difference in life between how you are born and how you live. This truth is apparent in today's passage, which begins a section of Amos dealing with hypocrisy. Amos was preaching to Israel, which had gone astray. The people were not living in their covenant relationship with God. God had instructed them to treat the poor with compassion and care. God had given the people a law that they were to treat others as they would like to be treated. In Leviticus 19:18, God told them, "You shall love your neighbor as yourself." Yet the people were far from following God and his law. The people were Israelites, descendants of Abraham, but they weren't living like it. The Israelites were ethnically God's people, but the poor who were being abused were economically God's people.

In other words, relying only on their DNA and heritage was not adequate for living a godly life. God had an ear and a heart tuned to the songs and cries of the poor and abused. As the genetic progeny of people who had been "chosen," Israel was failing. Not only were the people not hearing the pleas of the needy; they were trampling over them. In doing so, they were destroying the people God had told them to look after.

This should cause me to look beyond my parents and grandparents. My life is about my actions and attitudes. Anything I have in life, from genetics to status and all points in between, are only tools to follow the heart of God. If I am living for anyone or anything else, I am missing the mark.

Lord, give me an eye and heart for the things you treasure. In your name, amen.

MAY 18

"When will the new moon be over, that we may sell grain? And the Sabbath, that we may offer wheat for sale." (Amos 8:5)

In 1967, Truett Cathy founded and opened the world's first Chick-fil-A, a fast-food restaurant, in Atlanta, Georgia. As of the time I write this, Chick-fil-A is the world's largest quick-service chicken restaurant, if you go by annual system-wide sales. KFC has many more restaurants worldwide—almost ten times as many—but Chick-fil-A still outsells KFC. This is even more stunning when one realizes KFC is open seven days a week in most places, while all Chick-fil-As are closed on Sundays. The Cathys believed in a day of rest, a Sabbath, being more important than an additional day of sales.

In an interview late in his life, Truett, who lived to be ninety-three, told a reporter, "I think I'd like to be remembered as one who kept my priorities in order." He understood that money was a great tool but a harsh master. By earning money, he was able to put that money to great use. But he was careful never to let the money become a god, demanding and seeking more and more of it.

Today's passage reminds me of Truett Cathy but in reverse. Amos is calling out to a people who have lost their priorities. These people had to honor the Sabbath, for it was a national law. But they were eager for the Sabbath to pass; they wanted to get back to business. The next verses add the extra hypocritical element that the people would be pursuing that business the next day through cheating and deception.

Passages like today's should make all of us pause and examine our priorities. What is important to us in life? Where do the big five truly fall? The big five are the priorities of faith, family, friends, self, and money. How we list those—not only in our minds but in our lives—will determine what kind of people we are, how our families grow and function, and what kind of society we have. As I consider this, I need to not only ask what I believe should be my priorities, but I need to assess how my life reflects those priorities. How am I really doing?

Truett left a legacy, a business and family that carried on his priorities. God blessed that business immensely. I want my priorities to be right, and I can trust God will bless my life accordingly.

Lord, help me live the right priorities before you each day and in each decision. In you, amen.

MAY 19

"That we may offer wheat for sale, that we may make the ephah small and the shekel great and deal deceitfully with false balances." (Amos 8:5)

Leslie Thrasher (1889–1936) was an American illustrator who painted twenty-three *Saturday Evening Post* covers. In a year of great tragedy (a house fire destroyed much of his work and smoke inhalation led ultimately to pneumonia and his death at forty-seven), he painted my favorite of all his covers. The October 3, 1936, cover painting showed an old butcher selling an elderly woman a chicken. The chicken is on a scale, and if you look carefully, you will see that the butcher has his left middle finger on the scale, weighing it down a bit (and increasing the price). This careful examination also shows that the woman buying the chicken has her right index finger under the scale pushing the tray up, lightening the scale and lowering the price. These two would have fit into Israel in Amos' day.

In today's passage, Amos rails at the people of Israel for their hypocrisy. These people would close their shops on the Sabbath, presumably out of piety, and reopen them the next day to cheat the customers. They would sell an "ephah" of wheat (about the same as a bushel, more or less) that was less than a true ephah. Their scales were intentionally off. In today's legal parlance, this was basic fraud.

I don't want to be a hypocrite. I don't want people to have to double-check to see if I am dealing with them honestly. You may be with me in this and be tempted to skim over, if not totally skip, today's devotional teaching. Yet I need to check myself here, and you might need to also. Cheating and hypocrisy don't arise only in the business world.

How we treat others, both to their face and behind their backs, is rooted in the same ethic as expressed in today's passage. For example, do I say things about people when outside their company that I wouldn't say to their faces? Do I act as a friend to someone when my actions belie that supposed friendship? How am I in my life before God? Do I have a devotion in synagogue or church that is missing on Tuesday afternoon?

Sincerity begins in the heart, and it should express itself in our lives. It's a struggle for everyone but one worth engaging in. I can't judge Israel too harshly, for as the cover of the *Saturday Evening Post* portrayed, I may have a finger on the scale too.

Lord, forgive my hypocrisy, and help me grow in sincerity. In your name, amen.

MAY 20

Hear this, you who trample on the needy and bring the poor of the land to an end, saying . . . "that we may buy the poor for silver and the needy for a pair of sandals and sell the chaff of the wheat?" (Amos 8:4–6)

Confirmation bias is a phrase given to a cognitive process that social scientists have found is present in almost everyone. This bias is basically an instinct, something that automatically proceeds from one's mind without conscious thought. At its essence, confirmation bias means that we tend to interpret information, evidence, and arguments in ways that support our existing beliefs while we tend to ignore that which contradicts those beliefs. This isn't a new phenomenon; it seems as old as humanity. It was certainly there in Amos' day.

The odds are great that if you or I could have a conversation with the people in Amos' day and we asked them, "Do you think you're a terrible person?" they would answer truthfully, "No!" Somehow, in their minds and hearts, they would have justified their actions and lifestyle. Reading God's judgment voiced by Amos now—2,750 years later—makes them look bad, but they undoubtedly had reasons, a confirmation bias that not only excused but justified their behavior. It probably went something like this.

"Well, yes, we are selling the chaff, the nonnutritious, trashy part of the wheat plant that should be thrown away. BUT it's cheap and people are buying it! If they want to buy it, who are we not to sell it?" Or "OK, so we are abusing those who are so in debt that they can't even pay off a pair of sandals (about the least amount there was), but we are helping these poor people. As our servants, they will have a roof over their heads and we will be sure they are fed!"

We humans are a funny race. We figure out what we want and what we like, and then we set about justifying it. Amos tried to put a stop to that. He voiced God's message that humanity exists for much more than satisfying the drive of our own desires. People are called into a relationship with God to find God's values and heart. The desires and purposes of God should transform us. As we are transformed, the world around us will be transformed. Then this fallen and broken world will have a greater semblance of what it can be when the Lord is God rather than you and me. This will take prayer and work. We must defeat our own individual confirmation biases.

Lord, I need your work in my mind and heart to transform me in your name, amen.

MAY 21

The LORD has sworn by the pride of Jacob: "Surely I will never forget any of their deeds. Shall not the land tremble on this account, and everyone mourn who dwells in it, and all of it rise like the Nile, and be tossed about and sink again, like the Nile of Egypt?" (Amos 8:7–8)

Today's passage illustrates an important overarching promise of God's story with Israel. It's rooted in Israel's geography. An apt illustration is that of a bridge. Bridges are conduits, enabling people and materials to traverse from one side of a river or chasm to the other. With a bridge, commerce can thrive in lands that are now merged. Without a bridge, the lands stay separated, thwarting the growth of both sides. History is replete with examples. In a sense, Israel is one of those.

Israel was a geographic bridge from the thriving kingdoms to the north, in the Fertile Crescent of Mesopotamia, and the thriving Egyptian kingdom centered on the Nile. People, armies, and commerce going from one to the other naturally found their way through Israel. To the west of Israel was the Mediterranean Sea, which was an impediment to foot and animal traffic. To the east of Israel was the desolate desert, another impediment to foot and animal traffic.

As a land bridge, Israel was typically going to be one of two things: either a thriving independent state, with the great prosperity that came from being the land bridge, or a state paying tribute to the kingdom to the north or south that controlled this economy-generating bridge. History would show that Israel often vacillated between those statuses. There is a spiritual lesson here more important than the geography lesson.

God had promised Israel that if it reflected God's glory, if it lived by God's laws, if it was a testimony to God's reign and character, then Israel would be the first alternative: a thriving independent nation. If, however, Israel became like the other nations, living without God's instructions, character, and law, then God would deliver Israel over to the nations it copied. Sadly, that's what happened, as evidenced in today's passage. The "pride of Jacob"—the land that was a bridge—was on the brink. It was going to the nations.

God made a world with opportunity and consequence. With God is protection and blessing, even in hard times. Without him is the harsh world. I want God.

Lord, I want to follow you more carefully. Help me, please. In your name, amen.

MAY 22

"And on that day," declares the Lord GOD, "I will make the sun go down at noon and darken the earth in broad daylight." (Amos 8:9)

The musician Ray Stevens wrote a song entitled "My Dad." One repeated lyric is "My dad could beat up your dad, but he wouldn't." The old schoolyard taunt of "My dad (or brother, or sister, or mother) is better than yours" had many variations. In the early days of television, Ken-L Ration dog food even had a commercial with children singing, "My dog's better than your dog."

We are natural comparers. We see and rank things consciously and unconsciously. We also like to be affiliated with the things that are bigger and better. So today's passage should give everyone a bit of a pause. Amos was repeating God's declaration of profound power and authority.

In Amos' day, like today, certain people possessed great authority. A friend who is a federal judge teased, "I have the authority to shut down the electricity to a city block." He quickly added, "Now, once I did so, someone with greater authority would reverse me and likely strip me of my authority for abusing it. But I could shut it down for a time." He was right. Many leaders have sweeping powers, but I have never met anyone who could force a noon eclipse. Some might foresee it and announce it's coming. But who could actually cause it? No one.

But God can. God has command over all the elements in the universe. He made space, time, and matter. God can snap his fingers (speaking in human terms) and change any aspect of reality. God can part the waters. God can send fire or hailstones from heaven. God can bring light into darkness. God has majestic power beyond that which any person has had or could ever have.

What do we do before a God like this? I'd suggest several things. First and foremost, we should be on his side! In terms of schoolyard taunts, you could say, "My God is bigger than . . ." and finish that sentence with *anything* and be correct. Second, we shouldn't hesitate to go to God with our problems. He is bigger than any problem we might have. Additionally, we should worship and praise God for who he is. In the words of Scripture, we worship God because he is "worthy" of our praise. God is bigger than we are, more than we can even know!

Lord, I praise you for your grandeur and thank you for caring for me. I give you my life and heart, and I pray for strength to follow you. In your name, amen.

MAY 23

"I will turn your feasts into mourning and all your songs into lamentation; I will bring sackcloth on every waist and baldness on every head; I will make it like the mourning for an only son and the end of it like a bitter day." (Amos 8:10)

In the early 1960s, Ed Peterson was visiting some construction sites for dams in the northwestern United States when he found that a number of workers were getting killed by trucks backing over them. Ed then invented the backup alarm that goes "beep, beep, beep" when heavy machinery is shifted into reverse. It's a sound that even our three-year-old grandson makes when he's playing trucks on the floor and begins to back a truck up. The alert for "reverse" has saved countless lives.

In today's passage, Amos is sounding the backup alarm. The people are blithely going through their lives, feasting, singing, and wearing fancy clothes with no regard for God whatsoever. Yet God is a God of reversals. In a "beep, beep, beep" fashion, Amos is warning people that the feasting will become grieving. The singing will turn to sad songs of pain. The fancy clothes will be discarded for the rough sackcloth that people wear when distressed and heartbroken. Heads will be shaven to show inconsolable pain.

Yes, God is a God of reversals, but reversals work both ways. As the people had fled God's presence, their celebrations of life were hollow, and reversals would demonstrate that emptiness. But God also gives reversals the other way. To his people who are suffering, God promises reversals as well.

God can take mourning and turn it into dancing. God can remove one's sackcloth and clothe people in joy (Ps. 30:11). God can turn night into day and give shelter from the storm.

The backup alarm serves to modify one's behavior. If I know that reversals can come, I can seek to live under God's care. This is how I listen to his signals. Then, as God teaches me through his word and presence how to live, I can hear and respond properly. God's values become my values. God's priorities become my priorities. God's mission becomes my mission. Then I will see God's strength in my weakness, God's presence in my loneliness, and God's wisdom when I am lost. We have a God of reversals!

Lord, may I humbly seek you. Bring your peace into my life. To your glory, amen.

MAY 24

"Behold, the days are coming," declares the Lord GOD, "when I will send a famine on the land—not a famine of bread, nor a thirst for water, but of hearing the words of the LORD." (Amos 8:11)

Email—a blessing and a curse. Before email, I had to open and read countless letters all day. I was tied to the office because that is where the mail was delivered. It came once a day, and when I was finished with the mail, I was finished until the next day. Not so with email. I get them all day long. I can read and dispose of them all, only to have a full inbox an hour later. What's more, when people know you're reading their email, like when you answer one, they sometimes respond immediately, ready for you to carry on a dialogue via email. Hence email—a blessing and a curse.

Whether by email or letters (a.k.a. "snail mail"), we are people who need to communicate. We have important ideas, messages, and plans to share with one another. Scientists understand that human brains are hardwired for communication. It isn't simply a learned skill; it's embedded in how we think. Not surprisingly, then, the Maker of the Universe communicates with his creations. God speaks through his word.

God's word, delivered through tried, tested, and dedicated prophets over hundreds of years, has been secured for people. Translations into modern languages are on our shelves because people have dedicated their lives to producing them. It's one of life's greatest honors to have a chance to read, study, contemplate, and integrate the very words of God into our lives.

Today's passage notes a time when people would be without God's word. This famine from hearing God's revelation would be devastating. But sadly, often I self-impose this famine by ignoring his word. How many times have I failed to weigh God's counsel when relating with others or otherwise living my life? I have a friend who is a judge in Ohio. He told me recently that we are to read God's stories over and over in life. Not because the stories change but because we change. Therefore, we can hear something different in God's word each time. God's word can become a feast. Who wants to live in famine when a sumptuous meal awaits? I need to spend more time with God's word. Unlike email, it's only a blessing, not a curse!

Lord, may I always turn to your words for wisdom and life. By your grace, amen.

MAY 25

"Those who swear by the Guilt of Samaria, and say, 'As your god lives, O Dan,' and, 'As the Way of Beersheba lives,' they shall fall, and never rise again." (Amos 8:14)

My buddy was young, single, fresh out of law school, and making pretty good money. He decided to buy a small house in a hopping neighborhood, figuring it to be a better investment than just renting. He found a dilapidated house and planned to transform it into a dream house. The house was on the foreclosure auction market, and my friend needed to determine its value so he could submit a sealed bid. He hired an architect to help him assess the property. After examining the house, the architect said, "Take the value of the land and subtract $10,000 for your bid." My friend didn't understand. How could the house have a *negative* value? The expert replied, "Wait a minute, you are going to live in this house? It has no foundation. Look at the cracks in these walls! They start at the foundation and grow to two inches by the ceiling. It's a dump. Any money you spend on it will be thrown away. This house is suitable only for destruction. Tear down the house and build one that has value."

How often do we build our lives on things of no true value? You can take a sordid house and put on fresh wallpaper, and it might look presentable, even nice, for a few months, but the cracks in the walls will crack the wallpaper. The house will show its true condition before long.

Today's passage illustrates that lives built on falsehoods have no more lasting value than a trashed house without a real foundation. The people hypocritically acted religious, although their religion was one built to reinforce their poor behavior, not a true faith following the true God. They would take oaths by false idols, ascribing to their false gods in Dan, Samaria, and Beersheba the power to enforce an oath. This might have seemed pious, but it was fake. To use a Southern expression, they put lipstick on a pig and pretended it was a beauty.

Not surprisingly, this false and hypocritical piety wouldn't last. It was no better than wallpaper over massive cracks in the walls. In time, the cracks would show through. The people's false gods offered nothing real. The people's hypocritical behavior would catch up to them. This reinforces my need for a real, vibrant faith.

Lord, purify my heart and faith. Help me seek truth, not convenience. Authenticate my life. Make me wholly yours. In your name, amen.

MAY 26

I saw the Lord standing beside the altar, and he said: "Strike the capitals until the thresholds shake, and shatter them on the heads of all the people; and those who are left of them I will kill with the sword; not one of them shall flee away; not one of them shall escape." (Amos 9:1)

When I was in college, I attended a church with a godly preacher who had a profound understanding of God's word as well as insight into human nature. One night, he was speaking about worship. He explained, "We become like the gods we worship." His reasoning was that worship is ascribing worth or value to some thing or person. When we value something, we pursue it. So if we worship fame, placing value on prominence among others, we will pursue fame. If we worship money, we will prioritize financial pursuits. If we worship pleasure, then hedonism will be our hallmark.

Our preacher's point was that people are called to worship God in spirit (genuinely from our hearts) and in truth (John 4:23). When we do so, we seek to become like God not in some usurping terrible way but in humility as we find his morality, concerns, and goals worthy of our pursuit. We seek his guidance, protection, and fellowship. We want to understand him more and want that understanding to transform us. We find his consolation in life's rough times. We find his guidance when we can't find our way in the midst of our limited knowledge. This is how we should worship and live.

But alas, not for Israel at the time of Amos. They were worshiping gods of their own creation. These were gods that were not only useless as unreal idols but even destructive. These human-made gods approved of human cruelty. Thus, humans could likewise abuse people with trafficking in slavery, injustice in courts, and other social behavior that harmed others to enhance someone else's own prestige.

God was not going to sit idly by while this idolatry continued to ravage the land. God was going to destroy the idolators' fake religion. And he was going to destroy all who were relying on it as well. God is a pure God. He won't let fake and destructive actions destroy people he cares about. Actions have consequences, and so does worship. We become like the things we value. I want to value and worship the true God.

Lord, I want to know you better and worship only you. Help me see where I place my value so I can grow in worshiping you. In your name, amen.

MAY 27

"If they dig into Sheol, from there shall my hand take them; if they climb up to heaven, from there I will bring them down. If they hide themselves on the top of Carmel, from there I will search them out and take them." (Amos 9:2–3)

When I was in my first year of high school, I dropped the typical pursuit of athletics for debate. I enjoyed sports, and many of my friends played them, but I thought I could thrive in debate. Later that year, I found myself about to debate in a championship round, somehow having made it to finals against the senior team in spite of our youth. I wanted desperately to pray. I couldn't find a location where I could be alone to pray until it occurred to me that I might find solitude in the bathroom! So to the bathroom I went, wondering if God would listen to someone in the bathroom!

Of course, God was there. God is everywhere. We just don't often recognize it. Consider today's passage. Through Amos, God emphasizes his presence everywhere. Speaking in the people's language and understanding, God says if one digs into Sheol—the Hebrew word for the place where people went immediately after death—God will take them. Sheol was a place of shadows that was poorly understood. Later in Scripture, God gave more detailed teaching on what happens after this life, but in this prophetic passage, God was telling the people his power and presence extended everywhere.

From the highest places to the lowest and all places in between, God reigns supreme. This is important to me and should be to you. It means that anywhere we find ourselves, physically or metaphorically, God is there. If my day today entails the humdrum of normalcy that surrounds much of life, God is there. If I am called today to do unusual things, God is there. If work, home, or school demands my energy, God is there. If the stresses of life are mounting, God is there. If sickness and disease threaten, God is there. If money doesn't meet my needs, God is there.

In any problem, I need to turn to God. I get that. But sometimes the harder thing is turning to God when there isn't a problem. In Amos' day, it was the prosperity that turned the people's hearts from God, not the misery. Yes, as a high school student, I may need God before a debate round, but what about when I am simply eating lunch? God is to be our anchor for all we do, not simply the stressful situations. We can find God everywhere, even in a restroom.

Lord, I give you all I am and have today. May I live in your presence, amen.

MAY 28

The Lord GOD *of hosts, he who touches the earth and it melts, and all who dwell in it mourn, and all of it rises like the Nile, and sinks again, like the Nile of Egypt.* (Amos 9:5)

When I was a child, I loved to play in the dirt. At the end of most days, Mom would stick me in the bathtub, where the day's grime would wash away. I remember a game I would play in the tub. I would cup my two hands together and lift them out of the tub holding water. I would keep my fingers together as tightly as possible. Yet without fail, I couldn't hold the water. It would dribble through my tightest grip and make its way back into the tub.

As I got older, I realized that at times, life is like that water. The life we think we have in our grip, the life we expect, the life we have come to rely on, starts to slip away. We can cling to it as tightly as possible, but that aspect of life is going to disappear. Loved ones die. So do relationships. Careers take U-turns. Hopes and dreams turn upside down. These are times in life when despite our best efforts, what we want to hold slips away before our very eyes. What do we do then?

Today's passage speaks of a resource. Amos uses two titles to refer to God, translated as "The Lord GOD of hosts." The English translation can be confusing. Amos first uses the basic word *Lord*, which also could be used to address high-ranking humans. He then uses God's name *YHWH* (usually translated LORD, but here translated GOD, based on an ancient Jewish tradition), which references God as the "I AM" in life. Though as one can see in the passage, he combines the divine name *YHWH* with the word *hosts*. The one true God is the Master and Lord of Hosts. This is an army phrase. God is the commander, and his forces follow him. Then Amos takes it even further. He is the One who can melt the entire earth with a touch. He is the One who can bring entire nations to their knees. He can raise up, and he can bring down anything and anyone. God's power is beyond our ability to grasp or comprehend.

I need to know this. We all do. For when those really tough times of life come upon us or we feel we're losing touch with what we hold dear, we can call upon the Lord GOD of Hosts. We can find him as the one who is able to hold us up. We can rely on him as one who strengthens us in whatever stage of life awaits us. God has the power and desire to come to our aid.

Lord, thank you. I need you, and you are there for me. I am in awe of you. Amen.

Who builds his upper chambers in the heavens and founds his vault upon the earth; who calls for the waters of the sea and pours them out upon the surface of the earth—the LORD is his name. (Amos 9:6)

Our grandson John Henry was two when my wife first sang him the Beach Boys' "Barbara Ann." He fell in love instantly. Along with "Baby Beluga" (by Rafi), this song was not only his most frequent request; he would also sing along, at least to the "Bar bar bar, bar, Barbara Ann" chorus.

People have had songs they enjoy singing stretching back to the earliest recordings of society. Those songs may be hits because of catchy melodies. But we know many of the ancient songs because of their lyrics and structures. According to many scholars, today's passage (along with the prior v. 5) is such a song.

What's it in this song that was worth singing about? What made this song so prominent that Amos quotes it in his prophetic discourse? Amos wasn't after a catchy melody; Amos had the power of lyrics. This song describes God as omnipotent in power over both heaven and earth. He isn't uninvolved in our lives, but he "touches the earth" (v. 5) and "calls out for water and rain" (v. 6; my translation). This isn't indiscriminate by God as some random event. He can even use the weather with discretion and in judgment.

This song fits Amos' purposes because he's teaching and reminding the people that a real God exists who not only is over their world but is also involved in their world. This should alter what they believe and how they live. Amos wants this song to be a wake-up call that forces them to challenge how they go about life.

On the day I am writing this, I have a long drive ahead of me. In the car, I will be listening to the radio, flipping between stations to find the songs I enjoy. I doubt I will hear "Barbara Ann," and I'm rather certain I won't hear "Baby Beluga." But I want songs that stick in my head, with lyrics that will direct my focus. I'm going to find songs that awaken in me the realization of God and his presence in the world and my life. Those were in Amos. He sought to put them in his audience. I want to put them in me. If you don't have any songs that focus yourself on God, find some! If you do, listen to them! Sing them. Let them change you. Let God change you.

Lord, be the song in my heart and head today. May I sing in your power, amen.

MAY 30

"Are you not like the Cushites to me, O people of Israel?" declares the LORD. *"Did I not bring up Israel from the land of Egypt, and the Philistines from Caphtor and the Syrians from Kir?"* (Amos 9:7)

When our son was young, he and his friends would lapse into discussions about which superhero they might want to be. I have heard many similar arguments, even among those who are older! While many liked the mystique of Batman, I often heard Superman acclaimed. After all, who wouldn't want to be the fastest, strongest, gravity defying, überhuman hearing person who *also has X-ray vision*? Superman seems unbeatable, until one realizes that kryptonite renders him helpless. Just having a bit of kryptonite ends the super in Superman.

Sometimes people can begin to think of themselves as a spiritual superman. Amos' audience fell into this trap. They thought that since God had brought them out of Egypt, had given them the land where they dwelt, and had given them a good measure of prosperity and success over the neighboring tribes, they were almost untouchable. They had some spiritual superpower that put them atop others.

There's no doubt that God had made a promise that he would watch over his people. But that wasn't an unconditional promise without consideration. God would watch over *HIS* people. Israel had ceased to act as his people when they devoted their lives to their own pleasure and purposes rather than God's. They had manufactured gods (idols) that would approve of what they did. They had justified abusing the poor and downtrodden in ways that catapulted their personal power and prosperity. They had decided to be their own people, not God's.

This was their kryptonite, and I fear sometimes it is akin to our own. How often do we refocus our understanding of God in ways that justify what we want and do? How often does our faith in God rest upon our interpretation of him as approving our priorities and choices? Do we move from success to success, taking the minor setbacks in stride, because we figure we are owed or due as much?

Everyone should take time to assess God for who he is and for how he has revealed himself. Our superpower isn't anything associated with us. Our superpower is our super God. As we live in his will and seek his purposes, we will see his victory.

Lord, refine me to be in line with your focus and desires. In your name, amen.

MAY 31

"Behold, the eyes of the Lord GOD are upon the sinful kingdom, and I will destroy it from the surface of the ground, except that I will not utterly destroy the house of Jacob," declares the LORD. (Amos 9:8)

Becky and I were building a British-themed building in Texas, a good four thousand miles away from England. We needed certain things that we couldn't readily find in our home state. On a trip to England, we found certain businesses called "reclamation yards." These businesses salvaged certain features from walls to ceilings to radiators to knickknacks from buildings that were being destroyed. These salvaged items were then sold to those who would repurpose them. It was precisely what we Texans needed for our British building!

Salvage isn't a new thing. Recycling is big in certain places. Garage sales are also great ways to see unused items repurposed by someone else. eBay has made a megabusiness out of selling salvaged materials. As the saying goes, "One person's garbage is another person's treasure."

There is an echo of this in today's passage. Through Amos, God has spoken of Israel's coming destruction. God has determined that Israel was the building no longer serving its purposes. The building was going to be destroyed. However, God also promised to reclaim parts of the building. God would not let Israel be utterly annihilated; he would salvage a remnant for his purposes.

Today's passage teaches two important lessons. First, God says that his "eyes are upon" the people. God isn't blind or inattentive. He isn't so preoccupied with matters across the street or globe that he isn't also attentive to my life. God has his focus everywhere, including on me. God cares about everyone, including me.

Second, God is the master recycler. His destruction isn't about vengeance for vengeance's sake. God isn't throwing temper tantrums when he seeks to right that which is wrong. God will take that which is garbage and recycle it to good usage. He will destroy that which is counter to his will and repurpose what he can to further his will. God does that on a national stage, but he also does it in my life. God wants me living not a destructive life but a good, constructive life that furthers his will on earth. This should not only give me pause but should give me purpose. God can and will work in me today.

God, I am excited to give you my day for your good works! In your name, amen.

JUNE 1

"For behold, I will command, and shake the house of Israel among all the nations as one shakes with a sieve, but no pebble shall fall to the earth. All the sinners of my people shall die by the sword, who say, 'Disaster shall not overtake or meet us.'" (Amos 9:9–10)

I was trying the nation's first opioid case against three major pharmacies. My case centered on whether the pharmacies had properly applied their filters to keep rogue prescription opioids off the street. I needed a way to demonstrate their obligation. I ultimately opted to use a set of sieves my buddy Frank was able to find. These sieves had different-size screens. The larger screens would let through almost anything you placed in the sieve. The smaller screens might let through some flour, but rice was filtered out. I used these screens before the jury to demonstrate the idea that a good filter keeps out impurities whether in cooking or in prescriptions.

Sieves are not new inventions. They were used in Amos' day to filter grains. Sieves were set with holes large enough to let the grain through but small enough to keep the rocks and impurities out. Amos used this sieving process to illustrate how God was going to work his judgment on Israel.

God works on his people. He seeks to purify and grow his people into what they can and should be. I guess that is good. Well, not "I guess"; I *know* that is good. Yet it isn't what I always want. The growth process comes with growing pains. It isn't easy to shed bad habits. Getting moved from a comfortable chair to a strenuous workout isn't always what I desire.

In honesty, there are times and stages in my life when I'm not ready for God to change me. These are times when I could be happy coasting. Let me do the things that I'm doing without regard to growing and becoming a better person. "Leave well enough alone," as my father would say.

Yet I know this isn't God's way. Certainly, God moves in his good time and doesn't expect my full growth overnight. God knows there are times for shaking the sieve and times to let the dust settle. That is where trust comes in. I need to trust God to give me rest when appropriate but also give the sieve a shake when I need to grow. May God continue, and may I be grateful when he does.

Lord, I give you my life to grow me up in your good timing and name, amen.

JUNE 2

"In that day I will raise up the booth of David that is fallen and repair its breaches, and raise up its ruins and rebuild it as in the days of old." (Amos 9:11)

My buddy Louis loves fixing things. His love isn't just taking what is broken and making it work; he goes deep in "fixing." He will get on eBay or some similar site and find an old, broken-down piece of junk. He will take it apart piece by piece and work on each part, sanding, adding epoxy, painting, and putting it back together, good as new. Louis is the same with people. Trained as a counselor, Louis takes those who are broken or hurting, works with the pieces, and helps them get put back into good working order.

This is an admirable talent and trait, and on a small scale, it models what God does on a large scale. Amos was writing when God's people were broken seemingly beyond repair. They had abandoned God and his law and were abusing the needy, pursuing idols, and feasting on the fat of the land. They thought they were living their best lives, but in truth, they were destined for the dumpster.

Israel would soon experience how right Amos was in his declaration of what was to come. God's judgment would be swift and thorough. Yet God didn't leave his people thinking that would be the end for them. God left them with a promise.

God was going to restore his people in the fullest sense of the word. God would take the broken pieces and do the necessary work to have a rebuilt, repaired, and shiny kingdom. Out of brokenness would come healing. Out of pain would come joy. Times of mourning would become times of dancing.

This is the way of God. God despises evil and knows how it breeds misery. God will destroy evil even when it is found in people who claim to know God. Yet God will restore that which is right and good. The heart of God is for a pure and undefiled people to live in relationship with him. That means a productive life full of purpose, hope, and peace.

As I contemplate the heart and work of God, my desire is to be devoted to his cause. In my own life, I need to open myself to God's correction and guidance, seeking to be more like him in my actions. I should help others with the same goals.

Lord, purify my heart and mind. Polish my dinginess, freshen where I have turned stale, and make me useful in service to you. In your name, amen.

JUNE 3

"Behold, the days are coming," declares the LORD, *"when the plowman shall overtake the reaper and the treader of grapes him who sows the seed. . . . I will restore the fortunes of my people Israel, and they shall rebuild the ruined cities and inhabit them; they shall plant vineyards and drink their wine, and they shall make gardens and eat their fruit. I will plant them on their land, and they shall never again be uprooted out of the land that I have given them," says the* LORD *your God.* (Amos 9:13–15)

One of our daughters came to me in middle school, saying, "Dad, I've got bad news and good news. The bad news first: I got a bad grade on my report card. The good news: I have decided to be a missionary, so my grades don't count!" I replied, "Well, I have some bad news and some good news. The bad news: God doesn't want stupid missionaries. The good news: you will be grounded from TV and cell phones until you pull your grades up!" With indignance, she replied, "But Dad, that isn't bad news / good news. That is bad news and *worse* news!" I told her, "No, the grounding isn't worse news. It gives you a chance to be smarter! That is good news!"

Today's passage reminds me of my interchange with my daughter. These three verses conclude the book of Amos. The prophet spent nine chapters with the bad news, explaining how God was coming in judgment on the people who had abandoned him. But Amos didn't end with bad news. He ended with good news!

God said through Amos that he was working toward an ultimate good for God's people as well as God's kingdom. Using agricultural metaphors, Amos explains that no sooner will the plowman finish plowing than it will be time to harvest. Times will not just be good; they'll be great. God will secure a people who stay in his will and stay in his blessings.

I like the way Amos ends because it offers us hope. It shows God's overriding purpose for his people is their good, not God's vengeance. God isn't wanting to wipe out anyone, but he will do what is necessary to bring his ultimate good to his followers. Amos reminds us that God isn't finished with us yet, despite how bleak life may look. God is working out a much greater plan, a plan that ends with true good news.

Lord, bring light to the darkness and make my life shine for you. In you I cry, amen.

JUNE 4

The word of the LORD . . . (Hos. 1:1)

I have a friend who collects fine wines. His collection is quite large, and he stores the wines carefully, at the right temperature with minimal exposure to the sun. He can identify a wine just by its taste, smell, and texture. My friend doesn't collect wine based on the shape of its bottle or the contents of its label. The wines are special to him because of their taste.

Today's passage reminds me of my friend and his wine collection. These words—there are only two in the Hebrew original—are critical to what is to come. What we read in Hosea's book is the word of the Lord. This is what makes the reading of great value. The name of the human author, Hosea, comes later. Hosea is the wine bottle. He holds and delivers the word of the Lord, but the content is what counts. Without the value of the word of the Lord, Hosea's pen becomes just prattling ink, likely lost over time. But delivering God's word means the content is exquisite. It is to be tasted and remembered. It should be treasured and taken to heart.

It's not a mistake that the "word" of the Lord here is singular. Obviously, the book contains much more than one word. In the book, God's message comes in many forms, over different events, including narratives, prophesies, and commands. Yet the single God has a single word. The thrust of what God says is constant. All of the words dissolve into the singular event of God being God, calling humanity to be who he made us to be. God is about setting right to what is wrong.

The word of the Lord takes precedence over even the name of the author. The word of the Lord should similarly have priority over my life. As I go through my day, I should see things through the lens of God's word. I don't begin a day without grabbing my glasses. Without them, I have trouble seeing clearly if an object is more than two feet from my face. But once I put them on, I can see with twenty-twenty precision. So it is with God's word. I need the word of God to see clearly how to live my life.

Here the wine analogy breaks down. Today, I shouldn't store up the word of God in a wine cellar. God's word isn't to be kept for a special occasion. I am to feast upon it moment by moment, day by day. It is my treasure.

Lord, thank you for the treasure of your words. Speak to me. Help me hear and obey. In your name, amen.

JUNE 5

The word of the LORD that came to Hosea, the son of Beeri . . . (Hos. 1:1)

Our daughter Gracie was pregnant with her fourth baby and our tenth grandchild. By the time Gracie was three months pregnant, she and her husband, J. T., had narrowed the name selection to a few finalists. I asked her how they determined the name. She said, "We wanted a biblical name. We wanted a name that had a good meaning. We wanted a name that wasn't too bizarre." I thought about her desire for "a name that had a good meaning." Of course, that was important. Who wants to name a child something that means "She is going to wreck the world"? (They picked Zoey, meaning "life.")

In biblical times, names were more important than today. Biblical names weren't simply labels to go on a driver's license or passport. They weren't for identification in a national registry or census. They were statements of one's character or life. If a name didn't fit a person, the name was changed!

Biblical names have another important difference. Today the origin and meaning of names often needs to be traced back through other languages and traditions. My name—Mark—for example, goes back to the Roman god Mars, a god of war. (Some might say suitable for a trial lawyer?) In biblical times, however, names were statements in the original language. Today's passage is a great example.

Hosea's name is the Hebrew word for "rescued," "delivered," or "saved." His name and that of his family are in some ways prophetic messages wrapped up in labels. While the name of his wife and children will be identified in days (and verses) to come, a Hebrew reader of the opening line of the book would see a foreshadowing of an important theme. In Hebrew, Hosea isn't simply a name; it's a word with meaning. Likewise for his father, Beeri.

In English, the Hebrew reader would be reading, "The word of the LORD that came to *Rescue*, the son of *My Well* . . ." His name portends the message of God's word to the people. God's word will have a harsh judgment. It will presage pain. But it is a word that comes from a water source to offer deliverance, rescue, and salvation. Are you ready for God's word? Are you ready for a two-edged sword? It will come through Hosea, and it is for the nation's and our ultimate good!

Lord, may your words be my salvation and wellspring of life. I pray in you, amen.

JUNE 6

In the days of Uzziah, Jotham, Ahaz, and Hezekiah, kings of Judah, and in the days of Jeroboam the son of Joash, king of Israel. (Hos. 1:1)

Becky and I were having dinner with some dear friends when the conversation took an interesting turn. My friend was thinking about when he might retire. RETIRE? The mere mention of the word struck me as bizarre and unexpected. After all, old people retire, and we're not old. Then I started doing the math. Uh-oh. Retirement is a real option that, if people live long enough, they might consider. It might happen.

I began to think about how to view retirement. I got in touch with my preacher from my college days, Don Finto. I hadn't really spent much time with him in the last forty-five years, but God had used him in my life in mighty ways. I was curious how he had grown old. I asked him to come to Houston and give a lecture at our library. Don came at the ripe young age of ninety. He was spry, articulate, focused, and powerful. He chose his topic: "Don't retire; refire!" He then told how God was using him. No longer in the pulpit preaching, he was training missionaries for the Arabic Muslim world, making two to three trips a year placing these missionaries in remote villages in countries that I would fear entering.

Don likes his Bible, spending a good bit of his time memorizing large chunks, even passages in Hebrew, or as he calls it, "downloading Scripture into his brain." He reminds me in some ways of Hosea. Hosea kept his job as a prophet for many decades. We know this from the identities of the kings listed in today's passage. He prophesied for God while Jeroboam reigned in Israel and Uzziah, Jotham, Ahaz, and Hezekiah reigned in Judah. To have worked under all those reigns, Hosea kept at it for a long time. If he began his work as a sixteen-year-old, Hosea was prophesying into his eighties. What's more, Hosea's life was a difficult one. He dealt with personal problems most hope to avoid. Yet he did so with purpose. He didn't retire; he constantly refired!

Spending time with ninety-year-old Don blew me away. I listened intently to his words. He never stopped growing before God. He never quit daily study in God's word. He still committed vast swaths to memory. He still sought to mature in holiness. He still worked to align his values with God's. He still had a message. I realize that I have a lot more work to do!

Lord, keep your fire blazing in my heart every day of my life. In you, I pray, amen.

JUNE 7

When the LORD first spoke through Hosea . . . (Hos. 1:2)

Last week, I was set to deliver the keynote address at a seminar loaded with lawyers. As I was looking for a moment to get my head wrapped around my speech, I was approached by a lawyer I know but not well. She asked if she might have a moment. Sitting, she then began apologizing to me for a derogatory comment that she had made about me a year or so earlier. With a tear in her eye, she said she knew it was wrong but didn't put the brakes on it. She had wanted to apologize for some time but hadn't had a chance yet.

Passages like today's occurred to me at that moment. I readily understand that God has his word, what we call Holy Scripture. In these holy writings, we have God speaking to anyone who will read with an open mind and willing heart. Yet God speaks beyond the Bible. God also speaks *through* his people.

When those who are called by God's name interact with others, God can speak. As our behavior is godly, we reflect a message of godliness to those around us. The story of Hosea's life shows that a well-lived, godly life is a message in itself. Hosea's life unfolded in ways where God not only spoke *to* Hosea but also spoke *through* Hosea to Israel. In fact, in passages like today's, God is still speaking to us today *through* Hosea.

How we relate to people now takes center stage in life. We have a chance to be godly and, in that way, let God speak through us. Or we might choose a path of selfishness and stop God's message, promote an ungodly idea, or both. In New Testament writings, Paul contrasts those godly messages of "love, joy, peace, patience, kindness, goodness, faithfulness, gentleness, self-control" with messages of "sexual immorality, impurity, sensuality, idolatry, sorcery, enmity, strife, jealousy, fits of anger, rivalries, dissensions, divisions, envy, drunkenness, orgies, and things like these." Paul terms the godly set "fruit of the Spirit," while the others are "works of the flesh" (Gal. 5:19-23).

I told the lawyer that I appreciated her apology. I added that I had made so many mistakes in my life that if I ever withhold forgiveness, God should go ahead and strike me on the spot. I had a unique moment to explain God's forgiveness, and I wanted God to speak *through* me. Today's passage should be our goal!

Lord, speak through me today. To your glory and in your name, amen.

JUNE 8

The LORD said to Hosea, "Go, take to yourself a wife of whoredom and have children of whoredom, for the land commits great whoredom by forsaking the LORD." (Hos. 1:2)

Back in the 1960s and 1970s, Mennen Skin Bracer aftershave had a string of commercials where a man was a bit mentally foggy from waking up, from boxing, or from a number of activities. Skin Bracer aftershave was then placed on the man's hand, and then the hand slapped his own face. The man was then suddenly alert, and he said, "Thanks, I needed that." Half a century later, that ad still echoes in my mind at certain times.

Today's passage reminds me of the Mennen ads. This sentence is one of the last ones you might expect in Scripture. It seems like a cold slap in the face. God tells Hosea, one of his selected prophets, to marry "a wife of whoredom and have children of whoredom." What? Can this be? Why would God do such a thing?

Reading the Hebrew adds an interesting element to the story, one that gets subtly lost in the English. Hebrew had a word for a "prostitute." That word is *not* used here. The word used (*z^enunim*—זְנוּנִים) is a form ("plural abstract") that refers to a personal quality, not an active pursuit. In other words, Hosea was to marry someone with a tendency or experience of sexual impurity, not a practicing prostitute. Why does that matter?

Scholars debate exactly what Hosea's wife was vis-à-vis this word. Some note that in this instruction, God explains that Israel itself had the quality of unfaithfulness toward God. So Hosea was being told to marry one who was simply an unfaithful Israelite. In other words, this wasn't about the sexual impurity of Hosea's wife but about the nation's spiritual impurity. Others believe that Hosea was symbolically marrying a woman who had been initiated into some cultic sexual practice. Still others conclude she had a tendency toward sexual immorality.

Whichever our interpretation, this passage stands out like a cold slap in the face. Israel and maybe the prophet were more than mentally foggy about their relationship with God. This was no small matter. They had abandoned their fidelity to God, and judgment was coming. When we're numb to God, he may use life's circumstances to bring a cold—but needed—slap to our face!

Lord, forgive my tendencies to ignore you. Help me see you 24-7. In you, amen.

JUNE 9

So he went and took Gomer, the daughter of Diblaim, and she conceived and bore him a son. And the LORD said to him, "Call his name Jezreel, for in just a little while I will punish the house of Jehu for the blood of Jezreel, and I will put an end to the kingdom of the house of Israel." (Hos. 1:3–4)

One semester, I taught a law school course on jury selection. In preparation, I asked my friend Ernest about his approach. Ernest is a master at picking juries. Ernest told me he didn't like to put young people on his jury. When I asked why, he explained that he likes to see the road people have walked. He said, "When you can see where people have been, you have a good idea of where they are going. You know their road." Ernest makes a good point. The past can indicate the trajectory of the future.

So it was in Hosea's day. The ruling king, of the house of Jehu, was the beneficiary of a bloody massacre coup d'état that placed his family into power. That massacre had occurred at Jezreel (2 Ki. 9–10). The road that had led to Jehu's kingship was paved in blood, deceit, idolatry, and self-reliance. That road set a trajectory for his life. Instead of heeding the prophets' cries for Israel and the king to turn an about-face, the king continued to lead his people hurtling down this road. This road would prove to be a dead end. Literally.

Passages like today's remind us that actions have consequences. The consequences aren't always immediate, but they come. I have seen it over and over in my life as well as in other's lives.

Does any of this affect me today? Will knowing that I have a trajectory influence the road I walk? Do I understand that unfaithfulness to God affects the way I treat others? Will I pursue faith, hope, and love? Will I seek to influence others for good? Will I leave vengeance to God and prioritize mercy and forgiveness? Will I seek to build up rather than tear down? Will I spend my time and resources on things of eternal value rather than pleasures of the moment? Will I look to those in need with compassion rather than seek to avoid them? Will I put God first in my life, modeling his love to those around me? Will positive words come from my mouth? Will I flee gossip? Will I flee immorality? Will I . . . fill in the blank! My list could go on for pages! This is a question of action and also trajectory. The road continues with each new choice.

Lord, place my feet on the path you illuminate! In your name, amen.

JUNE 10

She conceived again and bore a daughter. And the LORD said to him, "Call her name No Mercy, for I will no more have mercy on the house of Israel, to forgive them at all." (Hos. 1:6)

One evening, at dinner with one of my daughters and son-in-law, the topic turned to people's names. They informed me of a certain media star who has fathered over ten children, each with somewhat unusual names. The names include "Beautiful Zeppelin," "Powerful Queen," and "Zillion Heir." Very descriptive indeed! These children and their parents might seem bizarre in an age of people named "Mary" and "John," but in ancient Israel, they would have fit in!

Today's passage describes the birth of a child to Hosea and Gomer. God instructed Hosea to name the baby "No Mercy." Now, in Hebrew, that would be *Lo Ruhama*, and had the translators simply used the Hebrew name, then most readers would be none the wiser. But the Hebrew name is simply the Hebrew words for "No Mercy" or "She has not received mercy." So Hebrew readers would understand the name's meaning.

I can imagine Hosea and Gomer bringing the baby to an event. Someone comes up and says, "Oh, she's adorable! What's her name?" At that point, Hosea would proclaim, "She's named, 'No Mercy!'" The friend would likely ask, "Why did you choose that name?" Hosea would then explain, "God gave me the name. God wants Israel to wake up to its sin and idolatry. He has judgment coming, and as things currently stand, he isn't going to have mercy on Israel." I wonder in that event what reactions might register. I suspect most would walk away, muttering, "That Hosea is a weird bird!" But in fact, Hosea was a walking prophesy.

Our children bear more common names. Yet even those names have meanings. We carefully selected each. They weren't drawn out of a hat. In our time, however, every person tends to make a name for themselves. We can name our children "Will," "Rachel," or "Sarah," but how they live and what they do will define who they really are. I wonder how differently we might live if we knew that at the end of each year, our names would change to reflect our choices or our reputations. Making my name a good name is important. It is my focus growing out of today's passage.

Lord, give me chances to make a good name for myself as a reflection of your goodness. In your name, amen.

JUNE 11

"But I will have mercy on the house of Judah, and I will save them by the LORD their God. I will not save them by bow or by sword or by war or by horses or by horsemen." (Hos. 1:7)

I went for about a decade reading through the psalms each month. There are 150 psalms and thirty days in most months. That means if you read 5 psalms a day, you get through all the psalms each month. (Suggestion: Rather than reading 5 successive psalms, read the psalm associated with the day of the month, add 30, and read that psalm, add 30, and read that one, and so on. So on June 11, I would read the 11th Psalm, the 41st, the 71st, the 101st, and the 131st.) I always loved reading on the twentieth of each month. Psalm 20:7–8 reads, "Some trust in chariots and some in horses, but we trust in the name of the LORD our God. They collapse and fall, but we rise and stand upright." What a verse!

Everyone lives in turbulent times. We may not realize it. We may not see it. Our days may be humdrum; our concerns may seem run-of-the-mill. But with one leaked virus, our world shuts down. We are one election away from a different direction or agenda for the country. We are one mad man away from nuclear war. We are sensitive to economic upheaval. We are a doctor's visit away from getting life-altering medical news. We have family turmoil, school and work messes, social mistakes, and so much more. The world can turn upside down and inside out on us at a moment's notice.

How do we live and navigate in this truth? When the foundations of life seem shaken, what can anyone do? We have options. Those options can be classified into several buckets. One bucket is simple despair. We can fall apart. A second bucket is idolatry. We can trust that our money, our resources, our talent, our relationships, and other temporal things that we value can pull us through. The third bucket is God. We can seek God in prayer and devotion. We can try to follow his will for us. Then we can trust as we do so that he will bless and protect us by his mercy. We can live in faith that come what may, our God will be with us. We will face nothing alone. Nor will we face anything that overcomes us.

Today's passage is like Psalm 20. It is the call to love and trust God. Whatever you or I face today, if we face it with God, we can trust it will work out.

Lord, I commit today to you. I need and trust you to be my deliverer. In you, amen.

JUNE 12

When she had weaned No Mercy, she conceived and bore a son. And the LORD *said, "Call his name Not My People, for you are not my people, and I am not your God."* (Hos. 1:8–9)

My buddy is a Mississippi State University fan. So one Saturday night in the fall, I found myself sitting in the stands of Davis Wade Stadium in Starkville, Mississippi, watching the Bulldogs play college football against Georgia. The game was OK (Georgia won), but the fellowship and atmosphere were incredible. Football fans in Mississippi tend to support either Mississippi State or Ole Miss. But not both! As loud as the cheering was that night when Mississippi State scored on Georgia, the cheering was just as loud, if not louder, when the stadium announcer declared that Ole Miss had just lost their game against Alabama. The Mississippi State fans were cheering because their rivals had lost!

The fanbase in Starkville, Mississippi, reminds me a bit of today's passage in Hosea. The people in Israel during Hosea's day had erected idols for worship. They found a religion that was comfortable to them, one they enjoyed, and they put their allegiance there. They had made their choice, and it wasn't the God of Abraham. It wasn't the true God.

God let Israel make its choice. When they chose to follow other gods, God didn't force-feed them himself. He let them go their own way. But their choice had consequences. The people were not God's people. They chose another team, and God let them. God was not their god.

I get to choose who I worship. I get to choose how I live my life and whether I live it trusting something greater than myself. These are my choices. I am not God's computer program that will run whatever functions he hardwires into me. Nor am I God's puppet, dancing to the tune of the moment, subject to his whims and string pulling. I am a real, acting, deciding, purposeful person. That is amazing in itself, but it also has amazing consequences. I choose how I live, and that means I can be one of God's people or not.

I don't want to earn the name "Not My People." I want God to call me "My People." More important than college football, I can be on God's team!

Lord, I'm yours. Be my God, and may I be among your people. In you, amen.

JUNE 13

Yet the number of the children of Israel shall be like the sand of the sea, which cannot be measured or numbered. And in the place where it was said to them, "You are not my people," it shall be said to them, "Children of the living God." (Hos. 1:10)

Most people find it easy to live for the moment or immediate future. What am I going to eat? What do I want to do this weekend? At times, most look ahead even further. What should I do after I finish school? What career do I want? Where do I want to live? Whom should I marry? Those are all important decisions and worthy of our prayer, contemplation, and careful discretion. But Scripture also calls on people to live with a very extended view of life. This is wrapped up in the word *legacy*.

A person's legacy is the long-term effect they have had on this world. For many, this is found in their families. My children, for example, are a part of my legacy. When I am long gone, my children will hopefully live and carry on a piece of who I am. Beyond my DNA, they will have stories and memories and will be shaped at least a bit by my influence in their lives. All of us have a chance at leaving a legacy—good or bad. It should be a focus point for all, even at a young age.

Today's passage speaks to legacy. God has already announced, through Hosea and other contemporary prophets like Amos, that judgment was coming on Israel. Israel had turned from God to worship dead and worthless idols. Israel was abusive to the poor and downtrodden. Israel lived for themselves and for the moment. God wasn't going to let that continue. So the legacy of Israel was God's coming judgment. But that judgment wouldn't be the end of things.

Centuries before, God promised Abraham a legacy. The legacy wasn't going to be erased by an immoral, anti-God generation. God would deal with that generation, but God would still bring about the legacy of Abraham's offspring as God's people. Interestingly, the legacy would also include those outside Abraham's DNA pool. Those who were "not my people" would be called "children of the living God." Hosea's listeners weren't concerned with their legacy, but they had one anyway. We are reading it. Their legacy of disobedience and paganism led to their own destruction and the edification of others (including you and me). Their destructive legacy, however, didn't win the day. God's legacy becomes the final story of victory.

Lord, I want to leave a good legacy to your honor and in your name, amen.

JUNE 14

Say to your brothers, "You are my people," and to your sisters, "You have received mercy."
(Hos. 2:1)

I've got a buddy who is married to a really strong woman. I am too. They can endure pain that would stop me dead in my tracks. I get a cold and feel like the world may come to an end. My buddy told me recently, "It takes a woman who has been through childbirth without an epidural to understand the pain of a man who has a cold." We laughed, but he wasn't far off.

This lighthearted story comes to mind as I read the encouraging passage for today. Israel is in a "good place" from an earthly perspective at the time of Hosea's prophesying. But times are going to do a 180-degree turn. Israel will soon be invaded and the people will be taken off and scattered, losing their money, comforts, homes, and families. This jolt is around the corner and will be life changing. The people will experience pain, misery, and death.

This is so important that God has prophesied through Hosea, giving him children named "Not My People" and "No Mercy." Every time those children are called by name, the confirmation of God's coming judgment is proclaimed. Yet even as the people secured their fate by ignoring these prophetic words, God was not done speaking. God knew that he would turn around the misery that was coming, bringing his ultimate promises of being God to the people and showing them his mercy.

The coming pain for Israel was going to be akin to giving birth without an epidural. The pain of childbearing, only really understood by those who have endured it, is excruciating. But if it ends with a newborn baby who will grow to be amazing, then the pain takes on a different significance. So Israel was warned by God that the coming misery of "Not My People" and "No Mercy" would give birth to children who are "My People" and "Received Mercy."

This happened to Israel on a cataclysmic scale. But it happens in everyone's life on a more individual scale. We all go through times of rebellion against God. We all find ourselves in difficult straits of our own making. We all need his mercy and lordship in our lives. His promise to us is to be there as we call on him. Pains of childbirth will be transformed into a brighter future when we trust and follow God.

Lord, please be my God and show me mercy! I need you. In your holy name, amen.

JUNE 15

"Plead with your mother, plead—for she is not my wife, and I am not her husband—that she put away her whoring from her face, and her adultery from between her breasts." (Hos. 2:2)

In courtrooms across the United States, witnesses can be divided into two groups. One group are "friendly" witnesses. These support your case, and it means that you can ask them only "open questions." The second group are "hostile" witnesses, and the law allows you to ask them "leading questions." Open questions are like, "What did you do next?" Leading questions are like, "You did ABC next, didn't you?" I often call hostile witnesses as my first witness, trying to get them to admit the core truths of my case or show themselves to be liars for failing to admit certain facts.

Today's passage begins with a courtroom scene, although the courtroom for ancient Israel would have been the city gates, where the city elders sat and through which all foot traffic flowed. The legal proceedings center on a wife's adultery, and the witnesses are her children. The Hebrew used indicates the children are "hostile" witnesses. (The word *plead* is used twice, an indication the witnesses aren't naturally the most forthcoming.) Hosea calls on the children to testify about their mother's infidelity.

The scene is a metaphor for Israel's sin. When God brought Israel out of Egypt, he had them come to Mt. Sinai in the wilderness for a solemn ceremony. The ceremony was structured like a wedding. God was the groom, promising to provide for, protect, and nurture Israel. Israel was the bride, promising to be faithful to and follow the lead of the Lord. By Hosea's day, Israel had abandoned the marriage. Israel followed other gods, not the Lord. Israel's unfaithfulness was going to be its undoing.

Israel wasn't living with malice toward God. Instead, its people were caught up in the daily routine of life, celebrating the good days, suffering through the sorrowful days, and worshiping the gods they imagined existed. Yet their life choices were not right. The evidence was found in their children. What we believe and where we place our faith determine who we are and profoundly influence our children. When I embrace God and his ways, the fruits of my life are different from when I live as my own moral compass based on my own strength. I need to live focused on the one true God, trusting in him.

Lord, may I see you in greater detail to worship and follow. In your name, amen.

JUNE 16

"Lest I strip her naked and make her as in the day she was born, and make her like a wilderness, and make her like a parched land, and kill her with thirst." (Hos. 2:3)

Over every court proceeding, a judge presides, designated as a neutral party. Then at the end of the trial, the judge pronounces the judgment. In criminal cases, the judge will enter a judgment of *guilty* or *not guilty*. In a civil case, the judge enters a judgment of *liable* or *not liable*. In cases where the defendant is either guilty or liable, the judge then announces the sentence (in criminal cases) or the amount owed (in civil cases). Over and over, for centuries, this process continues. But it wasn't invented in the United States. Far from it.

Yesterday's passage began with a courtroom scene painted by Hosea. As a metaphor, Israel was symbolically on trial as an adulterous wife to God, her husband. The evidence of her adultery was found in her life, the fruits of her actions (her "children" in the metaphor). Today's passage continues that metaphor with a slight shift. The woman is guilty, and in today's passage, the judge begins announcing the sentence.

The sentence is harsh, for the violation of adultery was significant. Israel's law was extensive, but this trial centered on one of the Ten Commandments. Number seven is "You shall not commit adultery" (Ex. 20:14). The husband, God in this analogy, was responsible under the law for providing marital intimacy, food, clothing, and provision for his wife. God had done so for Israel. Central to the wife's responsibility was fidelity. Israel had utterly failed over and over again.

The pronounced judgment was the removal of the husband Israel had shunned. God would put clothing on Israel no more. No longer would he provide her food and sustenance.

I fear sometimes we think of God relating to us on our terms and we fail to realize that any relationship is a two-way street. God doesn't shower us with blessings for us to squander them. God blesses us with the expectation we will use his blessings to bless others. God provides for his people, charging them to use those provisions for his kingdom's purposes. Our failure rightly forfeits our right to those blessings.

Lord, help me remember my charge before you. May I live rightly in you, amen.

"Upon her children also I will have no mercy, because they are children of whoredom. For their mother has played the whore; she who conceived them has acted shamefully." (Hos. 2:4–5)

My mom taught us proper nursery rhymes. My dad taught us his versions. From Dad, I learned, "Little Miss Muffet sat on her tuffet eating her curds and whey. Along came a spider and sat down beside her and she beat the heck out of him with the spoon." I taught the same to my children. Many of the "dad jokes" I told my children originated as ones my dad had told me. In many ways, we become our parents.

Our heritage can be a good thing when our parents train us up in the way we should walk. But when our parents train us poorly, we pay the price.

I had a case where a young girl of nine had gone into her basement and found that her mother had committed suicide, hanging herself from a beam. I thought about how tough that would be for the child to overcome in her life. Then I found out that the mother had been a drug addict who worked as a prostitute to support her habit. The mother's husband, the father to the nine-year-old, was the mother's pimp. With all that, it would take God's divine healing hand to bring anything close to normalcy in the life of that girl.

God does have compassion for children. But the problem is many children grow up to be their parents. That was the problem addressed by Hosea. The mother had played the harlot on God, and the children were growing up to do the same. God wasn't going to let that cycle continue indefinitely. He was intervening.

Becky and I had the blessing of rearing five amazing children. We are watching now as those five are rearing our ten grandchildren. I realize as I get older that even once our children are on their own and out of the house, we still affect them. The good things we pass on to our children are important. Unfortunately, the bad things are also. I want our children to know the importance of God when they are young and old. I want to pass on to my children the priorities of family and faith. I want to teach my children right and wrong. But all too often, this teaching comes from what I do, not what I say.

Lord, help me focus on you and grow in you. Then help me to pass this on to those around me, especially my family! In your name, amen.

JUNE 18

"She shall pursue her lovers but not overtake them, and she shall seek them but shall not find them." (Hos. 2:7)

I was jogging and listening to a playlist of songs from my youth. Many of them I loved but mostly for the melody, not really zooming in on the lyrics. I heard one of my favorite songs, "Strange Way" by Firefall. The lyrics are miserable! The song is sung from the perspective of a fellow who awakens from a great dream to his partner crying and depressed. The song is the man complaining about her raining on his parade. He says her sharing her sorrows is a strange way to tell him that she loves him. Evidently, he expects her to only be upbeat with him. One hears the song and figures he is moving on from that relationship.

The human tendency to look for something better has given birth to expressions like "The grass is always greener on the other side of the fence." It comes front and center with today's passage. God had called Israel into a relationship where each pledged their loyalty and faithfulness to the other. Israel had left God, however, pursuing other "lovers." But it became readily apparent that those other lovers would never satisfy Israel. We might think the grass is greener on the other side, but we will often find it isn't.

Many sages and writers in Jewish and Christian history have recognized that humans live with a vacuum in their hearts, longing for a relationship of love and meaning. The filling of that vacuum and satisfaction of that longing is found in the relationship with the God of heaven and earth and nowhere else. Israel left God for what they thought was a better deal, but they were never going to be satisfied. What they wanted could only be found in God.

The Firefall song I mentioned is one end of the story. The other end is found in a later Firefall song: "Livin' Ain't Livin'." In it, the songwriter, who couldn't put up with the woman in his earlier relationship, awakens to find himself alone. He knows it's his own fault for leaving the love he had found. He finds himself haunted by the loves he has pushed away in life, ending with the line "livin' ain't livin' alone."

I want to find my satisfaction with God. In seasons of joy and sorrow, in times of ease and difficulty, always, I want to hold tightly to God. No one else will do.

Lord, thank you for your unending love. I trust and live in it. In your name, amen.

JUNE 19

"And she did not know that it was I who gave her the grain, the wine, and the oil, and who lavished on her silver and gold, which they used for Baal." (Hos. 2:8)

I have a "no gifts" policy for my birthday. It's not that I don't like gifts. I love them! It's just that I have a challenging time writing thank you notes. The gratitude is in my heart, and I long to write the notes, but way too often, I fail to do so timely, getting caught up in the hustle-bustle of life.

At the time of today's passage, Israel not only failed to give thanks to God, but their failures went much deeper. Hosea began prophesying during the reign of the ungodly king Jeroboam II, who reigned over ungodly people. Yet the times were prosperous from a worldly perspective. Israel's territory expanded considerably, as Jeroboam was victorious on the battlefield. While Israel had its share of poverty, the rich were thriving. The Israelites not only ignored God but were irreligious. They set up a golden calf at Bethel and erected other sites of worship to idols and pagan entities.

Into this state of affairs came these words of God through his prophet Hosea. The Israelites had totally missed it! God was the cause of their blessings! He was the reason the sun was out and the wind was behind them. He produced the success and mitigated the failures. He made them thrive. He gave Israel these gifts. Yet Israel not only failed to thank God, not only didn't realize God was the source of their successes, but even worse, they also attributed the blessings in their lives to pagan entities. It's as if God had given them the greatest birthday gift, and they wrote the thank you note to someone else, ignoring God.

Today's passage is personal. It sharpens my resolve. I am reminded that God has given me every good thing in life. The people around me, the health I still have, the resources for living, the opportunities of the day, the hopes for tomorrow, all blessings come from God. How will I use those things? I don't want to take advantage of people. I don't want to mistreat my body or squander my God-given resources and opportunities on selfish wants. I don't want them given to useless idols or ideas. I want them used to bless God by setting in motion his plans for others in this world. God has blessed us to be a blessing for others.

I may have a no gifts policy on birthdays, but there is no such thing with our God.

Lord, with deep gratitude, I thank you and seek to serve you. In your name, amen.

JUNE 20

"And I will put an end to all her mirth, her feasts, her new moons, her Sabbaths, and all her appointed feasts." (Hos. 2:11)

Syncretism isn't a word most use daily. It's part of our lives but not so much in our conscious thought. Kind of like cellular usage of ATP (adenosine triphosphate), it's going on constantly in our bodies yet few outside of biology or the medical sciences know what it is. *Syncretism* is the blending of various religious schools of thought into a new thought. It's like taking Judaism or Christianity and putting it into a blender with some pagan religion. The end product has altered the purity of what started.

In some ways, syncretism is innocuous. Most in the United States, for example, will talk about what they're going to do on Tuesday without realizing the word itself originally recognized the old one-handed Germanic warring god Tiu. The Roman god of war was Mars. In Romance languages, therefore, "Tiu's day" is instead some variation of *Mars*, like *Martes* in Spanish or *Martedì* in Italian. Yet in other ways, syncretism is dangerous.

Consider today's passage. Israel started with a covenant God set forth on Mount Sinai, based on the Law that God gave through Moses. It included certain times of honoring God in celebration. These celebrations weren't established because God wanted a party thrown in his honor. They were times to recognize God and his blessings in ways that brought Israel into a holy and focused attention. They would make Israelites better people as they rightly worship the one true God.

Israel took those dedicated times and blended them with pagan religious notions. They distorted the focus God gave them and built their own religious focus, combining God's word with pagan elements of the surrounding cultures. Today's passage condemns her "feasts," which were the three annual celebrations honoring God with the agriculture or acknowledging his historical and current hand in their lives that had been corrupted. The "new moons" were monthly celebrations that were likely pagan in origin. The Sabbaths were supposed to be weekly times of rest but had been distorted into times to party. God was not going to let this continue.

The key to syncretism is the distortion of focus. I don't think of each day as a day for a pagan god. Dedicate each day to the glory of the true God. It's not a naming question; it's a mental decision. The true God should be my true focus.

Lord, I give you today and every day. To the honor and glory of your name, amen.

JUNE 21

"And I will lay waste her vines and her fig trees, of which she said, 'These are my wages, which my lovers have given me.' I will make them a forest, and the beasts of the field shall devour them." (Hos. 2:12)

Decades ago, the in-vogue thing to do at certain retreats and team-building events was the "trust fall." Someone would wear a blindfold, be spun around, and then fall back toward the ground, trusting another to catch them. Many people couldn't complete the challenge, catching themselves by moving their feet before they reached the point where they would really fall should the catcher fail to catch! What once was a team-building exercise has now become a practical joke. One can readily find YouTube videos where while the blindfolded person is spun around, they are subtly maneuvered toward a swimming pool. Then instead of being caught as they fall, they hit the water.

Those videos come to my mind as I study today's verse. The verse continues God-the-Judge's pronouncement of punishment against Israel in its trial for adultery. Hosea emphasizes this judgment with his Hebrew. God is going to lay waste to her fig trees, which she thought were fair wages earned by her worship—her prostitution—of other gods. To emphasize this point, Hosea alters the letters of a prostitute's wages (*etnan*—אתנן) by one letter (*etnah*—אתנה) to make it an anagram of *fig tree* (*tenah*—תאנה). Hosea doesn't want his point missed. The people thought they had provisions (fig trees) from the pagan idols (Baals) in which they trusted. Israel thought the gods were blessing them, but if they were, they would amount to nothing more than payments for their prostitution.

Israel was ludicrous for believing that they could live and trust in those supposed gifts. The idea that their invented gods were paying them for the homage was ludicrous, and the one true God would ultimately show it to be so.

This verse makes me stop and look around me. Where do I put my trust today? I trust in my car to drive me to work. I trust in my resources to see that I have food. I trust in my brain to figure out my challenges. I trust in my friends and family to give me companionship and good help in life. How did I get these things in which I trust? Was I clever? Lucky? Are these just rewards for my hard work? I should realize if I am trusting in anyone, myself included, for these gifts, I am lining myself up to fall into a swimming pool. God gives, and in him I should trust.

Lord, thank YOU for this life. May I always trust you foremost! Amen.

JUNE 22

"And I will punish her for the feast days of the Baals when she burned offerings to them and adorned herself with her ring and jewelry, and went after her lovers and forgot me, declares the LORD." (Hos. 2:13)

January 1, 1976, was a Thursday morning. I was fifteen. The night before, we had gone to a Wednesday night church service where our preacher, Joe Barnett, challenged us for the New Year. His challenge was to go the entire year reading a passage of Scripture every single day. He wanted us to see the importance of turning our minds to God every day, without exception. I don't know if any particular verse sparked his sermon or if it proceeded from his reservoir of wisdom and common sense. But if he needed a verse to support his challenge, today's passage would have been a good one.

Israel had forgotten God. In the business of life, they had gotten caught up in the latest theological fads, thinking themselves righteous and in good stead with the gods because they worshiped them appropriately, at least by their community beliefs. They looked to the Baals as their divine overlords who promised fertility for families and crops in return for worship. The Hebrew term *Baal* was rooted in the idea of an "owner" but was also used at times to refer to a husband or partner. For Israel, these Baals they worshiped were owners of power, and they would use that power to bless those devoted to them.

Caught up in what they thought was real life, the people forgot God. The God of their history; the God who made promises to Abraham, Isaac, and Jacob; the God who used Moses to bring Israel out of Egyptian slavery; the God who displayed his power in a miraculous escape; the God who gave them the Law on Mount Sinai; the God who overpowered the Canaanites and gave the land to Israel; the God who protected Israel against foreign powers; the God who answered prayers; the God who produced the prophets—the one true God was forgotten by Israel.

I can "Tsk! Tsk!" Israel with a shameful wag of my finger, or I can stop and realize how easy it is to forget God. Oh, it doesn't happen overnight or even in a week. But if I fail to spend time with him in his word, he begins to take on aspects of my personality, my wishes and wants, and then gradually, I find myself worshiping a god I created rather than learning and growing with the one true God. I think the counsel from my preacher was right. I better spend time each day in HIS word!

Lord, thank you for your words. May I learn from you daily. In your name, amen.

JUNE 23

"Therefore, behold, I will allure her, and bring her into the wilderness, and speak tenderly to her. And there I will give her her vineyards and make the Valley of Achor a door of hope." (Hos. 2:14)

I love a good television show, especially a courtroom drama. OK, admittedly, that may be because I make my living in courtrooms, but the great shows are . . . great! What makes them great? Of course it is the characters, the plot developments that twist and turn, the expectation, and for me, a good ending. I don't like shows where the ending leaves me dissatisfied or upset. I want the bad guys to lose and the good guys to win. If that isn't happening at the end of an episode, then the episode better continue to another where it resolves favorably.

Today's passage is like a courtroom drama. The entire chapter 2 of Hosea reads like a courtroom script. It began with the indictment against Israel as a bride who has committed adultery, selling herself as a prostitute. After being found guilty, God as the judge pronounces three judgments. Each begins with the Hebrew word *lachen* (לכן), translated as "therefore." These are the three results that bring this courtroom drama to an end.

The first "therefore . . ." judgment is in verse 6, where God says he will "hedge up her way with thorns." Israel would be lost and confused. The second "therefore . . ." judgment begins in verse 9, where God says he was taking back his gifts to her. God had provided for Israel, and Israel not only forgot God but attributed God's blessings to pagan idols instead. God was stripping those blessings away.

Then here in verse 14, Hosea begins God's third and final judgment. SURPRISE! It is the great ending! God promises mercy and restoration on Israel! God takes his wayward, unfaithful wife back and woos her. The translators say God will "speak tenderly to her." The Hebrew reads God will "speak upon her heart." God pursues even the unfaithful.

God wants you and me. God isn't in the business of culling his relationships. He wants restoration. He's full of compassion and ready to speak words of the heart into you and me, regardless of our sin. He is a God of good endings.

Lord, I confess my sins and seek your mercies and love. In your name, amen.

JUNE 24

"And there she shall answer as in the days of her youth, as at the time when she came out of the land of Egypt." (Hos. 2:15)

Keith Green was a musician who died in a plane crash on July 28, 1982, while still in his musical prime. I had seen him in concert just a few months before his death. Keith was a strong believer in God, having come to faith in his late teenage years. Shortly before he died, he wrote a prayer song that made quite an impression on me. He sang, "Lord, the feelings are not the same. I guess I'm older; I guess I've changed. And how I wish it had been explained that as you're growing, you must remember that nothing lasts except the grace of God by which I stand."

I'm personally blessed that Keith lived long enough to write, record, and publish this song before his death. What Keith wished others had explained to him, he explained to his listeners. So I had the benefit of the teaching that he had wished for when he was younger in his walk with the Lord.

The flavor of that teaching is in today's passage. The seminal event in the national heritage of Israel was the exodus out of Egypt. God took Abraham's descendants, who had been living in Egypt for centuries, and brought them out, making a nation of them. God didn't just plop the Israelites into Canaan, the land he was giving them as promised to Abraham. God first took them to Mount Sinai for a solemn ceremony. It was there that God gave a set of commands and terms for Israel. The decision Israel had to make was whether they would indeed enter into a covenant relationship, a wedding of sorts, with God. It was Israel's choice.

The covenant came with God's blessings and protection. But if Israel walked away from its covenant, God would remove those blessings. Israel agreed, the wedding took place, and God's hand blessed Israel. But things changed. Israel was not faithful. As the first generation died off, faithfulness to God was a struggle for the successive generations as well. By Hosea's time, it seems Israel had wandered so far that they would lose sight of God forever. But that was not to be. God was going to recapture their hearts and renew their covenant again. What started would return. The old would be made new.

Times do change, as Keith sang. With that, feelings change too. But the love and grace of God are constant. Our goal is to walk in that even as the days change.

Lord, I give myself to you anew today. In your name, amen.

JUNE 25

"And in that day, declares the Lord, you will call me 'My Husband,' and no longer will you call me 'My Baal.' For I will remove the names of the Baals from her mouth, and they shall be remembered by name no more." (Hos. 2:16–17)

Our daughter Gracie was about three and a half when we all went to an Indian food buffet. I had gone through the line with Gracie and gotten what I thought she might eat. Having set her at our booth, I went back to help Becky with Rachel (who was two) and Will, who at seven didn't really need help. As I walked back to our booth, Gracie was gone! I turned around to see her coming back from the buffet line carrying her plate. I asked her what she had done, and she told me innocently, "I took a bite of my chicken and didn't like it. So I put it back!" Now, the chicken dish was swimming in a brown gravy, so I couldn't determine which piece she had put in her mouth. What to do???

That story comes to mind as I read today's passage. Hosea is speaking of "in that day," a reference to a future time. At some future point, God's people will no longer call God "Baal" but instead will call him "my husband." This is a time when God's relationship will be restored to what it should be. The Hebrew word *baal* can mean "husband," but it generally means "lord" or "owner." It was also used for a pagan god. Here it indicates that God's people will not be substituting anyone or anything else in the place of a true relationship with God.

We have choices. In some ways, life is like a food buffet. But our choices hopefully reflect more than what we like. I want my choices about life to be based on truth. The truth is that there is one true God, who seeks to be in relationship with me. This relationship is to be on his terms, not mine. I can choose to have a true walk with him, or I can make him what I would like him to be and seek my religious truth accordingly.

An important part of this—one that can be lost because it is a bit subtle—is that one choice is better for me in the long run. Given a choice between being a bride to "my husband" or one to "my owner," who wouldn't take the husband? God longs to be in a right relationship with me and you. I fear at times, we take a taste and don't really like what we have, at least at that moment. Then we treat God like a buffet and return him to the pan, dining instead on what seems to fit our taste at the moment. I don't want a relationship *du jour*. I want a real one that lasts.

Lord, I repent of chasing after other gods and pledge myself to you. Amen.

JUNE 26

"And I will betroth you to me forever. I will betroth you to me in righteousness and in justice, in steadfast love and in mercy. I will betroth you to me in faithfulness. And you shall know the LORD." (Hos. 2:19)

A required course in almost every law school is "contracts." There, students learn general rules about how to identify, interpret, and enforce a contract. Some contracts are oral, and some are in writing. If the contract is in writing, it is interpreted by the words written. But sometimes those words can be ambiguous. The general rule in those cases is to interpret the ambiguity against the interests of the one who drafted the contract. This is because the drafter should be responsible for saying clearly what should be said. It also prevents the drafter from disguising a loophole through ambiguous language.

This contract rule comes to mind in today's passage because it's written in an ambiguous form in its Hebrew original and therefore can be understood in two separate ways. The key here isn't so much interpreting the writing against the one who wrote it. Instead, it is fair to read this poetically. In other words, this passage is properly read *both ways*. It is intentionally ambiguous because both readings are true!

The passage speaks of a day when God would be betrothed (a bit like a modern engagement but one that is a full-on commitment to marriage) to his people. To get betrothed, the bride's family was responsible for paying a dowry, a wedding payment to the groom. Here, God says that he will pay for his own bride's dowry! God will pay in "righteousness," "justice," "steadfast love," and "mercy." These are what God will pay to get his bride.

Yet the Hebrew can also be read to say that these traits will accompany the betrothal and marriage. So in the relationship with God will be found "righteousness," "justice," "steadfast love," and "mercy." Both are true! God pays in that currency, and the relationship is rooted in the same.

The basis for everybody's walk with God is found in the character of God. God's inherent traits include "righteousness," "justice," "steadfast love," and "mercy." So God reaches out to us in those valuable ways, and we walk with him in the same values. This relationship is *amazing*, and it comes from an amazing God!

Lord, may my life reflect righteousness, justice, steadfast love, and mercy. Amen.

JUNE 27

"I will betroth you to me in faithfulness. And you shall know the LORD." (Hos. 2:20)

I have a buddy who didn't grow up walking with the Lord. He lived a rough life, working in tough careers where the line between right and wrong was often fuzzy. Then, in his forties, he found faith. His life made a 180-degree turn in many ways, even though transforming who he was into who he needed to be was often painful. It was as if God had taken a huge chunk of marble and, with chisel in hand, began chipping off the stone, stroke by stroke, to reveal the man God knew was possible.

My friend invested his life in an adoptive daughter. He wanted her to have the life he missed. He gave her a good upbringing, but in spite of his best efforts, she did her own 180-degree turn. She took her life as deep into the sewer as one can, extending from prostitution to many other seedy things. She even taunted her father with what she had become. It was devastating for my friend. For two years, they had little to no relationship, and then out of the blue, she called him and asked to meet for dinner. She brought with her a young Christian man who was a new friend. Over dinner, she asked her father for forgiveness.

My friend was telling me the next day that he was going to tell his daughter that he forgave her but that he wouldn't forget what she had done. I told him, "Please don't say that!" I then explained that as her father, he was the ready representation of what she would understand God the Father to be. God the Father doesn't just forgive; he forgets. Today's passage is one of the many that indicate that truth.

The prophet Hosea accurately portrayed Israel as an unfaithful, adulterous wife. In this chapter of Hosea, God put Israel on trial for adultery and announced his judgments. While two of those judgments contain hard consequences, the third is one of future redemption. That is where today's verse is found. Here God says he will once again betroth Israel to himself and do so in faithfulness. The word used for "betroth" isn't the Hebrew for restoring an unfaithful wife. It's applied to the wooing of a maiden. It's a whole new marriage! God not only forgives his people, but the past is forgotten. It is altogether new.

No, God doesn't forgive and remember. God forgives and grants a brand new start!

Lord, thank you for forgiveness. May I forgive others in your name, amen.

JUNE 28

"And in that day I will answer, declares the Lord, *I will answer the heavens, and they shall answer the earth, and the earth shall answer the grain, the wine, and the oil, and they shall answer Jezreel."* (Hos. 2:21–22)

It was an ordinary Monday, by which I mean it was anything but ordinary. Thanksgiving had come and gone and, with it, an effective four-day weekend. I had taken off Thursday and Friday, and the work had piled up. High. As in more emails than anyone would want to answer. Additionally, all the meetings that somehow belonged in the preceding week had piled up to make Monday start early and be stacked with meetings that didn't end until late at night. I'm sure I'm not the only one with some Mondays like that.

The nice thing about my Monday, which was consumed with work issues, home issues, social issues, and even personal issues, is that all of those issues and projects, all of those meetings in person or via Zoom, all of the events were under the control and oversight of God. I didn't face anything that Monday alone. No child of God ever does. Today's passage is a big affirmation of that truth.

God is speaking through Hosea about the future blessings he would send to his people. God says that he will "answer the heavens, and they shall answer the earth." God has no limits. God controls the heavens, wrongly believed by Israel to be the province of Baal, the god who provided rains. God controls the earth, which the Canaanites also wrongly believed to be the domain of Baal as the fertility god. The one true God authored the entire cycle of life, from the rains of heaven to the fertility of earth, producing the crops for people. God is the one who sows and ensures sustenance. Hosea's comment that "they shall answer *Jezreel*" makes that point, for the Hebrew term *Jezreel* means "the Lord sows."

Nothing is outside of God's control. No one and no thing limit his jurisdiction. God not only has control over the elements of your day and mine; he has interest in our days also. God hears our prayers and stands ready to help and assist his children on Monday, Tuesday, or any other day ending in Y.

As I write and you read this day's devotional/teaching, it should comfort all of us to know that as we dedicate this day's activities to God and as we seek his help, he will answer. All of our days can be to his glory.

Lord, please touch my day. Infuse all I do with your purpose and name. Amen.

JUNE 29

And the LORD said to me, "Go again, love a woman who is loved by another man and is an adulteress, even as the LORD loves the children of Israel, though they turn to other gods and love cakes of raisins." (Hos. 3:1)

"Summer of Love" became the moniker for 1967, referencing the social phenomenon that sprung from Haight Ashbury in San Francisco. Massive numbers of young adults gathered for a countercultural movement during an era of a forced draft for the Vietnam War, civil rights battles seeking fair treatment for minorities, and exploration for a deeper purpose in life. The summer stressed unconventional and free housing, sharing food, free medical care, and more, all falling under the umbrella of *love*.

The Greeks were famous for dissecting the concept of *love* into many different vocabulary words. They had words for a service-rooted love (*agape*), parental love (*storge*), romantic love (*eros*), and brotherly or social love (*phileo*). While in English I can speak of loving apple pie, my wife, and my kids, ancient Greeks would use different words. The Hebrew word for love in Hosea's day was much like English: one word had the wide range of meaning given by many Greek words. That Hebrew word (*ahav*—אָהַב) referenced a love of service, parental love, spousal love, romantic love, and even a love of food. The Hebrew word for love is used four times in today's passage, packed and loaded with a range of meaning.

Hosea is told to "love" a woman "loved" by another man, as God "loves" the Israelites who "love" raisin cakes that they offer to other gods. Inherent in this verse, with the various meanings of the word *love*, are multiple concepts we shouldn't miss. Hosea is to "love"—or take care of, serve, and protect—a new wife. The new wife shares "love"—or affection, preference, and enjoyment—of another man. Meanwhile, the LORD loves Israel, in the sense that he is loyal to and provides for his people. Israel, on the other hand, sets their loyalty on fake gods, noted simply as "loving" raisin cakes. We learn here that God's love is certainly not earned!

This passage should cause all of us to ask ourselves important questions: "Who or what do I love?" and "What does that *love* mean?" God has a selfless, providing, generous love for you and me. Do we love him for our own selfish needs and wants (a raisin cake?) or do we return his love in higher ways?

Lord, I love you. May my love be purified as I learn true love from you. Amen.

JUNE 30

*So I bought her. . . . And I said to her, "You must dwell as mine for many days. You shall not play the whore, or belong to another man; so will I also be to you." For the children of Israel shall dwell many days without king or prince, without sacrifice or pillar, without ephod or household gods. Afterward the children of Israel shall return and seek the L*ORD *their God.* (Hos. 3:2–5)

I heard a blood-curdling scream from my three-year-old grandson. I went running into the room and saw him flailing about in absolute misery. Something horrible was happening. I didn't see what had precipitated this terrible moment, but I had a few guesses. My daughter was holding him in his moment of despair, explaining to him calmly, "You cannot do that to your sister. You are going to time-out." Yes, going to time-out was the cause of this three-year-old's tantrum.

Our grandson's time-out wasn't because his mother was cruel. It was for his own good. He was out of control and needed some time to calm down, think about his actions, and make deliberate decisions to be different.

Israel needed a time-out, as evidenced in today's passage. Chapter 3 of Hosea began with God instructing Hosea anew to acquire a wife. The Hebrew context makes it evident that this is again a woman who has a heart for others rather than for Hosea. This instruction to Hosea served as a metaphor for Israel, who would continue to find her heart invested in idols and gods rather than the LORD God who sought her, wooed her, and wedded her. God was going to put Israel into time-out. Hosea insisted that his wife must stay at home, unable to leave and play the harlot.

Israel needed to learn anew that it was living outside the propriety of God's people. It needed time to focus on what was important, on what was real, and on the implications of reality on their lives. Once they did so, they would return to God, and life would be different.

I relate to this passage. I'm not the nation of Israel, but I still need an occasional time-out from God. Sometimes I'm not walking as I should. I get a bit out of control. I find my priorities twisted. I find myself living out of focus. These are times when God has placed me in time-out. God has stopped me in my tracks and sat me on a bench where I can catch my breath, refocus, and do better. Like my grandson, I'm not a fan of time-out. But God knows when I need it.

Lord, help my focus stay on you and be reflected in what I do. In your name, amen.

JULY 1

Hear the word of the LORD, O children of Israel . . . (Hos. 4:1)

It was a busy morning filled with the greatest of intentions. I was out of town, in a different time zone, and my morning started much earlier than I would expect my wife to be awake. When I am out of town overnight, I always call my wife, Becky, the next morning and walk through the day's plans, but that had to wait a bit this time. I had already knocked out three meetings by the time I could call her. I was on my way to meeting number four and revising a PowerPoint I was using as part of a presentation when I was finally able to call her. We spoke of our days, and while talking (and listening), I kept making PowerPoint adjustments. At the end of the conversation, I told her that I loved her and that I would stay in touch, and we hung up.

That evening, I finally finished two days of work in one, and I called my wife again to see how her day had gone. She told me about a lunch she had with someone rather interesting. I was surprised and said, "Oh, I didn't know you were going to have lunch with her!" To this, Becky replied, "I told you that this morning when we were talking, and you acknowledged it with, 'Great!'" I confessed in reply, "Oh, I guess I was listening but not really paying attention. I was trying to get my PowerPoint finished while we were talking. I'm sorry!"

I was listening to my wife but not hearing what she said. Today's passage reminds me that I, and many of us, are guilty of the same thing with God. God has spoken, he has delivered important words to us, he has secured those words for the ages in Holy Scripture, and yet how often do I read them while I'm distracted or otherwise gloss over them? Or, heaven forbid, not read them at all!

Life can get crazy busy. Everyone can easily get caught up in life's hustle and bustle and fail to pay attention to the things that matter most. Our priorities get twisted. What could be more important than God's word?

God's word has amazing power. It can give direction to the lost and bewildered, purpose to the disillusioned, comfort to the hurting, balm to the wounded, love to the forlorn, and companionship to the lonely. It can lift heavy burdens and bring peace to those in turmoil. The key is to listen and hear the word. Let it change your life!

Lord, speak to me and open my ears and heart to listen carefully. In your name, amen.

JULY 2

Hear the word of the LORD, O children of Israel, for the LORD has a controversy with the inhabitants of the land. (Hos. 4:1)

Whoops! The lawyer who asked me to try his case had made a procedural error. Lawsuits begin with the filing of a written pleading in court, generally called a "complaint" or "petition." This document is then served on the defendant(s) as an itemization of the claims made in the suit as well as the basis for the claims and the sought-out relief. In this case, the lawyer had not asked for "punitive damages," nor had he alleged "gross negligence," which is the legal basis for punitive damages. I knew if he didn't plead it, I wouldn't be allowed to ask the jury and judge for it. The law requires proper notice of the claims before someone goes to trial.

Israel could never complain that God failed to give them notice before trial. Just as in Hosea 2, this fourth chapter begins another courtroom scene. God doesn't simply cast Israel aside without warning. God uses Hosea to bring definite charges against Israel. Those charges will be considered over the next several daily devotionals.

Today's passage is the setup for the charges. It begins God's "controversy" with the inhabitants of the land. "Controversy" translates to the Hebrew word *riv* (רִיב), a word that can also be translated simply as "lawsuit." (See, for example, the usage in Ex. 23:3 and 23:6.)

The lawyer in me appreciates this passage. God isn't lying in wait, looking to surprise you and me with a "gotcha!" God makes clear his will for us and his expectations for our moral choices. God tells us what it means to walk in relationship with him. This is sensible if one understands that God's goal is nothing less than our best. God's instructions for life are to make our lives abundant and to give us the greatest lives we can have. So it is natural and right that God would give us warnings when we ignore those instructions.

We then have choices. I can walk in God's wisdom and instruction, or I can freelance my own path and walk where I want. Of course, my vision is limited and my knowledge is incomplete, so to disregard God is not only shortsighted of me but plainly imprudent. God gives me notice; I should take notice.

Lord, may I listen and practice your words of instruction and guidance. Amen.

JULY 3

There is no faithfulness or steadfast love, and no knowledge of God in the land. (Hos. 4:1)

And it begins. . . . God's opening salvo against Israel in the "lawsuit" that began in yesterday's devotional set out three initial charges. Israel lacks faithfulness, steadfast love, and knowledge of God. Many sins in the Bible are sins of commission. Sins of commission are actions that violate explicit commands like "don't murder." These three charges God first lists against his people are sins of "omission." These are failures to do things that all of God's people should do.

The first is a lack of faithfulness (Hebrew *emet*—אֱמֶת). This marvelous and important Hebrew word has a wide range of meaning. It is hard to capture in a single English concept. It references "faithfulness" but also the ideas of "truth," "constancy," and "trustworthiness." The word suggests that God's people should be consistent and reliable in how they respond to and walk with God. In today's language, we might say that people shouldn't wear their "holy behavior" like a garment at church, in synagogue, or around certain people and then present a different behavior at work, at school, or in social outings. Faithfulness is a constant, reliable, genuine life of truth in all aspects of living.

The second sin of omission is failing to maintain "steadfast love." Books have been written on this single Hebrew word (*hesed*—חֶסֶד). I consider it one of the five most important words in the Old Testament Hebrew. At its core, it seems to reflect loyalty to an agreement, but it also includes keeping joint obligations between relatives, friends, a host and a guest, a master and a servant, parties to a contract, and more. It is loyalty between a husband and wife, between a king and his people, or within a community with a common goal of mutual protection. It includes the virtues of goodness, graciousness, and love.

The third sin of omission is failing to know about God. Humanity has a responsibility to seek out God. God has revealed himself in the world around us as well as in Holy Scripture. It is incumbent on us to learn of him.

All of these failures by Israel are important to me. I need to be reliable and faithful to him, to develop a love for him, and to pursue God and grow in learning who he is and what that means.

Lord, I commit to learning more of you and walking in your way. In you, amen.

JULY 4

There is swearing, lying, murder, stealing, and committing adultery; they break all bounds, and bloodshed follows bloodshed. (Hos. 4:2)

Dad jokes. I tell them; my kids groan in response. It is a cycle. My dad told dad jokes. I responded much as my kids do. Then I became a dad and started telling the same jokes. My most recent one is "If 666 is supposed to be all evil, then that would make 25.8069758011 the [square] root of all evil." Yeah, I know. Dad jokes.

Well, this particular dad joke makes a pun off evil, but evil is no joking matter. Still, that doesn't mean that humor can't be instructive. Combining yesterday's passage with today's teaches something about the root of evil, and it isn't 25.8069758011. Yesterday's passage dealt with sins of omission. Today's passage has sins of commission. Yesterday addressed good things that Israel was failing to do. Today, Hosea addresses evil things that Israel was doing instead.

Between those two passages is an important lesson. When we fail to follow the core spiritual practices we reviewed yesterday, it's not as if we just stay neutral in our behavior. Our failure to do those three key good practices negatively impacts the way we live. When one isn't faithful, loving, and growing in knowledge of God, one grows in evil, as set out in today's passage.

Hosea wasn't listing the only sins of Israel. He was giving an illustrative example, one that should be eye-opening to any reader. Several of these sins are violations of the Ten Commandments. In Hebrew, many of the Ten Commandments are a combination of two Hebrew words—*lo*, meaning "no" or "don't!" followed by the relevant word. For example, "Do not commit adultery" is just two Hebrew words: *lo* adultery. Hosea takes three of the Hebrew words that follow the *lo* in the Ten Commandments—murder, steal, and adultery—and lists them. In other words, the one thing they were told "don't do," they did. The indictment for swearing is likely taking oaths in God's name, a violation of the commandment to not take his name in vain. (Hosea isn't referencing speaking vulgarity, which also isn't a good thing, but rather, he intends something much more serious.) As for "breaking all bounds, and bloodshed follows bloodshed," scholars disagree on whether that is a catchall for violent behavior or a way of speaking about idol worship. Either way, we must be careful. For our failure to do right will lead us inevitably down a road to do wrong. There is a lesson here beyond a dad joke.

Lord, fill me with the good things in life. Help me avoid evil. To your honor, amen.

JULY 5

Yet let no one contend, and let none accuse, for with you is my contention, O priest. . . .
My people are destroyed for lack of knowledge; because you have rejected knowledge, I
reject you from being a priest to me. And since you have forgotten the law of your God,
I also will forget your children. (Hos. 4:4, 6)

Are you familiar with the phrase "circles of influence"? The idea is
that everyone has a circle of people that they influence in life. I take the
expression a step further. I think of a stone thrown into a placid pond.
The ripples are circles that are great where the stone went into the water
and then lessen as they continue manifesting beyond the point of impact.
We not only have an immediate circle of people who we influence in life,
but there are also lesser circles we influence. So, for example, I have a
pretty major influence on the lives of our five children. But my coworkers
and even opposing counsel are also people whose lives I influence.

Today's passage should give us pause and move us to reflect on how we
live oriented to those in our circles of influence. In the preceding verses,
God has indicted the people in the land first for failing to do good things
and, partly as a result, instead doing bad things. One of the good areas
where the people failed was learning truly of God. God's indictment for the
people who are ignorant of him doesn't stop there. He goes on in today's
verses to indict the priests who were to teach properly of God and oversee
Israel's worship. The priests had fallen down in their job, affecting a nation
in the circle of priestly influence.

God then loops this around, showing the effects on the circle. As the
priests failed to teach of God, their metaphorical children—the nation of
Israel—failed to honor and live right before God. The way we use our influence truly has a direct effect on those who are in our circle of influence.

This is seen early in life, as peer pressure affects teenagers. But it
goes beyond an adolescent concern. As parents, when we fail to teach our
children about God, the children will grow up differently than when we
teach them about God. As adults, when we live a life that fails to honor and
reflect God, we poorly affect the lives of those in our circle of influence.
How I live and how I teach doesn't merely affect me; it affects those around
me. This rightly gives me pause.

Lord, help me. Help me influence others for good. Let my life and words rightly teach
of you! In your name, amen.

JULY 6

My people are destroyed for lack of knowledge; because you have rejected knowledge. (Hos. 4:6)

Yes, this is a verse that was included in yesterday's reading! But as my friend N. T. (Tom) Wright told me once, some things bear repeating! While Tom was writing a book on Jesus, his sweet wife, Maggie, asked him, "Wait, didn't you write a book on Jesus about ten years ago?" Tom affirmed he had. Maggie then ribbed him, "Well, has Jesus changed?" To which Tom rejoined, "No . . . but maybe I have." We don't always have the same frame of mind from one day to the next. All valid reasons to pull out this section from yesterday's reading and see it through another prism.

Look closely at today's verse: God's people are destroyed for "lack of knowledge." Everyone reading this should immediately cry out, "I want more knowledge of God." So what precisely is "knowledge" of God, and how do I get it?

"Knowledge" is a translation of a great Hebrew word, built off the verb *yada'* (יָדַע), which has a range of meanings from "know" to "perceive" to "experience." The verb is used of Adam "knowing" Eve, his wife, and having children (Gen. 4:1). As used here, the noun carries a level of intimacy as well. Think of three aspects to knowing God: to "know" about God, to know God's ways, and to know God personally. The first two are vital to the third. All three aspects aren't simply intellectual exercises. These are practices; these are experiences. These begin with head knowledge, but they permeate into all aspects of life.

Understanding the breadth of the word *know* unlocks the path to acquiring it. We get knowledge as we learn about God and his ways. We do so by listening to godly people, by reading his word while praying for wisdom and understanding, by spending time in his presence through worship and prayer, by honoring those things he honors, by holy living, and so on.

One other important thing of note. Knowledge of God is an experience, and it goes beyond just doing good things. Knowledge includes an intimacy with the one we know. I can do all the things God instructs me to do, but if I fail to commune with him and know him personally, then I am not on the right road. The people in Hosea's day were caught up in their own lives and living without regard to God or his ways. I don't want to be that way.

Lord, be real to me. Let me see and know you better. In your name, amen.

JULY 7

The more they increased, the more they sinned against me; I will change their glory into shame. They feed on the sin of my people; they are greedy for their iniquity. (Hos. 4:7–8)

Toward the end of his life, Moses sang a song to Israel. In the song, Moses proclaimed the greatness of God. The faithful, just, upright, and loving God took Israel from a howling waste of wilderness, encircled them, cared for them, and guided them into a land of plenty. He gave them abundance, but they turned on him. Jeshurun (a name of honor for Israel) "grew fat, stout, and sleek." They "forsook God . . . and scoffed at the Rock of |their| salvation. They stirred him to jealousy with strange gods; with abominations they provoked him to anger. They sacrificed to demons that were no gods." They "were unmindful of the Rock that bore |them|, and . . . forgot the God who gave |them| birth" (Deut. 32:15–18).

Moses' song is echoed in today's passage. What Moses had prophesied had come true. God had done all he could possibly do for Israel. He made them, protected them, provided for them, revealed himself to them, and even warned them of their sinful tendencies. Yet Israel ignored him. Even the priests who God had put in charge of teaching and maintaining his law had abandoned him. As the prosperity grew, the distance of the people from the Lord grew.

The priests are singled out in these passages, but not to the exclusion of the people. What was true of the priests is true of others. Prosperity can do powerful things, either good or evil. On the good end, prosperity can create grateful hearts and be used to bless others. People with resources have access to help that others might otherwise not have. Yet prosperity can also drive people to independence from God. When you need God to provide your next meal, you are more carefully knit to following him than when you seem to have no manifest need for him. This independence is just one step away from the delusion that God has blessed you because of *you* rather than because of what you can do for others.

Additionally, prosperity is sticky. Once tasted, it's hard to imagine living without it. Once obtained, it's easy to get addicted and become greedy. Hence these ancient priests became greedy for the sin offerings of their flock, finding their own riches in the sins of the people. They should have all been singing the song of Moses.

Lord, purify my heart. May I use your blessings for others in your name, amen.

JULY 8

They shall eat, but not be satisfied; they shall play the whore, but not multiply, because they have forsaken the LORD to cherish whoredom, wine, and new wine, which take away the understanding. (Hos. 4:10–11)

My son turned me on to a foundational book I wish I had read years earlier. *Metaphors We Live By* (by G. Lakoff and M. Johnson) argues that the human mind thinks in metaphors. I know mine does. One metaphor that laces my thoughts is that of a wheel, one of humanity's most important inventions. I frequently use wheel metaphors—people who are a big wheel, not reinventing the wheel, something being in one's wheelhouse, and being a fifth wheel. Today's passage is one that reminds me of another wheel metaphor: people were spinning their wheels as they left God for seemingly earthly pleasures.

The idiom of spinning one's wheels speaks to putting in a great deal of effort without intended results. It is a fruitless pursuit. The people in Hosea's day didn't realize it, but their pursuit of the world's joys was not giving them any fulfillment. They had a never-ending appetite for wrong. Like the Rolling Stones, they tried and tried and tried but couldn't get any satisfaction. What's worse, their pursuit of the mundane pleasures of life hadn't given them insight into what they were missing. It had dulled their minds. It took away understanding that comes from God.

All of us crave meaning and purpose in life. That truly comes only from God. All of us crave acceptance and love. That also comes from God in our committed relationship with him. He loves us too much to let us squander away our lives in frivolity or self-destructive behaviors. He wants more for us.

One night, my high school daughter called me needing help. She had some friends who were "mudding." They had taken their four-wheel-drive trucks into a muddy field to enjoy sloshing around the trucks across the field. But they had gotten stuck. Their trucks were up to their axels in mud. They would push the gas, but the spinning wheels had no traction, and they just went deeper and deeper into the mud. They needed help.

I don't want my life to be spent spinning my wheels. I want my life to be fruitful. I need to pursue God and nothing less.

Lord, give me understanding. May I pursue only you. In your name, amen.

JULY 9

My people inquire of a piece of wood, and their walking staff gives them oracles. For a spirit of whoredom has led them astray, and they have left their God to play the whore. (Hos. 4:12)

In 1970, the game maker Hasbro began selling the "Prediction Rod." This combined the ancient usage of a stick to predict the future with a lode stone. Portraying itself as psychic science, the rod was supposed to help you answer life's basic questions. This usage of wood wasn't new to 1970. Divining rods had been used to help find water and gas for over a century. Even before that, magicians used wooden rods to gain insight and magical powers. Those practices date before the ancient Greeks (though they gave us the word for believing in magical powers of sticks—*rhabdomancy*). Those cultures around ancient Israel were famous for believing in such powers.

Israel had fallen under the mistaken belief that a stick would give them insight into issues—how to live, choices in life, and more. They consulted the sticks as oracles. God calls this a "spirit of whoredom." Why? The clear indication in Hosea is that people should be searching for answers to life's questions, for direction in life, and for meaning and purpose in one place only: God. Any other place is an investment in falsehood.

A question I am often asked—and one I used to ask myself—is "How do I know what God wants me to do? What decision does he want me to make?" This becomes really big when wondering what job I should take, whom I should marry, where I should live, and so on.

The Bible gives some exceptional messaging from God (Gideon's fleece, for example), but the general rules of Scripture are clear. First, read Scripture and learn God's heart. This is found in his instructions as well as the priorities reflected both in the instructions and the stories of God. When we spend our efforts pursuing his heart, we will find that answers most of our questions about what to do. With the remaining questions, pray. Seek godly counsel. Be open to whatever God might tell you. Then see if a way doesn't open up and make sense. Ultimately, remember that God made you able to choose, and sometimes he gives no direction beyond several good choices. God can say to you, "You decide; I will bless you either way!" Don't trust your future to a stick. Learn from God.

Lord, teach me your ways. May I follow you today. In your name, amen.

JULY 10

They sacrifice on the tops of the mountains and burn offerings on the hills, under oak, poplar, and terebinth, because their shade is good. Therefore your daughters play the whore, and your brides commit adultery . . . and a people without understanding shall come to ruin. (Hos. 4:13)

Influence. You and I have it. Some of it is direct and obvious (parents have it over children); some of it is indirect and not so recognizable. It can be good. (I sing the same ditties to my kids that my dad sang to me fifty years ago.) It can be bad. (I struggle to refrain from eating the same unhealthy foods that haunted my father's diet.) Harry Chapin's biggest hit was 1974's "Cat's in the Cradle," a narrative song about a father who had no time for his young son, even though the son begged for his father's time. The answer was always "soon." Then the boy grew into a man, and the father, in his elder years, sought out time with the adult son, who never had time for his father. The haunting refrain was "He'd grown up just like me."

In today's passage, a graphic illustration of this truth is presented. Israelite fathers were chasing after other gods, participating in cultic prostitution. Not surprisingly, then, their children were unfaithful to God as well. Hosea links it to ignorance.

Cultic prostitution was rife among the pagans. The idea was that by sacrificing to the gods, which included payment to their prostitutes, the gods would then bless the land and the families with fertility and growth. The Old Testament repeatedly shows that God's people succumbed to this abhorrent practice (see 1 Ki. 14:24; 15:12; 22:46; 2 Ki. 23:7; etc.). This false practice to false gods wasn't going to lead anywhere good. Instead, the people should have concentrated their efforts on following the instructions of the true God. Those instructions were for the good of the people, and they resulted in good things. It may not have meant the immediate fleshly gratifications, but each choice had long-term consequences. The consequence of the godly route was abundant life. That of the pagan route was death. The people should have known better.

The passage carries both points of emphasis: the need to know and walk in God's instructions and the influence our failures have. Eyes watch you and me each day. What those eyes see will influence what those people do. Influence. We have it. It's that simple and true.

Lord, teach me your ways. May I have a positive influence on those around me. For your sake, amen.

JULY 11

Like a stubborn heifer, Israel is stubborn; can the LORD *now feed them like a lamb in a broad pasture?* (Hos. 4:16)

I'm not a cattleman. Yet for some inexplicable reason, I once decided to buy two cows and put them in the backyard. (We live on a few acres without deed restrictions.) After the cows were delivered, I went to work getting them where they needed to be. They were not cooperative. At all. They ran out the open gate and onto the street. They had no interest in returning, and as I tried, they just started running away. They left our property, ran down the road, ran through a subdivision, and got near a highway before some friends and I managed to corner them. I got rid of them immediately.

While I'm not a cattleman, I learned what a stubborn heifer is and what havoc it can create. I now chuckle at Hosea's expression that Israel is a stubborn heifer who can't be treated like a cooperative lamb. The sad part is, while I laugh remembering my experience, I often tend to be like that stubborn young animal.

One important metaphor God uses to explain himself is that of a shepherd: "The LORD is my shepherd . . ." proclaims Psalm 23, perhaps the most famous psalm. God tells me where to lie down, where to graze, where to walk. He leads me, tends to my needs, and binds up my wounds. But I'm not God's puppet. I'm not a computer program he wrote and then watches run. I have choices. I can eat what he gives me or not. I can lie down where I choose and walk where I want to walk. I can follow him or make my own way. I can let him meet my needs or go after what I want on my own.

These are real choices. Everyone has a tendency to think that what they believe is right. With what social scientists call *confirmation bias*, we accept the evidence and arguments that support what we want and believe, and we disregard the rest. This tendency may work to our benefit where we are on solid ground. But the heart can be deceitful, and we often reckon our way right, even when it isn't.

The sad part is that the stubborn heifers are useless for many tasks. They really don't fit into the plan. I want God to give me the ability to see my rebellious nature and bring it to him to fix! I don't want to be running down the highway on my own.

God, please help me see truth and pursue it before you and in your name, amen.

JULY 12

I know Ephraim, and Israel is not hidden from me. (Hos. 5:3)

I make a living trying to determine who is being truthful and who isn't. I've read countless books on detecting lies. I've taught seminars on how to do so. Yet truth be told, when it came to my children as they were growing up, my wife rightly pointed out I was terrible at it. My kids could tell me the sky was green, and I would likely believe them. Fortunately, our children were usually deeply honest. Still, occasionally, they offered something less than the truth, and I was horrible at picking it up. Call it "Trusting-Daddy Syndrome."

Today's passage states what should be obvious. God knows. In the context of Hosea's prophecies, God knew how Ephraim (a tribe of Israel) and Israel at large had turned their backs on God. They had merged their historical religious faith with the contemporary cultures around them. They accepted that the God of the exodus was fine to celebrate and worship but not on his own terms. They redefined God based on the culture and religious thoughts of their day. They "modernized him" as they "learned more" from those around them.

This is a dangerous move. Yes, as culture changes, our understanding of how God relates to life within those cultures changes as well. Slavery is a great example. In historical cultures that used slavery as an economic tool, God spoke within those cultures, but the highest and most godly behaviors don't countenance slavery. Still, there is a difference between understanding God's character in light of culture and changing the essence of who God is. God doesn't change.

For example, regardless of the culture, the instruction stands that there is one God, and we should love him with all our heart, soul, and might (Deut. 6:4–5). Similarly, we should put nothing in front of him as worthy of our worship and pursuit: "You shall have no other gods before me" (Ex. 20:3).

God knows and sees what we're doing. He knows when we place him second in life. He knows when we seek our own values and interests and try to shift who he is to fit who we want him to be. We don't amble through life able to do as we please. God doesn't have Trusting-Daddy Syndrome. He has "Sees-the-Truth Syndrome."

Lord, give me a purer vision of you. May I always put you first. Prayerfully, amen.

JULY 13

Their deeds do not permit them to return to their God. For the spirit of whoredom is within them, and they know not the LORD. (Hos. 5:4)

We know the difference between a road and a parking lot. A road goes somewhere; a parking lot is a place to let your car sit without going anywhere. Life choices are roads we travel, not parking lots. That much is evident in today's passage.

The larger context beyond this verse adds important color. Like all of us, the Israelites of Hosea's day made choices in life. Their choices included ignoring God and his ways. The priests were of no help, for they taught and reinforced heresy adopted from the surrounding cultures. Pagan gods were celebrated in pagan ways, and the culture had denigrated into a selfish cesspool. I'm not suggesting the whole society was compassionless or without any goodness. But overall, they were rotten and getting worse.

Hosea points out that those choices would take them places. The destination was not one anyone would enjoy. The destination was death and societal destruction. The smart person would do a U-turn and find a better road. But the people didn't do this. Their choices were blinding them of their need for God and to their sin. Hosea says that the people were possessed by "the spirit of whoredom."

I am typing this book using the Microsoft Word program. It has a built-in grammar and writing filter that tells you when you misspell a word or when you might be making certain other writing mistakes. Each time the word *whoredom* appears in this message, it is underlined in blue by Microsoft, with the explanation, "This language may be offensive to your reader." Yes, the word *whoredom* should be offensive. The sad part is that the practices that Hosea labeled *whoredom* were not only unoffensive to the people; the people relished them.

That is often the way with sin. We think we have everything under control. We don't realize that the sin is in control. It possesses us; we don't have dominion over it. What we may think of as dabbling in disobedience, in reality, is something much worse.

Life is a road, and we get to choose how we live it. I want my deeds to lead me to God's goodness, not keep me from turning back to him.

Lord, forgive my sin, rescue me, bring me to you. In your name, amen.

JULY 14

The pride of Israel testifies to his face; Israel and Ephraim shall stumble in his guilt; Judah also shall stumble with them. (Hos. 5:5)

Many years back, a lawyer (now long deceased) asked me to represent him in a lawsuit filed against him by the State Bar, the group that licenses and regulates lawyers. This group sought to strip him of his law license, preventing him from practicing law. The State Bar had retained outside lawyers to prosecute the action. Those lawyers had the same type of trial practice as the fellow they sought to punish. I knew the allegations of wrongdoing, but I could tell the animus between these quasi-competitors was much deeper. I tried to understand why portions of the Bar were so upset with my client.

The one word that kept surfacing in my investigation was *arrogance*. People thought my client believed himself superior not only to other lawyers but to the system. One vignette seemed to illustrate this belief. After one particular high-profile court case where my client had won, my client went outside the courthouse to the street, lifted both his hands in the air, and began shouting, "I won! I won!! I did it! I. AM. THE. KING. OF. TORTS!!!!" The other lawyers, including those who lost, were not too happy.

Pride is one of life's most offensive sins. Think about it for a moment. No one picks their parents. No one picks their genetic code. So any giftedness and benefits of a good upbringing cannot form the basis of pride. But then one might ask, what about the person without the blessings of parentage, genetics, and a good upbringing? When that person succeeds, shouldn't that person be proud? Not by biblical teaching. God instructs us that he is the source of our successes. He blesses us so that we might bless others. When we do so, we give God the glory for success. We don't shout out our own value.

The northern kingdom of Israel was failing to give God glory. With hubris, they believed they had arrived out of personal greatness. But they weren't alone. In a prophetic book centered on the sins and future of Israel, Hosea notes that the godlier southern kingdom of Judah was also guilty of pride. Their inclusion in this warning should make the reader notice. Pride is not only the sin of some. It can invade all our lives. Everyone should be cautious. We shouldn't act like we are kings and queens. No one can write the book *Humility—and How I Achieved It.*

Lord, forgive my pride. May I find glory in you, praising you in my life. Amen.

JULY 15

With their flocks and herds they shall go to seek the LORD, but they will not find him; he has withdrawn from them. They have dealt faithlessly with the LORD; for they have borne alien children. Now the new moon shall devour them with their fields. (Hos. 5:6–7)

In the middle of a long trial in Dallas, the judge took a break for a "sentencing" hearing where various criminals who had already pleaded guilty were being assessed their sentences. Some got long prison terms, and some got shorter ones. It was sobering to hear what was said to the judge as well as the punishments meted out. Almost every criminal said, "I'm sorry. I won't do it again." These contrite words were even uttered by those who had been before the judge before for other crimes and sentencing where, presumably, they said much the same thing. The judge, a fair and just man, delivered appropriate sentences nonetheless. It's not that he wasn't merciful. It was just that the punishment was the right thing to do. The process had reached the point where the apologies were akin to the fresh haircuts it seemed each criminal had gotten for the hearing—a bit useless if not downright disingenuous.

The Israelites had hit that point with God. Over and over, God had sent his prophets proclaiming his pleas to Israel that they repent. God had warned them of the consequences of their actions. He had shown mercy upon mercy. Yet Israel spurned his love, ignored his cries, mocked and persecuted his prophets, and rushed speedily down the road of despising God.

Today's passage is God's proclamation that those days were coming to an end. Israel was going to be sentenced. It isn't that God wasn't merciful, for he had shown compassion for generations. It's just that Israel had made its choices, and those choices had gotten to the point where certain consequences were inevitable. Israel could bring flocks and herds to sacrifice to God, but they wouldn't find him at their holy places. God wasn't there. They were looking for God with the wrong attitude. Their apologies were hollow and misdirected. They were dealing with God "faithlessly." The fruits of their actions—the "alien children"—were manifestations of their blatant disregard of God.

I want to approach God honestly. I want to truly repent of my sins. I'm not looking to get a haircut to impress him. I want to be genuinely his.

Lord, I turn my heart and life to you. I seek you in your mercy. Amen.

JULY 16

When Ephraim saw his sickness, and Judah his wound, then Ephraim went to Assyria, and sent to the great king. But he is not able to cure you or heal your wound. (Hos. 5:13)

I was five years old, living in Memphis, Tennessee. My first-grade teacher explained to us that the earth was round! I hadn't had a clue. What was more, she explained that China was on the other side of the round world opposite us. This gave thought to one of my coolest ideas in my young life. I rushed home from school, found my dad's shovel, and went to the backyard. I started digging. I was going to China! I knew it might take a while, but all I had to do was dig through the round earth to get to the other side. Spoiler alert: I didn't make it.

My efforts were futile. Looking back as an adult, it's a laughable story of the naïveté of youth. Of course, I wouldn't be able to dig through the 7,900 miles of earth to get to China. I don't think I got much more than two feet.

Today's passage reflects a similar absurdity to my efforts to dig to China. Israel had irrevocably broken its agreement with God. They had spurned him, devoted themselves to false and evil gods, and strayed beyond the confines of being able to return. So God was going to bring judgment on them. This judgment was the only wake-up call left to allow God to establish his plans for the future kingdom he promised. The judgment was inevitable.

Yet Israel would try to get rescued from God's judgment. Israel was going to ask the king of Assyria to protect them and stop God. Think through the absurdity of this. That anyone or anything on this dirt clod called earth—one of innumerable planets around innumerable suns in innumerable galaxies in an unmeasurable universe, all of which fits metaphorically into the palm of God Almighty—would be able to counter the will of God is more laughable than a five-year-old boy with his dad's shovel digging to China through the backyard.

You and I have a choice. We can be on God's team today, or we can go our own way. God's team is unbeatable. It makes sense to spend my time and energy pursuing his plans, not my own. If I choose to fight him and his plans, I won't win, regardless of who I enlist to help me.

Lord, I pledge myself to you today. May my thoughts and my deeds focus on you and your will, and may I give you all my allegiance. In your name, amen.

JULY 17

For I will be like a lion to Ephraim, and like a young lion to the house of Judah. I, even I, will tear and go away; I will carry off, and no one shall rescue. I will return again to my place, until they acknowledge their guilt and seek my face, and in their distress earnestly seek me. (Hos. 5:14–15)

Years back, an insurance company conducted an ad campaign using a red umbrella. The ads ran for years, and the idea was that the company provided an "umbrella of protection." Umbrellas were already known by the time of Hosea, dating back thousands of years in Egypt and Assyria as well as in China. The purpose of an umbrella is to protect someone from the elements—sun as well as rain and snow. Umbrellas are also frequently used as metaphors for the way God protects his people. The metaphor derives its punch from the idea that often, people will step out from the umbrella of God's protection and subject themselves to the elements.

Hosea doesn't use an umbrella metaphor. His concern isn't just that Israel removed itself from God's protection. Israel departed from God, and God was not remaining passive. God was pursuing Israel, not to be an umbrella and protect, but like a lion pursues prey. God was going to reckon with Israel. God would then return, as a lion to its lair, to await Israel's genuine repentance.

This passage has a word that stands out within the larger context of Hosea, providing an extra emphasis. That word is *shuv* (שׁוּב), translated as "return." Hosea uses this word twenty-three times in his short book. Most of the time, the word is used in a plea for Israel to "return" or "turn back" to the Lord. Over a dozen times, Israel is urged to *return* to God. Here, the word is inserted with a different context. Because Israel would not heed the message and would not return to God, coming back under his umbrella of protection, God was going to venture forth and rain destruction on Israel. Afterward, God would *return* to his place and await the true *return* of Israel.

God's goal is always the best for his people and his purposes. But at times, God's people stray. God will not leave them abandoned forever. He will go out and do what needs to be done to get his people to turn back and find him. I am glad for this. A God who doesn't care enough to find his people, even when they stray, would leave me in trouble.

Lord, in genuine repentance, I seek your protection and restoration from all the sins that alienate me from you. In your name, I pray, amen.

JULY 18

*"Come, let us return to the L*ORD*; for he has torn us, that he may heal us; he has struck us down, and he will bind us up."* (Hos. 6:1)

It was middle school, and I got into a fight during lunch. Words were exchanged, challenges were made, and fists flew. After a few punches, the fight was broken up, and I was hauled to the principal's office, evidently a first for the Lanier children, according to my folks. The principal administered a stern talking to, which we admittedly deserved, but then he did something horrible. He called my parents. Mom and Dad were not amused. I was instructed that fighting was not acceptable school behavior, and I was appropriately punished.

Was the principal a rat for telling my parents? Were my parents mean for disciplining me? Of course not! I needed to have that behavior stopped before it became normal or repeated. The memory has lasted for now fifty years, with that being the last (and only) fistfight of my life. The actions of the principal and my parents were efforts to help me in discipline and motivation. They knew it was important that I follow a different course if I were to become the best me in this world. Some social workers call it *tough love*. I just call it love.

God loves his people. His love is not one that fosters destructive behaviors or reinforces bad habits. God's love seeks to pull people up and to build them into the best versions of themselves. God wants people to have lives of fulfillment and meaning. He wants his people to grow in love and holiness. He wants nothing less than the very best for us.

That is behind today's passage. God wasn't raining destruction on Israel because of a mean streak. God wasn't angry and seeking revenge. God was going to discipline Israel so that he could get their attention and bring them to the point where they would change and return to him. Any parent who has ever had to discipline a child understands this. Any owner who has trained a dog gets it. Any drill sergeant who has watched basic training deconstruct soldiers so they can be reconstructed with a military mind-set knows it.

God's goal is for us to be our best. He always puts that front and center in what he does and what he allows to happen in our lives. I must trust him there.

Lord, thank you for your love and, when necessary, your discipline. In you, amen.

JULY 19

"After two days he will revive us; on the third day he will raise us up, that we may live before him." (Hos. 6:2)

Racquetball is a great sport. You play in a court where there is no "out of bounds." You have a floor, four walls, and the ceiling. Your ball caroms off each surface and can produce some amazing spins as you try to figure out where it is going. When my buddy Louis and I play, sometimes the geometry will frustrate one of us, causing us to lose a point. At that point, we often complain loudly, "Ms. Bode!"

Ms. Bode was my geometry teacher my sophomore year of high school. She taught us advanced concepts but also the basics, like *parallelism*. Parallel planes never meet, for example. It wasn't until college that I learned that parallelism was also important in ancient Hebrew writing, especially poetry. Today's passage is a pristine example of parallelism, one that teaches an important truth.

The passage can be broken down into five clauses: (1) after two days, (2) he will revive us, (3) on the third day, (4) he will raise us up, and (5) that we may live before him. If you look carefully, you'll notice that clauses 1 and 2 are repeated, or "parallel" to clauses 3 and 4. So "after two days" is parallel to "on the third day," and "he will revive us" is parallel to "he will raise us up" or "make us stand." The "two" and "three" days are poetic; they're not to be taken literally. The passage says that God will take us from a dead state and give us life ("revive us"). He will take us from the supine position of the dead and make us stand ("raise us up"). There is a lot to be learned of Hebrew poetry in this passage, but I want to zoom in on the key, which is the fifth clause.

God calls us out of death into life "that we may live before him." God isn't interested in our lives being apart from him. God wants us before him, "before his face" in the Hebrew. You and I aren't God's hobby. God didn't bring us into a life to ignore him, a life we live focused on this world or its passions. God brings us to life and stands us up so that we might live in relation to him. That means that everything I do today has God in its field of vision. How I treat people, how I treat myself, what I choose, my priorities, and more—all these things are to be done with focus and recognition of the God who made me. I need to get the geometry straight!

Lord, let all I say, think, and do align with a life before and in you. Amen.

JULY 20

"Let us know; let us press on to know the LORD; his going out is sure as the dawn; he will come to us as the showers, as the spring rains that water the earth." (Hos. 6:3)

Benjamin Franklin was a publisher, businessman, and diplomat. He was also a quote generator. He gave us "He that lies down with dogs shall rise up with fleas," "No gains without pains," "Haste makes waste," and "Time is money." One of his most famous quotes was "In this world, nothing is certain except death and taxes." He was wrong on that one. Today's passage gives other certainties.

The Lord's "going out" is as sure as the dawn. The Lord's "coming" is as certain as rain. Hosea let everyone know that God is fully reliable and, as such, is available for people to "know."

To "know" God in the Hebrew means to be in a relationship with him. As Adam "knew" his wife Eve bringing forth children (Gen. 4:1), God calls us into a real relationship of intimacy. This is the challenge Hosea issued to his people. He called on them to know God. Not know *about* God but know God. This relationship certainly involves knowledge about God, but it is much greater than that. One can read Scripture, study theology, and know grand facts large and small about the Divine One but never know God! And without knowing God, all that knowledge is worthless.

I want to be in a relationship with God. I want to not only know about him; I want to walk with him. I want to understand his heart, know his compassion, and perceive his will. Then I want to be his servant, using the gifts and talents he has given me, combined with the doors he opens, to join him in his cause. And I will rightly praise and exalt him before this watching world. I want my life to show that the Lord is worthy of my best pursuits.

Some might say, "Who can have a relationship with the Divine One?" One major point of Hosea's passage is to affirm that it is possible. The God who created the universe is ready for humanity to want to be close to him. That's a stunning thought, but it's the truth. It's not Ben Franklin, but it is a worthy saying nonetheless: "Know God, for with him one finds true life."

Lord, I want to know you. Help me understand your priorities, pursue your agendas, model your love, and live in your care. In your name, amen.

JULY 21

What shall I do with you, O Ephraim? What shall I do with you, O Judah? Your love is like a morning cloud, like the dew that goes early away. (Hos. 6:4)

When I was thirteen years old, I began working in a local convenience store, owned by a truly marvelous fellow at church, Joe Stapleton. My job was three days a week after school, stocking the coolers and shelves, dusting the store, and mopping the floors. I got to know Joe, and I knew his difficulty at times finding the necessary people to work the register, especially on Saturday mornings. I couldn't understand why he didn't ask me to fill in occasionally. After all, I was really good at math!

When I became older and started running my own business, I figured out why. Although I would have denied it at the time, I was too young to be working the store as the cashier. The responsibility of being the person behind the register was too great. Age and maturity had not allowed me to grow into someone reliable enough to do so properly. With time, I came to work the register, and I worked for Joe when I was in town all the way through law school.

My story has a point in today's passage. Through Hosea, God expressed his frustration with Israel (called by one of its tribal names, "Ephraim"). Israel was totally unreliable. This passage contrasts with yesterday's passage. In Hosea 6:3, God is described as reliable as the dawning sun. Yet his people were as unreliable as dew, which disappears quickly once the sun comes out. It's as if when God appears, Israel evaporates. This verse expresses God's frustration with the nation.

At times, we forget the awesomeness of God's design. God has set this world into motion and given humanity the opportunity to work with him to bring goodness and light into dark and evil places. God wants everyone to work with him in furthering his kingdom and endeavors. We get to choose. It's up to us. But our choices are reflected in what we do, not what we say. Choices aren't lip service—"Yes, boss! We got that!"—followed by disobedience. That isn't mature or responsible. That isn't reliable. That leads to today's passage: "What shall I do with you?"

I had an excuse for my limited responsibility in my early teen years. But I have grown up. Now with God, it is choice and action.

Lord, I want to be responsible so you can trust me to help you. In you, amen.

JULY 22

For I desire steadfast love and not sacrifice, the knowledge of God rather than burnt offerings. (Hos. 6:6)

I love to study languages. English is so cool. We have words that came from Latin, Greek, Germanic tribes, and more. We have about one thousand words that came from the Vikings! The average high school graduate in the United States has an active vocabulary of around twenty thousand words. Recent research by UPI.com indicates the average person understands approximately 42,000 words but uses around half of those. The Hebrew Old Testament has only 6,259 different words, if you don't count proper names (8,674 words if you do). Not surprisingly, then, in translating the Hebrew into English, most Hebrew words express themselves through many English options.

Today's passage has an important Hebrew word that finds expression through many ideas and words in English. The Hebrew word is *hesed*—חֶסֶד (pronounce the *h* like the hard *c* in *cough*, gargling while you say it). In today's passage, the translators have chosen "steadfast love." The phrase and its meaning are extremely important because it is what God "desires" even more than sacrifice.

So if God desires *hesed*, what should that mean to us? In this verse, *Hesed* was translated by the Jews of 200 BCE into Greek using the Greek word for *mercy* (*eleos*—ἔλεος). Without a doubt, mercy is part of what Hosea is intending. Hosea was speaking to a self-centered people who abused the needy rather than exhibiting God's mercy. God was more interested in their actions than their ritual sacrifices.

But *hesed* means more than *mercy*; it includes the concepts of faithfulness, goodness, and graciousness. God is placing more value on our reliability, morality, and loving-kindness for others than on our attendance at a worship service. We can go to church or synagogue every time the doors open, but if we fail to treat others right, God is rightly displeased.

The root idea in *hesed* is being loyal to a covenant. For Israel, it wasn't that God didn't expect them to offer sacrifices as he instructed, but those were only part of the covenant relationship. God wants our hearts, not mindless obedience. God wants us to treat others well, not use them for our gain. God wants us to be holy, not vulgar displays of self-pleasure. This is *hesed*.

Lord, help me better live in mercy, graciousness, and steadfast love. In you, amen.

JULY 23

But like Adam they transgressed the covenant; there they dealt faithlessly with me. (Hos. 6:7)

Today's passage reminds me of *A Goofy Movie*. That 1995 animated Disney movie was a favorite among several of our children. They watched it. Then watched it again—over and over and over. And again. And again. They memorized it. Every line and song they could recite and sing. Two of those daughters are now in their thirties, and on occasion, they will still quote a line and laugh hysterically.

Now, you may wonder why this movie occurs to me in reading today's passage. It's because the story of Adam and Eve's rebellion in the garden of Eden is our story too; it gets more replay in our lives than even *A Goofy Movie*. This is remarkable, when one pauses and considers. Adam and Eve have it made. They're in perfect harmony with God, placed in an amazing world to explore and discover. The rules of nature and physics worked the same for them as they do for us, in that they could have created a civilization we can only dream of. God had an arrangement with them. They had no real limitations beyond not taking from one tree that belonged only to God. Both sides were clear on the terms of this agreement. God would take care of them perfectly. But to live in harmony with God, they must not steal and eat from his tree. Did I add that God warned them that if they did, they would bear the punishment? They would die.

Adam and Eve broke the covenant and, in doing so, challenged God. As they stole from his tree in seeming secrecy, they demonstrated a great distrust in God. They denied his words as they disobeyed his commands. Fear of God was replaced in their brains by personal desire. They believed some fake story rather than the plain words of the Lord.

This comes now to me. I can scoff at the sin of Adam and Eve, but if I look sincerely, it is plain to see that I break covenant with God too. How often do I ignore or set aside the words of God in favor of what I want or what I convince myself is right? It wasn't just Adam and Eve; it wasn't just Israel in the time of Hosea; it's also me today.

Yes, the movie seems to be on constant replay. It's a bit ironic that for my kids, it was *A Goofy Movie*. For me, it goes beyond goofy; it is senseless.

Lord, I repent of my rebellion, and I ask your forgiveness. In your name, amen.

JULY 24

But they do not consider that I remember all their evil. Now their deeds surround them; they are before my face. (Hos. 7:2)

Brevard Childs (1923–2007) was a marvelous Old Testament scholar at Yale University. He had authored a relatively obscure word study on the Hebrew word for "remember" (*zachar*—זכר). In the mid-'80s, I wanted to read his work, but it was long out of print, and the internet didn't exist for me to chase it down. Professor Childs had retired, but I managed to get his home phone number. I called him, and I asked him if he might have an extra copy I could buy. He told me that he did, but there was a much better publication in German. When I told him I couldn't read German, he cheerily replied, "Oh! Then you better read mine!" He sent it with a gracious inscription.

I wanted to read it because his work was an authoritative text for showing that the Hebrew word isn't precisely translated by "remember." Our English word calls to mind how one can "forget" and lose conscious memory of, or how one doesn't forget but keeps a matter fresh on one's mind. The Hebrew has an emphasis missing in the English. The Hebrew denotes *the action* one takes *because* of what is in one's conscious mind. This understanding makes today's passage stand out.

God said that the people were ignoring the truth that he "remembered all their evil." God wasn't saying that their deeds hadn't slipped his mind. The deeds "surrounded them"; no one looking could miss them! God was saying he wouldn't ignore or remain passive in the face of their evil. God was going to take action.

Today's passage both encourages and challenges me. It encourages me because God doesn't ignore evil. God detests evil. More than anyone, God knows the destructive power of evil. God sees the pain and misery brought about by sin. God doesn't get lost in the moment, like so many humans who choose sin. God will deal with sin.

This same truth also challenges me. God will deal with sin. It is true of the sin of those around me, and it is true of my own sin. God knows the destructive power of my sin and how it stunts my growth and prevents me from being all I can be. God is going to work on my sin, and that can be difficult, but it is a good thing.

Lord, I confess my sin to you. Please work in me so I can grow into who I can and should be before you. I pray in your name, amen.

JULY 25

By their evil they make the king glad, and the princes by their treachery. (Hos. 7:3)

Prisms are cool. A piece of glass cut in the right way bends the light going through it so that the light waves show their various colors. Looking at light without this hides the rainbow colors, but break it apart, and you see more fully the nature of light.

I think of prisms with today's verse because it breaks apart into constituent parts that help me more fully understand life's challenges. Israel had a problem with a secular, unholy lifestyle. The problem permeated the culture from the palace to the street and all stations of life in between. The people were evil, and the rulers didn't rein in the evil but instead reveled in it. The rulers were evil, and the people didn't reject it; they mimicked it. Hosea was watching the social breakdown with its inevitable consequences of social destruction.

Those in authority should expect goodness from those who report to them. This is true on all levels of submission and authority. Parents should seek goodness in their children's behavior. Bosses should set up a culture of goodness in workplaces. The idea that a person of authority would revel in the evil of others is reprehensible. This manifests itself in subtle ways. The boss who has an assistant lie for her or him is wrong. Anyone who has someone else "do their dirty work" is wrong.

Similarly, those who are under authority should cultivate goodness and righteous behavior and choices. Peer pressure should never operate to make someone transgress, but it should spur one another to good works. Life's choices should never be made on the lowest common denominator. Everyone should seek to do what is right and best.

My life can be a prism, for I, like most people, am both in a position of authority and yet also under authority (especially from judges!). I need to focus on living rightly in every capacity. I need to be an example that prompts others to be their best. I need to model and appreciate honesty and integrity. I need to support and applaud those holding on to good priorities as I seek right priorities as well. I need to delight in good, not evil.

Lord, teach me to model and applaud goodness. In your good name, amen.

JULY 26

They are all adulterers; they are like a heated oven whose baker ceases to stir the fire, from the kneading of the dough until it is leavened. (Hos. 7:4)

I have mentioned in an earlier devotional the foundational work of George Lakoff and Mark Johnson in *Metaphors We Live By*. In it, they discuss certain metaphors that are so ingrained in people that they pepper our expressions often without us realizing it. For example, like I used *pepper* in that last sentence, food metaphors are everywhere.

Today's passage uses food as a metaphor/simile referencing the oven in which the ancients baked their bread. Many people never work a wood-burning oven. But most are familiar with a fireplace. As I type this devotional, I have a roaring fire with real wood keeping my room toasty warm. But every hour or so, I have to replace the logs. An ancient wood oven for bread was built in a dome shape, like an igloo but with the opening at the top. The ancients would pile in wood, light it, and get the whole oven piping hot. While bread fermented and rose, the cook would tend the oven, replacing the wood. Today's metaphor draws on that practice.

The people's adultery—which was their spiritual adultery, or replacing the love of God with the love of other things—was an oven burning so hot that the baker didn't need to add wood or stir the fire. They had gotten to the point where, for example, their anger was out of control (as Hosea continued his metaphor in the coming verses). Their sins were raging, and they were destroying who they were and who they were meant to be. They wouldn't live their destiny because they burned with love for others over God.

This passage causes me to assess my temperature. Do I burn hot for God or for others? Do I tend to my walk with God like one tends to a fire? Am I carefully nurturing the fire as I make choices so my walk with God is growing, as the bread rises? Or is my fire raging out of control?

Hosea gives a food metaphor that everyone should chew on. My walk with God is never something on the back burner. It should be front and center each day. I want to burn for God, not for any other thing. That is Hosea's food for thought!

Lord, it's not always easy to stay on target. So many other things vie for my attention. Help me always to focus first and foremost on you! In your name, amen.

JULY 27

Ephraim mixes himself with the peoples; Ephraim is a cake not turned. (Hos. 7:8)

Riding with my buddy Richard is always edifying and instructive. He uses metaphors as well as anyone. We were recently in a car in Dallas, and I was bellyaching about my busyness and how much I had on my plate. Before I could say, "Yes, I know I do it to myself!" Richard responded, "You know, it's a volunteer army." Another of his metaphors concerned my devotional thoughts. He said, "Even the best has a half-life of about seventeen minutes, so don't hesitate to repeat a theme or message." He's right. I need constant reminders.

Today's passage contained ancient metaphors that work into modernity if we adjust them slightly. They also emphasize Richard's half-life theory. The first clause today—"Ephraim mixes himself with the peoples"—is a statement that the nation is "mixed up!" in modern speak. Just as in today's lingo, the phrase *mixed up* can have two meanings in the Hebrew. It can mean "mixed up" like the ingredients of bread, continuing the baking metaphor Hosea has been using. Or it can mean "mixed up" like "confused" or jumbled in thinking. As for the second clause—"Ephraim is a cake not turned"—we might use our modern metaphor to translate it as "Ephraim is half-baked."

Ephraim was living an unfocused and distracted life on a national level. It leaned on ungodly neighboring nations for stability rather than God as their rock. This left them in a precarious, half-baked position; they weren't who they should be. The next verse (Hos. 7:9) adds the consequences. Ephraim was wasting its energy on neighbors without knowing it. ("Strangers devour his strength, and he knows it not.") They were growing old without purpose. ("Gray hairs are sprinkled upon him, and he knows it not.")

Today's passage rings true as a warning to me. I get to choose how I live today—each day. I can muddle through life, busy or not, living in an unfocused way, frittering away the days. Or I can focus and live deliberately, seeking God at every turn and pursuing his purposes. I want clarity in my life, not confusion. Each day, I want to make choices that matter. This is my conviction. I just need a half-life on this pursuit longer than seventeen minutes.

Lord, help me to live focused on you and your will. I don't want to fritter away my days. I want them to count. In your name, amen.

JULY 28

Ephraim is like a dove, silly and without sense, calling to Egypt, going to Assyria.
(Hos. 7:11)

In 1980, I was studying to be a preacher. We students shared certain stories or parables that we thought were useful illustrations in sermons. One was this: A man was in his home when a flood came in to ravage his city. The man was told to flee to high ground but chose instead to pray for God's deliverance. The waters continued to rise. A rescue worker came to the man's home in a boat and told the fellow to get in. The fellow refused, explaining he had prayed and trusted in God to save him. The waters rose more. The man moved to his second story as the first story flooded. Another rescue worker with a boat came to save him, but the man still refused. He had prayed and knew God wouldn't let him down. The waters rose still more, forcing the man onto his roof. A rescue helicopter hovered above with a rope, urging the man to climb in. The man refused, noting he had prayed and trusted God to save him.

The waters rose; the man drowned and then appeared before God. The man challenged God for letting him down, at which point God said, "Don't blame me! I sent two boats and a helicopter!" The story makes a great point. Then step into today's passage.

Israel lived at a crossroads. To the north was the Assyrian powerhouse. To the south was the strong Egyptian Empire. Israel vacillated between serving Assyria for its protection and seeking protection from Egypt. Yet God was calling Israel to be an independent nation that relied on him for survival. In today's passage, God condemns Israel for looking to other nations to save it.

A fine line exists between my opening parable and Israel's behavior. The defining line is where we *first* turn for help in life. If we turn to God for help, then with open eyes, we will see God's rescue. His rescue will not be a path of ungodliness but one of wisdom and virtue. Israel hadn't turned to God at all. It sought only the rescue of this world. In that way, Israel had lost focus and failed to find the rescue that came from the Almighty God.

We all have struggles and needs in life. We should seek first God and his kingdom. He will then provide us with what we need, including boats and helicopters.

Lord, rescue me. May I walk in your rescue to your glory and in your name, amen.

JULY 29

Woe to them, for they have strayed from me! Destruction to them, for they have rebelled against me! I would redeem them, but they speak lies against me. They do not cry to me from the heart, but they wail upon their beds; for grain and wine they gash themselves; they rebel against me. (Hos. 7:13–14)

One of our daughters was in full mom mode. Her three-year-old son was misbehaving, as three-year-olds can do at times. She told him to stop, or she would have to put him in time-out. He looked her straight in the face and did what she had told him to stop doing. She had no choice then. She picked him up, explained he disobeyed on purpose, and placed him in time-out. You would have thought the world was coming to an end. He wailed like there was no tomorrow. She taught him at that critical age the basic obedience and behavioral traits that would serve him later in life. She was and is a great mom.

Her parenting comes to mind reading today's passage. Centuries before Hosea's era, God had made a covenant with Israel. God set out rules of behavior. God offered them to Israel with the promise that abiding by those rules would bring blessing and honor to the people. But flaunting and defying those rules would bring strife, trouble, and national disgrace. Israel made the covenant with God with its eyes fully open.

God upheld his end of that agreement and gave Israel second chances galore. But by Hosea's time, the people were so far from following the covenant that they had passed a point of no return. Their behavior left God no choice. The covenant terms were invoked, and Israel was headed to time-out. The punishment was coming. It caused God to say, in Hebrew, "Oy!"—a cry of lament. God took no pleasure in the punishment. God wanted to redeem his people. But the people were too far removed from God to genuinely care about him or seek his forgiveness.

God's punishment of Israel wasn't wasted. Like the time-out for our grandson, it had a future benefit. Those who read of it with eyes open and a willing mind can take the lesson to heart. I can learn from Israel. God calls me to obedience, with the promise of blessings. When I stumble, if I seek forgiveness with a genuine heart, he seeks to redeem me. Life isn't always easy, but I walk it with my loving God. This is the life worth living. I want to learn this lesson!

Lord, forgive my sin, and may I walk closely with you. In your name, amen.

JULY 30

Although I trained and strengthened their arms, yet they devise evil against me. (Hos. 7:15)

Dad would often speak of the importance of not taking things for granted. As I grew up, I understood he meant that we shouldn't just assume something as a matter of right but should always be appreciative. Admittedly, I was in my late teenage years before I realized the phrase was "Let's not take that for granted." Until then, I thought it was "Let's not take that for granite." I'm not sure why it took me so long to get the phrase right. I guess I assumed it derived from thinking something was granite when it wasn't!

In today's passage, reference is made to Israel taking God's gifts for granted. God points out through Hosea that God had trained and strengthened Israel's arms. The Hebrew word for "arms," *zero'a* (זְרוֹעַ), references the forearms of an individual, but much like the English word, it also can mean military power as well as simply "power" or "force." Hosea prophesied during an era of relative military strength for Israel. From a national perspective, Israel was doing quite well. They had enlarged their boundaries and instilled fear in the smaller nations/tribes surrounding them. This was a time when the international powerhouse Assyria was suffering internal civil wars and was not the strong presence it had been in the preceding centuries. Israel enjoyed the power and prestige, but it failed to appreciate that God was the source. So instead of acknowledging and praising God for his goodness, Israel pursued a course that set them at odds with God.

I can't type passages like today's without recognizing the many gifts God has given me that I take for granted. Go through your life in categories, and see if you don't find somewhere you are taking God for granted. Consider your physical health. I am not 100 percent where I'd like to be physically. I have aches and pains, but I am much better off than many! Thank you, God. Ditto for my emotional health and the workings of my mind. The same is also true for my relationships with others. They aren't perfect, but they are still amazing parts of my life. My job may not be without stress, but it is a great blessing nonetheless.

I take much for granted, and that isn't right. I need that "attitude of gratitude" to be more than a common platitude. I need it to be real in my life.

Lord, thank you! Your blessings are beyond my comprehension. I praise you with a grateful heart. In your name, amen.

JULY 31

Israel has spurned the good; the enemy shall pursue him. (Hos. 8:3)

My grandmother occasionally used the expression "Truth will out!" I understood what she was trying to say—that in time, truth will be revealed—but I had no idea of the phrase's origin. I figured it must be some country saying she grew up around in either Tennessee or Texas. Later in life, I discovered this was no colloquial country expression. My grandmother was quoting Shakespeare! In *The Merchant of Venice*, Shakespeare has the rascally Lancelot Gobbo offer, "Well, old man, I will tell you news of your son: give me your blessing: truth will come to light; murder cannot be hid long; a man's son may, but at the length truth will out."

In this world, cause and effect are not only laws of physics but also the way of morality. Sin cannot stay hidden. It isn't without consequence. This is indicated in today's passage.

Hosea prophesied to an Israel that had long abandoned God. The people pursued other gods, ignoring the covenant made with the one true God. Because we become like those we admire, that false worship caused a number of adverse effects. As Israel pursued gods who exalted selfishness, Israel became selfish. As Israel honored gods who cared little for the outcasts in society, Israel cared little for the outcasts. Israel chose injustice over justice. Israelites worshiped the gods of their desires, which in turn justified them in feeding their own desires.

In Hosea's pronouncement, "Israel spurned the good." And as certain as Shakespeare's observation that truth will out, the true effects caused by spurning the good were coming. Hosea pronounced this in the preceding verses, telling Israel to sound the alarm: "Set the trumpet to your lips! One like a vulture is over the house of the LORD, because they have transgressed my covenant and rebelled against my law" (Hos. 8:1).

Having read this passage for decades and translated it from the Hebrew forty years ago, I wonder why I have trouble remembering this principle. Why is it that I think I can spurn the good, pursue the wrong, and not have negative repercussions? When I spurn the good, I am setting myself in a position for the enemy to do me damage. Surely, I can do better!

Lord, forgive me. I need to be better about finding your holiness. Give me sight for the good and strength and courage to pursue it. In your name, amen.

AUGUST 1

They made kings, but not through me. They set up princes, but I knew it not. With their silver and gold they made idols for their own destruction. (Hos. 8:4)

The year was 753 BCE. For forty years, Jeroboam II had reigned in Israel. Upon his death, his son Zechariah took the throne. Zechariah was weak and unable to keep his kingship. After six months on the throne, he was assassinated by Shallum in a coup. Shallum lasted one month. Then another coup occurred, and Menahem set himself as king. Menahem was horrible. The Israelites that didn't follow his coup were assassinated, with the pregnant women ripped open and killed with their children as an example. Menahem kept the throne for ten years. When he died, he passed it to his son Pekahiah, who reigned for two years before a coup led by Pekah killed him.

It should never have been that way. Kings were God's representatives to dispense God's judgment and law. God was to choose them and, through his prophets, anoint them. The thrones were to be established by God. Had the people followed God's lead, their lives would have been much different. But the people chose their own path, and that path led to destruction.

Every one of us has tasks in front of us. Some may not seem as important as appointing a king to rule over a nation, but who is to say? How one treats a waiter at a restaurant might make a difference in that waiter's attitude for the rest of his or her shift. The waiter who leaves work after a difficult day without any kind words might decide to go to a bar to drink the poor feelings away. Several drinks later, the now intoxicated waiter might drive home, hitting and killing a family along the way. As a lawyer, I have seen this. Now, certainly, one cannot excuse the waiter who made poor choices. But one must wonder what might have happened differently had someone shown God's love to him or her rather than mistreatment.

The point of today's passage is that you and I are constantly making choices. We can make those choices by seeking God and his will, or we can make them on our own. I recognize that practically thinking, many choices are made nearly spontaneously, without time for devoted prayer. In those cases, it's important that we have drawn close enough to God for his character to have formed in us, such that we responsively make godly choices. The lesson is clear: I always want to build my life around godliness.

Lord, teach me your ways, renewing my mind in godliness, for your sake, amen.

AUGUST 2

I have spurned your calf, O Samaria. My anger burns against them. How long will they be incapable of innocence? For it is from Israel; a craftsman made it; it is not God. The calf of Samaria shall be broken to pieces. (Hos. 8:5–6)

Imagine a craftsman in Israel in 750 BCE. A merchant comes into his shop and says, "Hey, *shalom,* I need some goods to sell. Can you make me some calves out of gold for a reasonable price? They ought to go like hotcakes!" The craftsman replies, "Sure, why not? A buck's a buck!" He makes a mold, adds some gold and other metals to keep it shiny but not so pricey, and voilà—golden calves. The satisfied merchant takes them and resells them for a tidy profit. Enter some poor sap who buys a golden calf and starts praying to it, believing it to be a god. That is not far from what was happening in Israel, although the golden calves were larger and part of national worship. (Home idols were more commonly crafted out of clay.)

Fast forward almost 2,800 years. I haven't met any merchants peddling golden calf idols as if they are gods. But that doesn't mean this ancient event doesn't have relevance today. If we expand our understanding of what is a god, suddenly, today's passage speaks to us directly.

The objects of our worship are our gods. People worship things that they value, they believe can help them in life, they rely on, or make them feel good. These gods can be money, popularity, jobs, clothing, cars, and even food. (The Jewish-lawyer-turned-Christian-apostle Sha'ul, a.k.a. "Paul," would write to a group of Christians in Philippi of those whose "god" is "their appetite"!)

When we consider these gods, we now find plenty of merchants and craftsmen! These are the folks who convince us to buy that car, wear those clothes, eat that food, build that house, or whatever it may be all because it will make us feel better or give us inner satisfaction. These are fake gods giving fake sensations. Just as Hosea prophesied, these are gods that will be "broken to pieces."

My value needs to come from the one true God. My goal needs to be becoming the person God wants me to be. That doesn't mean I don't have a car or clothes, but I don't find my meaning or significance in them. It doesn't mean I don't trust door locks and seat belts. But I do so under the aegis of trusting in the one God before whom I bow.

Lord, may I seek only you as my God, living and praying in your name, amen.

AUGUST 3

For they sow the wind, and they shall reap the whirlwind. (Hos. 8:7)

Gardening is marvelous therapy. You prepare a plot of ground, you decide what you want to grow, and you plant it. Actually, there is a good bit more to it than that. You need to plant an appropriate crop for the area and soil type. You need to do it in the right season. You put the seeds at a proper depth. You tend to the garden with adequate water, remove weeds, and pay attention to pests and diseases. Then hopefully when the harvest is right, you reap what you've sown. If you sow tomatoes, you reap tomatoes, radish seeds make radishes—and so on.

In antiquity, large-scale farming, as opposed to a little garden plot, was done without machinery. Yet it was too inefficient to dig little holes and plant seeds one by one. So farmers would wait for the right weather, generally a gentle wind. They would then walk through the prepared field, throwing the seed in gentle back-and-forth motions. The wind would help disperse the seeds evenly.

Today's passage uses the farming metaphor but with a twist. Hosea doesn't mention any seed being sown. The people were simply sowing the wind. "Wind" here has a double meaning to the reader. Wind could be the breeze we associate with the word *wind*. So instead of using the wind to sow seed, they were doing nothing productive with the wind. But *wind* had a second, alternate meaning: *wind* can also be used, as it is in this passage, to represent foolish or worthless behavior or goals. In other words, the people were not living in fruitful ways. In foolishness, they lived worthless lives that would not produce a useful crop. They would reap a whirlwind.

Whirlwinds, or "storms"—an alternate way to translate the last word in this verse—were the bane of farmers. These were crop destroyers. In other words, the efforts of the people were not only dead ends, but they were destructive.

There is a lesson here. I have a certain number of heartbeats. We all do. Every day I have opportunities for love, service, and good seeds I can sow. Those seeds will produce good crops. Or I can live a fruitless life. I can live self-centeredly, seeking only what makes me happy. This will be destructive to me and others. I know what I want to do!

Lord, help me live productively toward your will and in your name. Amen.

AUGUST 4

For they have gone up to Assyria. . . . Ephraim has hired lovers. Though they hire allies among the nations, I will soon gather them up. And the king and princes shall soon writhe because of the tribute. Because Ephraim has multiplied altars for sinning, they have become to him altars for sinning. Were I to write for him my laws by the ten thousands, they would be regarded as a strange thing. As for my sacrificial offerings, they sacrifice meat and eat it, but the LORD does not accept them. Now he will remember their iniquity and punish their sins; they shall return to Egypt. For Israel has forgotten his Maker. (Hos. 8:9–14)

In my teenage years, I was invited to a dinner with the family of a friend from church. We went to the Lubbock Country Club, a new experience for me. I was out of my comfort zone, so I followed the lead of the young lady who had invited me. She had a baked potato with her dinner, and the waiter asked whether she wanted it "loaded." She said, "Yes," and so when my turn to order came, I ordered the same thing. I had never had a loaded baked potato before. It was huge!

Today's passage is a loaded potato. So much history and context is packed into these few verses that I am hesitant to write it in one devotional. Here is the context: Israel was a geographical bridge for traffic between Egypt to the south and Assyria to the north. God had brought Israel out of slavery in Egypt and put them in primo real estate. Both the Assyrian and Egyptian Empires wanted the land that was Israel's. God said he would protect Israel and keep the land for them as long as Israel reflected God by following his law. They would be blessed to be a light that blessed the darkness around them. Israel quit following God. They became like the pagans around them. They lost God's protection.

Israel then sought Assyria's protection to the north, paying tribute. But becoming a vassal to Assyria would result in Israel's return to Egypt and the slavery they escaped. The word *return* is key to this passage. Hosea had begged Israel to return to God, but Israel refused. They faked religion with sacrifices that were blatant disobedience in process, location, purpose, and attitude. God was having none of it. Israel forgot who was their real protector and why God protected them.

I don't want to forget God. I don't want my religion to be foreign to worshiping the true God. I don't want my mind to recreate God as I want him to be. God deserves better, and I need his protection that comes from following his will!

Lord, may I worship you truly for the great God you are. In your name, amen.

AUGUST 5

Rejoice not, O Israel! Exult not like the peoples; for you have played the whore, forsaking your God. You have loved a prostitute's wages on all threshing floors. (Hos. 9:1)

Ivan Pavlov was a brilliant Russian physiologist who, in the 1890s, did amazing experiments on classical conditioning using dogs. He began by thinking that dogs would salivate when food was set before them. But his experiments showed that the dogs salivated sooner! They would salivate simply hearing the footsteps of one bringing food. Then Pavlov experimented by ringing a bell before feeding the dogs. After a time, the dogs would begin salivating every time they heard the bell. The salivating wasn't intentional by the dogs. It was instinctive.

In certain ways, you and I aren't much better than Pavlov's dogs. Today's passage should remind us of this tendency, so our brains can engage and rise above these instinctive responses. Israel had experienced a few decades of worldly success. Their crops came through in abundance. They had relative safety in their borders, even expanding them through military conquest. The rich had built houses of stone, and those in the higher reaches of society seemed to have it made. The people were confident that this prosperity would continue, as they lived their pagan lifestyle in ignorance of God's instructions.

Into this bubble came Hosea's prophesy. Hosea told the people, "Don't rejoice in your successes!" They had betrayed their relationship with God. They might get temporary pleasure, but the long-term picture was bleak. Destruction was coming.

This is the Pavlovian lesson. When our immediate happiness and temporary pleasure become the directive for life, we are setting ourselves up for "classical conditioning." We believe that we will continue to have the blessings of the moment, and we emotionally salivate at the mere thought of momentary pleasure. But we do so blind to the long-term picture.

I should never let a momentary pleasure overcome my knowledge of what is right. Living for the moment has caused too many DUIs, fractured families, diseases, and other consequences of thoughtless living. I am not a dog. I don't need to act like one.

Lord, please renew my mind. Transform my tendency to prefer a moment's pleasure over the right course. I need your help and strength. In your name, amen.

AUGUST 6

The days of punishment have come; the days of recompense have come; Israel shall know it. The prophet is a fool; the man of the spirit is mad, because of your great iniquity and great hatred. (Hos. 9:7)

Bob Dylan, winner of a Nobel Prize in Literature, has written many insightful songs. In the early 1960s, Dylan was heralded as his generation's spokesman. Folk songs like "Blowin' in the Wind" and "The Times They Are A-Changin'" were seen by many as anthems of political and societal insights. Then in 1964, Dylan released his album titled, importantly, *Another Side of Bob Dylan.* This album had the song "My Back Pages," one of my all-time favorites.

The lyrics never say "back pages" and are hard to decipher in places. But the chorus is a simple two phrases with unmistakable meaning: "Ah, but I was so much older then; I'm younger than that now." In that repeated refrain, the title of the song comes into focus. Dylan lives in the back of the book and is singing about the previous pages of his life. He *used* to have the answers; he *used* to be so smart. He spoke for his generation. Yet as he aged, he realized he hadn't arrived where he and others thought. He characterizes his earlier preaching as hubris, thinking he had it figured out. As he aged, he realized he never had all the answers. He thought he was so much older in his earlier incarnation, but now he realized that he is younger and still searching for answers.

This song reminds me of today's passage. Israel had mocked Hosea and refused to listen to God's prophets. Israel believed they had the answers. In pride and arrogance, Israel dismissed any hint that God's judgment was coming. Yet the prophets were right. God's judgment was true. God was going to right what was wrong among his people.

This passage reminds me of the silly hubris often found in youth—at least, it was present in mine. If you ask me how many ways I have changed in my beliefs and understandings from my early days to now, if you were to get to the back pages of my book and read the earlier chapters, you would see similar hubris. What I need to remember, though, is that my book isn't over. I need to be old enough to recognize the permanent need to find God, follow God, and grow into a greater likeness of his character and love. I may only be midway through my book!

Lord, thank you for bringing me along in life. Continue to work in my life to mature me in thought and deed. I pray with love and appreciation in you, amen.

AUGUST 7

Like grapes in the wilderness, I found Israel. Like the first fruit on the fig tree in its first season, I saw your fathers. But they came to Baal-peor and consecrated themselves to the thing of shame, and became detestable like the thing they loved. (Hos. 9:10)

Don't be a Dufflepud! These foolish, self-reliant creatures are featured in C. S. Lewis' Narnian volume *The Voyage of the Dawn Treader.* They serve Coriakin, who seems to be a metaphor for God. Coriakin provides for them, treasures them, and instructs them on how to live. The Dufflepuds don't believe the obvious love and care of Coriakin is authentic and so live as if Coriakin is a trickster out to ruin their lives. So for example, when Coriakin diverts a creek to bring water near the Dufflepuds' home, they insist it is a trick and instead each day get their water by hauling buckets to a stream far away. I should add that the Dufflepuds are monopods, one-footed creatures who hop everywhere. So hauling water from far away in buckets causes most of the water to slosh out.

Israel was guilty of being Dufflepuds before God. God found Israel to be a rare thing (a "grape in the wilderness" or a "first fruit on the fig tree in its first season"). This refers back to the special relationship that God established with Israel in Sinai upon their liberation from Egypt. God treasured and offered Israel a position as his chosen people in order to be a blessing to the world.

Yet Israel didn't appreciate what God gave them. Instead, as recounted in Numbers 25, certain Israelites engaged in sexual rites with the Moabites, sacrificing to their gods. These Israelites bowed down before the Baal of Peor, apparently in hopes that the local gods would ensure fertility when the Israelites entered Canaan. God would have none of it. If Israel wanted to worship dead, unreal gods, Israel would become dead. After all, we become like the things we worship. As Israel "consecrated themselves to the thing of shame," they "became detestable like the thing they loved."

No, I don't want to be a Dufflepud. After all God has given me, all God has done for me, all God promises me, I don't want to think I know better than he does and go off on my own, freelancing my decisions based on what I think as opposed to what God says. That is foolishness personified!

Lord, give me faith to trust you and your words. In your name, amen.

AUGUST 8

Woe to them when I depart from them! (Hos. 9:12)

King David was Israel's greatest king. David was a successful king who accomplished glorious things in the service of God. David defeated Goliath. David defeated the Philistines. David conquered Jerusalem, known even today as "the city of David." God placed his Spirit in David, and David was even termed "a man after [God's] own heart" (1 Sam. 13:14). For good reason, his name is still present today. The King David Hotel in Jerusalem is one of its finest. The Star of David features on the Israeli flag. David is a popular name worldwide.

Yet David did some atrocious things. David's adultery with Bathsheba cascaded into sin after sin as David tried to cover up his misdeeds. Bathsheba was pregnant, and her husband couldn't be the father—he was away on military duty. So David tried to orchestrate a cover-up, having Uriah, the husband, return from the front lines for a weekend of R and R with Bathsheba. David figured that could act as a smoke screen to the fact that her pregnancy resulted from adultery. But Uriah refused to sleep at home because his men were in battle, and he felt a loyalty to them. So ultimately, David set Uriah up to be killed in battle. David became a murderer.

After the dust settled, David added the now widowed Bathsheba to his group of wives. Bathsheba gave birth to a baby that died, and David went into mourning. After the prophet Nathan brought conviction to David for all he'd done, David produced the Fifty-First Psalm. The psalm of repentance is memorable for many parts, but one section echoes today's passage from Hosea. Repenting and crying for God's mercy, David prays, "Create in me a clean heart, O God, and renew a right spirit within me. Cast me not away from your presence, and take not your Holy Spirit from me. Restore to me the joy of your salvation, and uphold me with a willing spirit" (Ps. 51:10–12). David doesn't want God to depart from him. That would be the worst of the worst.

Hosea notes that "woe" is the state of affairs when God departs. We want to think God is always there. We have a God we can abuse, ignore, distrust, and violate, and yet he will still take care of us because he is God. But God says that for those who leave God, there comes a time where God lets them go. He departs from them. I want to pursue God. I know he is always there for a repentant people. So I will repent like David, not shun him like Hosea's Israel.

Lord, in your mercy, forgive my foolish ways. Be my God, as I pray in you, amen.

AUGUST 9

Every evil of theirs is in Gilgal; there I began to hate them. Because of the wickedness of their deeds I will drive them out of my house. I will love them no more; all their princes are rebels. (Hos. 9:15)

Most of the people reading this are believers in God; otherwise they likely wouldn't still be reading in August! People who are believers in God have God imprinted into their lives, caring for the things that matter to God. As the psalmist said, "Those who know your name put their trust in you" (Ps. 9:10).

Therefore, most readers recoil in horror at today's passage. How can God hate people, drive them out of his house, and love them no more? After all, God is a God of love, not seeking to condemn anyone but hoping that all will have a relationship with and walk with him. How can one understanding of God coexist with the other? The answer lies in evil.

Evil isn't "just" a bad thing. Evil is a cancer. Evil takes what is good, what has near unlimited potential, and corrupts it, eventually destroying it. Evil may not do so in one small place here or there. After all, I have and still occasionally choose evil in my life. But I regret and repent from those choices. It isn't what I want to do and be, and I'm confident that God is at work growing me beyond that evil. But some people become so corrupted by evil that they pass the point of no return. They thrill in and thrive on evil and will not seek or want anything better. Think of serial criminals. Think of the ruthless devotee who purposes to destroy God and anything good.

Some might rejoin by saying, "But doesn't God himself do that in the Old Testament?" I believe that those Scriptures need to be read carefully to understand them properly. For in many, the people were given chances to turn to God or to flee the slaughter but chose not to. For example, God told Abraham that Israel would stay in Egypt—that is, not conquer the Promised Land—"until the sin of the Amorites has reached its full measure" (Gen. 15:16; my translation). Thus, the Amorites were given four hundred years to change their idolatrous, child-sacrificing ways. There comes a time when cancer needs to be cut out and destroyed. The tissue is too far gone for repair. This is the proper end of evil.

I don't want any evil in my life. I want holiness.

Lord, forgive my sin; help me grow beyond it. In your name, amen.

AUGUST 10

Israel is a luxuriant vine that yields its fruit. The more his fruit increased, the more altars he built; as his country improved, he improved his pillars. Their heart is false; now they must bear their guilt. The LORD will break down their altars and destroy their pillars. (Hos. 10:1–2)

Israel was taught to tithe to God. The Hebrew word translated as "tithe" means "a tenth part." Israel was to give to God the first tenth of what they received or made. This practice was carried into Christianity, not surprisingly, since the first Christians were all Jewish. Most churches still teach it today. I remember a pastor in a church who spoke of a member who told him, "Pastor, I used to tithe to the church, but now I make so much money that a tithe doesn't seem right." The pastor responded, "Well, I will pray that you make less money, so you can find obedience before God!"

That story comes to mind when reading today's passage. Israel had years of prosperity. Those years should've given Israel a grateful heart to pursue God as God had instructed. Yet Israel used their gains to fuel their own religious ideas and desires, even if they flew in the face of God's commands. God had instructed Israel to have one place of worship, one meeting place with God. That began in the wilderness with the tabernacle. It contained the singular ark of the covenant. With God's blessing, that location became permanent with the temple built by Solomon. God made it clear with smoke and miracles that his presence would be honored in that temple.

But after their civil war, the northern kingdom of Israel didn't want its people going to the southern kingdom of Judah to worship in Jerusalem. So the kings and priests in the north began to set up their own sites of worship, placing numerous altars in places of convenience and political expediency. Worship of God was reduced to what pleased the people and what helped build earthly kingdoms. The prosperity of the people fueled this disregarding of God. As the passage explains, God was not going to leave this alone. God is God, after all, regardless of what people think.

I learn an important lesson here. I need to be obedient to the Lord in all I do. The blessings of this life are given by God for his purposes, and I need to use them as he instructs.

Lord, teach me how to follow you more truly. In your name, amen.

AUGUST 11

For now they will say: "We have no king, for we do not fear the LORD*; and a king—what could he do for us?" They utter mere words; with empty oaths they make covenants; so judgment springs up like poisonous weeds in the furrows of the field.* (Hos. 10:3–4)

I have a wife and five children. So today's passage scares me and should put everyone who reads and understands it on notice. Read and consider it carefully. It takes a moment to digest it.

The passage begins with Hosea speaking of what Israel will say in the near future. Hosea prophesied during the last kingship of Israel (that of Hoshea, who reigned from 732–722 BCE). The conquering Assyrians were coming, and they would end the kingship, dispersing many if not most of the Israelites. Once that occurred, Hosea says Israel will say, "We have no king." They will also rightly say, "What did he ever do for us?" or "What could he do for us?" Notice in the English translation above, the quotation marks end there. That is because what comes next is from the mouth of Hosea, not the Israelites in the future. Hosea answers their future question.

What did the kings do? They uttered mere words! They made covenants with empty oaths. They led the people who lived without fear of God, bringing upon the people judgment and destruction. An extra level of condemnation is found in these words when one realizes that the purpose of a king was to lead Israel into battle and protect them (1 Sam. 8). The king was to follow God carefully and ensure God's provision and prosperity for the people. Yet Israel's kings were worthless. They spoke empty words. Following God wasn't their goal, and it left them as a bunch of hot air, able to do none of the protecting and providing that was supposed to occur.

I'm not a king. I don't know any kings. But God placed me into a life with my wife and five children. Part of my job is to provide and protect them. I don't want to do that with lip service. I don't want to write about it and talk about it. I want to *do* it. Everyone, whether a parent or not, should see in these verses the importance of doing over saying. People watch what we do more than they listen to what we say. I read this passage and take heed. We all should.

Lord, teach me your ways. Help me better follow you with what I do, not simply what I say. Help me walk with you in genuine faith and trust. In your name, amen.

AUGUST 12

The thing itself shall be carried to Assyria as tribute to the great king. Ephraim shall be put to shame, and Israel shall be ashamed of his idol. (Hos. 10:6)

In 1970, Canadian-born singer-songwriter Joni Mitchell wrote and released one of her biggest hits, "Big Yellow Taxi." I confess I was never a fan of the song, though the alliteration in its repeated phrase "Paved paradise and put up a parking lot" is quite clever. The line that stands out to me as most profound, however, is "Don't it always seem to go that you don't know what you've got till it's gone?" In her metaphor, it was some marvelous piece of land, realized as paradise after putting up a parking lot, something bland and mundane.

For Israel ("Ephraim"), the principle applied but in an almost opposite scenario. Israel had been worshiping and glorying in this fancy golden calf created as an idol. In spite of the Ten Commandments injunction "You shall not make for yourself a carved image, or any likeness of anything that is in heaven above, or that is in the earth beneath, or that is in the water under the earth. You shall not bow down to them or serve them" (Ex. 20:4–5), Israel did it anyway. They were so proud of it. The verse before today's passage, verse 5, explained that Israel worshiped the fake god Beth-aven in awe, trembling when they came before it. Hosea, prophesying the coming doom on the nation, proclaimed that the idol would be carted off as booty for the conquering king, and the people would then "mourn for it."

In time, Israel would come to realize the idol was a bauble, nothing to be proud of but something to be ashamed of. That's the way it is with anything we place in the stead of God. We can make or find an idol and think it awesome—it doesn't have to be a golden bull; it can be a career, money, prestige, or popularity. We can lose it and mourn. Yet in the end, when we come to our senses, we are rightly ashamed that we deceived ourselves. Of course, that is assuming we come to our senses!

I want to come to my senses today. I want to place God first in my life. I want my decisions about my career, money, prestige, popularity, and so on to be subject to my desire to serve God and him alone. If he blesses me with anything, I want to glory in him, not in what he gives me. I want to tremble before God alone. I don't want to wake up tomorrow and realize that what I had was a bauble.

Lord, please give me insight into my life to discern what I value in place of you. Help me perceive truth and place you first in my life. In your name, amen.

AUGUST 13

Samaria's king shall perish like a twig on the face of the waters. The high places of Aven, the sin of Israel, shall be destroyed. Thorn and thistle shall grow up on their altars, and they shall say to the mountains, "Cover us," and to the hills, "Fall on us." (Hos. 10:7–8)

I was about to try a case. Before the judge entered, the opposing lawyer asked for my "bottom line" number to resolve the case. I gave my lowest number, which the lawyer refused. I said that the number would go up once we selected the jury. We selected the jury, at which point the lawyer offered to settle for my pretrial demanded amount ($3 million). I informed the lawyer that I wouldn't alter my word. I said I would *not* take that number once we selected the jury. The lawyer pleaded with me, explaining that she really needed to resolve the case. The number was fair to my client, but I wanted to be a man of my word, knowing I would be dealing with that lawyer for decades to come. So with a chuckle, I told her the new amount—$3 million and one penny. She took the penny out of her purse, handed it to me, and said her client would pay the $3 million.

I'm glad that God is a God of kept promises. I rely on God's promises to love, nurture, protect, forgive, provide, and care for me and those I love. God's promises lace the pages of Scripture, and he is true to his word. As Bob Dylan sang so bluntly, "God don't make promises that he don't keep" ("When You Gonna Wake Up," 1979).

But there are two sides to God's promises. God promised blessing on Israel as Israel walked in obedience. Israel was to be God's blessing to the world, showing the beauty and holiness of God. This promise was clear in Leviticus 26:3–6: "If you walk in my statutes and observe my commandments and do them, then . . . you shall eat your bread to the full and dwell in your land securely. I will give peace in the land." Yet in Hosea's time, Israel had become as worldly as the next country. There was nothing special about Israel that positively imaged God to the world around them. They walked into the other side of God's promises. In the same Leviticus 26 speech, God said, "But if in spite of this you will not listen to me, but walk contrary to me, then I will walk contrary to you in fury, and I myself will discipline you sevenfold for your sins. . . . I will lay your cities waste and will make your sanctuaries desolate" (vv. 27–31). Today's passage confirms God is a God of promises. That can be good. It can also be a wake-up call!

Lord, I need to walk in your grace and mercy, each day. In your name, amen.

AUGUST 14

Ephraim was a trained calf that loved to thresh, and I spared her fair neck; but I will put Ephraim to the yoke; Judah must plow; Jacob must harrow for himself. (Hos. 10:11)

Among the most overused clichés in the movies must be "We can do this the easy way or the hard way." The phrase is in the lighthearted *Back to the Future Part II* and the thriller *The Patriot*. But my favorite is in the kid's show *SpongeBob SquarePants* when SpongeBob says, "Now, Gary, we can do this the hard way or the easy way. Or the medium way. Or the semi-medium-easy-hard way. Or the sort-of-hard-with-a-touch-of-awkward-easy-difficult-challenging way." The phrase works because it's true. Some things are easy, yet people choose to make them hard.

Today's passage teaches the lesson even though it doesn't use the cliché. Calves were beasts of work in Hosea's day. They functioned as tractors, plows, harvesters, threshers, and all sorts of other ancient machines. A well-trained calf could be used on the threshing floor. Here the young cow was often not even yoked but was tasked with walking around the threshing room floor and trampling the grains underfoot. This would separate the kernels from the stems. The cow would even be allowed to eat as it did its work. It was good, fruitful work and resulted in happy, well-fed cows! The passage indicates that this was Israel (called Ephraim here) in her early years. God didn't have to place a yoke on Israel's "fair" neck (a "strong" neck).

But cows that weren't so trained had yokes placed on their necks. They were set to plow the fields. These cows wouldn't be given pleasant, productive tasks where the animals can walk at leisure, eat at leisure, and still accomplish their work. These cows had the harsher, more controlled jobs where the master strictly governed and oversaw the hard work of pulling plows through dirt and fields. This was what Israel had become.

God doesn't ignore you and me. God is not simply tuned into the world, binge-watching as one does a show. God has a vested interest in humanity. He calls you and me to participate in his kingdom and his work. His people can do so in pleasant obedient ways, or he will discipline us and bring us into obedient service. It's our choice. We can do this the easy way or the hard way!

Lord, I want to be productive for you. I want to know and do your will in my life. Help me, please. In your name, amen.

AUGUST 15

Sow for yourselves righteousness; reap steadfast love; break up your fallow ground, for it is the time to seek the LORD, *that he may come and rain righteousness upon you.* (Hos. 10:12)

I was four years old and living in Abilene, Texas. Mom told me about gardening. We had a little part of our backyard where Dad had removed the grass. Mom told me we were going to put tomato seeds in the ground. They would grow into plants that would give us tomatoes to eat. Mom also explained that Native Americans would prepare the ground by placing parts of fish into the soil to enrich it. I wanted to put a can of tuna fish in the dirt, but she told me that wouldn't be necessary. So I dug a little hole, placed a seed in it, and went back the next day to look for tomatoes. She then taught me the lesson of patience, explaining the time needed for growth.

Mom was showing me the principle in today's passage. You reap what you sow. Israel was being taught by the prophet, in words that speak to people of all ages, that if you sow for yourselves righteousness, you reap steadfast love. Righteousness (*tzedaqah*—צְדָקָה) is an important Hebrew word with a wide range of meaning. It includes our English ideas of honesty, justice, and loyalty to God and community. Living right before God produces "steadfast love," another important Hebrew word (*ḥesed*—חֶסֶד). It includes our ideas of loyalty, faithfulness, goodness, graciousness, and much more. We should all hope for such a harvest!

To get this steadfast love, we need to sow the right seed of righteousness. We also need to get our ground ready to receive it! For me, that might still include a can of tuna, but the passage "breaking up the fallow ground" is a metaphor for getting myself in a position to do what is righteous. This is self-work. This isn't something that I wait for others to do. The job is mine.

I think that ground is broken for sowing righteousness by setting aside all pride and hubris and coming before God in humility, expressing regret for our sins and disobedience. Then we can seek his help in living right before him, following his instructions on how to be holy in the midst of an unholy world—how to be in the world but not live like the world. God will then rain righteousness upon us in all that it means—honesty, justice, and loyalty included.

Lord, I repent of my sin and seek your help in righteous living. I can't do it without you, but it is the desire of my heart. In your name, amen.

AUGUST 16

You have plowed iniquity; you have reaped injustice; you have eaten the fruit of lies. Because you have trusted in your own way and in the multitude of your warriors, therefore the tumult of war shall arise among your people, and all your fortresses shall be destroyed. (Hos. 10:13–14)

People who know me well know I loathe nutgrass (scientific name, *Cyperus rotundus*). These sedges are weed grasses that escape most common weedkillers. They have this little nut that is often two to three inches under the ground, and from it grows a thin stem into a weed grass. You can pull the weed up, but nine times out of ten, you will leave the nut, and the weed grows back almost instantly. What is worse, the nut sends out minute tendrils horizontally to establish new nuts and weeds. Once you get one nutgrass, you're about to get a bunch, and good luck getting rid of them.

The metaphor in today's passage reminds me of my hatred of nutgrass. Hosea speaks of Israel at a time when Israel had for many years plowed iniquity. They were now harvesting injustice. Think about that for a moment. The problems for Israel didn't spring up out of nowhere. They were their own worst enemy. They went to the trouble to prepare a field, but instead of sowing it with good seed, they threw in a bunch of weeds! It's like me planting a garden and, after getting it ready, throwing in a bunch of nutgrass kernels. When you think about it, it's idiocy, and it permeated their society. They were all eating the "fruit of lies."

At this point, Hosea moves beyond metaphor into clear facts. Israel had trusted in its own way, including its own army. One might pause here and say, "Wait a minute, is *that* that big a deal?" Answer: YES! Trusting in oneself rather than rooting one's life in trusting God is planting a small kernel of nutgrass. It may seem to be a little thing, but from self-trust over God-trust comes reliance on our own wisdom rather than on God's wisdom. Selfish priorities take over. Right and wrong begin being defined in day-to-day life by what benefits the individual. Wake up, and one day the entire garden is overrun with nutgrass. In Israel's case, the tumult of war was arising. The people who trusted their own judgment over God's were going to reap the consequences.

I see a clear lesson for myself here. I want to lean on God, not myself. What a pity to go to all the trouble to sow a field and sow it with weeds!

Lord, illuminate my eyes to your ways. I trust and pray in your name, amen.

AUGUST 17

When Israel was a child, I loved him, and out of Egypt I called my son. The more they were called, the more they went away; they kept sacrificing to the Baals and burning offerings to idols. (Hos. 11:1-2)

Adam and Eve messed up, no doubt about it. They were told clearly by God, as they were placed in God's garden, about their great liberty and opportunity. They were to work and watch over the land and could enjoy all of God's delights, except for one tree. That one tree belonged to God, and they weren't to eat from it. Yet one day, they decided to steal God's fruit and, in blatant disobedience, live beyond their boundaries. As God had foretold, that brought about death to them both—spiritual death and the beginning of their physical death. God removed them from paradise but not without making a promise. From the offspring of Eve would come one who would crush the serpent's head.

As Scripture continued, God made clear his blessing for the earth would come through Abraham, then Isaac, then Jacob. God's promise was not thwarted by the Israelites' subsequent sojourn in Egypt. While Israel languished for four centuries in Egypt, they grew into a nation. Then when the time was right, God called them forth. In love, God kept his commitment and called Israel out of Egypt as a son. As God said to Pharaoh through Moses, "Thus says the LORD, Israel is my firstborn son, and I say to you, 'Let my son go that he may serve me'" (Ex. 4:22-23). God had a grand purpose for Israel. He also provided Israel with an amazing opportunity. The Israelites could fulfill their role through blessing, or they could opt for God disciplining them and thereby squeezing them into fulfilling their role.

Israel was called out of Egypt as a son but too often chose the path of rebellion. In Hosea's day, they were repaying God's goodness with their own foolishness, thinking themselves wise while chasing fake substitute gods. They failed miserably in the process. The Christian writer Matthew contrasted Israel in Hosea's day with the Jewish Jesus. Matthew references the second part of verse 1—"out of Egypt I called my son"—noting that Jesus came from Egypt choosing faithful obedience rather than flagrant disobedience.

Like Israel, I often have a tendency to take God's blessings and disregard his will for how I walk in those blessings. This is a mistake I don't want to make. I need to focus on gratitude and obedience; God calls me to trust and obey.

Lord, let my focus be truly on you. May I walk in your ways and name, amen.

AUGUST 18

Yet it was I who taught Ephraim to walk; I took them up by their arms, but they did not know that I healed them. (Hos. 11:3)

When I was contacted by the American Association of Justice and told that they wanted to give me their lifetime achievement award, the first two thoughts that crossed my mind were truly, "Am I that old?" and "Have they run out of people to give it to?" I suspect the answer to both was "Yes!" I remember well my days as a young lawyer. I thought God had called me into law and had instilled in me the talents for what I was to do in the courts of justice. Yet at one point, I lost several cases in a row. I was reeling, thinking I had chosen the wrong career. I thought I was useless and lacked the necessary skill set. I remember precisely where I was when I expressed to God my exasperation, asking him to please teach me, to help me, to place the right people in my life to mentor me. I didn't want to continue. I was fearful of getting the lifetime loser award!

As I went in for the ceremony, I realized that God had answered those prayers. God had taught me to walk, even to run, in his will. That doesn't mean I didn't lose more cases. I certainly did. But through them, I learned more and more that as I walked in God's will, I walked in his blessings.

My life isn't unique. My life isn't made by me. God is at work, and I get to continue the most amazing journey that he orchestrates. This story should be true for everyone. As today's passage points out, it was God who grew Ephraim (one of Hosea's pet names for the northern kingdom of Israel). But over time, Israel's gratefulness and obedience dissolved into blindness. Israel began to think they had navigated their own ship. Any role divine help had played, Israel assigned to fictional gods.

If I scoff at Israel, thinking them fools, I have taken a step down their road. I have begun thinking myself responsible for the blessings in my life. As if I know better, as if I respond to God better, as if my memory and gratitude exceed those of others. Here lies pride and hubris. Here sin crouches at the door.

God is the source of all life's blessings and all of our good accomplishments. He gets all lifetime achievement awards. We get to humbly say, *thank you!*

Lord, we are honored to get to follow you. May we walk in your blessings as we pray in your name, amen.

AUGUST 19

I led them with cords of kindness, with the bands of love, and I became to them as one who eases the yoke on their jaws, and I bent down to them and fed them. (Hos. 11:4)

On one great family vacation, many of our grandchildren came along. We had five age two and under. During that time, it was all hands on deck. One day, a number of the parents were out, and Becky and I were playing zone defense, trying to take care of the children. The next day, my back was a bit sore! With toddlers, almost everything happens within a few feet of the ground. I had to bend over to play with them, to change their diapers, to give them a snack, and of course, to pick them up. Maybe that is why I pause at today's verse in Hosea.

God is continuing a metaphor of the Israelites but with a slight shift from a child he has reared to a young animal he has cared for. In the prior verse, God spoke of teaching Israel (a.k.a. "Ephraim") to walk, of lifting them, of healing them. In today's passage, he adds that he led them with cords of kindness and bands of love. This is a tender way of rearing and training a baby animal. God didn't rear them with a shock collar. He led them gently. He used "cords of kindness," which literally means "human cords." (English has the same play on "human" with an animal when we speak of treating an animal "humanely.") He made life comfortable for Israel.

What is more, God "bent down" to feed them. This shows the effort of God. God didn't leave Israel to their own devices. The holy and awesome God bent down. At his own cost, he worked to help Israel and meet their needs. This is the loving and caring nature of God, who is willing to nurture his children at his own expense.

As part of the overall book of Hosea, I find this passage stunning. It shows the compassion of God among a people with a very rebellious and callous heart. God prospered Israel, but they credited pagan gods. God corrected Israel, but they ignored his correction. God punished Israel, but they sought help from foreign powers. All of this God did in loving-kindness, bending down to love and care for them.

I want to learn from this. I want to respond to God's care. I want my arms uplifted for God to bend down and pick me up.

Lord, teach me, and give me a willing spirit to learn. In your name, amen.

AUGUST 20

Assyria shall be their king, because they have refused to return to me. The sword shall rage against their cities, consume the bars of their gates, and devour them because of their own counsels. (Hos. 11:5–6)

On October 13, 2016, the Swedish Academy announced the awarding of the 2016 Nobel Prize in Literature to American singer-songwriter Bob Dylan. They credited him for "having created new poetic expressions within the great American song tradition." For over fifty years, Dylan was a thoughtful lyricist, giving insights into life through his work. One of my favorite albums was 1979's *Slow Train Coming* and the song "Gotta Serve Somebody." The Bob (as he is affectionately known in the Lanier household) explained that no matter who you are or what your station is in life, you have to serve the devil or the Lord. You have to serve somebody.

God's people in 700 BCE were no exception. God had called Israel to service. Israel had responded in a covenantal promise that they would serve God and him alone. Over time, the descendants of that original covenant changed their minds. They decided that they would go a different direction. They served the gods of their day rather than the God of their fathers.

Hosea told the people that they weren't going to be on their own. While God had promised them autonomy among the world's governments, that independence came with serving God. If the people weren't going to serve God, his protection and their liberty would evaporate. This doesn't mean that they were freewheeling through life. As Bob said, they were going to serve somebody!

In today's passage, Hosea speaks for God when he declares the people will be serving the king of Assyria. If they weren't going to serve God, they were losing their independence. War was coming, and they were going to be the losers.

I don't fear Assyria today. But I do know that I'm going to serve somebody. I can choose to serve the Lord, or I can go it alone. But "alone" means that I'm serving the enemy, and it will not go well with me. I don't understand why I have trouble thinking in these terms in the daily decisions of life. I can choose God, or I can defy him. Those are my real choices, and they have real consequences. I gotta serve somebody.

Lord, I commit to serving you, but I need your help. In your name, amen.

AUGUST 21

My people are bent on turning away from me, and though they call out to the Most High, he shall not raise them up at all. (Hos. 11:7)

Over my lifetime, I have been blessed to work with a lot of people. At my law firm, many of the folks are incredibly smart, with degrees from some of the best schools in the country. It is an honor to work with them. Interestingly, however, one of the very best people working at my firm is a woman who went to college, but I was never clear on whether she graduated. Her school isn't a famous academic institution. Sometimes it makes the list as a top party school, but that is about it. This woman has worked for me longer than anyone else at the firm—well over three decades. Why?

When I assign a task to this person, she gets it done. It's that simple. I don't need to follow up, I don't need to guide her through it, and I don't need to worry she will drop the ball. It's like the old commercial: I set it and forget it.

This admirable trait was missing from Israel in Hosea's day. They weren't pursuing God and his goals; they were turning away from him. They never said this to God, but it's what they did. They paid God lip service.

The expression "lip service" first appeared in English print in the late 1500s. It developed into an expression for those who would pray with their mouths but stray in thought and deed. Another early usage, in 1662, has it in conjunction with Jesus quoting the Old Testament prophet Isaiah: "This people honors me with their lips, but their heart is far from me" (Matt. 15:8; Isa. 29:13).

I don't want to give God lip service. I want my life to be authentic and real. God knows my heart. He sees my deeds. He knows my imperfections and blemishes, but he also knows whether I am trying to follow him or not. I want my efforts, my choices, and my actions to be consistently true to him.

I may not have attended the best school or have the best pedigree or résumé, but I have a heart and life to give to God. He deserves nothing less. No lip service, just genuine serving.

Lord, may my life reflect my words as I seek to follow you truly. In your name, amen.

AUGUST 22

How can I give you up, O Ephraim? How can I hand you over, O Israel? . . . My heart recoils within me; my compassion grows warm and tender. I will not execute my burning anger; I will not again destroy Ephraim; for I am God and not a man, the Holy One in your midst. (Hos. 11:8–9)

My buddy Vaughan periodically sends out email quizzes. Recently he sent one that asked, "What is the missing number in this series? 1, 64, 125, 216, 729, 13,824, 15,625, _____, 132,651." I tried a bit before Googling the answer (117,649). I'm still not sure how that's the answer, but alas, some things are hard to understand.

God isn't always easy to understand either. Oh, in some ways, he's as clear and basic as two plus two is four. Yet there are times when human words, human thoughts, and human experience fail us in understanding or explaining God. God isn't some supersized human or a megacomputer program. He's a being that is beyond all we know. After all, he knows the past and future of all things and fathoms all we think and feel. How could anyone know this God?

No one can understand God fully. But that doesn't mean that we can't understand him truly. For he has revealed himself through the universe as well as his direct communication in Scripture. But sometimes the under-standing is tough. The interpretation of Scripture isn't restricted to human language, with all its limitations. At times, it requires considerations of human experience. In discerning important truths about God, we must read using common human expressions and thought forms.

Today's passage illustrates the point. How can an unchanging God, an omniscient God, seem to fluctuate like the weather? At one point, his heart is cold; at another point, it grows warm and tender. His "heart recoils," or in an equivalent English idiom, "God changes his mind." How can that happen?

These are human expressions to explain that the unchanging God is compassionate and has plans and desires to win the hearts of people. He has always been that way. To human eyes, his redemption of his people after first punishing them may seem to be a change of heart, but it's really the consistent nature of a compassionate, loving God. It's the logical number in a series, even if I don't understand it fully.

Lord, your ways are beyond me, but I trust your unchanging love. In you, amen.

AUGUST 23

The LORD has an indictment against Judah and will punish Jacob according to his ways; he will repay him according to his deeds. In the womb he took his brother by the heel, and in his manhood he strove with God. (Hos. 12:2–3)

Someone dear to me works on a minimal salary plus commission. Recently, I asked him how work was going. He told me that his company had just pulled out of two major jobs. Those two jobs accounted for half their revenue and half his commission. "I am a bit freaked out," he told me. The next day, I was talking with Becky, my wife. We were both concerned for him. I decided to tell this young man about the many times where I had no idea when our next nickel might come in. Yet in it all, God was *more than* faithful. He always provided in abundance, all while he taught me to rely on him.

Past acts of God's faithfulness should help inform our present. Today's passage is a graphic illustration. Buried in the twelfth chapter of Hosea, the prophet appeals to the historic ancestors of Israel. Israel as a people descended from Abraham through his son Isaac. Isaac had twins, Esau and Jacob. The second twin, Jacob, struggled with his brother, as seen by Jacob coming out of their mother hand first rather than headfirst. It was as if he was "grasping the heel" of firstborn Esau. From this he drew the name Jacob, which derives from the Hebrew word for "heel holder." It also meant to cheat or deceive.

Jacob was a troubled youth. A mama's boy, he was never as solidly in his dad's graces as his older brother, the hunter and man's man Esau. Jacob leveraged his brother out of his birthright and then tricked his dad into giving him the blessing and inheritance of the firstborn. Jacob's mom sent Jacob away to get a wife and mature, while Esau was thinking of killing him. Almost two decades later, Jacob returned, having tricked his father-in-law in the process. (In fairness, it should be added that his father-in-law had deceived him in a major way as well.)

This middle-aged man, whose name could be understood as "Trickster," grew to rely on God. He encountered God in an all-night wrestling match with an angel, and in the end, God gave him a new name. No longer Jacob the trickster, he was now Israel, the father of a nation and one who contended with God but grew from it.

Israel needed to heed that lesson. I need to heed that lesson. I can rely on God, not to keep me where I am, but to grow me to where I need to be.

Lord, give me faith, hope, and trust in you and your name, amen.

AUGUST 24

He strove with the angel and prevailed; he wept and sought his favor. He met God at Bethel, and there God spoke with us—the LORD, the God of hosts, the LORD is his memorial name. (Hos. 12:4–5)

It is false to say the human body regenerates itself every seven years, as I had heard once. But the body is constantly renewing itself. Skin cells rejuvenate every two to four weeks. The liver renews itself every five to eighteen months. Bone regeneration takes around ten years, although that slows as we age. As I type this, I can figure most of the thirty trillion cells in my body aren't the same ones they used to be! My body changes as much as my mind!

God isn't that way. God is the same today, yesterday, and tomorrow. Today's passage bears that out. The passage flows from yesterday's passage, where the prophet uses the ancient ancestor Jacob as a model for how Israel should grow out of rebellion and into a vibrant faith walk with God. But in this passage, Hosea illustrates an important truth placed in the original account of Jacob and God. God changed Jacob's name to Israel but did so as a revelation and confirmation of God's name as "YHWH" (יהוה). This name is almost always translated as "LORD," using all capital letters to distinguish it from the general Hebrew word for "lord" (as in a human master) or "Lord" (as one may use when addressing the king or another superior).

This name was of utmost importance to Israel. One of the Ten Commandments is not to take the name of the Lord "in vain," meaning lightly. For millennia, careful Jews wouldn't even pronounce the name. In the existing copies of the Hebrew Bible—copies that date back over the last thousand years—there are special marks (vowel signs) that indicate how to pronounce the words in a language whose alphabet is made up only of consonants. Yet these manuscripts don't have the vowel sounds for the name of God because no one was to be pronouncing it.

I am certain that many thinking Israelites and Jews would have thought about the meaning of God's name. The letters YHWH would have indicated a meaning of either "I am" or "I will be." They are one and the same. For God doesn't change. Israel needed to learn that lesson. The God of Jacob was still God over a thousand years later. He is the same God today. This is the God I want to learn about, even as my cells keep changing!

Lord God, I praise you as the unchanging God. I rely on you as the keeper of your promises and the one constant in life. I praise and pray in your NAME, amen.

AUGUST 25

"So you, by the help of your God, return, hold fast to love and justice, and wait continually for your God." (Hos. 12:6)

I read through the fantasy genre at an early stage in life, starting with *The Chronicles of Prydain.* Gobbling up not only *The Lord of the Rings* and *The Chronicles of Narnia* but also the *Earthsea* trilogy, *The Wheel of Time,* and all books in between, I read more fantasy genre books than I can remember. I devoured them. My kids' generation entered that genre through the *Harry Potter* series. The genre is alive and well today.

Many people love the ideas inherent in fantasy books. They escape into another world, closer to *Alice in Wonderland* than reality. It's a world of imagination loaded with things that are impossible in our world. I like this escapism. (It's found also in the science fiction genre, which is popular in books and movies.) But in enjoying the escapism, I must never confuse it with reality.

The Bible isn't a book of fantasy or science fiction. It isn't rooted in a fictional world where up is down and down is up, where little is big and big is little. It's a real-world book with authentic life. I recognize that God works miracles, as the Bible records. Some of those miracles involve making something out of nothing. But more often, God's miracles are the effects of his moving hand in the real stuff of the world. God was going to use Assyria, for example, to conquer Israel and teach them necessary lessons. God didn't create a fictitious army of invaders.

This real-world stuff of Scripture is where I find God in my life today. As a younger man, I wanted to experience biblical miracles. Like Elijah, I wanted to call down God's devouring fire to prove his realness. I wanted to see the Moses who brought water out of rock. But those rare miracles from God's hand are few and far between in the Bible. Most of God's working is in this world, as his hand moves in the hearts and minds of people. God walked Israel from Egypt to the Promised Land. He didn't beam them there a la *Star Trek.*

This truth is rooted in today's passage. God was working in Israel to turn their hearts. He wanted their return to love and justice. He wanted them to rely and wait on God. This is what real-world life is about— real actions, real decisions, and real results. I can enjoy fiction, but I want to live in reality.

Lord, give me an authentic walk with you in this world. In your name, amen.

AUGUST 26

A merchant, in whose hands are false balances, he loves to oppress. Ephraim has said, "Ah, but I am rich; I have found wealth for myself; in all my labors they cannot find in me iniquity or sin." (Hos. 12:7–8)

A number of years back, a food company hired me to evaluate its food practices and see whether it had any legal exposure for how it did business. In the United States, food and its labeling are governed by law. If a package says it has twelve ounces of product, then it must have within a margin of error of that twelve ounces. If a label says that a product serving has 180 calories, then the product has to be within 10 percent of that 180 calories.

Food weights and measures have been issues for almost as long as human civilization. In Hosea's time, people bought much of their merchandise by weight. Scales were used to measure spices, price bread and meat, and more. If a merchant used a false scale, it would increase the merchant's profit to the detriment of the purchaser. This is dishonesty at a fundamental level.

The passage today speaks to cutting corners. Merchant scales were balances where the product was placed on one side and weights on the other side. Merchants who used false weights could make an extra profit from each transaction. There were no government regulations on scales, so no one was catching them! Their falsely earned wealth would enrich them, while no person was readily able to point to their sin.

As Hosea pronounced this, however, he made it clear that the merchants weren't really getting away with it. God saw their cheating. God was calling them to account. Under God's eyes, no one cheats and gets away with it.

Several of our daughters run marathons. Becky and I love to go watch and cheer, finding ourselves better at supporting than running! Marathons are just over twenty-six miles, and with a course that long, there are plenty of places where the runners could cut corners, shaving just a bit off their time and distance. That is cheating, of course, and would be a basis to disqualify anyone who tried.

In my life, in my dealings with others at work, at home, with the IRS, and in the grocery store, I need to be careful. Cutting corners is wrong. Period.

Lord, open my eyes to where I need to be more diligent in life. In your name, amen.

AUGUST 27

I spoke to the prophets; it was I who multiplied visions, and through the prophets gave parables. (Hos. 12:10)

I'm not a Wikipedia fan. On the surface, it looks like a community encyclopedia where people in the know can write, edit, and publish facts that keep it utterly current. In actuality, I have found it agenda-driven on many important topics, with editorial control held by a shadowy troop of unknown people. I have found so many entries that are both wrong and biased, yet attempts to edit those entries are unwound by some anonymous police force that has absolute control. If I'm going to rely on something, I want to know its source, and I want to know it's authoritative.

Hosea's prophetic announcements and the many metaphors in his book are not Wikipedia. These are the ramblings of some fellow from the 700s BCE. Hosea was a high-fidelity speaker. He was accurately reproducing the words of God. The metaphors he used—for example, God as a husband and Israel as an adulterous wife—weren't ingenious ideas created by Hosea. They were God's metaphors. (The Hebrew word translated as "parables" could also be translated as "similes and metaphors." It is the Hebrew *damah*—דמה, and it covers a range of meanings in which one thing is indicated to be like or resemble another.)

Because we live in an era when almost everyone has an available Bible, and multiple translations can be accessed via the internet, we might lose sight of how profound and important God's words are. The Almighty God, King of kings and Lord of lords, Maker of the Universe, the unchanging, unfathomable Spirit, decided to speak through a fellow living in the hills of ancient Israel to a people who had strayed far from who they were meant to be.

God's words were so important that he uttered them through Hosea, even though he knew the first generation of listeners would by and large ignore it. Their importance lies especially in the coming generations, including people like you and me, and is the reason these words and metaphors are studied in this book. These words are the basis for the devotional encouragements and warnings written here. We aren't looking at some internet page of questionable origin. We are absorbing the important words of God!

Lord, thank you for the words of Scripture. Thank you for making available to us pictures and images of your love and concerns. May we read with open minds and hearts. In your name, amen.

AUGUST 28

Jacob fled to the land of Aram; there Israel served for a wife, and for a wife he guarded sheep. By a prophet the LORD *brought Israel up from Egypt, and by a prophet he was guarded.* (Hos. 12:12–13)

When our son was two, he was adept at climbing out of his baby bed. I had visions of him falling in the process, so I decided it was time to get him a "big-boy bed." Without much money to go buy a new bed, I thought I could make one out of a bit of lumber, reusing the mattress from the crib. My hope was to get him a bed for less than twenty dollars! The problem was I didn't have many tools at the time. I got the bed made, and it worked, but I readily admit it was laughable to look at! The task was important, but I didn't have the tools and know-how to do it well.

So it is with today's passage. In the beginning of Scripture, God placed Adam and Eve in a garden and gave them two tasks: to "work" (*'avad*, עבד) and "keep" (*shamar*, שמר) their abode. "The LORD God took the man and put him in the garden of Eden to *work* [*'avad*; emphasis mine] it and keep [*shamar*] it" (Gen. 2:15). In time, Adam and Eve sinned and left paradise, but their charge never changed. They were told to continue their work, but now instead of the ease of Eden, they would be working among thorns and thistles (Gen. 3:17–18). So it was in the time of Jacob, as indicated in today's passage, and so it was in the time of Hosea.

Hosea uses these two paired words—*work* and *keep*—when speaking of Jacob. This patriarch had gone to the land of Aram and found his desired wife, Rachel. To get Rachel, Jacob had to serve her father, with "work" and "keep." The word *keep* is translated as "guard" here, which is what Jacob did with the sheep.

The passage then takes a slight turn with the example of Moses and the exodus from Egypt. There, God did the work of bringing Israel out of Egypt, using Moses in the process. God was at work in Moses to guard or "keep" the people. This turn in the passage reminds me of something important. In the work and keeping I have to do among the thorns and this-tles of this world, I can rely on my own efforts, resulting in limited success. Or I can do it hand in hand with the power, insight, and direction of God, resulting in godly success! That seems a no-brainer to me. He will give me the tools and know-how to achieve his will in my work, all to his glory. We can glorify God in everything from making a bed to making a life.

Lord, please give me wisdom and strength to work for you today. In you, amen.

AUGUST 29

It was I who knew you in the wilderness, in the land of drought; but when they had grazed, they became full, they were filled, and their heart was lifted up; therefore they forgot me. (Hos. 13:5-6)

In 2013, Forbes ran an article entitled "Money, Sex, Power: How to Get Plenty of One." The article speaks of the desire for those three objects as great motivators, things that few have but many want. The author added that typically, if one can get one of the three, then the other two will soon follow. He then went on to tell people that the power of being a good negotiator will help you acquire one, and then you can get all three. What was never addressed in the article was whether one should even seek the three desires. He spoke of them as great motivators but failed to give any context for why they are good to have.

Today's passage reminds me of why those three desires need to be treated carefully in life. The root of today's passage, especially in its broader Hosean context, is that prosperity made Israel proud, and their pride became an accelerant to their downfall. God explains in these verses that Israel started with nothing. In the land of drought, all they really had was a God who knew them and sought to take care of them. Then prosperity came, and in their pride, the people spent their energy patting themselves on the back and forgetting God.

It's axiomatic that when we have levels of success, we are walking a tightrope in our reliance on God. When I'm broke, I cry out to God for the next meal. When I'm enriched, I don't need to cry out to God for the next meal. I may not even think to thank him for it. When I'm alone, I cry out to God for companionship. But as I get companionship, I don't feel that need to call out for God's presence. When I'm abused or rejected, I cry out to God to sustain me and to deal with my enemies. But when I have authority and people are under my thumb, I might deal with them as I choose and see no need for God to teach me how.

Having money, sex, and power is not always a bad thing. They have a time and place. They have a purpose. But how we deal with them and how we decide whether to chase after them depend on whether they have become our god or we see them as tools God has given us to bless and nurture others. Prosperity is never the goal. Serving God is always the best road, whether we're rich or poor or somewhere in between.

Lord, may I seek to serve you above all other things. In your name, amen.

AUGUST 30

Return, O Israel, to the LORD your God, for you have stumbled because of your iniquity. Take with you words and return to the LORD; say to him, "Take away all iniquity; accept what is good, and we will pay with bulls the vows of our lips." (Hos. 14:1-2)

Legos—what an invention! Those little plastic blocks create sensational projects. Bellaire, Ohio, is home to a Legos museum of sorts (the "Toy and Plastic Brick Museum"). The museum contains works by "brick artists," people whose artistic works aren't watercolors or acrylics but simply blocks built one by one. Our son and several of our grandchildren found Legos fascinating and were able to follow the instructions and build spectacular items. Every Legos set came with step-by-step instructions. That made the work—if not easy—at least easier.

Step-by-step instructions should always help us in whatever we endeavor to do. Of course, those instructions only work if we follow them. Today's passage sets out God's instructions to a wayward people who need to change their lives.

It begins with "return!" The Hebrew word (*shuv*—שׁוּב) is used twenty-three times in this short book. It forms a drumbeat that keeps playing throughout the book. It's the word of U-turns. It speaks of changing course. Israel was to stop, turn around, and go back to what was right. This is what all should do as they wander in their service to God. Walking away from God and his purposes for your life is the quickest way to stumble, as the passage also relates. So the Lego instructions begin with "Stop! Turn around!"

The instructions then say to take "words" and return to God saying, in essence, "Forgive me!" This is the next step in repentance. First, we stop what we are doing and turn our lives around. Then we confess our sin to God and know that he is faithful to forgive us.

Too often, when God's children get caught up in sin, they stumble through a vicious cycle of more sin. God's plea is simple. Return to him in heart and mind. Say true words of regret, and show yourself penitent. This is the beginning of getting right with God. These are instructions for building back a relationship.

Lord, I confess my sin to you. Take away my iniquity, and help me follow you in word and deed. To your credit, in your love and your name, amen.

AUGUST 31

"Assyria shall not save us; we will not ride on horses; and we will say no more, 'Our God,' to the work of our hands. In you the orphan finds mercy." (Hos. 14:3)

Growing up in Lubbock, Texas, we always went to the Bailey Bookstore for religious books. I was fifteen when I bought my first Bible on my own. Walking through the section on Greek and Hebrew books gave me the original desire to get a degree in those languages. The store also had a records section. I was introduced to a whole new genre of music. Albums by new artists like Keith Green, the 2nd Chapter of Acts, and others soon touched my life. I also bought two albums from another group called Lamb. Featuring the voice and songwriting talents of Joel Chernoff, who in my adult life would become a friend, these were Jewish works but based on a belief that Yeshua (Jesus) was the Messiah.

A number of Joel's works were songs half in Hebrew and half in English. Many of them also were just Jewish Scriptures (the Old Testament) put to music. The album *Lamb III* featured a number of songs that were based on Hosea. After a beautiful song entitled "Ephraim," which is rooted in Hosea 11, comes a song "Eli Eli," built around a Hebrew phrase, *Eli, Eli, Eli y'didi*, which means "My God, my God, my God my beloved." Aside from the irony of this protestant *goy* (non-Jew) walking around singing a Hebrew song in his mind, the English portion of the lyrics rightly touched my heart.

Joel sings of "my God" as "my light in times of darkness. My strength in times of weakness. My joy in times of sadness. My God my God, my God my beloved. A Father to the fatherless. The comforter to sorrowing. The singing of the nightingale, my God my God, my God my beloved." That is the root of today's passage. It's the root of truth in life.

Our light in darkness, our strength in weakness, our joy in sadness—none of this can really come from anywhere other than God. Not just "God" but a personal relationship with God: "*My* God. *My* beloved." Don't look to the works of your hands to be God. Walk with the one true God. In walking with God, the orphan finds family. God makes the crooked way straight. God gives direction to the lost. God lifts up the fallen. That is *Eli, Eli, Eli y'didi*—my God, my God, my God my beloved.

Lord, may I hearken to your word and embrace your love. In your name, amen.

SEPTEMBER 1

I will heal their apostasy; I will love them freely, for my anger has turned from them. (Hos. 14:4)

Anyone who followed baseball had to love the many expressions of Yogi Berra. Humor stood front and center in statements that were also insightful. "Baseball is 90 percent mental," he would say, then adding, "The other half is physical." Or I always liked this Yogi-ism: "You can observe a lot by watching." Or in speaking about a restaurant, "Nobody goes there anymore; it's too crowded." Perhaps his most famous expression, however, was "It ain't over till it's over." That statement has found its way into pop culture through movies, songs, and general conversation. It also applies to today's passage.

Hosea is nearing the end of his prophetic proclamations. The book has contained a vast swath of insights into the many moral cancers plaguing Israel, explaining the work God would need to do to cut those cancers out. The judgments about to befall Israel were severe and necessary. But as Hosea nears the end of his proclamations, he does so indicating that God wasn't going to bow out of the picture after these judgments. God wouldn't allow the story to end there.

Instead, God was going to turn the page after the judgment on Israel. The purpose of the judgment wasn't the destruction of God's people. God brought judgment with another purpose in mind. The judgment was necessary to get God's people back on track. God was going to write another chapter. God would return to heal their apostasy. God would be dispensing love freely and bountifully as his repulsion to their sin was satisfied. In Christian teaching, this is seen most clearly in the blessings of God's people following the final punishment of sin in the death of Jesus.

I like that God doesn't end his story with sin winning out. In my personal life, I have seen God's hand extend his mercy to me, even in my life with sin that needs his strict attention. He isn't looking to destroy you or me. He is seeking to heal us. The Hebrew word here for "heal" is *rafah* (רפא), the word for healing from disease. Wrapped in this expression is another Hosea metaphor seeing apostasy and sin as a sickness, a cancer. The cancer may be destructive to the uttermost degree, but with God the Healer, it ain't over till it's over. When it is over, God will be in victory, and his people will dwell in his loving-kindness.

Lord, thank you for loving and healing me through my sin. In your name, amen.

SEPTEMBER 2

Whoever is wise, let him understand these things; whoever is discerning, let him know them; for the ways of the LORD are right, and the upright walk in them, but transgressors stumble in them. (Hos. 14:9)

Travel books and articles often highlight scenic trips. Some are stunning drives, while others are great train rides. Regardless, these lists highlight not only a destination but the journey to the destination. Driving up the Pacific Coast Highway in the western United States is one such stunning drive. So is the Amalfi Coast in Italy. Its beauty can be appreciated not only during a drive but through spectacular photos and videos on the internet.

For an extended time in this book, I have taken the reader on a drive through Hosea. The views are striking and impressive. They aren't always views that are easy on the eyes, as the judgments and declarations of Israel's apostasy are decidedly blunt. But seeing the sins motivates me, even as sadness stirs my heart.

A reader of Hosea might think, "Oh, those foolish Israelites. If only they had heeded the word of God." Twenty-three times the book used the word *shuv*, seen in our English words as "repent," "turn away," and "return." Why was it so hard for Israel to do that? Why couldn't they just come to their senses? If we read the book and then leave the conversation saying, "Those tragic folks!" then we have missed a major purpose—if not *the* major purpose—of the book. The book and the prophecies were recorded for *us*, the readers!

Here in the last verse of Hosea, the prophet makes this clear. "Whoever is wise, whoever is discerning" should hear and heed the book's message. It wasn't simply a projection of what was going to befall Israel. It was a cogent and compelling account of the gravity of sin, the way sin infiltrates one's life as well as the culture and society. The subverting power of sin that blinds the eyes of sinners isn't innocuous. It's a rancid disease that requires serious treatment. That treatment comes from God and will be as thorough as necessary to allow people to live in God's love.

With that journey in hand, the reader is encouraged to take life seriously, to learn the abhorrence of sin, and to find the ways of God. Walking in God's will and righteousness is the voyage of a great lifetime.

Lord, may I walk in your joy and holiness today. In Jesus, amen.

SEPTEMBER 3

The word of the LORD *that came to Micah of Moresheth . . .* (Mic. 1:1)

Do you know the word *clickbait*? It is an internet word referencing something you see that causes you to click on a website. It might be a picture or a headline, but it's the enticement that prompts you to click on the link. For example, I saw a picture of the inside of a van that stunned me! The van looked like a living room in a nice house. I thought, "Who is selling *that* van? That is way cool!" I clicked on the title that went with the picture: "Incredible vans for sale." The title took me to a website populated with normal, everyday, run-of-the-mill vans. Nothing like the picture existed. That said, sometimes the title or picture is real. It isn't just something to trick you into going to a website. That real deal is what we see in these first words of the prophet Micah, especially in the original Hebrew.

The English translation faithfully reproduces the Hebrew word order. The book begins in Hebrew with the pronouncement "*devar YHWH*" (דְּבַר־יְהוָה), meaning "The word of YHWH." This signifies the book is one of prophecy. The words are not someone's musings but the very oracles and words of YHWH, the name God assigned himself in the Old Testament when speaking with Moses at the burning bush (Ex. 3:14). Because that name is so holy, our translators do not attempt to translate it, and many will not ever attempt to say it. Instead, it is given the word "LORD," written in all capital letters.

The Hebrew continues, "That came to Micah." In Hebrew, the name *Micah* is a sentence. It combines three different Hebrew words. The Hebrew *mi* means "who," the Hebrew *ca* means "is like," and the Hebrew *h* is shortened from *yah*, which itself is a shortened form of "YHWH," God's name.

Putting this sentence together, now the reader is ready for this book's teaching. This isn't clickbait; this is real content. This book is, in a sentence, a reproduction of the words of YHWH by one whose very name means "Who is like YHWH?" The bold question is answered by YHWH himself.

If I spend time on a van website, tricked by some fake picture, how much more should I readily go to the words of the Lord, when those words are faithfully reproduced? Time spent in Micah is important and transforming. It is a chance to realize the answer to the most important question: Who is like our God??

Lord, show me who you are more and more each day, please. In your name, amen.

SEPTEMBER 4

The word of the Lord *that came to Micah of Moresheth in the days of Jotham, Ahaz, and Hezekiah, kings of Judah, which he saw concerning Samaria and Jerusalem.* (Mic. 1:1)

If I look back on my life, I can find times that were comfortable and relatively stress free. These were days of clear sailing when the proverbial sun was out and the wind was behind me. But I can also remember times that were remarkably different, times as stressful as the other days had been pleasant. These were periods when health, relationships, work, and even school seemed dark and rainy. The storms brought dread and concern and drove me to my knees in prayer. Micah is writing during stormy days.

Micah delivered God's words during the eighth century BCE, at a time when Judah (commonly called the southern kingdom) and Israel (a.k.a. the northern kingdom) faced ominous problems nationally and internationally. The national problems stemmed from the people's overt disobedience. The international problems dealt with Assyria's resurgence. This was a time when Assyria was rapidly becoming the largest superpower humanity had ever seen, using imperial expansion to destroy smaller nations and incorporate their peoples as transplants elsewhere in the empire. Micah was a contemporary prophet with Isaiah, another of God's prophets. Not surprisingly, the two wrote commonly of many ideas and even words in the face of these internal and external issues.

Crisis is a driver. When faced with calamity, options become stark. For some, it brings out the claws. Like a cornered cat, they are ready to fight. For others, it brings out the Nikes. They don't go into fight mode but go into flight mode. Yet others find refuge in pills or drinks, hoping to numb any experience of misfortune or tragedy. For some, the fallback includes "comfort food," indulging in less-than-healthy foods consumed in an excess manner, hoping to find some contentment. Others do therapy shopping.

Micah reminds us that God speaks into our crises. When confronted with the deep problems of life, we needn't flee or fight, and we don't need to find refuge in a bottle, pill, donut, or shopping mall. Instead, we go to the word of the Lord. God will give direction, comfort, and above all else, peace. Sometimes God's words may not be the most pleasant, but we can be assured that they're precisely what we need.

Lord, speak to me and give me open ears and heart to listen. In your name, amen.

SEPTEMBER 5

Hear, you peoples, all of you; pay attention, O earth, and all that is in it, and let the Lord GOD be a witness against you, the Lord from his holy temple. (Mic. 1:2)

The thousands of lawsuits over the dangerousness of Vioxx were the focus of my practice for years. I had to try cases from Texas to New Jersey. Our disputes lasted over a decade. After my first trial, the company hired a new star witness to bolster their defense. I needed to know why this witness was expected to be so effective, so I had him carefully researched. We discovered his academic qualifications were strong, and he spoke with a charming Scottish accent, but I thought his ideas of science and medicine were out of whack with the most reputable sources. He was also relatively unknown in the field. Learning that, I wasn't worried. He didn't help the company one bit.

Contrast my experience in those trials with the trial about to begin in the book of Micah. (Yes, Micah is writing about an ancient trial like we might see in our courts today.) The earth is on notice, the trial is about to begin, and the star witness is none other than God himself. In the verses that come after today's passage, Micah details that God will descend from his holy abode to tread upon the earth. In his presence, the mountains will melt, and the valleys will split apart. God is no ordinary witness.

Today's passage serves as an attention-getter. The reader or listener is about to hear the word of the Lord. When God's word comes forth, we have a few choices. We can ignore it and pretend it isn't there, we can look at it and maybe even think and talk about it, or we can respond to it, honoring it in our lives as we seek to live under it.

Recognizing that God will be the ultimate witness should get our attention. It should be a sharp wake-up call. The voice of God isn't to be ignored or made simply a matter of discussion. We should attentively seek to make it the goal of our day and the measure of our life.

This causes me to read Scripture in a focused way. I always want to understand Scripture rightly, discerning what it meant in its original setting, but I also want to hear what it says to me. I should never be satisfied with anything less.

Lord, may your word captivate my heart and direct my life. In your name, amen.

SEPTEMBER 6

All this is for the transgression of Jacob and for the sins of the house of Israel. What is the transgression of Jacob? Is it not Samaria? And what is the high place of Judah? Is it not Jerusalem? Therefore I will make Samaria a heap in the open country. (Mic. 1:5-6)

In modern court proceedings, different people have roles. The lawyers represent the parties at interest. The judge presides over the proceeding, announcing the ultimate judgment and applying the law to the facts as given. Sometimes juries decide the facts; sometimes judges do (the parties can pick either option). Witnesses play the role of testifying to what occurred. They are the keys to establishing the facts. Each of those roles is distinct.

But ancient trials in Israel and Judah weren't held in a courtroom; they were typically held in the city gates. The jury or judge would come from the city or town's elders. The witnesses would give testimony, questioned often by the judges themselves but also by the parties or their representatives. As the hub of activity, the city gates as a setting would ensure that the trial got public attention and everyone would know what was going on.

In that typical scenario, Micah begins his prophetic book with a trial. But in this trial, God plays two different roles. God is both the key witness and the judge. God will be testifying against the people, and he will then assess and enforce the punishment.

This is quite provocative if one steps back and considers the larger world. During this century, Rome was founded—an event with a massive footprint on history. The Greek colonies were established, setting in place a language and people that would permeate culture and the Bible. In the Far East, the Zhou capital at Hao was destroyed by barbarians who killed the king Yu. In Egypt, the Kushite ruler Piankhi sailed down the Nile and took control of Egypt, establishing the Twenty-Fifth Dynasty. And while all of this was going on, God was descending to testify against a small, hilly nation in a corner of the Middle East, with judgment in hand.

A lot of events are happening in the world today. But I should never think that God has his hands full. God cares about you and me in our corners of the world. He is witness, judge, protector, mentor, Lord, God, and friend all rolled into one.

Lord, thank you for your love and care. May I live responsively. In you, amen.

SEPTEMBER 7

All her carved images shall be beaten to pieces, all her wages shall be burned with fire, and all her idols I will lay waste, for from the fee of a prostitute she gathered them, and to the fee of a prostitute they shall return. (Mic. 1:7)

A number of years back, we had a case that was rooted in deception. The opposing side produced millions of pages of documents, and I had a team responsible for combing through those millions of pages to find critical documents that would prove the bad conduct. The investment to get to the root of the behavior and find the proof would be sizable. Someone asked me once how I could be so confident that we would find proof of the misconduct, and my reply was simple: "You can't practice vice virtuously." It was clear to me that the conduct was reprehensible, so the evidence would bear that out. You couldn't have done such dirty work with clean hands.

Today's passage has a similar message. God was pronouncing a judgment and destruction upon Israel, but it didn't come out of thin air. Israel had long before sown the seeds of conduct being judged. The vices of Israel had not arisen mysteriously. They were products of an underlying vice.

In the words of the prophet, Israel had gathered her idols, prosperity, and resources through sordid means. In today's parlance, they were "ill-gotten gains." In Micah's parlance, they were "fees of a prostitute." Micah used expressions well understood in his day, although not as readily in ours. He wasn't saying that all Israel had accumulated and all they had invested in their idols were generated by prostitution income. He was saying that Israel hadn't been faithful to God. Israel dallied with other gods and sold their fidelity to God's laws for what they could gain in their immediate lives. Those vices were going to be destroyed.

No one can practice vice virtuously. When we invest in things of this world, they will meet the end of things of this world. They will decay, rust, and fade away. That is why God calls us to invest in him and his ways. God endures forever. His ways are ways that last. His faithfulness and steadfast love should be our guiding lights as we walk in response to him.

I have choices today. I can make godly choices, or I can go in my own direction. Each choice will bear its own fruit.

Lord, may I build my life on you, not the vices of the world. In your name, amen.

SEPTEMBER 8

For this I will lament and wail; I will go stripped and naked; I will make lamentation like the jackals, and mourning like the ostriches. For her wound is incurable, and it has come to Judah; it has reached to the gate of my people, to Jerusalem. (Mic. 1:8–9)

Tragedy comes in all shapes and sizes. The word itself comes straight from the Greek (*tragōdia*—τραγῳδία), which was a drama or play where horrible events cause human suffering to the main character. These horrible events can befall an individual, family, community, and even nation. These events rightly bring forth lamenting and wailing.

In writing this devotional, I reflect on my life, and I invite the readers to think through their lives. Recalling tragedies, I also recall my reaction to those events. Like the prophet, I have lived dark days of sadness and tears. I have not cared about my appearance. I have hurt. This is true for almost everyone.

Today's passage authenticates the propriety of lamenting over tragedy. The passage's backstory is important. God gave the Promised Land to the offspring of Abraham on the condition of living under God's covenant. After King Solomon, the nation split into two, the northern kingdom ("Israel") and the southern kingdom ("Judah"). In the North, the people and kings had times of prosperity, but they rejected God's covenant and chased idols. God sent prophetic warnings to the people, but the prophets were ignored. Then God brought judgment, and most of the people of the northern kingdom were deported.

Undoubtedly, many of the people fled south to Judah as the conquering Assyrian army blistered through Samaria's country. Those people brought with them idol worship and attitudes of rejection of the covenant of Moses. Judah already struggled against those same vices and surely didn't need any help. Micah saw that the fate of Judah was similar to that of Samaria. Judah would also fall to foreign powers. The prophet equates the people's sin to a wound, one that was so serious that it was now incurable.

This situation was rightly a cause for wailing and lamentation. I know I will see tragedy in my life. I am glad that I don't wail without a God of comfort who walks with me even in dark valleys.

Lord, be with me each step of life, I pray. I need your touch. In you I stay, amen.

SEPTEMBER 9

Tell it not in Gath; weep not at all; in Beth-le-aphrah roll yourselves in the dust. Pass on your way, inhabitants of Shaphir, in nakedness and shame; the inhabitants of Zaanan do not come out; the lamentation of Beth-ezel shall take away from you its standing place. (Mic. 1:10–11)

Kevin Parker was legendary in high school. He led a group of folks who took the art of puns to another level. Kevin still punctuates his conversations with plays on words today. He can make a punch line out of almost any word or subject. Most of Kevin's puns are delightful plays that bring a smile or perhaps a groan. Kevin comes to mind and becomes the introduction to today's devotional because Micah here plays the punster.

Micah speaks of the coming punishment of Judah, and he does so with puns. His puns are made on the names of twelve cities that the Assyrian king Sennacherib would encounter in his march to Jerusalem, likely during his invasion of 701 BCE. Unlike my buddy Kevin, Micah isn't making the puns to get a laugh. He's speaking in a memorable way of punishment that is both tragic and lamentable. Not all of the puns are readily recognizable, even to the best Hebrew scholars, but several stand out so clearly that their message can't be missed.

The town Beth-le-aphrah was a sentence name in Hebrew. That name literally meant "House of Dust." Here Micah tells the people in the House of Dust to roll in the dust, an expression of great distress and mourning (see, for example, Jer. 6:26; Ezek. 27:30). The next town mentioned is Shaphir, a word that means "beautiful." Micah details that the people of "Beautiful" will instead be naked and shameful in appearance as they pass over into exile. The next town, Zaanan, is also punned in its name, which means "one who goes out." Yet those people will be reduced to not coming out. They will lose the claim of their name. As for the town Beth-ezel, its name means "House by the Side of Another." Yet it will lose its place of standing.

These puns of Micah's aren't mirthful; they are sorrowful. They speak of ruin and reversal of fortune. All of these puns reflect what happens due to the disobedience of Judah and its people. It's the way of sin. Sin takes the promised blessings of God and what could be and contorts them into a destructive reminder of God's goodness. I need to keep this in mind as I make my choices today.

Lord, show me the fruit of my actions. May I walk in you, as I pray in you. Amen.

SEPTEMBER 10

For the inhabitants of Maroth wait anxiously for good, because disaster has come down from the LORD to the gate of Jerusalem. Harness the steeds to the chariots, inhabitants of Lachish; it was the beginning of sin to the daughter of Zion, for in you were found the transgressions of Israel. Therefore you shall give parting gifts to Moresheth-gath; the houses of Achzib shall be a deceitful thing to the kings of Israel. I will again bring a conqueror to you, inhabitants of Mareshah; the glory of Israel shall come to Adullam. (Mic. 1:12–15)

I first translated these passages under the watchful eye of Clyde "Mad Dog" Miller. Now, I should add that no one called him "Mad Dog" other than me, but he was rabid for the Hebrew text! I was the only student in the Minor Prophets class. It was a chore and delight. One of the fun moments was working through these pun passages of Micah. I have each day been quoting from the wonderful English Standard Version. Yet if the Hebrew town and city names are translated into their English meanings, the passage takes on a bit more of its Hebrew shine.

One could easily translate the first of today's verses as follows: "For the inhabitants of Bitterness Town (Maroth) ache for pleasantness, as calamity has come upon them from the Lord, even to the gate of Jerusalem." The name of the town Lachish makes a Hebrew pun of "harness the steeds to chariots," as the word for "steeds" (*larechesh*) sounds like the name *Lachish*. Lachish was the second largest city in Judah, next to Jerusalem. Micah describes it as the head or beginning of where the sins of the northern people of Israel had first appeared.

Moresheth-gath is Micah's hometown. The name *Moresheth* sounds like the Hebrew word for a dowry or gift. So the prophet puns that the town of dowry itself will be the gift, departing for captivity to the conquering king. Achzib is akin to the Hebrew word for "lie" or "deceit." One might translate this passage as "The houses of Deceptionville will themselves be a deceit." In other words, that town and its people will be of no help in staving off the conquering army. As for Mareshah, that town name is similar to the Hebrew for "possessor" or "conqueror." That town would itself be conquered.

While I enjoy the translation task, I'm also wary of the text's message. How we live before God gives true meaning to our lives, even if it turns them upside down. I want God's goodness expressed in my life.

Lord, use me to spread your message of fullness and peace. In your name, amen.

SEPTEMBER 11

Woe to those who devise wickedness and work evil on their beds! When the morning dawns, they perform it, because it is in the power of their hand. They covet fields and seize them, and houses, and take them away; they oppress a man and his house, a man and his inheritance. (Mic. 2:1–2)

My schedule can vary greatly day by day. But many days are what I consider "normal." On those days, I get up and get ready, read my Bible and work on my devotional, eat breakfast, and start work. During the day, I try to get in my allotted work and some exercise and juggle in a bit of interpersonal time (phone calls). As the day winds down, I have dinner with family, finish up a few chores, and read, relax, or catch up with the internet. Of course, in our electronic age, I also monitor emails and texts well into the evening. My goals each day fold around the priorities of faith, family, work, and friends.

Today's passage highlights the actions of another approach to life. The passage shines the spotlight on wealthy and powerful people who take the quiet downtime of night, and instead of relaxing and investing in their family and friends, they contemplate how they can accomplish evil deeds that meet their sinful desires. Specifically, the subjects of Micah's warning were men who were trying to think of how to seize the land that belonged to the families of others.

A bit of context is helpful. God set up a legal scheme where all of his people—the Israelites—were entitled to land. The land was distributed based on family units. This land was to stay in the families' hands and, if pledged away, was to be restored during years of Jubilee. This was one of the obvious ways that God demonstrated to the Israelites that God valued each and every one of them, not simply the successful ones that the world often values.

In Micah's time, certain rich and resourceful people were subverting God's plans and values. God pronounces his "woe" upon them. These people may have been gathering earthly wealth but not because God was blessing them. To the contrary, God saw woe coming their way.

I don't live with Micah's land laws, but I still live where I can choose to value people or use people to further my selfish desires. I need to spend my time at night figuring out how to help others, not take advantage of them.

Lord, give me insight in healing and helping others. In your name, amen.

SEPTEMBER 12

Therefore thus says the LORD: behold, against this family I am devising disaster, from which you cannot remove your necks, and you shall not walk haughtily, for it will be a time of disaster. In that day they shall take up a taunt song against you and moan bitterly, and say, "We are utterly ruined; he changes the portion of my people; how he removes it from me! To an apostate he allots our fields." (Mic. 2:3–4)

I don't believe in reincarnation—that an individual's soul comes back in another life-form over and over. The religions that teach this usually link the next incarnational form to how well a person lived in the previous life. This is generally termed *karma*. Now, while I don't believe in reincarnation karma, I do believe in what one might call *cosmic karma*. God has set up a system in this world where what one does echoes back in life. I have seen this over and over. It is also shown in today's passage.

The people against whom Micah is prophesying have heaped sin upon sin, all in arrogant and selfish disregard of God's clear law and instructions. The sin that Micah is highlighting was discussed in yesterday's devotional. This sin destroyed society's inheritance and property ownership system to enrich the powerful at the cost of the typical person. God says not only will this not be allowed, but if the nation won't enforce God's laws, God himself will enforce them by punishing these bad deeds.

The punishment God was promising to mete out is the punishment that was fitting to the crime. In arrogance, the powerful were pulling property away from certain victims. In turn, God was going to destroy the property holdings of these perpetrators. God would take their wrongly acquired fields and give them to these apostates. The schemers themselves would suffer, as they had caused suffering to others.

Not all suffering in this world comes about because of our bad deeds. But some does. We sometimes bring some damage upon ourselves by our sinful actions. Yes, God is loving, and he is certainly merciful. But God is still one who doesn't countenance pride, selfishness, and sin. He doesn't feed the beast. He brings the beast to heal. Call it cosmic karma, or call it the justice of God. Either way, we should never think he turns a blind eye to our evil.

Lord, forgive me, and teach me to walk rightly before you. In your name, amen.

SEPTEMBER 13

"Do not preach"—thus they preach—"one should not preach of such things; disgrace will not overtake us." Should this be said, O house of Jacob? Has the LORD grown impatient? Are these his deeds? Do not my words do good to him who walks uprightly? But lately my people have risen up as an enemy. (Mic. 2:6–8)

I was interviewing a marvelous godly woman who had been through a devastating marriage. Her ex-husband had continually beaten her up, once sending her to the emergency room with a broken nose. She finally divorced him after one of the times he tried to kill her. I was interested in her comment that ten days before her wedding, she was confident that while she was praying about her prospective marriage, God had communicated to her that she shouldn't marry her fiancé and that he wasn't the right husband for her. She said that God also indicated that he knew she was going to go ahead with the marriage anyway. She then went through with it, thinking, "Oh, it may not be right, but God will be OK with it." She felt like a fool later.

This was one of many tragedies that befell her in life. She went on to get degrees in theology and specialized in studies on God and suffering. I have never discussed today's passage with her, but I can guess what she would say.

In today's passage, Micah quotes the very people he is preaching against. Micah is telling certain schemers of evil that God will bring their evil back on their heads. He is telling them, "Rest assured, what goes around comes around!" The schemers didn't want to hear it. Ironically, they were preaching to Micah, "Don't you preach to us! It isn't right to preach such things!" It's as if they were saying, "God is letting us do this, so it must be OK with him. Quit saying God will judge us and bring calamity our way! God is loving and patient!!!"

Yes, God is loving and patient. But God also stands up for those wronged by the sin of others. God also stands for righteousness and blesses those who bring peace. God is not beguiled by our mental gymnastics that let us get away with contortions of right and wrong. God's eyes see right through our actions and motives. His gaze pierces into the heart of the matter. We may not want to hear it, but if we don't listen, like the woman I interviewed, it is to our own detriment. God wants the best for us and will not tolerate our sin when we set ourselves against him and his will.

Lord, I don't want to be against you. I want to live for you. In your name, amen.

SEPTEMBER 14

If a man should go about and utter wind and lies, saying, "I will preach to you of wine and strong drink," he would be the preacher for this people! (Mic. 2:11)

Shows are remarkably different today from when I grew up. In my youth, most houses had one television, which was fine because there were only three real stations. (We didn't count PBS.) Furthermore, there were certain days when people stayed home in the evening because they didn't want to miss that night's shows. If you missed them, you might not get a chance to rewatch them, and there was no internet to tell you what you missed.

The world is very different now. We sit around and discuss what good shows are out there and then can binge-watch them whenever we choose. With such a wealth of shows on ready demand, some homes have tons of screens so people can watch whatever they choose whenever they wish. In a way, this had become the state of religion in Micah's day. Let me explain.

Israel started their independence as a nation with one God, the Lord who revealed himself to them and then rescued them from the Egyptians. On Mount Sinai, God entered into a covenant with the people, promising them their land and his blessings in return for their devotion to only him. He gave them the laws to govern life and behavior. They agreed to the covenant and thus began their life in the Promised Land. God would send his prophets to correct and aid the people in life.

But years grew into decades and centuries, and the generations changed over and over. In time, the people left their commitment to the Lord and began selecting a different voice from the Lord's as their source for life's decisions. No longer were the prophets of God held in high esteem. Instead, people based their choices and walked according to the instructions of whoever told them what they wanted to hear. As today's passage reads, if someone told them, "Life is better if you get drunk!" the people would choose that person as their preacher to follow.

We have choices about where we get our guidance and what to do. God's voice is one of many options. God may not always tell us what we want to hear, but he will always tell us the road that blesses life most. Yet too often, I feel we treat life like TV. We choose what we want and claim that is the right way. Not good!

Lord, may I hear and follow you and not be seduced by other voices. In you, amen.

SEPTEMBER 15

I will surely assemble all of you, O Jacob; I will gather the remnant of Israel; I will set them together like sheep in a fold, like a flock in its pasture, a noisy multitude of men. (Mic. 2:12)

Have you ever messed up? Really messed up? Sometimes we make mistakes, and they are fixable. We may need to backtrack, apologize, or do some repair work. But there are occasions where the error is so great that there is no fixing it. Sometimes, Humpty Dumpty's fall is so great he's smashed, and everyone's best efforts can't put him together again.

Here is where God shines brightly. When all the king's horses and all the king's men can't put aright that which has been broken, God can work his ways. This important biblical principle is laced throughout the stories and narratives of the Bible, and today's passage is a classic example.

Destruction was around the corner and wouldn't be avoided. The victorious king would be dispersing Israel to the ends of his kingdom, knowing an unsettled people are less likely to rebel in the future. When you lose your neighbors, culture, religious moorings, and resources, it's difficult to organize and revolt. Israel would be a strange people in strange land. Their life as a nation and their culture as a common people was as gone as gone could be. Truly, Israel's sin had taken them past the point of return. A simple "I'm sorry, God; let's start all over" was not in the cards.

Yet God wasn't going to let Israel's punishment be the end of the story. Israel may have thrown themselves off Humpty Dumpty's proverbial wall to their own great destruction, but God is a God who repairs and restores. God had a plan in place even before the nation's fall. God would use the destruction of Israel as a winnowing process, finding a remnant of people who would live in covenant with him and bringing them back together.

This is the way of God. You and I can mess up, and God will be able to work out a Plan B (or in my case, he is on at least Plan ZZZ). God has his fallback position ready to go for those who turn and call on him with a sincere heart. I have seen God do this over and over in my life. I wish I were better at walking in his presence, but I seem to have Humpty Dumpty syndrome. Thankfully, God the King is better than his horsemen at putting things back together!

Lord, I confess my sin and error. I seek your help in living life. I pray in you, amen.

SEPTEMBER 16

And I said: Hear, you heads of Jacob and rulers of the house of Israel! Is it not for you to know justice? (Mic. 3:1)

My first job was throwing newspapers. Next, I worked in a convenience store. Following that, I managed an apartment complex. My final job is as a trial lawyer. I remain in that job today. My goal in throwing papers was to get the paper on the front porch by the door of each customer each day. My goal in the convenience store included ensuring stocked shelves, clean products, rapid service, and a till that balanced at the end of the day. As an apartment manager, I collected rent, filled vacancies, and got problems repaired. In the legal field, I am to pursue justice.

American courts are fashioned for justice. Sometimes they seem to favor the rich, who can hire teams of legal talent, but the judges presiding over the courts are supposed to be impartial. Judges are rightly doing their job when they ensure a level playing field. Courts aren't supposed to be tools of oppression or playgrounds for the resourced few to trample over those who are weaker. Instead, courts should be bastions of right and wrong, giving justice to everyone, regardless of wealth, race, nationality, gender, education, occupation, or social status.

Some of America's biggest societal changes have been wrought by the courts. In 1954, the Supreme Court's landmark decision *Brown v. Board of Education* pronounced that racial segregation in America was unconstitutional and opened up schools to everyone, regardless of race. This decision reflected a judicial attempt to fulfill the American pledge of "justice for all." It was pronounced by a court, but it dealt with everyday life.

Today's passage doesn't refer to American courts but does refer to everyday life. People are to treasure justice. Yes, it starts with the rulers referenced in the verse, but those rulers were presiding over people living ordinary lives. The rulers were to oversee justice when the people failed to achieve it on their own. This means when I delivered papers, I should have given people their due: a paper on their porch. Doing so was justice. As a clerk, I wasn't to pocket the money meant for the register, nor was I to overcharge the customer. This was justice. As a manager, I was to fill vacant apartments with good renters as soon as I could, not wait simply because it wasn't my money. This was justice. God wants all his people to live justly. May I do so!

Lord, give me eyes and a heart for justice. In your name, amen.

SEPTEMBER 17

You who hate the good and love the evil . . . (Mic. 3:2)

Over two thousand years ago, the Greek philosopher Plato wrote up a dialogue his teacher Socrates had with a young man named Euthyphro. The irony of the dialogue is found in the young man's name, Euthyphro, which in Greek means "a straight or rightminded thinker." The young man Euthyphro, however, was anything but. In the story, Socrates is headed to court to be tried for corrupting the youth of Athens. Euthyphro is a corrupted youth who is headed to court to push for his father to be tried and convicted for alleged bad deeds. In another twist of irony, Socrates tries to reform rather than corrupt Euthyphro.

Early in the dialogue, Socrates seeks to have Euthyphro define what is good and what is evil. Euthyphro tells Socrates that his court case against his father is good. Socrates dismisses that answer by pointing out that Euthyphro is merely offering an example of good, not a definition. Euthyphro then tries defining good as what is pleasing to the gods. Socrates reminds Euthyphro that the gods often disagree, so that definition also falls flat. Euthyphro then tries the position that what *all* the gods love is good, while what they *all* hate is evil. Socrates then famously asks, Is the good good because the gods love it, or do the gods love it because it is good? This question, "Euthyphro's dilemma," as it is termed, has become one of the most debated ethical questions in history.

Today's passage speaks to moral ethics, but not as Socrates and Euthyphro did. Today's passage reflects the biblical teaching that the one true God has determined what is good. Good is part of who God is, part of his very character. Goodness is interlaced with what will bear the greatest fruit for people in their lives, resulting in fulfillment and peace. The problem Micah points to is that people didn't accept that good. Instead, they sought to define good by what they wanted and liked. In this way, the people would call what is good *evil* and what is evil *good*. This was a tragedy of biblical proportions (literally).

Since what is good is actually what God has designed as healthy for people and society, when the people redefined good by their own desires, they and their society headed away from good into evil. This moral lesson reminds me that my goal should be finding what God says is good and pursuing that. I must carefully avoid that human tendency to consider something good because it's what I want.

Lord, give me insight into your nature and your good. In your name, amen.

SEPTEMBER 18

Then they will cry to the Lord, *but he will not answer them; he will hide his face from them at that time, because they have made their deeds evil.* (Mic. 3:4)

One of my buddies called me in tears. He was a single parent who had sent his daughter off to college. She was a smart, kind young lady who seemed well on the road to success. Yet in college, things took a terrible turn. She fell in with the wrong group, dropped out midsemester, and started down a road of drugs. This devolved into a sordid life with things too wretched to detail here. At times, she would call her father, but only when she wanted money. My friend knew he couldn't fund her reckless, dangerous life. He lived in fear that one day, a call would inform him of her death.

I am reminded of my friend's pain as I read today's passage. Read on its own, the passage seems to fly in the face of the biblical teaching of God. It reads that the people will cry to the Lord and that God will ignore them. It makes the reader wonder, "Don't we have a forgiving God? Doesn't he await the call of his people to answer them in love?" Space prohibits me in this short devotional from putting the whole context into place along with the verse.

But context is important here. Earlier, the prophet used metaphors to show what the people were doing, and the metaphors sound atrocious. Micah spoke of the people tearing the skin from God's good people, ripping the flesh from the bones and eating it, then breaking up the bones and making soup from them. These people were deeply disturbed. Like my friend's daughter, they were only calling to God to ask for something that would propel them further down the road of destruction.

My friend knew better than to give his daughter money when that money would be spent not on rent but on drugs. He couldn't support his daughter's life choices at that time. He wasn't going to feed the beast.

So it is with God. When the repentance isn't genuine, when God is sought at times and in ways simply to further a broken life and its poor choices, God won't answer. God doesn't feed the beast. My friend's daughter reached the end of her road and, in despair, truly repented. My friend was there at that time. Similarly, we can be assured that God does answer the truly repentant, giving life in the face of despair. That is our loving God.

Lord, keep me near your heart. May I pursue you earnestly. In your name, amen.

SEPTEMBER 19

Thus says the LORD concerning the prophets who lead my people astray, who cry "Peace" when they have something to eat, but declare war against him who puts nothing into their mouths. Therefore it shall be night to you, without vision. (Mic. 3:5–6)

As the owner of a business (OK, a law firm), I sometimes read articles and books on good business practices. One day, I came across an article entitled "Why Entrepreneurs Should Never Hire a Yes-Man (or Woman)." It presented a number of great reasons to avoid hiring those who will always agree with the boss rather than give their own judgment and reasons. The article made sense.

When people say only what they think others want to hear, judgment gets skewed. The wisdom and resulting success that come from honest discussion and debate get lost. Today's passage is a riff off the same idea, and it shows the dangers of disingenuous attitudes.

Micah lived in a day when a prophet was often a paid profession. People were paid, often by the government, to declare what God (or the gods) thought best. These were the government's "go-to" wise men. These were the folks that people could ask to seek the gods on their behalf. Micah pointed out that the nation had false prophets who weren't speaking the truth, really seeking God, or really hearing from God. Instead, these were yes-men, in their own way.

As long as these so-called prophets were well-fed and paid, they would say whatever anyone wanted to hear. They would predict peace and prosperity regardless of what was true. When the prophets weren't paid, their counsel took a darker turn. Advice hinged not on truth but on the payment offered.

This passage reminds me of the importance of genuine friendship. Everyone needs people around them—at work, at home, and at play—who speak candidly. I don't want friends who tell me what I want to hear. I don't want workers who think all my ideas are brilliant. I don't want a preacher or teacher to pat me on the back and make me feel good. I want to hear truth. It will help me build a better life, do better work, be a better husband and father, and better pursue God. And I want to be the kind of person who truthfully, lovingly, and gently speaks into the lives of those I touch.

Lord, help me to be genuine and loving in my relationships. In your name, amen.

SEPTEMBER 20

But as for me, I am filled with power, with the Spirit of the LORD, and with justice and might, to declare to Jacob his transgression and to Israel his sin. (Mic. 3:8)

Superman has been a show in one incarnation or another for over seventy-five years. In *The Adventures of Superman*, the announcer began the show by proclaiming, "The adventures of Superman. Faster than a speeding bullet! More powerful than a locomotive! Able to leap tall buildings in a single bound!" Superman was able to save the day, despite all that was going wrong. He would use his superpowers to change the course of rivers, bend steel with his hands, and in one movie, fly around the earth so fast that he reversed time itself. Many a kid pretended to be Superman (or Superwoman) at some point growing up.

Contrast Superman with the prophet Micah. Micah was also filled with power and might, being infused with the Holy Spirit. Micah's superpower, however, wasn't to move a river or bend a gun. Micah had the superpower of proclaiming the word of God. Micah was empowered to preach justice, proclaiming to Jacob and Israel their moral failures before God.

Today's passage impresses me in multiple ways. I am fascinated and challenged by the Scripture's teaching of what Micah's superpower was. My tendency is to see power as doing something more visible. A powerlifter can muscle big weights. A superpower is seeing through walls, disappearing into thin air, or being able to stretch out beyond physical reach. In contrast, the power of the Holy Spirit to proclaim the word of God is scarcely visible, if at all. Yet Scripture clearly indicates this is a potent power.

Another impression from this passage is how important the word of God is in everyday life. God's word has the power to soften one's heart and realign one's mind and give willpower to the weak, comfort to the hurting, inspiration to the deflated, value to the dejected, direction to the lost, shelter from the storm, mercy to the wounded, humility to the proud, and more. By hearing and applying the word of God, we receive power to live godly lives. This superpower can alter humanity and change the course of history.

This passage makes me want this superpower. I want the Spirit of God to enrich my life as I seek to understand and follow God's word.

Lord, empower me with your words and your Spirit. In your name, amen.

SEPTEMBER 21

It shall come to pass in the latter days that the mountain of the house of the LORD *shall be established as the highest of the mountains, and it shall be lifted up above the hills; and peoples shall flow to it.* (Mic. 4:1)

It was shortly after 6 a.m., and I was headed to the office. My first order of business, before a full day of work, was praying through and writing two of these devotionals, starting with today's verse. While still in the car, I got a phone call everyone dreads. One of the firm's talented young lawyers died unexpectantly the night before. He was playing with his four- and two-year-old daughters when he abruptly collapsed and died.

Tragedies like this are hard to grapple with. They stun us with the pain and grief that befall the family and all of us who knew and loved the person. They show the frailty and brevity of life. They affirm our need for God's love and care, even as they challenge us to understand God. They leave us helpless to aid the family, except for by showing them love (hopefully in practical ways) and praying for them.

Today's passage gives a measure of comfort to the hurting as well as insight into God. Micah has spent the last chapter writing about the severe impact of God's coming judgment on Israel. His language was difficult, as he proclaimed, "Zion shall be plowed as a field; Jerusalem shall become a heap of ruins." Unlike my young lawyer, Israel had brought judgment upon themselves. They had rebelled against God and violated his justice with utter disregard to how it affected others. Yet even after proper judgment, God speaks of his future work as positive, uplifting, and beautiful. Judgment doesn't win; it doesn't end the story.

God stands on the other side of death, despair, and desolation. God wins over misery, anguish, and distress. This was true in ancient times, and it is true today. It was true in the national identity surrounding Jerusalem and the Jews, and it is true in our individual lives.

As the future unfolds, the grief from the unexpected death of my lawyer can't be erased from the lives of his family and loved ones. But God doesn't end the story with grief. One day, God can and will still bring joy and peace, even as he promises a future where all his faithful are united in his love and care. I am thankful for that.

Lord, give comfort and solace to the hurting. Give them your peace in you, amen.

SEPTEMBER 22

Many nations shall come, and say: "Come, let us go up to the mountain of the LORD, *to the house of the God of Jacob, that he may teach us his ways and that we may walk in his paths." For out of Zion shall go forth the law, and the word of the* LORD *from Jerusalem.* (Mic. 4:2)

Sometimes my grandmother surprised me. Well into her nineties, she would suddenly quote some Latin sentence she had memorized in high school. When she walked by me while I was working on a crossword puzzle with a pen, she touched my shoulder and gently said, "Mark, it is a sign of arrogance to be seen working on a crossword with an ink pen." Another one of her phrases, which I referenced in an earlier devotional, was the simple proclamation "Truth will out" from Shakespeare's classic *The Merchant of Venice!*

Grandmother knew that truth had a way of coming to the surface. It rarely stays hidden. I think of that phrase as I look at today's passage. It's a positive proclamation from a prophet who frequently pronounced doom to the people of his day. Micah knew and plainly proclaimed that God's story wasn't always going to be one of doom and judgment. God was going to bring about an awesome change. Though Jerusalem might be laid desolate by invaders, a day would come when Jerusalem would bring life and light to the world. Nations wouldn't come to Jerusalem to destroy it; they would come to learn. From Jerusalem, a new age would usher forth God's word to the masses.

History shows the truth of Micah's words. While Israel was invaded and destroyed by Assyria, and Judah suffered a similar judgment from Babylon, restoration did indeed come. From a Christian perspective, this prophetic word saw direct fulfillment in the coming of Jesus, the word of God incarnate—given to all the nations from Jerusalem.

We live in blurry days. It's a bit like a glass of water with silt and mud swirling around. Then God brings peace to the water, the muck settles on the bottom, and the water can be seen clearly. God can do that in our lives. He can work through our messes, bring his peace, and transform our days. These are the genuine lessons we can learn from God. Give God time. Truth will out.

Lord, please take the messes in my life and shine your truth into them. Bring me the truth of your love and peace in your name, amen.

SEPTEMBER 23

He shall judge between many peoples, and shall decide disputes for strong nations far away; and they shall beat their swords into plowshares, and their spears into pruning hooks; nation shall not lift up sword against nation, neither shall they learn war anymore.
(Mic. 4:3)

My daughter called her husband in a panic. They were in a foreign country, and she had gone to the grocery store. She had their four-month-old in her arms and had been pushing the empty stroller. My daughter exclaimed into the phone, "Someone has stolen the stroller!" She had no clue what to do. She was beside herself. Her husband was about to head to the store when Gracie meekly stated, "Oh, here it is. Never mind." She had left it further up the aisle.

Gracie comes by this honestly. As I have referenced earlier in this book, I have a history of misplacing things and being unable to find them. Our family trait comes to mind as I read today's passage. Micah is speaking to God's faithful people, who are to read and heed his words. In this prophetic passage, Micah is speaking about the future. God *shall* judge. . . . People *shall* beat swords into plowshares. . . . Nations *shall* not lift up sword. . . . These were future events for Micah.

But if we look for them in the pages of history, we don't find them fulfilled. These are future events that are still to come. These days didn't go missing. They weren't stolen. They were written but are yet to be fulfilled. These are words of hope that inspire generations. If you go to the United Nations building, you see outside a marvelous sculpture by Evgeniy Vuchetich of a mighty man with a hammer, beating the metal of his warring sword into the metal of a plow to be used in times of peace. This 1959 work expresses the beauty of God's promise here. This promise is found in not only Micah's prophecy but his contemporary Isaiah's similar assurance (Isa. 2:4).

God can and does engage in conflict. He battles evil and its ills. He is against the injustices of the world. He is against the purveyors of wickedness and malevolence. He leads his people to battle evil. Yet he promises an important goal, that one day, those conflicts will cease. God will win over evil, and peace will reign. We glimpse that in our lives, even if we don't see it worldwide. No one has stolen this promise of God. It will come; it's just a matter of time.

Lord, may I join you in your fight for peace, here and all around. In you, amen.

SEPTEMBER 24

But they shall sit every man under his vine and under his fig tree, and no one shall make them afraid, for the mouth of the LORD of hosts has spoken. For all the peoples walk each in the name of its god, but we will walk in the name of the LORD our God forever and ever. (Mic. 4:4–5)

When I was in third and fourth grade, I was often scared at night. I had dreams that were haunting and often had difficulty going to sleep at night for fear of what might happen. Everything from vampires to mass murderers invaded my thoughts. I may have passed that on to at least one daughter, who had trouble going to sleep for fear that a nearby train might leave its tracks and come through her bedroom. The train got no closer than one-quarter of a mile.

Those memories are in the past, but they return, albeit with some humor, as I read today's passage. The verses come in the midst of Micah talking about the future day of the Lord, when all that is wrong will be made right. Amid his description of that glorious time is today's verse: "They shall sit every man under his vine and under his fig tree, and no one shall make them afraid." "Sitting under one's vine" was an ancient expression of experiencing peace and prosperity. And all our fears will disappear. Micah emphasizes the certainty of these promises by declaring, "For the mouth of the LORD has spoken it." In other words, God has said this; you can take it to the bank.

God's promise that we will live in a secured future without fear is comforting. But it also speaks to me about today. This is in the following verse. The reason that people aren't sitting under their vines today, aren't living in peace and prosperity, and aren't living without fear is because they are walking "each in the name of its god." "Name" in Hebrew was more than a title. It meant who you are and what you've done. It was, in a modern sense, your résumé. When we live in the security of anything but the true God, we live an insecure life. Everything in life can fail us. We know the frailty of life, and so we fear much. Yet if we walk or live in the name of the LORD, we are living under the care and instruction of one who is able to secure our hearts and our minds. We have peace. Gone are our fears.

When my nightmares occurred, Mom taught me in those early years to pray. She knew if I sought God, I would find peace from fear. I tried to teach the same to my daughter. In God is peace, and that is a life changer.

Lord, be my strength, wisdom, protector, and guide. In your NAME, I pray, amen!

SEPTEMBER 25

In that day, declares the LORD, *I will assemble the lame and gather those who have been driven away and those whom I have afflicted; and the lame I will make the remnant, and those who were cast off, a strong nation; and the* LORD *will reign over them in Mount Zion from this time forth and forevermore.* (Mic. 4:6–7)

The Holocaust is properly named. Called *Shoah* in Hebrew, the word for "catastrophe," the Nazi regime and their collaborators during World War II enacted a gruesome extermination program that sought to destroy those deemed racial and social polluters of the master race. This horrifying murder scheme killed countless Jews (roughly six million) as well as millions of prisoners of war, Roma people, same-sex-attracted people, Jehovah's Witnesses (who wouldn't swear allegiance to the state), and disabled people, who were called "useless eaters" and "life unworthy of life."

How different was the Nazi approach from God's approach? The Nazis wanted to purify and secure the future by getting rid of those they deemed undesirable. How does God treat those deemed "undesirable"? As today's amazing passage details, God does so differently. God offers love and mercy and is always approachable whether one is deemed worthy or not.

So as this future passage explains, God will not eliminate those who are lame, have been driven away, or are afflicted. Rather, God will take them, bless them, and use them to form a strong nation. These are God's people. As a remnant, they will assume their position as the blessed of God. God isn't purifying his people by some genetic scheme. God is taking what is broken and fixing it.

I love that our God is a God of restoration. It is framed here in the future work he will bring to fruition, but I have seen it in my life too. Over and over, God has taken what is broken, undesirable, and seemingly beyond repair and has made something beautiful, useful, and worthy of respect.

This is God's goodness and steadfast love. He cares for those of us who are hurting, even when the hurt is brought on by our own stupidity. He longs for a people who will lean on him for life. He seeks to restore what is lost and brings value to that which is despised. He does that to everyone who turns to him.

Lord, I turn to you. Give my life meaning. Heal what is damaged, and make me fruitful for your work. Give me a heart for the broken. In your name, amen.

SEPTEMBER 26

Writhe and groan, O daughter of Zion, like a woman in labor, for now you shall go out from the city and dwell in the open country; you shall go to Babylon. There you shall be rescued; there the LORD will redeem you from the hand of your enemies. (Mic. 4:10)

Life choices have consequences. Think of all the sayings brought about by this truth: If you stick your finger in the fire, you're going to get burned. If you want to dance, you gotta pay the band. Don't do the crime if you can't do the time. What goes around comes around. The sayings are plentiful because the truth is obvious and verified over and over. This truth isn't new to the twenty-first century. It was no less true in Micah's day.

Today's passage paints an interesting picture onto that truth. Micah and his contemporary prophets Isaiah, Amos, and Hosea have been prophesying that Israel's and Judah's actions were going to bring their destruction. God had warned his people of the consequences of disobedience centuries earlier through Moses. God had also instructed the people to teach each successive generation this truth. Yet the people had strayed and strayed far. They not only disregarded God's warning, but they engaged in the very behavior that God had warned would bring their downfall. Micah now warns them of the result. The people would lose their homes, their cities, and their towns and would be either deported to a faraway place— Babylon—or be desolated, living in the barren open country.

Micah could have left the story line there. Maybe he would have added a final refrain like "You were warned!" "You brought this on yourself!" "You get what you pay for!" or "You reap what you sow!" Yet that isn't what Micah does because with God, the horrid consequences of our sins don't need to be the final word. God has something more to say, and it isn't "You've got no one to blame but yourself!"

God tells the people through Micah that even though their sin was bringing the consequence, the story wouldn't end there because God is a redeeming God. God is a rescuing God. God is a saving God. God would be at the end of the story bringing his people back into homes, a relationship with him, and a world of blessing and opportunity. I am thankful for this God of redemption. My life would be a wreck without him. But with him, the possibilities are endlessly good.

Lord, thank you for redeeming me. I need your salvation. In your name, amen.

SEPTEMBER 27

Now many nations are assembled against you, saying, "Let her be defiled, and let our eyes gaze upon Zion." *But they do not know the thoughts of the* LORD; *they do not understand his plan, that he has gathered them as sheaves to the threshing floor.* (Mic. 4:11–12)

Confession: I am a word nerd. I love language and words. (Even if you don't, please keep reading! I make a point.) Take, for example, the Latin word *stringo*. The verb conveys the idea of stretching or drawing something tight. Add to it the Latin prefix *di*—which denotes twice, two, or even once every two—and you get the Latin word *distringo*, which in its past participle form is *districtus*. This is the idea of being drawn tightly in two directions. It means being ripped apart. As Latin became more regionally adjusted and slurred, in old France, this word became the Old French *destresse*. In English, it became *distress*. Yes, from its roots, distress conveys the idea of being ripped apart.

Everyone experiences distress in life. We are pulled in different directions. We have pain, suffering, concerns, and longings that seem to stretch our minds and hearts apart. We aren't at peace. We struggle. These are the difficult times in life that we wish we never saw. For those times in life, passages like today's become a balm.

Israel and Judah were going into a time of great distress. They would lose in conflicts with the Assyrian and Babylonian empires. They were going to be driven off into foreign lands and enslaved. They were losing happiness and security.

In light of that future, Micah writes these words to encourage the people and give them hope. While distress was definitely coming, they were not going to experience it in isolation. God was at work. God had plans that would work through and in spite of the difficulties coming their way. God was going to bring his people through their distress into a place of peace.

This is the way of the world and the way of God. In the world, we will have tribulations and distress. Our lives will be pulled apart in many ways. But we need never be pessimistic about it. God is an overcoming Lord whose thoughts and plans are for the ultimate good of his people and kingdom. He will bring peace to those in distress.

Lord, please bring peace to my distress. I need you. In your name, amen.

SEPTEMBER 28

Now muster your troops, O daughter of troops; siege is laid against us; with a rod they strike the judge of Israel on the cheek. But you, O Bethlehem Ephrathah, who are too little to be among the clans of Judah, from you shall come forth for me one who is to be ruler in Israel, whose coming forth is from of old, from ancient days. (Mic. 5:1–2)

I write from the United States, a place where, as of now, people are relatively safe in their homes. In this world, there are people who are displaced from their homes and are refugees on the run. I am thankful for our safety. In contrast to me, Micah prophesied at a time when Israel and Judah were unsafe. Conquering armies were going to decimate their countryside, ransack their villages, and displace their people. Their lifestyles and sin had corrupted their society on all levels and sent them down a road of no return. Horrors were on their way. What made things worse is that rather than returning to God and seeking his rescue, the people pushed the pedal to the floor and accelerated to their own ruin.

Into this certain near-term future, Micah pronounced God's just as certain long-term salvation. These are some of the key verses. The passage begins by noting that the destruction of Israel would hurt but wouldn't be a death blow. It would be a hard smash across the face with an iron rod. But the story wouldn't end there. For God would one day call forth a ruler from Bethlehem Ephrathah. He was a restorer of life, deeply rooted in Israel's past, even from the ancient days.

The prophet is rather specific in this affirmation. Many villages and towns were named *Bethlehem*, a word for "house of bread" or "bakery." But Micah specified one from the region of David. Bethlehem Ephrathah was where Ruth met and married Boaz, as told in the book called Ruth in the Hebrew Scriptures.

To Christians, this passage is understood as a prediction of Yeshua (Jesus), who would come as the Messiah not only to Israel and Judah but to the world. Both Matthew and Luke set the birth of Jesus in Bethlehem, and John references it as well. In Matthew 2:5–6, the wise men quote this verse to King Herod as a reference point to where the Messiah would be born.

God is never out of the picture. In our lives, in our world, God will have the final say. He assures everyone the final say will be his victory. Amen!

Lord, I need your victory in my life, today and every day. In your name, amen.

SEPTEMBER 29

And he shall stand and shepherd his flock in the strength of the LORD, *in the majesty of the name of the* LORD *his God. And they shall dwell secure, for now he shall be great to the ends of the earth. And he shall be their peace.* (Mic. 5:4–5)

The 1960s were turbulent times in the United States. The Vietnam War was responsible for the deaths of over fifty thousand Americans. The civil rights movement saw the assassination of Martin Luther King Jr. The rioting and civil unrest from large swaths of America arose out of mandatory drafts for the war, the unfair life assigned to minorities, and important social issues like why eighteen-year-olds were deemed old enough to die for America but too young to vote. Two Kennedys were murdered in their prime—one a sitting president, the other a leading candidate for that office.

Into this turmoil came a John Lennon song that became an anthem for many protestors. In "Give Peace a Chance," the lyrics included small verses like "Everybody's talking 'bout . . . this-ism, that-ism, is-m, is-m, is-m." But the main mantra of the song, the hook that stays in your brain and was sung across the land, is the repetitious affirmation "All we are saying is give peace a chance!"

Peace is something everyone craves. We want peace from social turmoil. We desire peace among the nations. We long for peace in our families. We yearn for peace in our hearts. We desperately need peace with God, our Maker. Where is this peace to be found? Micah says it will come from God.

Micah proclaims that a day would come when peace would abound. That peace would be full peace in the Hebrew sense of the word *shalom* (שָׁלוֹם). It conveys prosperity, success, and a mental state of health considered "happy" and "well." This peace would come with security. Micah says this peace would come in the future for Israel and Judah, when one would come forth from Bethlehem to shepherd the people and deliver this peace.

Many Jews today await this peace. To the Christian, the peace is found in Yeshua (Jesus), who offers internal peace as well as peace with God. Christians also await the end of days when this peace will expand around the earth. Micah speaks of peace proceeding from God. Only God can bring full and final peace in our hearts, relationships, and world. Everyone should long for God's peace.

Lord, bring your peace into my heart and shine it into the world. In you, amen.

SEPTEMBER 30

And in that day, declares the Lord, *I will cut off your horses from among you ... and I will cut off the cities of your land and throw down all your strongholds; and I will cut off sorceries from your hand ...; and I will cut off your carved images ..., and you shall bow down no more to the work of your hands; and I will root out your Asherah images from among you and destroy your cities.* (Mic. 5:10–14)

My mother-in-law was diagnosed with a pernicious and growing cancer. It was isolated to a section of her body, and the oncologist had a specific treatment regime. It started with surgery. His team went into her body and cut out the cancer. They sought to remove every cancer cell, knowing even one left behind could grow into an untreatable cancer. The regime included chemotherapy and radiation to destroy any unseen cells left behind. It was thorough. She was cured.

This experience and similar stories from others around the globe serve as a metaphor in my mind for how God deals with sin and disobedience. Let me explain.

Commonly termed malignant, cancer is destructive to the body. Left unchecked, it leads to death. Cancer grows and consumes or replaces healthy tissue. Cancer isn't a new invader in the body in the sense of a foreign virus or bacteria (although viruses are known to cause some cancers). Cancer takes normal functioning cells and perverts them, in a sense. Those cells are turned against the body they are meant to fortify.

So it is with sin. Sin is malignant—that is, harmful. Left unchecked, it leads to death. Sin can take what is healthy and distort it, turning it into something horrid. Most sin has its root in a good thing. Eating, for example, is a source of health. Yet the sin of gluttony is eating gone amuck. Similarly, words can be used to build up and encourage another to achieve great things. Yet words can also be used in countless ways that destroy another. In this sense, sin takes that which is good and twists it, distorting it into a perversion.

Today's passage is set in the "God is going to deliver his people" passages that I have covered in the preceding days. Today's passage explains that even in deliverance, God will be at work cutting out the cancer of sin in his people. God will take out the root of the problem. He isn't satisfied with a band-aid on cancer.

Lord, root out my sin, and help me grow in holiness to your glory and name, amen.

OCTOBER 1

"O my people, what have I done to you? How have I wearied you? Answer me!" (Mic. 6:3)

One of the required classes in law school is "Contracts." One of the first questions in that class is whether a valid contract exists. Certain things must be present for an enforceable contract. Among those necessary elements is a "meeting of the minds," which generally means that the parties involved in the contract have agreed on the key terms. Another element is "consideration." This term means that each party contributes something of value or commits to doing something in a contract. Additionally, the parties must have "mutual consent"—that is, they must agree to be bound by the contract. American law didn't invent these elements; they've been around for a long time. Today's passage echoes those elements.

In this chapter of the prophet Micah, God is speaking in the framework of a lawsuit. God is suing his people for violating their covenant, an agreement akin in many ways to a modern contract. The chapter began with the legal "pleading." God indicts or sues Israel for violating the covenant, calling on the hills and mountains as a jury rather than the normal jury of a village's elders. The hills and mountains have been around for a long time. They can be witnesses and jurors with deep historical perspectives. They are also clearly neutral and unbiased.

The basis of the lawsuit is Israel's failure to live up to the terms of the covenant entered into on Mount Sinai under the leadership of Moses centuries earlier. The contract terms had specified actions required by God—to provide, protect, and even punish Israel. Israel had, in turn, agreed to certain rules of treatment of one another, foreigners, and God. But Israel had failed miserably, abdicating justice for selfish gain, doing whatever pleased them in the moment rather than what was right and substituting idolatry for worship of God. The agreement had also said if Israel pursued such a course, God would punish appropriately. In today's passage, God raises a possible defense of Israel. Could Israel possibly accuse God, as if God had done something wrong? Of course not!

Yet this passage leaves me wondering, How often in my life have I made bad choices that resulted in bad consequences and then blamed God? In my self-righteous moments, I might feel God is the one who has failed me, but truth be told, God has never been unfaithful. His mercy is why I am alive today.

Lord, please forgive my failures before you. I seek your love in your name, amen.

OCTOBER 2

"With what shall I come before the LORD, and bow myself before God on high? Shall I come before him with burnt offerings . . . ? Will the LORD be pleased with thousands of rams, with ten thousands of rivers of oil? Shall I give my firstborn for my transgression, the fruit of my body for the sin of my soul?" He has told you, O man, what is good; and what does the LORD require of you but to do justice, and to love kindness, and to walk humbly with your God? (Mic. 6:6–8)

"You don't have to come pick me up at the airport," my daughter told me on the phone. "Traffic will be terrible, and I can get an Uber!" I replied that of course I didn't "need" to. I "got" to! For me, having the chance to do that was a blessing, not an obligation. It brought joy to my heart to serve her and show her my love by making that drive and valuing that extra time with her.

I am reminded of that story as I read today's passage. Israel asks the question of what will satisfy God in the framework of the breach-of-contract lawsuit reviewed in yesterday's devotional. Would God accept as a remedy for Israel's conduct a penalty of burnt offerings? What if Israel offered thousands of rams? Would God be satisfied if Israel gave God ten thousand rivers worth of oil, an extravagant hyperbole? Or what if Israel offered up to God the nation's firstborn children?

In the Old Testament, God had repeatedly instructed Israel to sacrifice rams, goats, and more. God also called on the people to give oil and dedicate their children to him. But those deeds were not the full picture. God's interest was never in Israel doing things out of obligation. God's desire was that Israel's heart of love for him would manifest itself in obedience. Sacrifices weren't so much what Israel *had to do*; they were what Israel *got to do*. The attitude made the difference.

The prophet frames an answer to Israel's question. God laid out what was required of Israel, and it began with the heart. Doing justice, loving kindness, and walking humbly with God are attitude driven. Justice is rooted in believing that others are equally worthy of fair treatment in life. To care about kindness is a heart matter. A humble relationship with God places all of life in its right perspective.

My obedience to God should never be out of obligation. I obey and walk with God out of love and devotion. Like getting my daughter at the airport, it is a blessing, not a burden.

Lord, I love you and want to serve you. May I bless you in your name, amen.

OCTOBER 3

"Shall I acquit the man with wicked scales and with a bag of deceitful weights? Your rich men are full of violence; your inhabitants speak lies, and their tongue is deceitful in their mouth. Therefore I strike you with a grievous blow, making you desolate because of your sins. You shall eat, but not be satisfied, and there shall be hunger within you; you shall put away, but not preserve, and what you preserve I will give to the sword." (Mic. 6:11–14)

I've been in courthouses across the United States. Many of them feature "Lady Justice." Robed in the garb of Ancient Greece, this statue is usually holding a set of scales. The scales are even, neither side weighing more than the other. This is to reflect the foundational truth that justice is an even playing field. In a courtroom, everyone should be treated fairly. What's more, the statue usually is blindfolded, a further symbol of the fundamental fact that justice should be blind, no respecter of persons. Everyone should be treated evenly in a court of justice, or justice doesn't exist.

The most important task of a judge is to enforce fairness and justice. In a courtroom, the rich shouldn't have an advantage over the poor. The connected shouldn't get benefits not accorded to the unconnected. Justice is at its best when it is blindfolded. This isn't a new concept. It's inherent fairness built into our DNA. It's inherent in the character of God.

This leads to today's passage, where God is the judge getting ready to announce his sentencing. Like the judge I spoke of before, God is just and must enforce his just penalty, even though he has a heart of mercy. Hence God asks the hard question, Should he let off a cheat and fraud who is abusing his neighbor for selfish gain? Should God just pat him on the shoulder and say, "Go on about your business, but just try not to cheat so many people anymore!" Should God let the liar continue in lies? Can God condone the violence? No, a just God will not judge unjustly. In God's judgment, the guilty will not enjoy the fruits of their crimes. They may have plenty of food, but their hearts and minds won't find satisfaction.

As a Christian, this passage heightens my appreciation of what God did with the death of Yeshua (in Greek, "Jesus"). The just God transferred the ultimate penalty for my sin onto Jesus as my substitute. He paid the debt I couldn't pay. But this passage puts everyone on notice: our actions have consequences before a just God.

Lord, I pray for forgiveness as well as strength to live better in your name, amen.

OCTOBER 4

"You shall sow, but not reap; you shall tread olives, but not anoint yourselves with oil; you shall tread grapes, but not drink wine. For you have kept the statutes of Omri, and all the works of the house of Ahab; and you have walked in their counsels." (Mic. 6:15–16)

Certain parenting sayings have been around as long as there have been parents. OK, not really, but many parents have found themselves with a child who has done something clearly wrong. At times when that child is corrected for the mistake, the child produces the excuse "But Johnny was doing it!" or "Come on! Everyone does it!" Then comes the eternal parenting line "Well if Johnny was going to jump off a bridge, would you do it?"

One reason the parenting line has been around so long is because the excuse for poor conduct has been to blame each other since the beginning of time. Go back to the garden of Eden story. Adam is before God, confronted with his sin. Adam blames Eve (with a slight dig at God himself): "The woman *whom you gave* to be with me, she gave me fruit of the tree" (emphasis mine). Then when God turned his attention to Eve and questioned her, she deflected also, saying, "The serpent deceived me, and I ate" (Gen. 3:12–13). In Texas colloquial parlance, that dog won't hunt. Excuses are just that—excuses.

Today's passage speaks to the same age-old attempt at deflection. Israel had been walking in great societal and individual sin, rebelling against God, his statutes, and his values. They replaced God's goodness and truth with selfish, destructive lies and idolatry. One might say, "Well, it wasn't their fault. Look at the kings they had!" King Omri was atrocious, having gained the throne by assassinating King Zimri. When Omri died, his son Ahab assumed the throne, leading Israel to even more sin, including even child sacrifice (1 Ki. 16:34). Israelites had choices. They could follow the ways of the evil kings, or they could follow the ways of God, the King of kings.

You and I are confronted with similar choices every day. We can follow the ways of the world, or we can pursue God and his paths. But we have no excuses when we choose the wrong path. The choice is ours. I want to have the strength and presence of mind, the maturity and wisdom to choose rightly.

Lord, I need your strength and wisdom to walk holy. Please lighten my path and give me the vigor to walk it. In your name, I ask, amen.

OCTOBER 5

Woe is me! For I have become as when the summer fruit has been gathered, as when the grapes have been gleaned: there is no cluster to eat. . . . The godly has perished from the earth, and there is no one upright among mankind. . . . Their hands are on what is evil, to do it well; the prince and the judge ask for a bribe. . . . The best of them is like a brier, the most upright of them a thorn hedge. The day of your watchmen, of your punishment, has come; now their confusion is at hand. (Mic. 7:1–4)

Everyone needs an older sister. Kathryn, my older sister, has been a source of wisdom for me from day one. She was in kindergarten and first grade before I ever started school. She would come home each day, and we would play school. She would teach me whatever she had learned. So when I started kindergarten, in a sense, I had already been there! I lasted one day because my teachers told my mom that I had already learned kindergarten, and they wanted to move me to first grade instead. Thank you, Kathryn!

With a wise bigger sister, I learned much, and one of her many pearls of wisdom surfaces in my mind as I read today's passage. I had had a few rough days, and I was complaining to my sister. I added the somewhat common refrain, "Well, it can't get any worse." At this, Kathryn got a serious look on her face and sternly told me, "Never challenge worse!" She knew that it could indeed always get worse. She was right.

Consider living in the times of Micah. He goes looking for someone—anyone—who is righteous and reliable. Zero. Zip. Nada. It's akin to walking in a field to gather fruit after it has already been fully harvested and only twigs remain. From the bottom of the socioeconomic ladder to the top was evil. Even the trained and schooled princes and judges sought bribes for discharging their duties. Go to them for help, and you might as well recline on thorny brambles for a good night's sleep.

I've had bad days. I've grieved the deaths of loved ones. I've seen evil triumph in the short term. I've been stuck in sin and all its pain. I've been betrayed by people who I thought were my friends. Yet I have never been in a time as bad as Micah's. Knowing our God was present then and was set to clean up the land gives me confidence to live today. For while it can always be worse, I know it will also get better. That is the way of God.

Lord, thank you for turning night into day and weeping into dancing. In you, amen.

OCTOBER 6

Put no trust in a neighbor; have no confidence in a friend . . . for the son treats the father with contempt, the daughter rises up against her mother, the daughter-in-law against her mother-in-law; a man's enemies are the men of his own house. But as for me, I will look to the LORD; I will wait for the God of my salvation; my God will hear me. (Mic. 7:5-7)

"What are you going to do about it?" I'll bet that this sentence has been uttered hundreds of millions of times. Think about the many contexts where one might hear it. A bully takes a kid's lunch money and stands over him, asking, "What are you going to do about it?" Or in an altogether different context, someone is faced with a hard choice and seeks the advice of a friend. Acknowledging the difficult predicament, the friend asks earnestly, "What are you going to do about it?" You might be faced with a moral challenge, and in self-talk, you say, "What are you going to do about it?"

Today's passage answers that question for many situations. Micah has been speaking to a people and society that's wrecked. As the last several days' devotionals have noted, morality is nowhere to be found. King Omri sacrificed his son to dedicate a city. The princes and judges took bribes. Neighbors cheated neighbors. Everyone was out for themselves, even at the expense of their families. As today's passage noted, sons treated fathers with contempt rather than respect. Daughters trashed their mothers. Society needed a full cleansing. So then the question is fairly asked of Micah, "What are you going to do about it?"

Micah answers the question, and his answer should inform all of us. Micah says he will look to the LORD. Not only will he look to God, but he will *wait* for God, knowing that God's salvation comes at God's carefully chosen time. But let there be no doubt: God will come.

Everyone faces difficulties in life. Some days aren't as bad as others. But often we find ourselves set in a struggle just trying to set one foot in front of another while life cascades around us. As we face life, we can fairly ask ourselves, "What are you going to do about it?" Now we can answer, "I have the prescription for that. I found it in Micah. I will look to the Lord! I will wait for the God *of my salvation*, nothing less. God will hear me!"

Lord, make this lesson real in my life. Take all my problems and difficulties, and come to save me. Hear my plea in your name, amen.

OCTOBER 7

Rejoice not over me, O my enemy; when I fall, I shall rise; when I sit in darkness, the LORD will be a light to me. I will bear the indignation of the LORD because I have sinned against him, until he pleads my cause and executes judgment for me. He will bring me out to the light; I shall look upon his vindication. Then my enemy will see, and shame will cover her who said to me, "Where is the LORD your God?" (Mic. 7:8–10)

There's a fine line between being right and being harsh. Let me explain. How often have you seen someone make poor choices that had poor results? Maybe someone got into an ungodly and destructive relationship when they knew better. I know one fellow who defrauded the government, thinking he was just taking advantage of opportunities and not realizing he was blatantly committing a crime. Maybe it's something as simple as cheating on an exam at school and getting caught.

When someone does something wrong, makes poor choices, or walks in sin before God, and when the just consequences follow the conduct, how easy it is to say, "Well, he had it coming!" or "It serves her right!" There may be truth in that statement, and maybe the consequences will teach an important lesson, but that fine line between being right in judging another and being harsh becomes apparent. We are not to relish in another's comeuppance. We are to always seek others' best.

This comes front and center with today's passage. Micah is speaking of the nations around Israel and of Israel itself, but Micah does so in the first person. This makes it echo in one's personal life as well as have meaning on an international scale. Micah wrote of an enemy who taunted Israel and Judah (represented by Micah) over their coming fall. These other nations derisively mocked Israel and Judah over their discipline from God. Micah (Israel/Judah) had steeped itself in sin, and God's judgment was righteous. Still, laughing wasn't the right response, and Micah knew the enemy would not get the last laugh.

Micah affirms that God is a forgiving God. He lifts the fallen. He brings his people from darkness into light. This isn't because the people deserve it; it's the hand of God working from God's loving and giving nature. This should stir how we react to people who suffer, even when justified. I need to be more merciful.

Lord, thank you for my deliverance. May I use it to serve you all my days. In your name, amen.

OCTOBER 8

Shepherd your people with your staff, the flock of your inheritance, who dwell alone in a forest in the midst of a garden land; let them graze in Bashan and Gilead as in the days of old. (Mic. 7:14)

As I read the email, I had a pit in my stomach. A marvelous young Christian couple in New Zealand with a bright future, young children, and joy on the horizon had asked for prayers. The vibrant young husband, a friend of our son from university days, had a life-threatening case of leukemia. The family was desperate and uncertain about what to do. They sought prayers but also were investigating whether better cancer treatment might be available in the United States. We relayed information about M. D. Anderson, maybe the best cancer care in the world. But we also prayed for them. We asked God Almighty to intervene, with or without medical treatment, to restore health to this friend.

I can happily report that just this morning, as I type this devotional, I have received the latest email from the family noting that M. D. Anderson is off the table because the cancer is in full remission. I am rejoicing! Now, I recognize that many times, I and others have asked God to provide similar remission, only to have God answer those prayers with a sad, "No, not this time." I seek to rejoice then as well, knowing God is in control. But I don't let those times inhibit my praise and thanks to God when he answers the prayers with "Yes!"

In today's passage, Micah prays on behalf of the people who have been conquered and ousted from their cities and homes and are now trying to live in a metaphorical wild forest rather than tilled and tended gardens. In other words, stripped of their homes and towns, they live a wretched life trying to eke out an existence. Micah's prayer is that God will be a shepherd to the people and that he will lead them back to a fruitful and beautiful life.

The next verses—verses 15 to 20—affirm that God will hear that prayer. God will bring his people out of their desolation into a life filled with marvelous things. The enemies will suffer, but God's people will be rescued.

We can and should seek God for ourselves but, importantly, for others as well. Think through your life today. Who is suffering in darkness? Pray for God to shepherd them into the light. Then when he does, praise him for it!

Lord, please shepherd (fill in the blank) with your care and love. In you, amen.

OCTOBER 9

Who is a God like you, pardoning iniquity and passing over transgression for the remnant of his inheritance? He does not retain his anger forever, because he delights in steadfast love. (Mic. 7:18)

Last month, as I began this devotional study in the book of Micah, I pointed out the potential "clickbait" at the start of the book. If the book is read in Hebrew, it begins as a prophecy of "Micah." The name *Micah* is a shortened form of a Hebrew question. Fully translated out, the question asked by the name of Micah is this: "Who is like the LORD?" With that question set forth in the Hebrew meaning of the name *Micah*, the book works through the question in a variety of forms—metaphors, a lawsuit, poetic expressions of judgment and mercy, instructions in life, warnings, and more. Then the book draws to a close in today's passage and over the next two verses.

As the book draws to a close, Micah addresses the question asked in the beginning by his name. Here, Micah is blunt: "Who is a God like the LORD?" Who indeed! Micah declares that God pardons iniquity. Full stop. God is a forgiving God. He doesn't invalidate his promises because of human error and frailty. He doesn't excuse sin; he deals with it. But God is constantly seeking to bring people into his saving love rather than hoping for their destruction.

Micah explains the uniqueness of our God, who passes over transgressions because he is calling out his people, his "remnant" of those who would follow him rather than dedicate life to destroying God and his work. Sin does bring out God's anger—of that there is no doubt. Yet this anger against the cancer of sin doesn't get the last word. For God is a God who delights in steadfast love, and he seeks to bring life from death. The next verse affirms that he throws "all our sins into the depths of the sea" (v. 19).

Who is like God indeed? No one! His love and compassion need to be models for our lives. Too often, we live and dwell in grudges and anger over those who sin against us. I don't minimize the hurt that can cause such feelings. Yet the goal needs to be modeling after our God of steadfast love to move beyond anger to a genuine desire for the good of others, even our enemies. This is hard, but we have the perfect model in our God.

Lord, there is no one like you, but I long to grow to be more like you. In your name, amen.

OCTOBER 10

An oracle concerning Nineveh. The book of the vision of Nahum of Elkosh. (Nah. 1:1)

Thus begins Nahum, thirteen short words in English and only six in the Hebrew original. But these words provide the setting of this small three-chapter book. The words also direct the careful reader's attention to important truths about God.

The first word in Hebrew, meaning "oracle," is a word of burden. By that I mean that the word itself can mean "burden" as well as "utterance" or "oracle." The oracle concerning Nineveh was a burden that needed to be lifted. The oracle couldn't remain unuttered. It weighed heavy on Nahum, ready to come forth.

Yet the burden or oracle wasn't about Israel or Judah. God's people aren't the subject of the oracle. This oracle concerns the pagans of Assyria, the world's superpower to the north. Ruled from the capital city of Nineveh, the Assyrian Empire was at its zenith. It spanned from the Tigris and Euphrates all the way into Egypt. It contained much of the modern Middle East, including parts of Turkey, Syria, Iran, Iraq, Lebanon, Jordan, Syria, Egypt, Saudi Arabia, and Kuwait.

The burden is a vision recorded onto a scroll (translated as "book"). This vision showed the coming destruction of Nineveh and Assyria. History verified the vision incredibly; in just twenty-five years' time, Assyria went from being the world's largest superpower ever at that point in history to total destruction.

God gave this burden and vision to Nahum, a prophet whose name means "full of comfort." Where is the comfort in this word of destruction? The comfort comes from knowing that history is not a spectator sport for God. The pages of history turn, but not without God's active involvement. He isn't interested only in those who know him (or should know him). His interest is in the entirety of humanity. He is Lord of the Earth, not a geographic region or certain population.

Sometimes I act like life is my bubble. I have my job, my community, my family, and my friends. But things are happening all over the world, and I always need to educate myself about them. I believe that when ungodliness reigns, I should have a burden about it. I should be seeking God in prayer, ready for his hand to work.

Lord, give me a burden for others. May I pray for your love to invade the world. In your name, amen.

OCTOBER 11

The LORD is a jealous and avenging God; the LORD is avenging and wrathful; the LORD takes vengeance on his adversaries and keeps wrath for his enemies. The LORD is slow to anger and great in power, and the LORD will by no means clear the guilty. (Nah. 1:2–3)

Think about a hammer. "What a wonderful tool!" you may be thinking, if your mind is worried about having to drive a nail through a piece of wood. But that same hammer can be a terrible weapon if it is used to destroy something or someone. Same tool, different value—good or bad depending on the circumstances.

So it is with "jealousy." It can be virtuous or destructive, depending on the situation. In situations when a third party intrudes on a relationship, a righteous jealousy for the good of a loved one is fully appropriate. To be apathetic in the face of another's damage to a relationship isn't true love. On the other hand, petty jealousy isn't a value but likely stems from one's own insecurities.

Scriptures like today's attribute to God a righteous jealousy. This jealousy doesn't stem from God's ego being damaged. It stems from God's intense love for his people and his desire for their best. When evil forces damage his people and cause them to stray from his tender love, God rightly reacts to protect those he loves.

It's easy to read passages like today's and not dwell on the words long, for the words are hard ones. To call God jealous, wrathful, or avenging doesn't fit the image of God we like to think about. Yet these are clearly traits of God that come into play in defense of his people.

Righteous jealousy, righteous wrath, and even righteous vengeance act as God's hammer to build his people as well as destroy those things that entice his people to stumble. These aren't traits that God lashes out inappropriately or without compelling need. They go hand in hand with God's slowness to anger. But this passage shows that in the end, God doesn't countenance evil.

I am glad that God loves me fiercely. I am glad that his love is protecting, seeking only what is best for me, often in spite of myself. I need that from God.

Lord, protect me in your love as through your name, I pray, amen.

OCTOBER 12

His way is in whirlwind and storm, and the clouds are the dust of his feet. He rebukes the sea and makes it dry; he dries up all the rivers; Bashan and Carmel wither; the bloom of Lebanon withers. The mountains quake before him; the hills melt; the earth heaves before him, the world and all who dwell in it. (Nah. 1:3–5)

Have you ever gotten into a GOAT debate? I don't mean judging a contest at a county fair over who raised the best goat. I am referring to the acronym GOAT: "Greatest of All Time." Like "Who is the greatest basketball player of all time? Michael Jordan? Wilt Chamberlain? Kobe Bryant? Lebron James?" Those debates rage back and forth among sports enthusiasts. Some played better defense than others. Some won more championships. Some had more total career points. The factors that go into the debates range far and wide, affecting the outcome of the winner.

Today's passage is one that sets out an absolute truth. Among the pantheon of gods that many believed worthy of worship, God reigned supreme. God is the ultimate Greatest of All Time.

Today's passage is built into a hymn of praise found in the first part of Nahum. Part of the praise stems from God's role as the God of creation. Whirlwinds, storms, clouds with all their chaos and mystery (to the ancients) are nothing to him. Water is fully under his control, as are mountains and hills. God is over the whole earth, including everyone in it.

In the days of Nahum, many people believed in regional gods. They believed that a god had a certain area of the world carved out for him or her, such as a geographic region or an element of life (fertility, for example). This is a reason ancient kings warred on behalf of their gods. They sought their god's blessing by seeking to extend their god's reign over neighboring gods.

Not so with the one true God. He is God over all things and all people, whether anyone acknowledges him or not. This makes God worthy of my praise and respect. It also removes my fear, as I realize that this God loves me and wants what is best for me. Let there be no debate about who is truly the Greatest of All Time.

Lord, I worship you for your greatness and thank you for your love. In you, amen.

OCTOBER 13

The LORD is good, a stronghold in the day of trouble; he knows those who take refuge in him. But with an overflowing flood he will make a complete end of the adversaries, and will pursue his enemies into darkness. (Nah. 1:7–8)

When I was young, I heard a friend explain that a mutual acquaintance was in a world of hurt. As my friend put it, "He's too godly to have fun in the world, but he's too worldly to have fun in God." People who straddle a fence aren't sitting in a comfortable seat. There comes a time where people need to take a side and stick with it.

In PE classes when I was young, we had pullover sleeveless shirts that were blue or red and were used to divide two teams. The different colors made it easy to know who was on which team. On the playground away from school, we guys would frequently divide up into "shirts and skins," with one team removing their shirts to make it easier to see in a split second if someone was on your team or not.

Today's passage sets up a question for everyone who reads it. When it comes to life and its focus and choices, people can choose their team. They can choose their side of the fence. That choice isn't made for us. We make that choice ourselves.

The passage makes it clear that God operates on both sides of this fence. On one side, he is protecting, supporting, and uplifting those who love him. On the other side, God is a raging flood, pursuing his enemies. When the choice is that graphic, I know which side I want to pick!

Yet over and over, in the small and large areas of life, we tend to forget this dividing line. We might become a bit like the acquaintance I described in the opening paragraph—too worldly for faith and too faithful for the world. That is a path to misery.

I want to be God's, and I want to dwell deep in his care. That isn't a life free of hurt and pain. It's one where when I hurt or suffer, I have a God of refuge. When days of trouble come, I can rest in the arms of one who overcomes trouble. That's the side of the fence where I wish to dwell: with God—my light in times of darkness, my strength in times of weakness, and my joy in times of sorrow. My God.

Lord, I live and trust in your goodness. Be my stronghold. In your name, amen.

OCTOBER 14

What do you plot against the LORD? He will make a complete end; trouble will not rise up a second time. For they are like entangled thorns, like drunkards as they drink; they are consumed like stubble fully dried. From you came one who plotted evil against the LORD, a worthless counselor. (Nah. 1:9–11)

Imagine this: a four-year-old kid has learned how to play basketball with an indoor nerf basketball hoop that is three feet off the floor. For some reason, this child has a real arrogant streak. The child makes a few baskets, perhaps because a parent doesn't really play defense. The child then approaches Michael Jordan in his prime and asserts that on a real court, with a full weighted basketball and a ten-foot rim, the child could beat Jordan. Absurd, isn't it? No one would ever bet on the child. The child has no chance against Jordan playing full out.

Now imagine this: an ancient empire arose in the Middle East that, by the seventh century BCE, conquered and subjugated its surrounding neighbors. Then the empire's military leaders decided they would take on God—the maker of heaven and earth; the one who was, is, and is to come; the one who knows our every thought; the one who knows a word before we form it on our tongue; the one who knows the future with perfect clarity, just as well as he does the present or past. Absurd, isn't it? No one should ever have bet on the earthly empire. The transient military leaders had no chance against the eternal Lord of all.

Yet today's passage indicates this attitude and planning of Assyria. The leaders were plotting against the LORD. Nahum states the obvious. God will put an end to Assyria once and for all. No one can overcome the Lord God.

Now transition this to you and me today. Isn't it equally absurd that we would make our own plans in life without seeking God's plans? If our plans don't align with his, we are setting our plans against him, even if by accident or ignorance. Either way, our plans will not succeed against the plans of the Lord. God will bring our plans to naught. It is the way of things.

This leaves me with a conviction that I need to better seek the Lord with my plans. I need to apply Proverbs 3:6: "In all your ways acknowledge him, and he will make straight your paths." This is the way to success.

Lord, I want to follow your will and guidance in my life. Give me eyes to see and ears to hear where you lead me. In your name, amen.

OCTOBER 15

*Thus says the L*ORD*, "Though they are at full strength and many, they will be cut down and pass away. Though I have afflicted you, I will afflict you no more. And now I will break his yoke from off you and will burst your bonds apart." (Nah. 1:12–13)*

Mr. Mars was my high school drama teacher. But he did more than teach acting and give roles in plays. He had us read plays, do play reports, and study the history of theater. That was where I first met the phrase *deus ex machina*, Latin for "god from the machine." Dating from the fifth century BCE, the Greek playwrights would set an impossible situation before an audience. The difficulty would then be resolved by a god appearing in the sky via the use of an ancient crane (the "machine" in the phrase). The phrase has stayed in modern usage to mean some unlikely resolution that resolves the unresolvable, usually at the end of a show or movie.

The Greek playwrights may be responsible for our phrase, but God was stepping down to solve the unsolvable long before Sophocles wrote his *Philoctetes* (one of the first plays to use the convention).

Look at God's track record. God promises to make a great nation from Abraham, one through which the whole earth will receive a blessing. Yet his offspring spend four hundred years in Egypt as slaves to Pharaoh and don't hold fast to the faith of Abraham. Yet deus ex machina, God rescues the people, gives them land, and makes a nation of them. The story continues to be repeated over and over as God rescues the nation up to the passage today in Nahum. It comes at a time when the mighty Assyrian Empire rules over Israel and Judah. What's worse, many of God's people aren't faithful to him, seeking to worship idols instead. Yet deus ex machina, God promises he will cut down and abolish the mightiest army on earth. God will break the bondage of Assyria.

This is who God is, and I am glad. More times than I can count, I have been in impossible situations where chaos seems to reign, events spiral out of control, and tragedy and doom seem impending, and yet, deus ex machina, God comes to the rescue. In the words of the song "Came to My Rescue" by Hillsong United, "I called, he answered, and he came to my rescue." Don't ever be daunted by the impossible. There's no such thing to God.

Lord, I place my life in your hands. I bow down before you. My prayer in your name is that you be lifted up, even as you come to my rescue. Amen.

OCTOBER 16

The Lord has given commandment about you: "No more shall your name be perpetuated; from the house of your gods I will cut off the carved image and the metal image. I will make your grave, for you are vile." (Nah. 1:14)

I can't tell you much about Dr. Henry Talley (1778–1862). He and his wife, Mary, had a daughter named Susan. Susan married Matthew Dixon (1817–1878), of whom I also know very little beyond the birth of their son, James, in 1841. James and his wife, Eugenia, had a daughter, Ellen, who married a Tennessee boy, William Bray (1857–1938), and beyond basic birth and death data, I know little of him. But in 1894, they gave birth to a daughter named Tommie Lee, and of her I can tell you a ton! She was my great-grandmother, who lived long enough that I performed her funeral. I knew her well.

Even though I didn't know my forebears, without each one I wouldn't be here today. They were real people rooted in real history who're critical to my life today. My life, your life—we're all rooted in history, which brings me to today's passage.

God and Scripture are rooted in history. They aren't mystical vibrations that echo through time. They have a place of origin as God involves himself in human history and life. This passage is a judgment oracle against the king of Nineveh and, by extension, the Assyrian kingdom he ruled.

God was writing a history that the king's lineage would not "be perpetuated" but would cease. The king's gods would fail to perform, and the king wouldn't have a massive memorial for a grave. Instead, God would decide where his body would rot. He wasn't as important as he thought.

Knowing that God is involved in history means that I can be assured that God is involved in today. History is built one day at a time. I live my history, but as I interact with others, directly or indirectly, I'm affecting their histories as well. Not only should I trust God with my history, but I should work with God to make good histories for others. This brings me to the all-important question of how I am going to treat others today. But it also leaves me seeking God in prayer to work in my history for his good purposes. In a few hundred years, no one may know of me, but I want God to be praised because of how I lived.

Lord, use me to sculpt your history for your glory. In your name, amen.

OCTOBER 17

Behold, upon the mountains, the feet of him who brings good news, who publishes peace! Keep your feasts, O Judah; fulfill your vows, for never again shall the worthless pass through you; he is utterly cut off. . . . For the LORD is restoring the majesty of Jacob as the majesty of Israel, for plunderers have plundered them and ruined their branches. (Nah. 1:15; 2:2)

"Keep the faith" is an expression whose roots are lost in history. The phrase is an encouragement to be optimistic about a situation (or person) despite how pessimistic the situation may appear. "Keep the faith" was popularized in the 1960s during the civil rights movement. The phrase was the title of a hit song for Bon Jovi in 1992 on an album also named *Keep the Faith*. The ubiquitous nature of the phrase stems from the importance of remaining confident that the morning is coming, even on the darkest night.

"Keep the faith" is a biblical concept for God's children. It reminds us that those who oppose God are foolish even when they first succeed. Any success opposing God is a temporary illusion. Today's passage lies in the context of God judging the king of Nineveh/Assyria in the preceding verse and God judging the Ninevites in battle in the successive verses.

So these verses set out two camps. For God's people, it's the camp of "keep the faith." Even though they were underdogs who had suffered and were subject to the Assyrians, God wanted them to keep the faith. They should continue their feasts of celebration and fulfill the vows they made as they sought God's deliverance. God was going to redeem his people, and the enemy would be lost.

There was no faith for the enemy to keep. Their confidence was misplaced. Their arrogance and pride would precede their downfall. Their destruction was certain.

I'm confronted by this passage in my life as I seek God and his will. I know that I'm to keep the faith. Evil might win a battle, but evil won't win in the end. God can be trusted with those things tendered into his care. He may not draw the results I want when I want them (and I do want everything most immediately!), but I need to keep the faith. For God is at work in me, you, the loved ones I pray for, broken situations, life's griefs, and the losses we mourn. God is moving, and I need to keep the faith!

Lord, inspire greater faith in my heart as I await deliverance in you, amen.

OCTOBER 18

The shield of his mighty men is red; his soldiers are clothed in scarlet. The chariots come with flashing metal on the day he musters them; the cypress spears are brandished. The chariots race madly through the streets; they rush to and fro through the squares. (Nah. 2:3–4)

"Put on your Sunday best," I was told when younger. By that, my mom meant I was to wear nice clothes like I would wear to church. The idea being that in church, we wanted to present God with our best. Not a bad idea.

Recently, I was on a Zoom call with some potential clients. One of the men asking for my legal help cussed a decent bit on the call. He later emailed me an apology, noting that he didn't realize I was a minister as well as a lawyer, or he wouldn't have cussed. I replied via email that God knows who we are and expects authenticity, not fakery, so when dealing with me, he needn't try to be someone he isn't. Again, not a bad idea.

The interesting thing to me is that God is as genuine and authentic as can be. Today's passage begins a narrative of the final attack that would destroy the city of Nineveh. If the language were put into a movie, it would carry a PG-13 rating for its unvarnished portrayal of violence. The biblical account in Nahum of the battle and destruction is much more graphic than the Babylonian chronicle now housed in the British Museum.

I haven't presented the entire text of Nahum's account, but he graphically described the total destruction and desolation of the city, including officers stumbling (perhaps drunk or injured) to their stations, the city flooding, the palace's destruction, the harm to the city's women, the plundering, the piles of dead bodies, and the animals feasting on the dead flesh. God didn't tone down his language and description for Nahum, and Nahum set it forth in alarming language.

God isn't fake. He doesn't put on airs. He isn't interested in painting a picture that isn't reality. You can't get more authentic than God, even when that requires hard-to-digest information. God isn't going to sugarcoat for you or me. That is a good thing. We live in times where fakery abounds. But with our God, everything is 100 percent real. It makes me want to know him better and be more authentic myself.

Lord, open my eyes to truth in this world. May I live honestly before you and spread your honesty to others. In your name, I pray, amen.

OCTOBER 19

Woe to the bloody city, all full of lies and plunder—no end to the prey! ... *Behold, I am against you, declares the* Lord *of hosts, and will lift up your skirts over your face; and I will make nations look at your nakedness and kingdoms at your shame. I will throw filth at you and treat you with contempt and make you a spectacle.* (Nah. 3:1, 5–6)

When really tough things happen, my Jewish buddy Rick will frequently exclaim, "*Oy veh!*" or "Woe is me!" *Oy* is akin to the ancient Hebrew word for "woe" (*hoy*—הוֹי). It is used often in the Hebrew Bible, including at the start of today's passage. But the prophet isn't proclaiming "woe is me." Rather than *oy veh*, this Hebrew reads *hoy 'ir*, or "woe to the city!" Today's passage is another judgment oracle against Nineveh, the administrative capital of the evil Assyrian Empire.

For centuries, Assyria had reigned over great swaths of the rich soil called the Fertile Crescent. They conquered nations, enslaved people, extracted ransoms, enforced paganism, established puppet governments, and ruled with a harsh and violent hand. Their own history tablets record that they dragged women and children back to their empire as slaves after killing their fathers in battle. They excelled in the evil God hates, and God was going to punish them.

It is a fearsome thing to fall under the judgment of God. The prophet uses a strong metaphor proclaiming that God would lift Nineveh's skirt over its head, revealing its nakedness and shame. The city is going to become a spectacle and example for everyone. The book ends with God noting the failures of people to stop the evil.

No one should mistakenly believe that the kind and loving God will look the other way when people practice deceit, injustice, violence, and abuse. No, God doesn't tolerate evil, and the promise of Scripture, over and over, is that evil will consume itself. Its end will never be victory but utter defeat. Today's passage is a snippet of this eternal truth. God has set his face against those who practice evil as well as those who look the other way and allow evil to thrive. God's call to his people is to not only turn from evil but seek God's justice and will. God's will should be sought on earth, not simply in heaven.

Hoy ir, woe to the city, but by God's grace, as we turn to his mercy with repentant hearts, it needn't be *oy veh*, woe to me. Thank you, God!

Lord, I do seek your mercy as I seek to live in your will and name, amen.

OCTOBER 20

The word of the LORD *that came to Zephaniah the son of Cushi, son of Gedaliah, son of Amariah, son of Hezekiah, in the days of Josiah the son of Amon, king of Judah.* (Zeph. 1:1)

Today is my birthday! Of course, I have no memories of being born, but I do remember my mother and father, both sets of grandparents, and even one great-grandparent. I can trace my lineage going back multiple generations. I can speak to their faith journeys as well as the various places they lived. Our family has often chosen family names for children. My true first name is William, same as my father's. My sisters were named after grandparents.

These things occur to me as I read this passage, what scholars call the "superscription" to the prophet Zephaniah. The prophets almost without exception give the name of their father, but Zephaniah gives four generational names in his lineage, going back to Hezekiah. Many believe that this is a reference to the good king Hezekiah, who reigned over Judah in the days of the prophet Isaiah. Whether it is or isn't, I find it fascinating that each name save one ends in -*iah*. This ending in English references the Hebrew *yah* (יָהּ), an abbreviation of YHWH, the holy name of God.

For four generations, the lineage of Zephaniah cared enough to include the holy name in the naming of their children. Zephaniah's name seems to mean "YHWH treasures" or "YHWH hides." His grandfather's name, Gedaliah, means "YHWH is great!" His great-grandfather Amaziah's name proclaims, "YHWH has spoken." Then finally, Hezekiah's name conveys, "YHWH is my strength" or "YHWH strengthens me."

Zephaniah will come from this carefully named family and be used by YHWH. The Hebrew text begins with the holy name speaking, "The word of YHWH." This word that came to Zephaniah over 2,600 years ago comes to me today. It affirms the one true God who treasures his children. Our great God speaks and is available to be our strength as we walk before him.

This inspires me to not only read these words in the coming days but apply them. If I could give myself a birthday gift, it would be this: I want to know the LORD better, follow him more closely, and become the person he can make me.

Holy Lord, be as integral to me as my name. May I find life in your name, amen.

OCTOBER 21

"I will utterly sweep away everything from the face of the earth," declares the LORD. *"I will sweep away man and beast; I will sweep away the birds of the heavens and the fish of the sea, and the rubble with the wicked. I will cut off mankind from the face of the earth," declares the* LORD. (Zeph. 1:2–3)

"Clean the what???" I whined to Mom in my youth. It was spring cleaning time, and I was assigned to clean our bathroom. I could wipe down the sink. I could sort of clean the commode and tub. But it never occurred to me to get on my knees and wipe down the baseboards, especially behind the toilet! "But Mom, *no one* will ever see that!" She laughed and said cleaning is to get it clean, not to show to other people. Mercy! When Mom cleaned, Mom cleaned it all! She left no dirt!

So it is with God. Today's passage begins the prophecy of Zephaniah announcing God's universal judgment. God will be the ultimate cleanser of all that is dirty and deficient. He will sweep the whole earth from corner to corner. Nothing will escape his broom, not even the birds and fish.

This beginning of a short three-chapter book should grab everyone's attention. One might read quickly over Nahum, the prophet covered in the previous weeks. After all, his prophesy of doom was over the pagan nation Assyria and its capital Nineveh. But no one dare take this lightly. This cleaning is thorough and reaches everyone.

After this strong attention-getter, Zephaniah then zooms his focus in on the nation of Judah, the southern kingdom still under the rule of King David's descendants. God is going to cut off the priests and people that are worshiping the idol Baal. These people have turned their backs on the Lord, for we can't worship anything other than the one true God without turning our backs on God. God rightly deserves first and only worship from his people. Anything less is nothing at all.

The Hebrew text of Zephaniah shows that this prophetic word is written as poetry. As such, its descriptive language should be read poetically as hyperbole that expresses strong emotions and the heart of the message rather than literally. Thus, the prophesy about the destruction of all flesh is poetry intended to grab our attention. We should not let anything but God take the first place in our hearts and minds.

Lord, I give you my heart and my life. Take first place. In your name, amen.

OCTOBER 22

"I will cut off from this place . . . those who bow down on the roofs to the host of the heavens, those who bow down and swear to the LORD and yet swear by Milcom, those who have turned back from following the LORD, who do not seek the LORD or inquire of him." (Zeph. 1:4–6)

Decision time: four doors are in front of you. One door is marked "flu" for those who pass through it. A second door is labeled "COVID," while the third door is marked "pneumonia," indicating the diseases awaiting those who enter those doors. The fourth and final door is marked "health." It signifies good health for those who enter. Which door are you going in? I am taking health, every time.

In a similar fashion, Zephaniah explains that there were four doors in front of Judah, three of which would lead to God's fierce judgment. The first door was for those who "bow down to the hosts of heaven." This references people who went up on their roofs at night and worshiped the stars, thinking them a heavenly entourage of gods. The second door was those who swear to both the LORD *and* Baal ("Milcom"), blending the religion of antiquity given through Moses with the modern religious expressions of Baal. The third door was those who don't seek the Lord but have turned their backs to him.

All three of these groups/doors were going to be subject to God's judgment. Not knowing or seeking God is not better than worshiping others. It's a dead end. All these doors are set out by God as dead ends. The judgment of God would be coming soon. The implied fourth door was for those who dwell with and worship the Lord. They are in a different camp altogether; they would be untouched.

I read this and wonder about which door I am seeking to use today. I can pretty much exclude doors one and two. I'm not into worshiping stars or Baal. But turning back from God, not seeking God, not inquiring of God—those are stumbling points for the best of us on the worst days. Actually, on the worst days, we might seek God more. Some find this stumbling more on the good days! Either way, I may play with that door, but reading this passage, I definitely want to avoid it!

This makes my commission today simple. I will seek God today. I will set before him my decision points and seek his wisdom and guidance. I will set my hope on him.

Lord, please give me wisdom and guidance to follow you today. In you is my amen.

OCTOBER 23

Be silent before the Lord GOD! For the day of the LORD is near. (Zeph. 1:7)

Did you ever wonder where the word *hush* comes from? Scholars can trace it back to the 1600s, but the word has been around longer than that. A prominent scholarly opinion is that the word originated as a hissing sound that would get attention yet takes only the slightest effort and makes little noise. I think those scholars have it right. Because the ancient Hebrew word used in today's passage and translated as "be silent" is the simple *hus*! The ancients made the same basic sound to tell people not to make any noise!

While the word *hus* is interesting to me, the *most* interesting part of today's passage is *why* the people were instructed to hush. They were to hush before the Lord GOD, whose day was near.

Why do people get quiet? Some are silent to remain hidden, but that isn't the case here. The people aren't hidden, for they are being spoken to. Sometimes, people are silent out of awe. We have the expression "She was speechless!" That certainly might be a reason to be silent before the Lord and his coming day. Still others get silent before a momentous event. At many a sports event, when the game is on the line, the home crowd will get raucous to disturb the opposing team but dead silent to allow the home team to concentrate. I can see that being part of the meaning here. Not that God needs to concentrate but that the people need to hush and watch what is about to happen. Still yet another time of quiet is in a place of reverence and worship. This certainly could be a reason for the instruction in today's passage. While Scripture teaches that there are times of worship that include singing, clapping, and shouting for joy, Scripture also teaches that there are times to be silent in worship. This is akin to being silent out of awe.

I suspect a combination of factors are at play in today's verse. We become silent and pay attention as we contemplate in awe God's mighty works, wait for him to do something momentous, and worship him. If we aren't careful, we can get so caught up in the racket and clamor of life that we fail to focus on what God is about to do.

Hush! Listen to God. Watch God at work. Sometimes, that is the right thing to do.

Lord, I am quiet before you. Help me see your hand at work. In your name, amen.

OCTOBER 24

Seek the LORD, *all you humble of the land, who do his just commands; seek righteous-ness; seek humility; perhaps you may be hidden on the day of the anger of the* LORD. (Zeph. 2:3)

One of my buddies, Larry, emailed me about his faith walk. He was working through the Minor Prophets and told me, "I'm still working through daily how I should be living if (since) God is king and I'm living in his kingdom. I can't think of anything in my fifty years as a Christian that has had a greater effect on my everyday life." Like many of us, Larry would love the simple manual that has clear and concise steps for spiritual growth: (1) do A, (2) do B, (3) do C, and so on. While Scripture isn't so plain, there are a few passages that do give us glimpses and guideposts to follow. Today's is such a passage.

This passage comes at the end of Zephaniah's section on the coming day of the Lord. That day would bring harsh judgments and wouldn't be easy. After detailing the fallout from the fearsome day of judgment, the prophet tells the "humble of the land" to seek God, continue to do God's just commands, and seek righteousness. To emphasize the point, he tells the "humble" to seek more "humility."

The prophet's call shows his own humility. The prophet doesn't pre-sume to say that God will hide the righteous on the day of anger. Rather, the prophet says *might.* Using the word *perhaps* (Hebrew *'ulay*—אוּלַי), the prophet knows that God's ways aren't our ways. Obligating God here would be presumptuous.

This passage speaks to me, as it does to my buddy. I need to know how to walk humbly before God. I can't say for certain whether his day of judg-ment is today, tomorrow, next year, or next century. I can't say what form it might take. But I know that I can trust God to take care of me in whatever form is best. My goal needs to be a humble walk in his righteousness. I want to do as God instructs me.

This is a reason for this devotional book. My writing forces me to read and contemplate how to apply the word of God each day. God's word teaches me more of him, refocuses my priorities and righteousness, and transforms my life.

Lord, I have so far to go to find you in each day's choices. I want to know you more, to be absorbed in seeing your greatness, and to be faithful to you in your kingdom. Please help me in your great name, amen.

OCTOBER 25

This shall be their lot in return for their pride, because they taunted and boasted against the people of the LORD of hosts. The LORD will be awesome against them; for he will famish all the gods of the earth, and to him shall bow down, each in its place, all the lands of the nations. (Zeph. 2:10–11)

Traveling the streets of London in a cab, the conversation with the driver turned to Premier League football (the top level of soccer played in England). I asked the driver his favorite team. He told me he always roots for two teams each week: the Tottenham Spurs and whoever is playing Arsenal. I get that. There have been years when, in college football, I would root for Texas Tech and for whoever was playing the University of Texas. There is something about seeing our adversaries lose that is almost as pleasant as seeing our own team win.

A bit of that was at play in the world of the prophet Zephaniah, although it was no game. Judah was selected by God and given the Promised Land. But Judah was not alone in the Middle East. God's people were surrounded by neighbors. Those neighbors weren't generally allies. They were competition. The neighbors naturally cared for their own borders and people. But there was often an element of jealous hatred toward the people of Judah. Today's passage sets out such a time.

As God was bringing judgment on Judah, the neighbors weren't lamenting. Nor were they coming to Judah's aid. Instead, they were rejoicing over Judah's hard times. They relished Judah's defeat and suffering. They raised taunts and showered Judah with hatred.

God wasn't pleased. Even though God was bringing the judgment on his people for their idolatry and abject disobedience, it should have been a warning to others and cause them to mourn, not rejoice. God's judgment was necessary but wasn't pleasant. So the judgment hammer of God was set to swing toward others.

I might root against teams in football but not against people. I need to think carefully on tragedy that befalls people, even my enemies. I should be seeking good for others and learn to lament when disaster befalls them. That's not easy, but it's right.

Lord, give me a heart for others. Help me to see those set against you as people worthy of my prayers rather than my hatred. Purify my thoughts in your name, amen.

OCTOBER 26

This is the exultant city that lived securely, that said in her heart, "I am, and there is no one else." What a desolation she has become, a lair for wild beasts! Everyone who passes by her hisses and shakes his fist. (Zeph. 2:15)

The dangers of hubris are a recurrent theme found in the Bible and in life. How many times in a movie do you see the seemingly invincible fall? How often in life does the same happen? Jesus told a parable of a rich and foolish farmer who had such a bumper crop that, rather than reduce prices, he built bigger barns so he could continue to command premium prices. The man said to himself, "I have ample goods laid up for many years; I shall relax, eat, drink, be merry." Jesus pointed out the foolishness, saying, little did he know, but he was set to die that night. Jesus taught we should live each day with an eye toward investing in God's work rather than seeking personal enrichment. But the crux of the story remains that it's foolish to ever think we've arrived.

Today's passage has the prophet echoing the same basic sentiment. In this concluding passage on God's judgment against the foreign nations, he speaks to the arrogant city of Nineveh, where people considered themselves untouchable. It was going to be destroyed. No one's untouchable, except when they're in the bosom of God.

Zephaniah's oracles against foreign powers are *not* directed against the foreign powers directly. Zephaniah wasn't going to the foreign lands to speak to them. He didn't have the internet to post his prophetic pronouncements. Zephaniah's prophecy against the foreign powers was for the benefit of Judah. God's covenant people were his audience. These passages had at least two other purposes.

First, the passages spoke to God's sovereignty in the world. God's people should never think God is only concerned with them or others of their tribe. God's hands reach throughout the earth. He is the Lord of all, not the Lord of any limited group.

Second, the passages inform God's people of the right attitudes and behaviors we are to have. If pagans will be judged for pride, arrogance, and hubris, we should never think God suddenly likes the traits when they're found in us! This passage should cause each of us to pause, reflect, and live for God.

Lord, forgive my hubris. I want to live to glorify your greatness and name, amen.

OCTOBER 27

Woe to her who is rebellious and defiled, the oppressing city! She listens to no voice; she accepts no correction. She does not trust in the LORD; she does not draw near to her God. (Zeph. 3:1–2)

Do you have a "life verse"? By this, I mean a passage in the Bible that has been a compass needle in your life, directing you on a good path. I have a host of friends who have such verses. They are found in calligraphy hanging on their walls. They are engraved in wood or even stone. These are touchstones by which people keep their focus on God. Among many Jews for millennia, that verse might be the *shema*, which begins in Deuteronomy 6:4–9 with, in English, "Hear, O Israel: The Lord our God, the LORD is one." This passage is frequently inscribed on parchment and attached in a small box to Jews' doorways to remind them as they come and go that the Lord is their God. It's a "life verse" in this way.

When I am asked for my life or favorite verse, I readily confess that mine depends on the day and what I have been reading! Today, for example, this passage might be my life verse! Why does it speak so profoundly to me? Look at it carefully. The prophet is indicting the city of Jerusalem. But this indictment isn't of the buildings in Jerusalem; it's of its citizens. God's judgment will fall on the people, not an impersonal "city."

So the indictment is against those in a covenant relationship with the Almighty. These are the people who are "rebellious and defiled." Those are clearly terms I hope don't ever apply to me! I don't want to be part of that! Who, then, are these rebellious and defiled people? The passage clarifies they're people who don't listen and don't accept correction. OUCH! How often do I get my mind made up, do I get set in my ways, and regardless of what God and his word says, regardless of the good counsel of godly friends, I stay on my course?

Then the passage continues, explaining that these are people who aren't trusting in God. Their trust is in others, or in things, or in nothing! Put this all together, and these people aren't drawing near to God but are rebelling and defiled.

So if this is my life verse today, I want to listen to God, accept correction, trust in God, and draw near to him. That is my goal today and in my life.

Lord, I repent of rebellion and long to draw close to you in trust. In you, amen.

OCTOBER 28

"For at that time I will change the speech of the peoples to a pure speech, that all of them may call upon the name of the LORD and serve him with one accord. From beyond the rivers of Cush my worshipers, the daughter of my dispersed ones, shall bring my offering." (Zeph. 3:9–10)

There seems to be a basic principle in life that everything wears out. My clothes aren't as fresh as when I bought them. The bread in my pantry molds over time. My body isn't in the shape it was in my youth. Decay happens on a grand level and even on an atomic level. It's a principle of life.

Yet God is a restorative God, not a God of decay. Scripture teaches that decay doesn't touch God. He's the same today as he was yesterday. He will be the same tomorrow. What's more, even as we earthly and fallen folks tend to decay into rot, God surprisingly uses that decay to restore and build us. Consider today's passage within the larger context of Scripture.

In early Genesis, the story is told of a united humanity building a tower that will reach up to God in the heavens. God sees that people have become united in their efforts to climb up and become like God, and so God disperses them by confusing their speech. Instead of one language, they now have many. As their communication suffers, the people divide, and their united effort to be a god fades into chaos.

Yet in today's passage, with a strong echo of the Tower of Babel story, God promises that he will bring his people from the dispersal around the earth and unite them again into a single pure speech. They will be of one "lip," the term translated as "speech." Their speech will unite them not to become a god but to serve the one true God.

I am thankful God is a restorative God. I have made a lot of chaos in my life through poor choices and self-seeking behavior. Left to my own devices, I would wither into oblivion, wearing myself out like a pair of jeans. I would be that moldy bread suitable for feeding birds or, more likely, going in the trash. But God recycles. God will take the yuck I've created and call me back into a restored relationship with him. He will make right what I have made wrong. What a God!

Lord, I lean on you to take me and my failures and use me for your good purposes. I pray this in your mighty restorative name, amen.

OCTOBER 29

"On that day you shall not be put to shame because of the deeds by which you have rebelled against me; for then I will remove from your midst your proudly exultant ones, and you shall no longer be haughty in my holy mountain. But I will leave in your midst a people humble and lowly. They shall seek refuge in the name of the LORD." (Zeph. 3:11–12)

My sweet wife and I have had a long-standing debate about dish washing. I believe in hand-washing dishes. She believes in the dishwasher. She is especially concerned that hand-washing doesn't get hot enough to get the dishes clean.

With that background, we were in England on a family vacation. We returned to the home where we were staying one night. I had a drink of water, and rather than put the glass in the dishwasher, I proudly took some soap and a sponge and hand-washed it. All was good until the glass broke in my hands and cut a massive chunk out of my right ring finger. Wrapping it in a towel, off we went to navigate an emergency room visit late on a Saturday night in a foreign country. Many stitches later, I was forced to reconsider the debate on hand-washing versus dishwashers.

This is a paltry example that comes to mind when praying through today's passage. Because in this passage, God is promising to restore that which was rebellious. God will make the proud and arrogant suffer a corrective and attention-getting judgment. But he will leave some who, after being humbled, he will restore.

The proud have no reason or basis for being with God. God seeks those who look to him and depend on him. If we're proud and haughty, we don't perceive our need for God. We might haul him out on occasion, perhaps even for show, but day-to-day prayerful dependence *on* God is found among those who understand their daily need *for* God. These are the ones who seek refuge in God and desire to dwell deep within his love and care.

My emergency room visit turned out great. I have a nice long scar on my knuckle that I can look at and remember that pride has no place in my life, not even when it comes to dishwashing. I want to be smart, and that means I need to be humble and lowly before and dependent on God.

Lord, without you I am nothing, but with you, I am all you need me to be. May I always remember that and seek you out. In your name, I pray, amen.

OCTOBER 30

"Those who are left in Israel; they shall do no injustice and speak no lies, nor shall there be found in their mouth a deceitful tongue. For they shall graze and lie down, and none shall make them afraid." (Zeph. 3:13)

I was staying in a home in a foreign country. I was alone. I had just finished eating at a restaurant and drove back to the house, which was at the end of a dark street. There might have been a neighbor or two, but I wasn't certain if they were home. And they weren't exactly "next door," as I was staying in basically a farmhouse. Alone in this old three-story house, I started to climb into bed. As I lifted my feet off the floor, I heard a BAM! The loud noise seemed to clearly be someone or something in the house. It wasn't a creak; it was as if someone had jumped on the floor above me.

Zephaniah's prophesy that the people wouldn't be afraid did *not* jump into my mind. The adage that God's people will "graze and lie down, and none shall make them afraid" didn't apply to me! Oh, I had grazed, and I had laid down, but not be afraid? I wanted to know who was in the house and what they were doing! Ultimately, I decided that 11:00 p.m. was not the time to investigate, and I didn't know the foreign equivalent of dialing 911, so I just decided to keep my bedroom door locked and let them have the rest of the house!

My story is unique in some ways, but I am certain that everyone has had times of fear and doubt in life. We fear that which is outside our control, and since no one can control everything, fear is an emotion we all share at some point or another.

Importantly, however, we worship a God for whom *nothing* is outside his control. This is why the prophet, as well as the whole of the Bible, teaches us to reside in God, to take up our residence in his love and care, and to "fear not." This passage urges God's people to avoid injustice and lies. To not practice deceit. This is part of dwelling within God's care. God isn't going to countenance us claiming to be in his care with one breath while we are acting unjustly, deceiving, and lying with another breath.

After my night of loud noise, I eventually went to sleep. The next morning, I discovered that a beam had fallen from the ceiling. I guess I didn't need to fear after all! I just need to stay in God's care.

Lord, I give you all my fears and doubts. Please handle them! In your name, amen.

OCTOBER 31

"The LORD your God is in your midst, a mighty one who will save; he will rejoice over you with gladness; he will quiet you by his love; he will exult over you with loud singing. I will gather those of you who mourn for the festival, so that you will no longer suffer reproach. Behold, at that time I will deal with all your oppressors. And I will save the lame and gather the outcast, and I will change their shame into praise and renown in all the earth." (Zeph. 3:17–19)

Don't you hate Russian nesting dolls (matryoshka dolls) because they are so full of themselves? (Yes, that was purposefully an *inside* joke.) Or might you enjoy them? I kind of find them fascinating. They remind me of so much of life, where you dig deeper and find more to a situation than you thought. They are like onions you peel back layer by layer.

Today's passage reminds me of this principle of more and more as I work through it. The passage is within the last few verses of the prophet's book, and it could have been written with one phrase: "The LORD your God is in your midst." That itself is marvelous to behold and a cause for rejoicing. God at your dinner table. God in your home. God at your school or job. God in the car with you. Who could ask for anything more than God in our midst? Yet there's more!

Peel back another layer, look inside the nesting doll, and see that God is "a mighty one who will save." God isn't just walking beside us in our lives. He isn't just monitoring the situation. He is active and seeking to use his might on our behalf! God is here to save. Great, right? But wait! There's more! He will also "rejoice over us with gladness." Wow! God rejoicing over us is an amazing thought! Then we peel back the onion further and see he will "quiet us by his love." Think of the mother holding her crying infant, soothing him and giving him solace. That is our God to us! But hold on, there's still more! He will also exult over us with loud singing! The world will hear God living in us in victory! Then as the nesting dolls continue, we see God fathering the mourning and removing the cause for their pain. We see God dealing with our enemies. We see God taking that which is inadequate or damaged, gathering the land and outcast, and making them great and marvelous for the world to see.

This is the final word from God. So the days might be tough, but with God in our midst, we rejoice. Layer after layer, he drives this point home.

Lord, thank you for your love and mercy, layer upon layer. In your name, amen.

NOVEMBER 1

O LORD, how long shall I cry for help, and you will not hear? Or cry to you "Violence!"
and you will not save? (Hab. 1:2)

How good is your memory? A lot of people use acronyms or other aides to help them remember information. A common one is HOMES for remembering the great lakes (Huron, Ontario, Michigan, Erie, and Superior). In seminary, many are required to deliver shorthand summaries of the various books in the Bible. The Minor Prophets are particularly difficult because so many are similar, and they aren't generally studied in great detail. Habakkuk, which begins today, wrote during the same time period as Nahum, which we just finished in this book. How can students remember the difference?

The simple mantra many learned was "Habakkuk talked back-uk." The idea was that Nahum explains a sinful situation and announces the judgment of God along with his ultimate victory. In Habakkuk, the sinful situation is also explained, but with a catch! Habakkuk challenges God, in a way, asking God to explain why he allows this world to run as it does.

God doesn't slap Habakkuk down for his questioning. God works in Habakkuk's life to help him understand how to live faithfully, even while he doesn't understand this world and the way it unfolds. In doing so, God gives us a prophetic book that bears his thumbprint affirming to us, the readers, how to live faithfully.

I have a lot of friends who have been through great tragedies. I have lost count of how many friends of mine as parents have had to bury their adult children who died too young. Even though most of them are followers of God, they all sustain unbearable grief. God is not offended if they or any of us close to the situation question God about what is going on. God can handle our questions, and he appreciates our authenticity.

Today's passage cries out, "How long shall I cry for help, and you will not hear?" It is an acceptable and holy cry to the God who knows our hurt. We are OK when we bring our sincere hearts to God. He will hear our cries, and he *will* answer, regardless of how it seems.

Lord, hear my cries. Know my heart. Give aid to those who hurt and reassurance
that you hear our prayers. Bring your comfort. We pray in your name, amen.

NOVEMBER 2

Why do you make me see iniquity, and why do you idly look at wrong? Destruction and violence are before me; strife and contention arise. So the law is paralyzed, and justice never goes forth. For the wicked surround the righteous; so justice goes forth perverted. (Hab. 1:3–4)

Rabbi Harold Kushner got news all parents fear. His three-year-old son had an untreatable degenerative disease that meant the young boy had only ten more years to live. It rightly threw the rabbi into a tailspin. From that experience came his 1981 best-selling book *Why Bad Things Happen to Good People*. The title alone drove many to read the book. But Rabbi Kushner was not the first to ask the question. Habakkuk asked the same question. But Habakkuk also added a second question: why do good things happen to bad people? Today's passage sets out both questions.

Habakkuk challenges God to explain the destruction and violence in Israel. The word translated as "iniquity" (*'aven*—אָוֶן) has a full semantic range. It includes our ideas of sin, injustice, disaster, and deception. Habakkuk sees that wretched things are occurring, but at the same time, the wicked seem to have the upper hand. The wretchedness isn't happening to the wicked. The wicked surround the righteous!

Habakkuk knows that life shouldn't be that way. Justice demands that the wicked have adversity pile high upon their heads, while the righteous should walk in life with a song in their mouth and a smile on their face. Habakkuk doesn't reject God over this injustice, but he does question God. He wants to know what God is doing. God gave the law to his people with promises that following the law would give blessings, while violating the law would bring curses. Yet when Habakkuk lives, the law seems paralyzed. God's righteous justice appears perverted.

Live long enough, and these questions will surface in life. I love the way they surfaced in Scripture and aren't squelched. These are important questions that God wants us to ask. As we ask them, we begin to sensitize to the issues. Of course, the answers are important too. To some, it seems Rabbi Kushner's conclusion—that God is good, but not all-powerful when it comes to stopping evil—is correct. But I think the coming days will show a better answer through Habakkuk. Importantly, we should never think the question is invalid! To have a full relationship with God, we must ask him our honest questions.

Lord, please open my eyes to better see and understand you. In you I pray, amen.

NOVEMBER 3

"Look among the nations, and see; wonder and be astounded. For I am doing a work in your days that you would not believe if told. For behold, I am raising up the Chaldeans." (Hab. 1:5–6)

Our daughter Gracie loved to swing. One Saturday, we were in the backyard, and I was pushing her in the swing. "Higher, Daddy! Higher!" she exclaimed. She was only three but already had me ready to do almost anything for her. So higher she went. But as she went higher, she lost her grip on the swing and flew out, hitting her head on a brick walkway. She got a huge gash on her head, an inch inside her hairline. I scooped her up and drove straight to the emergency clinic, forgetting I had chocolate chip cookies in the oven.

The clinic physicians saw her immediately. The blood seemed immense, and it was clear that she needed stitches. Because she was three, they knew she would squirm, so they strapped her to a board, making her immobile. She cried out, "Make them stop, Daddy. Make them stop!!!" She was crying, and I was too. I tried comforting her, saying that they had to do this for her own good, but she was barely three and didn't understand. She just knew they were hurting her, and I was doing nothing. Yet I was her dad; I was supposed to be able to fix things. She kept crying out, "Daddy, *please* help me!!!"

I still hurt thinking about that day, even though the doctor patched her up, I got to hold and comfort her, and she healed completely. (Not so the cookies. It turns out that if you cook chocolate chip cookies in the oven for over an hour, they look like charcoal briquettes.)

This story is fresh in my mind as I read God's initial reply to Habakkuk's complaint about bad things happening to good people and good things happening to bad people. Habakkuk is told to look at the bigger picture. God was at work in ways that Habakkuk wasn't able to understand. God was working in the world, not simply in Habakkuk's community. God's concerns were much greater than just what was immediately before Habakkuk.

There are times when the temporary moment is one of suffering. We're strapped to the board of life as God works to an important and great end. Healing can hurt in the short term. But God is doing something, even if we don't understand.

Lord, give me faith and trust in the midst of life's events. In your name, amen.

NOVEMBER 4

Are you not from everlasting, O LORD my God, my Holy One? . . . You who are of purer eyes than to see evil and cannot look at wrong, why do you idly look at traitors and remain silent when the wicked swallows up the man more righteous than he? (Hab. 1:12–13)

One of my favorite activities is to watch a show with my wife. We find a series we haven't seen, designate it "our show," and then only watch it together. Part of our ritual is that Becky asks me periodically to pause the show while she asks questions. She loves to guess what will happen and speculate about whether the show contains hints of what will happen. She can be quite persistent. Of course, I have no clue; the answer hasn't yet been revealed. So in this ritual dance we have, I say, "That's why it's a show instead of a five-minute miniclip. They expect you to watch the whole show to get your questions answered!"

I'm reminded of this routine with Becky as I read today's passage in its original context. Most of the other prophets spend their time proclaiming the word of the Lord. Habakkuk spends a good bit of his time questioning the acts of the Lord. It's as if he is watching a show but keeps hitting the pause button to question what is going on. Habakkuk already did that earlier in this chapter, but after receiving his answer, he persists in asking God again.

Habakkuk wants to know how God—the Holy One, the one who is everlasting—can look at the evil on earth and allow it to happen. This is an age-old question. How can an all-powerful God, who is also all good, allow evil to befall people on earth?

Some might think it wrong to openly question God like this. God doesn't think so. God has Habakkuk's repeated questions preserved in Scripture for all people of all ages to read. God will have answers, and they will come in the study of the coming days, but it is important to first see that God didn't record just the answer and insight for posterity. God also recorded his holy prophet asking the perplexing question.

We are rightly bothered by evil in this world. We rightly understand that God is not only pure and good but all-powerful. This struggle is something we can pause and ask about before our God.

Lord, help me understand your toleration of the evil in this world. In you, amen.

NOVEMBER 5

I will take my stand at my watchpost and station myself on the tower, and look out to see what he will say to me, and what I will answer concerning my complaint. (Hab. 2:1)

William Langland is believed to be the author of the poem "Piers Plowman," first written around 1365. Written in Middle English, like Chaucer's *Canterbury Tales*, it tells the story of Piers, who falls asleep on the Malvern Hills and dreams a series of dreams that set out allegorical commentary on the life and politics of his day. One of the key characters in the dreams is a fellow named Patience. Patience teaches the keys to living a life of faith. Before introducing the character, Langland quoted a proverb, *Bele virtue est suffraunceu,* or as we have evolved it into modern English, "Patience is a beautiful virtue."

The poem, when translated into modern English, is fascinating. The character Patience has much to teach. Patience is where grace grows. At one point, a feast is held, and the character Conscience serves Patience and the author. Patience declares that the food and drink he serves—a sourdough bread of repentance and a mug of long-suffering or endurance—are fit for a king.

The poem is worth a careful read. The same principle is buried in today's passage. Habakkuk has spent the preceding verses questioning God about the unfairness of life. The evil people are winning in the fight against those less evil. Then after lodging his questions, the prophet goes into watch mode. Ascending the metaphorical watchtower in life, he carefully looks out to see how God is going to answer him. He waits patiently.

Simply waiting in faith for God to reveal his answers is a virtue. It produces good fruit in the faithful. Langland in his poem says, at one point, that patience will "prove thee and perfect thee make." He was right.

I have many questions for God. I want to know what he is doing in my life and the lives of many others. I want to know why I have prayed for the souls of many, and yet they have strayed even further from God. I want to know why I have sought God's release from bondage for many friends yet see them chained tight. I want to know . . . and yet God is teaching me patience. He says, "Watch!" In his time, he moves. That is a hard lesson, but one that I am trying to learn.

Lord, I wait and watch for your mighty hand. In your name, amen.

NOVEMBER 6

And the Lord *answered me: "Write the vision; make it plain on tablets, so he may run who reads it. For still the vision awaits its appointed time; it hastens to the end—it will not lie. If it seems slow, wait for it; it will surely come; it will not delay. . . . The righteous shall live by his faith."* (Hab. 2:2–4)

The next generation amazes me. I was in New York visiting our son, daughter-in-law, and two grandchildren. Our granddaughter said to her mom, "Mom, I really want *xyz*." Our daughter-in-law said, "Well, that would be a great thing to add to your birthday list!" Our six-year-old granddaughter said, "Yes! Let's do that!" Of course, her birthday was many months away, but she was learning that great virtue of patience. A short time later, I found myself in Florida with one of our daughters and one of our grandsons, who proclaimed his great desire for a certain truck. Our daughter responded, "That would be a great thing to put on your Christmas list." Christmas was several months away, but our three-year-old grandson was content to put it on his list and wait. Such wise parenting!

Their parenting wisdom reflects a bit of God's response to Habakkuk in today's passage. Habakkuk has declared that he wants God to answer the question of why he is allowing evil to triumph over good, and Habakkuk has set himself upon a watchtower to see God's answer. God tells Habakkuk, "Write this down! Others need to read this!"

God's answer was simple: time is not over. In accounting terms, God doesn't balance the books each microsecond, but when the time is right, an accounting will be made. The responsibility of those who walk with God is to wait in faith, knowing that God will be God and he will make things right.

My grandchildren were great about putting their wants on the list and awaiting the right time to get them. I'm not so patient with God. I live a fast-food life. I can get food immediately, I can get data from Google with a few strokes of the keyboard, and I can buy almost anything using the internet. I'm not patient by nature. Yet God says that things occur in the right time, and my job is to trust him in that while I wait. The righteous will live sitting in faith and trust. Here is a lesson for me from God, the ultimate parent.

Lord, I confess impatience. I confess my tendency to think my timing best. I confess difficulty in trusting you with my limited vision. Grow my faith in you, amen.

NOVEMBER 7

"Woe to him. . . . But the Lord *is in his holy temple; let all the earth keep silence before him."* (Hab. 2:6–20)

I've seen it over and over in life. People beg, scrape, and claw for this, that, or the other, only to get something that winds up biting them in the end. In one particular trial, my goal was to prove to the jury that a certain kind of talc powder had asbestos in it and would cause ovarian cancer. The lawyers arguing that the powder was safe wanted to put on a company witness who was a medical doctor to testify that the powder was safe. The lawyers wanted to have the doctor testify that her mother used the powder all the time. The lawyers' point to the jury would be that the doctor would never let her own mother use the powder if it indeed caused ovarian cancer.

I argued that the witness should not be allowed to testify to personal usage, but the judge overruled me. The doctor took the stand, testified as predicted, and my time came to cross-examine her. In cross-examination, I asked if her mother was still feeling OK. Then the witness seemed to twitch as she told me her mother had died. I asked what her mother had died from, and she confessed, "Ovarian cancer." In my mind, the case was over at that point.

The lawyer never should have taken the risk of pursuing that line of questioning. I filed that away as "Be careful what you ask for; you might get it." In the same vein, today's passage is the culmination of five woes listed by Habakkuk. He pronounces multiple woes on people who gain the property of others through wrongful means, abuse others for personal enjoyment, and worship idols. In each case, what they seek becomes their demise.

Why does it happen this way? Why, when we seek vice or evil or act with greed or selfishness, does it come back to bite us? This is summed up by the end of the passage. It comes back negatively because God is in his holy temple. God is watching. God knows what is happening. God will see to the consequences in his timing. This should cause everyone to stop; quietly observe this truth; think about God's ultimate, final justice; and live accordingly. Live as if God is watching each moment because *God is watching each moment!* This truth transforms me.

Lord, please give me the presence of mind to know each moment of the day, each choice I make, each difficulty I face happens with you watching, waiting, and responding. May I walk by faith in you, as I pray in your name, amen.

NOVEMBER 8

I hear, and my body trembles; my lips quiver at the sound; rottenness enters into my bones; my legs tremble beneath me. Yet I will quietly wait for the day of trouble to come upon people who invade us. (Hab. 3:16)

The news was not good. The doctor came in and explained that someone dear to many was too ill for treatment. It was time to get his house in order because death was around the corner. But wait—we serve the God who can reverse the irreversible. Our God is able to topple mountains. He can revive that which is beyond revivable. With a snap of his fingers, he can make the old new. But our gut told us his time was imminent. What God *can* do and what God *will* do aren't always aligned.

Today's passage comes toward the end of Habakkuk. The third chapter is a prayer put to music. It begins with musical instructions, then proceeds to prayerfully speak of God's coming judgment. The scene will be terrifying to those involved, and it is inevitable. *Could* God refrain? Yes. *Would* God refrain? No. After detailing what was coming, Habakkuk declares, "I hear, and my body trembles." The translation "body" loses a bit of the graphicness of the Hebrew word *beten* (בֶּטֶן). The word references the belly. To use the equivalent modern expression, Habakkuk knew it in his gut. It made his lips quiver, like the chattering of teeth or the trembling that precedes crying. He couldn't stand up because he was so upset.

Habakkuk's response is notable. It begins in today's passage and will continue through the next two days of devotionals. Habakkuk will wait quietly for God's work to be finished. In Habakkuk's response, we see acceptance and faithful trust. His response is inspiring.

Certain times will come in life that are dramatically different from how we would write the script. People dear to us die. Those we love go through great difficulty, and we are unable to aid them. Innocent victims suffer at the hands of others, leaving deep scars. God doesn't ignore these situations, and he certainly teaches his people to do all they can to alleviate pain and hurt. Yet in the end, when our efforts are unsuccessful, we don't sit in anger. We sit in faith, knowing and trusting that God isn't fully finished. For when the end comes, everything will be set right by God, whether we see it or not.

Lord, please give me faith to wait for you in the toughest of times. In you, amen.

NOVEMBER 9

Though the fig tree should not blossom, nor fruit be on the vines, the produce of the olive fail and the fields yield no food, the flock be cut off from the fold and there be no herd in the stalls, yet I will rejoice in the LORD; I will take joy in the God of my salvation. (Hab. 3:17–18)

As little children, we were taught a song with the lyrics "I've got the joy, joy, joy, joy down in my heart, down in my heart, down in my heart; I've got the joy, joy, joy, joy down in my heart, down in my heart to stay." Needless to say, the tune was cheery, and the lively rhythm matched the happy melody. That was decades ago, yet the song lingers in my brain. It resurfaces as I pray over today's passage.

Habakkuk's prayer in his third chapter is drawing to an end, and he has recognized that incredibly tough and hurting times are imminent for his people. He has seen what's coming, and it isn't pretty. People will be in tears as families are destroyed, crops and possessions are stripped, homes are burned, and people are carted off in slavery.

But somehow, with all that is coming, Habakkuk is able to affirm his joy. Nothing is going to strip that joy from him. He can be without food and without the basics of life, but his joy isn't going to be gone. Why? His joy isn't found primarily in his worldly possessions. His joy is found in the LORD. God isn't absent when everything falls apart. God is still present, and God is still working. This is why Habakkuk can confirm the LORD as the God of his *salvation*. Even the worst of times are not the end of times. For God will redeem his people.

This affirmation allows faith in spite of life's circumstances. God's love and presence are the source of a joy that no one can strip. When I trust in God to be there when nothing else is going right, I will find joy. This joy isn't the same as happiness. This joy is deeper and less transient. It can even be a joy with tears. It is faith in the midst of heartache.

The children's song isn't pablum. It's not some meaningless mantra to give false hope. It is a truth that should seep deeply into our minds, resurfacing in times of difficulty. I may be in a wretched season, but I'm not alone. God walks it with me, and that produces joy in the midst of sorrow.

Lord, teach me your joy. Let it run deep in my mind and heart. In you I pray, amen.

NOVEMBER 10

GOD, the Lord, is my strength; he makes my feet like the deer's; he makes me tread on my high places. (Hab. 3:19)

My high school friend told me, "You must read *Hind's Feet on High Places* by Hannah Hunard. It will change your life!" I found the small paperback and loved it. It tells the story of Much Afraid, who was in the service of the Great Shepherd. She lived in a village of Much Trembling, and her flocks were found in the Valley of Humiliation. As you might recognize, the book was an allegory of all the things that hold people back in life, keeping them from being all they can be.

As the book progresses, little Much Afraid grows and learns. The inspiration and result of her growth through the difficulties of life are expressed in the book using this last verse from Habakkuk. God makes her feet like those of a doe (or a "hind" in the old King James Version), which can nimbly jump over obstacles. Thus, God teaches her to skip on the mountain peaks of life.

Today's passage suited Hunard's purposes and title for the book, for there are few places in Scripture that affirm faith so eloquently. This verse closes a book that includes many questions about God and his justice. Over and over, Habakkuk peppered God with probing questions of why evil is allowed to hurt good people and why evil people are allowed to experience goodness and success. It doesn't seem right, nor does it seem a righteous God would allow it.

Yet the lessons Habakkuk teaches from this interchange with God include that (1) God allows questions asked in faith; (2) God's timing isn't the same as human timing, so although weeping may come, the story isn't over until God is finished; and (3) when God is finished, everything will be made right. His faithful children will be made whole, and his enemies will suffer righteous punishment.

As Habakkuk internalized these lessons, he found strength in God, even in the midst of difficulties. This strength produced joy and an ability to live well today. So that even while the strains and stresses of life abounded, Habakkuk was able to maneuver through life like a deer is able to prance around in the mountains, bounding from rock to rock. God put a skip in his step, and he knew everything would be OK. This is a profound lesson of faith for me, because I'm too often more like Hunard's character Much Afraid.

Lord, place the skip in my step that comes from faith. I trust and pray in you, amen.

NOVEMBER 11

In the second year of Darius the king, in the sixth month, on the first day of the month, the word of the LORD came by the hand of Haggai the prophet to Zerubbabel the son of Shealtiel, governor of Judah, and to Joshua the son of Jehozadak, the high priest. (Hag. 1:1)

A long time ago, I began my faith walk with God. Maybe the time wasn't that far back compared to most of history, but it was to me! I was a kid when I started down this path. I'm still on the same faith journey that I began some fifty years ago. Memories of those early days seem a lifetime away. Many events have come and gone, yet my faith is still real and strong. Time continues forward. That is life.

I reminisce about time as I focus on today's passage because a huge shift happened to Israel between the last prophetic book in this study (Habakkuk) and the book of Haggai, which we begin today. The previous prophets had spoken of the downfall of the Hebrew people in Israel (the northern kingdom) and Judah (the southern kingdom). Those downfalls happened at different times, as the prophets had foretold. The last to fall was the kingdom of Judah, which had been conquered by Nebuchadnezzar, the king of Babylon. Judah had suffered greatly. Jerusalem was devastated, with its walls pulled down and the temple destroyed. Many survivors were carted off to Babylon, a journey of nine hundred miles on foot.

Those taken into captivity lived in and around Babylon for sixty-plus years. Toward the end of that time, Babylon itself was conquered by Cyrus, king of the Persian Empire (in October 539 BCE). Cyrus announced that the captives from Babylon were free to return to their homelands, and many Jews left Babylon to go back to Jerusalem. There they found devastation, not the beauty that their grandparents and great-grandparents had described. The city was in ruins. Homes were destroyed. No walls existed to protect from marauders, animals, or thieves. No temple existed for worship. No fields were ready for planting. Life was in shambles.

But the same prophets who predicted Judah's downfall also prophesied of its restoration. God was still working generations later. Time didn't rob him of his promises, nor should it rob his people of their faith. Time moves on, but one constant through all time is God. To him we direct our faith, today and forever.

Lord, grow my faith in you day by day throughout all days. In your name, amen.

NOVEMBER 12

"Now, therefore, thus says the LORD of hosts: Consider your ways. . . . You looked for much, and behold, it came to little. And when you brought it home, I blew it away. Why? declares the LORD of hosts. Because of my house that lies in ruins, while each of you busies himself with his own house." (Hag. 1:5, 9)

In law school, I got a coveted spot on our moot court team. We had to try out to get one of these three positions, and I was a bit nervous when we first met with our coach, the marvelous appellate lawyer Don Hunt, who, in addition to his private practice, coached our law school's teams. Lawyers are famous for overworking. "Sweatshop" is a common name for many law firms. Of course, law professors seem to think you should spend all your time on law school. I was mildly surprised and very impressed when at our first meeting, Coach said, "Here's what I expect on your priorities: First you place your faith and family, then you place your schoolwork. After that, I want all your time." Putting faith first was not what I expected to hear, but it was the right priority then and in life ever since.

Coach Hunt would have fit well with the prophet Haggai and God's message to the people. The people had returned to a Jerusalem that had been desolate for almost a century. The temple was destroyed, their homes were in ruins, and their farmlands, vineyards, and orchards were weeded over. The people were setting about working on their homes, some with plans of luxury. But no one had a mind to also be working on the temple, the place where the people were to meet God in worship and sacrifice. Their efforts at farming the land were not meeting great success. Their sheep weren't breeding prolifically enough for wool supplies to keep the people clothed warmly. They were struggling daily.

God then speaks through Haggai to the people: consider your ways! The people had their priorities wrong. They needed Coach Hunt. If they put their faith first, followed next by their families and then their work, God would bless what they were doing. Their daily needs would be met. Life would grow. They would prosper, all to the glory of God.

This is a reminder to me to live with God as the hub of my heart and life. Then like a wheel, life becomes spokes that proceed from faith as the center. He helps me love my family. He helps me do well at work. He is present in all I do.

Lord, give me wisdom and presence to seek you and your will as most important in life. Help me with my family, and help me work to your glory and in your name, amen.

The people, obeyed the voice of the LORD their God, and the words of Haggai the prophet, as the LORD their God had sent him. And the people feared the LORD. Then Haggai, the messenger of the LORD, spoke to the people with the LORD's message, "I am with you, declares the LORD." (Hag. 1:12–13)

From an early age, I loved the music of Bruce Springsteen. He came out of a working community in New Jersey to sing of the plight of everyday people struggling to get through life with a smile. Living in Lubbock, Texas, I couldn't really relate to the Jersey scene, but the songs spoke to me nonetheless. A few days after I graduated from high school, Bruce dropped his album *Darkness on the Edge of Town*. It was a dark album but contained glimmers of promise, as if the town with light and life was perhaps attainable.

In the song "Badlands," Bruce sings about the difficulties of life. When the lights are out, things don't make sense, you fear each day, you work yourself to death and seem to get nowhere, your heart's broken, your back's broken, and you never feel satisfied with your lot in life—these are the "badlands" of which he sings.

These were also the badlands where the Jews returned after a century of captivity in Babylon. They had gone to the home country that they had grown up hearing was beautiful and flowing with milk and honey. But in truth, it was in shambles. It didn't seem a Promised Land; it seemed more like Badlands.

But there is a bright spot in the Badlands. Bruce sings a refrain that says, "I believe in the love that you gave me; I believe in the faith that can save me; I believe in the hope, and I pray that someday it may raise me above these Badlands." He was right to believe!

Today's passage follows Haggai's rebuke of the people for fouling up their priorities, thinking they needed to fend for their security and material needs before seeing to their faith and service of God. Haggai rebuked them, they listened, and they heeded what he said. Then they found life! God declared that he himself was present with them.

When my days seem dark and I dwell in darkness, I need to recheck my priorities. God will be my light. God will make my badlands good!

Lord, I turn to you. Be my light and bring goodness to my days. In you, amen.

NOVEMBER 14

"Yet now be strong, O Zerubbabel, declares the LORD. Be strong, O Joshua, son of Jehozadak, the high priest. Be strong, all you people of the land, declares the LORD. Work, for I am with you, declares the LORD of hosts." (Hag. 2:4)

One of the best singer-songwriters in my generation is Paul Simon. He had a special gift for writing a first line that was a real attention-getter. Song openings like "Well, I would not give you false hope on this strange and mournful day" draw you in and make you stay. One of my favorites is from "The Sound of Silence." Simon begins the song, "Hello darkness, my old friend." You know you are in for quite a song when the lyrics start that way.

This occurs to me within the context of today's passage. The prophet Haggai addressed the people at a time when they were struggling mightily. They had trouble getting their lives on track. Poverty and lack were the main descriptors of their daily lives. They awoke each morning to darkness, their old friend! Haggai urged the people to make God their first priority, assuring them if they did so, then they would be living rightly, whether in poverty or plenty. God would be their light and dispel the darkness of each day. The people heeded Haggai's correction, and God came to them and again promised, just like he did in yesterday's devotion, his presence during these difficult days.

In today's passage, God then assured the people that because they had sought him first, he would ensure that their work would be strong. God told them, "Work! For I am with you!" This is a positive plot twist in their lives! When they earlier worked with God as a low priority, they got nowhere fast. But see the change: when they made God their top priority, God didn't stop them from working; he began working with them. The work may have been virtually the same but with a different attitude, and consequently, their world was about to dramatically improve.

I like this on many levels. I find it encouraging and "real world-y." I know I need to work. (This is true even for students. School work is real!) But sometimes, work can seem dark and full of drudgery. That's a sure sign we need a God infusion. If we make our work something done in service to God our king, suddenly we discover that we aren't working alone or in silence. We have God himself working with us. Now that is a turnaround.

Lord, I give my work to you today. I want to work to your glory, doing that which you made me to do. Be with me, empower me, give me your peace! In you, amen.

NOVEMBER 15

"Is the seed yet in the barn? Indeed, the vine, the fig tree, the pomegranate, and the olive tree have yielded nothing. But from this day on I will bless you." (Hag. 2:19)

I was worried. It was near the end of my college education and the first time in forever I didn't hold a job. I was trying to cram in too many hours so I could graduate early, and I didn't see how I could work at the same time. But I wasn't without resources. My grandmother had promised me some funds, and I knew she was reliable. The problem was this preceded the days of easy electronic funds transfers. So I was waiting on a check in the mail. I didn't know if it would come in time, however, because I needed to buy gas for my car and a few other necessities. Lo and behold, the check came right before I ran out of funds. Perfect timing! (Thank you, Grandmother!)

Timing is God's specialty. Because of that, we are called to run on his time; he doesn't run on ours. Today's passage is an encouraging reminder of that truth. God had promised to restore Judah in prosperity. As of Haggai's prophetic ministry, Jews were restored to the land, but they were far from prosperous. Their crops were failing, and they were worried about food on the table.

Enter into the picture Haggai. Haggai came in and declared that the wait was over. God's blessings were going to be seen in tangible ways. The people would prosper again. That word from Haggai was perfectly timed, as were the blessings of God.

Sometimes we need a word of encouragement to continue in faithful service when times are bleak. It helps to know that God hasn't fallen asleep. God isn't false to his promises. God doesn't fail to attend to his children in need. God is faithful in his love and devotion.

The key for us is to recognize that his timing isn't our timing. God will come: God will deliver, God will provide, and God will amaze and stun. But God will do so when the moment is absolutely right. We can stand in expectation and amazement as we faithfully await our God.

Lord, sometimes my patience wears thin. I worry when I shouldn't. Fear sometimes invades my faith. Yet you have sustained me in all my days, so I give you thanks as I wait for you, praying as always. In your name, amen.

NOVEMBER 16

"On that day, declares the LORD *of hosts, I will take you, O Zerubbabel my servant, the son of Shealtiel, declares the* LORD, *and make you like a signet ring, for I have chosen you, declares the* LORD *of hosts."* (Hag. 2:23)

In the legal world, I sign many documents under oath with a notary's affirmation attached. This is a legal verification that my signature is genuine. The notary also stamps the document with the notary's seal, affirming the notary's authority. Similarly, seals were used over five thousand years ago, as early as 3,500 BCE, in Mesopotamia. Kings used seals to confirm that the document came from them. Pharaohs of Egypt adopted seals but stamped documents using a seal that was placed on a ring that they wore. No one could wear the seal on his finger except the pharaoh. By the time of Haggai, these rings were common among many kings.

Before Judah was taken into captivity by the Babylonians, some one hundred-plus years before Haggai, the prophet Jeremiah declared to the king of Judah that God said that the king had been like a seal or signet ring that God had on his own (metaphorical) finger. Yet God was going to tear the ring off his finger and give it to Nebuchadnezzar, the king of Babylon. God was no longer going to wear (using the ring metaphor) the people of Judah as his own.

Today's passage is the last verse of Haggai, and in it, Haggai harkens back to this interchange between God and the people of Judah. Looking to the future, God declares that he will take Zerubbabel, who was of the lineage of King David, and would make him like a signet ring that he would again wear. At the time of this prophecy, Zerubbabel was a governor at best and certainly not the head of a kingdom. But in Hebrew thought, when Haggai spoke of Zerubbabel's future, he spoke also of those in the lineage of Zerubbabel.

In today's passage, Haggai is speaking of the future. Many understand this to refer to that Messianic age when God will restore the line of David to a throne to reign forever. But it also says something more. It affirms that God is a God of reversal. God takes bad things or events and can reverse them into good. The way things aren't the way they will always be. God knows what the future holds, and he holds that future. This should reassure everyone. There's a difference between how things are now and how they will be in the future.

Lord, I trust you with my tomorrow, leaning on you to reverse those things that need reversing and bringing life where things are dying. In your name, amen.

NOVEMBER 17

In the eighth month, in the second year of Darius, the word of the LORD *came to the prophet Zechariah, the son of Berechiah, son of Iddo, saying . . .* (Zech. 1:1)

In April 2021, Apple began selling the AirTag, a device that helps you find lost items. You can attach it to your key ring, slide it in your purse or wallet, or put it almost anywhere. Then when you lose or misplace the item, you can more readily find it. (I have yet to figure out how to attach it to my glasses, something I lose often.) Within the first year, Apple sold about fifty million of these devices, which shows that I'm not the only one who constantly loses things.

My poor memory of where I put things seems to be in my DNA. I have always been this way. But not God! God remembers, and more than that, God acts on his memory. We are reminded of that in today's passage.

Today we begin a series of devotionals from the book of Zechariah, often described as the most obscure of the Minor Prophets. Zechariah's name, however, gives a clue to a good bit of the content. Zechariah is a combination of two Hebrew words: (1) *zechar* (זכר), which is typically translated as "remember," and (2) *iah*, which is an ending often attached to a name and is a shortened form of YHWH, the "name" of God. In Zechariah's name, one is encouraged by the truth expressed in the name: God remembers!

Our English word *remember* doesn't quite give the full flavor of the Hebrew word. In Hebrew, the word, especially when used in reference to God, doesn't reference remembering something that had previously been forgotten. The word emphasizes taking action on something that's present in your mind.

I like the way today's verse launches the book. For the book came at a time when the Jews had returned to their lands and towns *after* having spent sixty years in Babylonian captivity. They returned home as God had promised because of one simple truth: God remembers. God took action based on his promises long before.

Of course, God hasn't stopped. He still remembers. He will still act faithful to his promises today. He will act for you and for me. We can trust him, because God remembers!

Lord, please help me today. Take action in my life! In your name, amen.

NOVEMBER 18

"The LORD was very angry with your fathers. Therefore say to them, Thus declares the LORD of hosts: Return to me, says the LORD of hosts, and I will return to you, says the LORD of hosts." (Zech. 1:2–3)

The judge called six of us into his private conference room. He was clearly angry. We went in, and the judge followed, sitting at the head of his conference table. The judge then looked at one of the lawyers and called him down for a fairly egregious judgment call the lawyer had made. The judge pointed out not only the error but that the lawyer had done it intentionally, thinking he could get away with it.

The judge looked at the lawyer and asked what he had to say for himself. The lawyer began stuttering, trying to justify his actions. The judge interrupted sternly and said, "I only want to hear three things from you." Then holding up one finger, then two, and then a third, the judge said, "One, I am sorry; I was wrong. Two, I won't do it again. And three, what can I do to make it right?" The lawyer didn't get it and kept trying to justify himself. But the judge would have none of it and kept interrupting, saying, "I only want to hear those three points. Make them or face the consequences." The rest of us listened, with heads bowed, lest we make eye contact with the judge!

That memory and those three steps were seared into my mind that day. The judge, a devout man raised by a preacher, knew a thing or two about repentance and the Bible. When people offend and sin against God, the judge's three-point response works well.

Zechariah is about to launch into a number of oracles. Before doing so, however, he wants his audience to be of a right mind. He begins by reminding them of the people's offense against God. He tells them to "return" or repent. He wants them to do their three steps!

I know that I'm far from perfect. I tend to live with self-centeredness, which often drives me to say and do selfish things. I don't have the self-control I would like. I'm not as kind or patient as I should be. The list can go on and on. But I know how to come before God in repentance.

Lord, I am sorry for my sin. I don't want to sin, and I will work to fix what I have done wrong. In your name and by your power, amen.

NOVEMBER 19

*"Do not be like your fathers, to whom the former prophets cried out, 'Thus says the L*ORD *of hosts, Return from your evil ways and from your evil deeds.' But they did not hear or pay attention to me, declares the L*ORD*." (Zech. 1:4)*

Have you ever considered yourself obstinate? The word comes from the Latin verb *obstinare* (which means to persist). An obstinate person is stubbornly determined to continue along with an opinion, plan, or purpose despite good reasons to change. Sometimes in my life, *obstinate* might as well be my middle name. From simple and insignificant areas to those much more notable, I have doggedly kept opinions that are unreasonable and pursued goals that aren't worth pursuing. Like a dog that can't drop a ball, I have held on to things that are useless in life.

Today's passage is one about obstinacy. Zechariah's audience were people fresh back from sixty years of forced exile. The exile should have stunned no one. The people of Judah weren't living in a vacuum where exile jumped up and surprised them. The people had stubbornly lived bowing to idols and ignoring the God who had called them, saved them, delivered them, protected them, and cared for them. God had put an umbrella of protection over the people, and the people refused to stay under that umbrella. Instead, they ventured out into the storm.

God had sent prophets to warn the people. These prophets declared God's truth, announcing that the course being chosen was one that stripped the people of God's protection. By leaving God's umbrella, the people were going to get caught up in huge storms. God, therefore, urges the people to get back under the umbrella and worship and serve him.

The people didn't respond with repentance to the prophets. They mocked, ridiculed, ignored, and in some cases, persecuted God's chosen prophets. Rather than return to God, they strayed even further, obstinate in all their ways. Zechariah reminds the people of their dreadful history and urges them not to be like their fathers.

Obstinacy is an enemy of growth. It stems from not only rebellion but also pride. We should not only be willing to change our ways before God; we should seek to do so. Our goal should be to grow before him. I have some work to do.

Lord, forgive my pride, my obstinacy to sin, and my all-too-frequent focus on myself and what I want. Give me a heart for you and your will. In your name, amen.

NOVEMBER 20

On the twenty-fourth day of the eleventh month, which is the month of Shebat, in the second year of Darius, the word of the LORD came to the prophet Zechariah, the son of Berechiah, son of Iddo, saying . . . (Zech. 1:7)

If you are reading this devotional by the calendar entry, then today is November 20. I put these devotionals in my best estimate of chronology, meaning I started the year and book with the earliest prophets and have continued through time to the later ones. In a way, that is a pity, especially today.

Why? Today's passage references a vision that God gave to Zechariah on the "twenty-fourth day of the eleventh month, which is the month of Shebat, in the second year of Darius." Scholars have determined the exact date; it was February 15, 519 BCE. If I had been clever, I would have figured out how to read it on its anniversary, but I couldn't make that work with the chronology.

Even without nailing the anniversary of the passage, Scripture's identity of this specific date shows us something about God. Falling one day after our modern celebration in the West of Valentine's Day, this was a red-letter day for the prophet. He had no apparent reason to be so specific, yet he was. The specificity focuses my mind on how God reveals and works in this world each and every day, whether people realize it or not.

On February 15, November 20, or any other date for that matter, God is at work speaking to and seeking out his people. Our brains are hardwired for communication. Even the youngest baby can be soothed with sound or touch, both forms of communication. We want to know that we aren't alone. We want to know that others are in contact with us. It not only brings out the best in us, but it also makes us sane. There's a reason the ultimate punishment in the penal system is solitary confinement that limits communication with others.

You and I are not in isolation today. We may feel it. We may wonder why we don't have close friends, why we don't have a significant other, or why we face life alone, but the truth is, we don't have to. God seeks a relationship with us each day. He's never further than a prayer away. His word has been secured for us to read and pray through any and every day. This is remarkable and shouldn't be missed.

Lord, thank you for being there. Thank you for wanting to communicate with me. I bless you as I seek you today. In your will and in your name, amen.

NOVEMBER 21

*"And the L*ORD *answered gracious and comforting words to the angel who talked with me. . . . Cry out again, Thus says the L*ORD *of hosts: My cities shall again overflow with prosperity, and the L*ORD *will again comfort Zion and again choose Jerusalem."* (Zech. 1:13, 17)

If you are traveling away from home, you can choose to stay at a Comfort Inn. If you are stressed, you might choose to eat some comfort food. If someone has lost a loved one, you might be in a position to offer them comfort. While visiting a friend, they might urge you to make yourself comfortable. I like to sleep in my bed at night because my sheets and pillow comfort my head and body. Some people draw comfort from a dog, others from a cat, and others from no pet at all.

Comfort is a good thing. No one recoils from comfort. The word comes from two Latin words: *com,* meaning "along with" or "together," and *fortis,* meaning strong. To comfort is to strengthen, support, or console another.

The two verses in today's passages speak of comfort, but not of one person comforting another. The passages speak of God comforting. God spoke to an angel in "gracious and comforting" words in verse 13 and explained that he would "comfort Zion" in verse 17.

God wants to comfort his people. God wants to come alongside and share our lives with us. He wants to strengthen us in our weaknesses. He wants to support us in our godly endeavors. He wants to console us in our losses. The comfort of God comes from his compassionate heart. It is worth noting that the Jews who translated this passage into Greek in the centuries before Jesus used a form of the Greek word *parakletos* for the "comforting words" that God speaks in verse 13. Jesus would use this same word to speak of God's Holy Spirit. God comes alongside his people in comfort.

I need God's comfort. I need his gentle touch in my life. I need him more than a comfortable bed and pillow, more than comfort food, and more than a pet. When God touches our lives with kindness and gentleness, we are stronger. We are able to find joy in sorrow. We function much better in times of stress. We serve an amazingly loving God!

Lord, I desperately want your comfort in my life. I seek you and your touch today. Thank you for your love and compassion. In your name, amen.

NOVEMBER 22

"Jerusalem shall be inhabited as villages without walls, because of the multitude of people and livestock in it. And I will be to her a wall of fire all around, declares the LORD, *and I will be the glory in her midst."* (Zech. 2:4–5)

In 2023, the Kansas City Chiefs defeated the Philadelphia Eagles to win the National Football League's fifty-seventh Super Bowl. The Chiefs sported a great quarterback, Patrick Mahomes, who unfortunately had sustained a high ankle sprain just weeks before the big game. His health for the game was a major focal point. Football aficionados knew that the Chiefs could win only if both the offensive line protected Mahomes and Mahomes shined in his performance. Both happened, and the rest is history.

In 586 BCE, the Babylonians destroyed Jerusalem, pulling down the city's walls, dismantling the temple, and carting the residents off into captivity. The injury was great. But for the Lord, the Babylonians would have permanently destroyed the nation. Yet by God's hand, the Jews survived and returned to Jerusalem, a city in ruins. They began to rebuild. During this time, God, through night visions, gave eight oracles to Zechariah. Today's passage is the second of those oracles.

This vision began with a man going out over the city with a measuring line in hand. This indicated that rebuilding the city was part of the dream because a measuring line was used in building. An angel then told Zechariah today's passage. The angel explained that Jerusalem would be as a village without walls, with masses of people and livestock living there. Normally, walls were necessary for protection, but the angel explained that God would be the protection, like a wall of fire. Furthermore, God would place his glory inside the city.

If Kansas City needed an offensive line to protect a glorious quarterback in order to win the Super Bowl, that is small potatoes compared to the need of a city to have God protecting it and placing his glory within it.

This brings me to you and me. We will be attacked on many fronts in our lives. We will face moral, physical, and emotional onslaughts. We will never have the level of protection we need unless we have God as our protecting wall and his glory dwelling within us. Only then will we rise up to live how we should.

Lord, please be my protection. May my life reflect your glory, and may you shine from me into the darkness of the world. In your name, amen.

NOVEMBER 23

For thus said the Lord *of hosts, after his glory sent me to the nations who plundered you, for he who touches you touches the apple of his eye.* (Zech. 2:8)

Stevie Wonder, in his 1972 song "You Are the Sunshine of My Life," sang, "You are the apple of my eye; forever you'll stay in my heart." I first heard the phrase "apple of my eye" then. I wasn't conversant enough in Shakespeare to know *A Midsummer Night's Dream*, where, in Act 3, Oberon exclaims, "Flower of this purple dye; Hit with Cupid's archery; Sink in apple of his eye" (i.e., cupid drops love juice on Demetrius' eyelids). Nor did I know that Anglo-Saxon King Alfred had used the phrase "*æppel* of the eye" to translate a Latin passage. Yet the earliest use of the phrase is actually in multiple Old Testament passages, including today's! (To be fair, that is the common English translation of the Hebrew phrase that more accurately might be translated as the "pupil" of one's eye.)

The point of the expression is one of endearment. This makes today's passage rather touching and profound. Many people suffer from a poor self-image. We see this in the ways people try to compensate for low-self-esteem: they become tough to hide weakness, become self-absorbed to disguise self-disgust, become bullies to overcome self-limitations, become liars for fear the truth isn't important enough, and so on. Inferiority complexes are big drivers of the way people act at any age.

Yet no one should ever feel inferior. For the biblical truth is that we're created in God's image, and God has made each person to be in a relationship with him. God seeks to hold each person as the apple of his eye. God wants to endear himself to us, as we are very dear to him. The value of each person is incomprehensible.

If each of us could see ourselves in this way, this world would be radically different. My perspective on the world changes as my perspective of who I am changes. When we find ourselves as the apple, or pupil, of God's eye, we find an indescribable peace. We realize that God will go to the greatest lengths on our behalf, always seeking what is best for us, even when it isn't what we might choose for ourselves. We begin to see the world in a new light. We begin to treat others with the same love that our loving God has for us. Our impatience fades away into meaninglessness. Our anger resolves into contentment. Problems become opportunities. We are transformed. May God give us this grace.

Lord, I treasure being the apple of your eye. May I know that truth. In you, amen.

NOVEMBER 24

"Sing and rejoice, O daughter of Zion, for behold, I come and I will dwell in your midst, declares the LORD.*" (Zech. 2:10)*

Once talking films were invented, musicals became a top-selling genre. Even before talking films, operas and operettas popularized certain songs and music. Typically, some event causes the characters to break out into song. For example, in 1978's blockbuster hit *Grease*, the greaser Danny Zuko, played by John Travolta, and the Australian transfer student Sandy Olsson, played by Olivia Newton-John, proclaim their attraction for each other by passionately singing "You're the One That I Want." The song hit number one in many countries and was certified platinum, selling over two million copies.

Some things in life make you want to sing. That's not a recent phenomenon, as today's passage portrays. God is declaring to Zechariah the ways he is going to bless his people. The very same tribes that had been sent into captivity, losing their land and being plundered by their enemies, were going to see a huge reversal. God would not only be bringing a generation back to their land but be blessing them immensely and enabling them to plunder their enemies.

These events should certainly make one want to break out into song. So in the passage, God instructs the Jewish people to "sing and rejoice." Interestingly, though, this singing and rejoicing isn't because the people get to return to Judah. Nor is it because God is going to bring tragedy on their enemies, giving their wealth as plunder. The reason for singing and rejoicing is because God is going to be in the midst of his people.

God isn't proclaiming a summer romance, like Travolta and Newton-John. God is declaring a restoration of a relationship for the ages. From the very beginning, God sought to be in a relationship with his creation. He walked and spoke with Adam and Eve in the cool of the garden. Yet humanity often wanders from God, sometimes in outright rebellion. God's love story doesn't end with rebellion; it ends with restoration. That's the promise in today's passage, and that's a reality worthy of songs of rejoicing. Find a song that rejoices before God, and sing it today.

Lord, I seek to be in a direct relationship with you. Guide me into that, and put a song of rejoicing in my heart and on my lips. I praise you as my Lord and God, and I do so in your name, amen.

NOVEMBER 25

Be silent, all flesh, before the LORD, for he has roused himself from his holy dwelling. (Zech. 2:13)

Who goes first? The decision is often decided by the flip of a coin. In the Super Bowl, for example, a special coin is used. It has the Super Bowl insignia as well as the logos for the two teams playing. Before the coin flip, the official tells the team captains which side will be considered heads and which side will be considered tails. The double-sided feature of every coin has given birth to common expressions like "There are two sides to every coin." It's a simple and obvious truth.

Today's passage read by itself might not evoke the truth of two sides to a coin. But if one reads it in conjunction with the passage used in yesterday's devotional, the dual nature becomes apparent. Both yesterday's passage and today's are part of the same vision and instruction from God to Zechariah. Yesterday, we saw the people are told to "sing and rejoice." Today, they're told to "Be silent" or "Hush!"

It doesn't take rocket science to read these two passages and see that there's a time to sing and a time to be silent. The singing was the appropriate response for God returning to his people to dwell in their midst. The command for silence also has a reason: God has "roused himself from his holy dwelling."

Using a verb aspect called the *niphal*, Zechariah is declaring that God has stirred himself and he is on the move. God has chosen this time to begin what he has earlier planned. The time is ripe, and God is about to do something spectacular.

When God is moving in a special way, sometimes it isn't a time to sing but a time to watch. God rightly commands our focus and attention. This was true as God oversaw world empires overthrown, but it isn't exclusively for events on a world stage. We experience God's movement in our lives as well. When God is afoot in special, direct ways, we may hear his inner voice as he rouses us from our slumber into a more direct walk with him or may sense his presence when life events seem to turn upside down as God commands our attention. In these situations, we should be silent, listen, and watch. God is a moving God who takes action at the right time and in the right ways in our lives. After those actions are done, we can sing and rejoice, but sometimes we need to be still, listen, and watch first.

Lord, move in my life and world to your glory as I pray and watch. In you, amen.

Then he showed me Joshua the high priest standing before the angel of the LORD, and Satan standing at his right hand to accuse him. (Zech. 3:1)

Keith Green wrote a song entitled "Satan's Boast." The song portrays Satan, who proudly proclaims, "My job keeps getting easier as time keeps slipping away. I can imitate your brightest light and make your night look just like day. I put some truth in every lie to tickle itching ears. You know I'm drawing people just like flies 'cause they like what they hear." Then he brings the repeated chorus lines emphasizing, "I'm gaining power by the hour. They're falling by the score. You know, it's getting very simple now 'cause no one believes in me anymore."

It is amazing how much evil is in the world and yet how many people don't believe in Satan. Today's passage shines a spotlight on him. It's one of the rare passages in the Old Testament where he is called Satan. He is called a "serpent" in the garden of Eden. He is called an "evil spirit" repeatedly in the Old Testament. But here, he is called by the Hebrew word שָׂטָן, which is literally pronounced "Satan."

Our label or name *Satan* comes directly from the Hebrew word. The word references one who is hostile to others and accuses others. The verb form of the word is used in today's passage and translated as "accuse." One could easily translate today's passage as "Satan standing at this right hand to satan him." Or one could say, "The Accuser is standing at his right hand to accuse him."

I find the reality of Satan obvious, even as others find him unbelievable. We live in an age of deception. I have seen clear evil. There are horrid influences that seek to control us. I've seen people change as influencers lead them astray. Some might think this is all of human origin, but I believe there are dark spiritual powers beyond our human race.

Does this frighten or discourage me? Not at all. I know there's one greater than Satan. Satan is not equal to God. He is much below God. He is portrayed in this passage as on the level of the high priest but far below God. I won't ignore Satan. I won't give him his way unabated. I will watch for him and his wily ways and, with God's grace, seek to thwart him in this world.

Lord, reveal my enemies, and be my strength today. In your name, amen.

NOVEMBER 27

Now Joshua was standing before the angel, clothed with filthy garments. And the angel said to those who were standing before him, "Remove the filthy garments from him." And to him he said, "Behold, I have taken your iniquity away from you, and I will clothe you with pure vestments." (Zech. 3:3–4)

I dreaded those days when Mom would declare, "Clean up your room!" Sometimes it was even worse. Mom would instruct me to clean out my toybox. Oh my. (It wasn't until I became a parent that Mom told me that was her ploy when I was bored. She found that as I cleaned out my toy chest, I found toys I hadn't played with in some time, and I would play much more than I would clean. It kept me distracted for hours!)

Some things we can clean. Some we can't. Today's passage speaks to the latter situation.

Consider the passage in context: Zechariah is having a fourth vision in the night. In this vision, a high priest named Joshua stands before God's representative, an angel. "Joshua" is both a famous Old Testament character who led Israel into the Promised Land but also a common Hebrew name. The name means "Yahweh (the LORD) is my salvation." Also standing before the Lord's angel is Satan, the accuser. The passage indicates that Satan is accusing the people through their high priest Joshua.

Normally, one would simply say, "Away with you, Satan!" but there's a problem here. The accusations do not seem false but seem true. Joshua stands before the Lord's representative in filthy clothes! The filth reference isn't simply to the clothes but to what they represent. The dirty clothes are metaphors for the people's sinful deeds. In other words, Satan's accusations are well grounded! The people have been vile and filthy in their behavior, not something that sits well with a pure God.

Neither the high priest nor the people are able to clean themselves up. It's like using a dirty hand to wipe dirt from one's face. It doesn't work. But Satan doesn't win the day. God intervenes. He washes the people clean from their iniquity and gives them pure, clean clothes to wear. Only God can purify us from sin.

Lord, I turn to you and your forgiveness. Please take away my iniquity and place your purity in my life. I seek this in your name and holiness, amen.

NOVEMBER 28

"This is the word of the LORD to Zerubbabel: Not by might, nor by power, but by my Spirit, says the LORD of hosts. Who are you, O great mountain? Before Zerubbabel you shall become a plain." (Zech. 4:6–7)

I'm a list guy. Give me a list of things to do, and I will get a lot more done than if no list is in front of me. I will get it done more efficiently too. I tend to order my lists, often putting the easier things at the top to give me momentum as I get into the harder things. The key is getting done what needs to be done.

Zerubbabel had a list. The number one thing he had to do was rebuild the temple. But that chore was impossible, regardless of where it was on his list. The temple site was a wreck from its destruction a century earlier. The site was doubtless overgrown, and Zerubbabel had volunteer workers, no real budget, and no modern machinery. And he would have to import temple stones, which were massive. I wonder if Zerubbabel even knew where to start.

Into this moment in history, God gave a dream to Zechariah. The dream concerned a lamp—a key symbol of the temple. The temple itself was God's presence with his people in a way that showed God to the world. The lamp had extra arms for pouring the oil in so they wouldn't run out. Oil was frequently a symbol of God's Spirit moving and working in and on people. Zechariah was befuddled about the dream and needed God's angel to explain it.

The angel explained that the rebuilding of the temple wouldn't be easy. It would be a mountain of a chore. But the task was God's task, not just that of Zerubbabel. The temple would be built not by might or by power but by God's Spirit. God was at work on this task. Zerubbabel wasn't going it alone. The mountainous obstacles would become flatlands for Zerubbabel. As my dad would say, those obstacles are "no hill for a stepper."

This dream must have boosted Zerubbabel's resolve and helped him get through his mountainous chore. It also boosts me. As I face my "to-do" list today, I can know that when my jobs are done before and for God, he will be my strength and help. I can do my list by his Spirit, and the challenges will be overcome. Thank God!

Lord, I set my list of things to do before you. I pray that my list will match your list for me and that you will empower me to do your will. In your name, amen.

NOVEMBER 29

"The hands of Zerubbabel have laid the foundation of this house; his hands shall also complete it. Then you will know that the LORD of hosts has sent me to you. For whoever has despised the day of small things shall rejoice, and shall see the plumb line in the hand of Zerubbabel." (Zech. 4:9-10)

I started throwing papers as a paperboy in fourth grade in Rochester, New York. The first few years were easy because the *Times Union* came out in the afternoon and only on weekdays, so I would throw them after school. When we moved to Lubbock, I got a paper boy job delivering the *Avalanche Journal*. It was an early morning delivery, seven days a week. Every morning for several years, I would awaken at 5:00 a.m. to deliver my papers. From there, I took a job at a community store, sweeping, stocking, and so on. After that, I managed an apartment complex and from there went to lawyering.

Each job taught me something. I learned responsibility from throwing papers early every morning. I couldn't call in sick. I couldn't go out of town without setting up someone to take my place. I learned how to clean at the community store. Each job taught me an important life skill.

That is the way of life. That is a lesson from today's passage. Zerubbabel is tasked with rebuilding the temple of God. It wasn't going to be done in a day, a week, or even a year. It was an awesome task, made even more difficult by the circumstances. Each day would provide an observer plenty of reasons to scoff. The passage refers to "the day of small things." The work done each day undoubtedly seemed small—incremental at best. Yet over time, day by day, the building progressed. Like weight loss (or gain), it might not be noticed each day, but it adds up over longer periods of time. The key was to keep working.

God is at work in the lives of his people. God's work in your life and mine is also incremental. Each day we follow God, we find his hand working to fashion us, rewire our brains, train our will, teach us godliness, guide us into the works he has set apart for us, and empower us to do those works. God is at work daily. We may not see the big results for some time, but as we stay faithful in our walk, we find God more than faithful in his work. Don't ever despise the small things. They build the future.

Lord, work in me today to your glory! In your name, I live and pray, amen.

NOVEMBER 30

"This is the curse that goes out over the face of the whole land. For everyone who steals shall be cleaned out according to what is on one side, and everyone who swears falsely shall be cleaned out according to what is on the other side. I will send it out, declares the LORD of hosts, and it shall enter the house of the thief, and the house of him who swears falsely by my name. And it shall remain in his house and consume it, both timber and stones." (Zech. 5:3–4)

In 1978, Bruce Springsteen released the album *Darkness on the Edge of Town*. The album was dark, no mistake about that! The album's title song spoke to the darkness on the edge of town where everybody's got a secret that they can't face, yet they carry it with them, trying to hold it private all their lives. He sang of repeating the sins of the fathers in "Adam Raised a Cain." In "Streets of Fire," Springsteen set the song in the night, when "you don't care anymore," you're tired, and you just want to let go. In the song, he's been lied to, tricked, and deceived. He has no desire to live. What a dark album!

The album comes to my mind as I read today's passage, which describes one of two visions Zechariah has in chapter 5. The visions concern the darkness on earth as people steal, lie, swear falsely, and live wickedly and "iniquity" reigns over "all the land" (v. 6). So God in the vision sends out judgment, bringing down physical darkness upon those who live in moral darkness. As Springsteen sings in "Prove It All Night," also on his *Darkness* album, "You want it, you take it, you pay the price."

People can choose to live in darkness, but it comes with a price. God ensures that. The curse that goes out over the earth is one that brings down the houses of the wicked. One cannot practice vice virtuously. One can't sow seeds of wickedness and reap a crop of righteous joy.

This truth has two sides. In the midst of his darkness, Springsteen also sang of "the Promised Land." Acknowledging the "twister" coming, he noted that it would "blow everything down that ain't got the faith to stand its ground." But with faith, truth can remain even as the lies and brokenness are revealed and destroyed. In faithfulness to God, one finds life. That is the good news about choice!

Lord, I want to choose you. Forgive my sin and teach me righteousness. In your name, amen.

DECEMBER 1

Then I lifted my eyes and saw, and behold, two women coming forward! The wind was in their wings. They had wings like the wings of a stork, and they lifted up the basket between earth and heaven. Then I said to the angel who talked with me, "Where are they taking the basket?" He said to me, "To the land of Shinar, to build a house for it. And when this is prepared, they will set the basket down there on its base." (Zech. 5:9–11)

Few things excited me more as a third grader than the news that my grandparents were coming to visit. We usually only saw them once a year because travel was expensive and we lived almost two thousand miles away. Before they arrived, however, we always had an important task. Mom put everyone to work cleaning the house. From top to bottom, we cleaned until no dirt could be found.

Different people have different standards for a clean house. For some, clutter is normal; for others, it is taboo. Some don't mind a small amount of dirt and grime, while others want sparkle and shine. Today's passage gives a moral equivalent to cleaning the house immaculately. The message comes in the form of a vision.

In the vision, which begins several verses before today's passage, a woman represents evil. That woman is in a basket found in Judah among God's people. God has two women—with strong wings of a stork—arrive, pick up the basket, and fly it to Shinar, an ancient name for Babylon. There, evil is to stay. In Babylon, it can have its home.

God used this vision to teach that evil has no place among God's people. Like the grime in our house growing up, it is to be eliminated! There are places where evil is honored, emulated, and encouraged, but not in the house of God.

This is an important moral lesson for us. Our lives can always use some spring cleaning. We need to examine our lives for sin and seek, with God's transforming power, to move them from our homes to a faraway place. This is what God is working toward, and it should be our project as well. Evil doesn't belong in God's house.

Lord, I want to live in your holiness and goodness. Please help remove any evil from my heart and mind and bless me in your holiness. In your name, amen.

DECEMBER 2

Again I lifted my eyes and saw, and behold, four chariots came out from between two mountains. And the mountains were mountains of bronze. The first chariot had red horses, the second black horses, the third white horses, and the fourth chariot dappled horses—all of them strong. Then I answered and said to the angel who talked with me, "What are these, my lord?" And the angel answered and said to me, "These are going out to the four winds of heaven, after presenting themselves before the Lord of all the earth." (Zech. 6:1-5)

Our son obtained three degrees in philosophy, including a doctorate from Oxford University. His focus was the logic behind language. His doctoral dissertation was long, and I asked him if I might read it. He responded it was rather technical and not the kind of philosophy that I typically read—that is, not that of the classical philosophers looking at life and culture. I knew that but told him I still wanted to read it. What I didn't tell him was my true goal in reading it. I wanted to see if I could truly say that I *fully* understood every word for two entire consecutive paragraphs. Answer? I couldn't.

But my failure to understand all the nuances didn't stop me from appreciating what I read, nor from learning a few things too. I am reminded of that when I study today's passage. The passage is obscure, as is much of Zechariah. It's open to a wide range of interpretations. It moves into the realm of my son's dissertation. I may not understand it all, but I can still see things in the passage that touch me and make me grow.

The passage is the final of eight (some count them as seven) visions Zechariah had in the night. What the chariots and the horse colors represent, no one knows for sure. But one thing is certain: these present themselves to the Lord and then go out to all corners of the earth. This is right and seemly because the Lord is the Lord of *all the earth.*

God's rulership over all the earth causes me to examine my life. If God is the Lord of all the earth, how much of my life I have surrendered in obedience and faith to him? Do I hold back corners? Are there spots that I keep to myself and dare not let him near? Heaven forbid! I need God to roam freely throughout all that I am and all I do. He is Lord of all the earth and should be Lord of all my life. Even if I don't understand all the details and nuances.

Lord, take all of me, all my desires and moments, and make them yours. Amen.

DECEMBER 3

"And those who are far off shall come and help to build the temple of the LORD. And you shall know that the LORD of hosts has sent me to you. And this shall come to pass, if you will diligently obey the voice of the LORD your God." (Zech. 6:15)

I want to lose a few pounds—well actually, more than a few. So as I type this, I am eating a healthy meal. In preparation, I went into the kitchen to get a can of tuna and some crackers, my intended meal. I saw this box of toffee. It looked really good. I almost could hear it whisper my name. So I reached out my hand . . . and got a can of tuna. Whew. Crisis past, I sat down to eat and type.

I could have grabbed a piece of toffee. I still could. But if I did, my diet would be shot. I find sweets to be like the Lay's potato chip commercial from days gone by: "No one can eat just one." Now, there may be nothing wrong with me eating one piece of toffee, but I just wouldn't get the diet results I'm seeking. What I eat and do makes a difference in what I weigh and how I feel. It is that simple.

God made people with a remarkable power—the power to choose. We take actions based on our own thoughts and desires, and those actions have consequences. This was laid out in the earliest pages of the Bible. Remember the story of creation? God made light and separated it from darkness. God called the light *day* and the darkness *night*. God continues to ascribe names to his creation as each appears. So when God made Adam in his image, this meant, in part, that Adam reflected some of God in the world. This is shown when God brought the various animals before Adam and, for the first time, God doesn't assign the names, *Adam* does. Adam chose those names, and Scripture teaches that whatever Adam named the animals became the animals' names.

This remarkable power to choose is real. You have it. I have it. It's evident in today's passage. God promises certain events will occur if the people "diligently obey" what God says. God's promise gave the people a choice with consequences.

So it is with you and me. Today we have choices—not only in how we eat but in how we treat people, in what we do, and in our priorities and values. Our choices will have consequences ranging from great to terrible. I want to make good choices today.

Lord, give me wisdom and strength to make good choices today. In you, amen.

DECEMBER 4

*And the word of the L*ORD *came to Zechariah, saying, "Thus says the L*ORD *of hosts, Render true judgments, show kindness and mercy to one another, do not oppress the widow, the fatherless, the sojourner, or the poor, and let none of you devise evil against another in your heart." (Zech. 7:8–10)*

Snapshots, photographs, and pictures that capture a moment—we all take them, some more than others, and we enjoy going back through the memories those pictures bring. But there is a difference between a photograph and a movie. Movies and shows tell a story. They develop characters, follow plots, and engage the audience in ways that a photo can't. In a sense, a movie is a massive series of photographs put to sound and placed into a specific context.

Shows tend to be a bit more reflective of life to me. Life isn't a snapshot moment; it has movement. One thing flows into another. I have noticed this over and over. A moment comes and goes, but the movie of life continues unabated until it ends. We have no ability to hit a pause button on life and stop things. It moves on.

Today's passage highlights for me the difference between a photo and a show. If I look at a moment in my life, I might lose the truth that comes with the flow of a movie. God sees the flow of life, not only a moment here or there. I am called to render true judgments—not on certain occasions but as a lifestyle. Kindness and mercy aren't traits to be exercised only when I'm happy, well-fed, and feeling particularly generous. These are to be traits that are so bound up in who I am and how I think that they pervade every moment in my life—even when I haven't slept much, am in the midst of struggles, or find life's pressures folding down upon me. There are no excuses. Kindness and mercy should be my movie.

God follows his command to live a life of kindness and mercy with a specific application: no one should oppress the widow, the fatherless, the sojourner, or the poor. These people are often disenfranchised by society. They're easily overlooked, if not downright exploited. But God sees them, and he cares for them as much as he does for the married, the child of prestige and promise, the citizen, and the well-to-do. The movie of God's people should include God's concern for those faced with life's difficulties.

I want the movie of my life to reflect God's compassion and love.

Lord, grow your love in me. Teach me holiness at all times. In your name, amen.

DECEMBER 5

But they refused to pay attention and turned a stubborn shoulder and stopped their ears that they might not hear. They made their hearts diamond-hard lest they should hear the law and the words that the LORD of hosts had sent by his Spirit through the former prophets. (Zech. 7:11–12)

When I started playing guitar, I was good for about fifteen minutes of practice. Then I had to quit. The strings were killing my fingertips. Over time, however, I got to where I could play as long as I wanted without fingertip pain. The reason? Callouses developed on my fingertips from pressing them over and over on the steel strings. Those callouses were good things for guitar playing. However, if I needed those fingertips to read braille, I would be in trouble. They were no longer sensitive enough to discern the letters.

Consider this idea when reading today's passage. Zechariah explained that the people had developed callouses on their hearts. But these callouses had no good purpose; they were destructive. They deprived the people of knowing the reality that was the voice of God.

How did the people develop these callouses on their hearts? When they would hear God, they would ignore what they heard. Like a child who hears his parent say "Come here" and yet pretends not to hear and doesn't obey, so the people turned away from God's instructions for their lives. Over time, these small acts of disobedience became a horrible habit and made the people insensitive to God. They began to live as if there was no God. They heard and understood nothing from him.

I read this with melancholy feelings. I know there are times when God's clear instructions and voice are apparent to me, and yet I sometimes ignore them. Like a child who puts fingers in his ears to try to shut out a parent's directive, I push on as if I hear or know nothing. This isn't simply detrimental in the moment. Over time, it makes me insensitive to God's word in many arenas. I begin to lose touch with my God as my spirit becomes calloused to him.

This moves my prayer for a more sensitive and soft heart, even as it incites me to be more deliberative about hearing and obeying God. "Listen the first time!" as my dad used to say.

Lord, I repent from times I have ignored you. Please soften my heart and tune my ears to hear your voice. In your name, I pray, amen.

DECEMBER 6

And the word of the LORD of hosts came, saying, "Thus says the LORD of hosts: I am jealous for Zion with great jealousy, and I am jealous for her with great wrath." (Zech. 8:1–2)

Did you have a high school sweetheart? Perhaps a college romance? Maybe some other time when you were in love (or at least serious like!) with someone who then received attention from another? If so, you are likely familiar with feelings of jealousy. If not, watch a romantic comedy and you will often find jealousy rearing its ugly head.

Thinking of human jealousy "rearing its ugly head" makes passages like today's seem a bit off-putting. No one likes to think of God as someone experiencing the petty jealousies of human romance. This might move someone to conduct a word study on the Hebrew word translated as "jealousy" (*qana'*—קָנָא) to see if perhaps it sheds greater light on what is meant by "jealous." But the Hebrew word simply means "jealous." There is no hedging to be found.

The key to understanding God's jealousy is in *when* and *why* he is jealous. God's jealousy is a protective desire for what is best for people. God is jealous for our own good. God isn't pleased when ungodliness becomes the desire of our hearts. If we chase after false gods—idols that reflect our personal cravings instead of God's truth—then God's righteous love for us rises up. He is "jealous," seeking our good and imposing his holy wrath on sin, which is destructive to what God created us to be.

God's jealousy is not something that should drive anyone away from him. It should move us with responsive love toward him. Knowing God as a protecting God who seeks the very best for us isn't a bad thing. It's a marvelous safety net in life. As we walk confidently in his caring love, we're shielded from much of the pain of this world. It doesn't mean pain can't come into our lives for other reasons, but when that happens, we have a compassionate God on whom we lean and from whom we derive comfort.

This is part of faith, knowing that God cares for us with a possessive love. But this love is a good thing, and it secures our steps each day. I don't want to chase after other gods. I want to pursue the one true God, who loves me despite myself!

Lord, thank you for your love. Thank you for seeking my best. In your name, amen.

DECEMBER 7

*In the fourth year of King Darius, the word of the L*ORD *came to Zechariah on the fourth day of the ninth month, which is Chislev. Now the people of Bethel had sent Sharezer and Regem-melech and their men to entreat the favor of the L*ORD*, saying to the priests of the house of the L*ORD *of hosts and the prophets, "Should I weep and abstain in the fifth month, as I have done for so many years?" Then the word of the L*ORD *of hosts came to me: "Say to all the people of the land and the priests, 'When you fasted and mourned in the fifth month and in the seventh, for these seventy years, was it for me that you fasted?'"* (Zech. 7:1–5)

People are often driven by desires. The desire for money is the basis of capitalism, an economic system where people work and keep capital. Some work overtime to get more money for one purpose or another. People will dress a certain way to be attractive to others, seeking benefits from a relationship. Top athletes practice out of a desire to win. Desires are in focus in today's extended passage.

Some readers will notice that today's passage is the only one in the book that is out of order. Today's reading should have been on December 4. Why the adjustment? It struck me as seemly, since this is one of the few passages in the Bible that can be dated with precision. Scholars know that the "fourth day of the ninth month" in the "fourth year of King Darius" is December 7, 518 BCE. So as of this book's 2024 publication, today marks precisely 2,542 years from the day referenced.

The people of Bethel (which was in Israel, the northern kingdom) sent two men to ask Zechariah if they should continue fasting during the fifth month of the year as they had done during the captivity. Symbolism is rampant in what is done and said here. Bethel was a seat of idolatrous worship that had caused Israel's downfall. The named men who were sent to Zechariah had Babylonian names, symbolic of the country that had defeated and transported away those of Judah (the southern kingdom). The fifth month marked the month when the Babylonians had destroyed the temple over seventy years earlier. People remembered that by fasting during the fifth month for some seventy years. They also fasted in the seventh month, when the indigenous government of Judah had come to an end.

Zechariah answers by questioning their motives. Why were they fasting? For God or themselves? God cares about motives, even when we are doing something "good." We should always be looking to do good for the right reasons!

Lord, help me see my true motives as I seek to be pure before you. In you, amen.

DECEMBER 8

"Thus says the LORD: *I have returned to Zion and will dwell in the midst of Jerusalem, and Jerusalem shall be called the faithful city, and the mountain of the* LORD *of hosts, the holy mountain." (*Zech. 8:3)

The 1964 movie *A House Is Not a Home*'s theme song, written by Burt Bacharach, has been a hit twice, first sung by Dionne Warwick, then later by Luther Vandross. The lyric affirms that having a loved one present changes a house to a home: "A chair is still a chair even when there's no one sitting there. But a chair is not a house, and a house is not a home when there's no one there to hold you."

People long for the presence of love in their life. Not a temporary, come-and-go presence, but a permanent presence. The idea of God dwelling with people in a permanent fashion is an important and repeated biblical narrative. In the story of creation, people are different from all else God made. From the sun and moon to the birds and beasts, God made many good things. But only of man and woman does God say, "God created man in his own image, in the image of God he created him; male and female he created them" (Gen. 1:27). While God pronounced all of creation "good," he called only the creation of people "very good" (Gen. 1:31). Then in the garden of Eden story in Genesis 2–3, God actually walked through the garden, speaking and engaging with Adam and Eve.

The rebellion of Adam and Eve disrupted this close relationship and erected a barrier between people and God. But the promise was always one of God returning to dwell with his people. When God instructed Israel to make the tabernacle in the wilderness, he added, "Let them make me a sanctuary, that I may dwell in their midst" (Ex. 25:8). In building the temple, Solomon sought a house where God might "dwell forever" (1 Ki. 8:12–13). The prophet Ezekiel told of God departing from the temple and leaving his people as part of the destruction allowed upon Jerusalem (Ezek. 10). Yet the prophet Zechariah has already promised God would again return to his people (Zech. 1:16).

Today's passage affirms that God will dwell with his people. The Christian Scriptures echo this in Revelation 21, when the promise is made that with the New Jerusalem, God "will dwell with them, and they will be his people" (v. 3).

The presence of God turns a house into a home. That's a song worth singing!

Lord, I welcome you into my life. I long to live with you. In your name, amen.

DECEMBER 9

"Thus says the LORD *of hosts: Behold, I will save my people from the east country and from the west country, and I will bring them to dwell in the midst of Jerusalem. And they shall be my people, and I will be their God, in faithfulness and in righteousness."* (Zech. 8:7–8)

Our three-year-old grandson did *not* want to go to bed. He wanted to play all night long. I explained to him that once he went to sleep, the next day would come, and after his school was over, I would be at his home ready to play trains with him. He liked that! So off he went to bed. The next day, after school, he was ready to play. He doesn't forget promises like that, and it didn't matter how tired or busy I was; I wasn't going to let him down.

If a human grandfather can remember and keep a promise to his grandson, how much more will God be faithful to his promises? God assured the Jews that he would not only return to Jerusalem but bring back his people there as well. He would save them "from the east country and from the west country." He would bring his people to dwell in Jerusalem and be his people once again.

Interestingly, though, there is an important tagline. God says, "They shall be my people, and I will be their God, in faithfulness and in righteousness." Does God mean that God will be faithful and righteous? Or that the people will be faithful and righteous? The original Hebrew language can be read either way, and so can the English. This is because faithfulness and righteousness are rightly a two-way street between God and his people.

God models both traits. Over and over, Scripture points to God's character as faithful. If people aren't as close to God as they used to be, it isn't because God moved. God will stay faithful to his promises. As Dylan sings in "When You Gonna Wake Up," "God don't make promises that he don't keep." Similarly, righteousness is a definition of God's character and morality. He gives the word meaning.

But the second part of the tagline is important too. God's people are called to replicate God's faithfulness and righteousness. This is part of bearing God's image to the world. A fruit of being God's people is learning to be like God.

Lord, thank you for your righteousness and faithfulness. Teach me to be like you in these ways. May my life reflect your goodness to this world. In your name, amen.

DECEMBER 10

*Thus says the L*ORD *of hosts: "Let your hands be strong, you who in these days have been hearing these words from the mouth of the prophets who were present on the day that the foundation of the house of the L*ORD *of hosts was laid, that the temple might be built."* (Zech. 8:9)

When our son was three or four, he would often sing a church song that went "Rise and shine, and give God the glory." At that age, he couldn't yet pronounce his hard *G*, so the song sounded more like "And div Dod the dory." It gave the impression one was giving God a boat (a "dory"). When I was the same age, I still remember walking around singing the church song "Trust and Obey." The song's message is that when we hear God's word, our job is to trust it and live accordingly. I didn't really get the message; I just liked the melodic hook. Only when I got older did I begin to understand the song's message.

Today's passage is a marvelous one for both songs, that of my son and that of the four-year-old me. This passage comes in the midst of a set of promises that God is making through the prophet Zechariah. These promises included God calling his people back to populate Jerusalem, dwelling again in the temple, making his presence among his people, and faithfully and righteously securing his people against enemies. The people were charged with rebuilding the temple as they walked with God, also in faithfulness and righteousness.

Then in this flow of promise, God tells the people to "let" their hands "be strong." They were to work hard in what God charged them to do. This, of course, first involved trusting God to be true to his word. But within that trusting, the people had a job to do. They were to obey God and get to work. "Trust and obey" could have been their song and mantra.

Could God have built the temple himself? Could he have caused the wind and ground to shift and construct it? Could he have pronounced it into being, as he did creation? Of course. But that isn't the way God typically works. This earth was made for humanity to work in it, bringing God glory in that process. We "rise and shine," going about his business in trust and obedience, and seek to bring him glory rather than taking credit for our work. That is the point of this passage, which is the same as the two songs my son and I sang in youthful times.

Lord, I want to trust in your promises, stand on your word, and do those tasks you have set before my hands. Give me wisdom, inspiration, and strength in you, amen.

DECEMBER 11

"For there shall be a sowing of peace. The vine shall give its fruit, and the ground shall give its produce, and the heavens shall give their dew. And I will cause the remnant of this people to possess all these things." (Zech. 8:12)

Gardening is an amazing chance to understand God and life. It's taken me a while to figure it out. I've learned to prepare the ground, get rid of weeds, break up the clumps, ensure adequate drainage, and get the acidity right. Then I learned that you have to use the right kind of seeds for the weather and plant them at the right time to ensure they not only grow but have time to ripen. When all of this comes together, the harvest is plentiful and a time of great rejoicing! It's fun to rush to get corn boiling within minutes of being picked, knowing the sugars in the corn begin depleting almost immediately. We try to beat the insects and birds to the ripe tomatoes. We get the okra in the heat that few other plants can bear.

Gardening teaches us not only about life but about God. Not surprisingly, God uses gardening/agricultural metaphors throughout Scripture. I like the way he does so in today's passage.

The passage illustrates the importance and beauty of sowing "peace," a very important Hebrew word—*shalom* (שָׁלוֹם). The meaning of the Hebrew *shalom* spans a wide range of ideas in English. It includes peace but also indicates a wholeness, an intactness, the prosperity and success that come with good welfare, and a good state of health. It even includes the idea of friendliness, as peace is experienced with your neighbor. *Shalom* can mean peace among nations, tribes, and families as well as internal peace. It also includes peace with God and so can mean a deliverance and a salvation as well.

With all these traits wrapped up in that word, it's really important that we sow shalom! And when it is sown, it will reap a harvest. That harvest is described as the vine producing fruit and the heavens giving dew. Life is rich. Provisions arrive. Peace is experienced.

I want to sow peace. I want to be friendly, seek the success of others, try to put good things together rather than take them apart, help mend broken relationships, see the good in people, and so much more. I want to sow shalom.

God of shalom peace, help me be a shalom peacemaker. To your glory, amen.

DECEMBER 12

"And as you have been a byword of cursing among the nations, O house of Judah and house of Israel, so will I save you, and you shall be a blessing. Fear not, but let your hands be strong." (Zech. 8:13)

My sister Kathryn has always been a giver. Her compassionate heart is constantly looking to give to others. Whether providing material things, a listening ear, or time or energy for a task, I have seen my sister invest in others during my entire life. This is a godly trait and one that is emphasized in today's passage.

Judah had been through the wringer. They had left God, destroyed their covenant with him, defied his warnings, and paid the price. But God never abandoned them, and in today's passage, God promises a blessing for Judah. God says he will "save" Judah and Israel. "Save" is a word of deliverance. God was going to bring health, peace, and opportunity to Judah. God would rain upon the people his goodwill.

A very important principle follows God's promise of saving Judah. God says he will deliver them so that Judah will be a blessing to others. That is the way of God. God sends his blessings on his people for a reason. God isn't simply looking to reward certain folks with a cushy life. God is wanting to entrust blessings to his people with the expectation that those so blessed will share those blessings with others. We are blessed to be a blessing.

I find it useful to take a personal inventory periodically. What has God placed in my care or custody? What do I "have" that could be used to bless others? This doesn't just mean material things, although those are hugely important. It also includes time and talents. It includes access to opportunities. What emotional support, advice, or encouragement might I have for others? What deeds of service could I do for others? How can I pray for them?

If we live our lives trying to bless others in God's name, not for our own honor, then we will see God pouring more blessings into our lives. Now, we don't do it to get more blessings! Instead, we want to glorify God. As God's blessings come, we use them to bless others. It's a wash, rinse, and repeat process!

Lord, thank you for the many blessings in my life. Give me eyes to see the opportunities to bless others and the energy to do so. May it always be to your glory and in your name, amen.

DECEMBER 13

For thus says the LORD *of hosts: "As I purposed to bring disaster to you when your fathers provoked me to wrath, and I did not relent, says the* LORD *of hosts, so again have I purposed in these days to bring good to Jerusalem and to the house of Judah; fear not. These are the things that you shall do: Speak the truth to one another; render in your gates judgments that are true and make for peace; do not devise evil in your hearts against one another, and love no false oath, for all these things I hate, declares the* LORD*."*
(Zech. 8:14–17)

So much of the Bible reminds me of raising our five children. One parenting story I can readily tell without identifying the child involved because it happened with all five. I gave them a set of instructions, they blatantly disobeyed, and they were corrected to help them learn. Or I could give another parenting story that happened much more frequently. I gave them a set of instructions, they gave great effort in following them, and they were praised and affirmed.

The principles in my examples are found repeatedly in Scripture. Israel had wandered far from God in blatant disobedience. God warned them, trying gentle corrective measures, but nothing worked. Eventually, God brought disaster on the people, setting a course for later generations to follow God in faith rather than abandon him in rebellion. God was ready for his people's return. Indeed, God had orchestrated their return. Their return was God's goal from the beginning.

Then, having orchestrated their return, God assured the people that if they would walk in his ways, their paths would be blessed and marvelous. Their instructions weren't elaborate or hard to understand. Today's passage sets them out: speak the truth, deal with one another fairly and honestly, and be good to one another. As the people lived within these guardrails, they would be fulfilling the great commandment of God to love their neighbor as themselves (Lev. 19:18). This idea, together with the instruction to love God fully, wraps up the teachings of the Bible in a nice bow. The details get fleshed out more fully through other passages, but this is the root of it all. This is the path of blessing and affirmation.

The Bible teaches why God sets out the proper path for his people to follow: he is showing the path of blessing. This is the path that makes life better. A society of selfish lies will never stand. Nor will a life lived that way. God's way is the right way. Why would I ever choose another?

Lord, I want to follow you. Give me help to do so. In your name, amen.

DECEMBER 14

"Many peoples and strong nations shall come to seek the Lord *of hosts in Jerusalem and to entreat the favor of the* Lord. *Thus says the* Lord *of hosts: In those days ten men from the nations of every tongue shall take hold of the robe of a Jew, saying, 'Let us go with you, for we have heard that God is with you.'"* (Zech. 8:22–23)

We were living on about thirty acres, and I decided we had room for two cows. I bought two, got a cowboy hat and some boots, and I was ready to go. It was less than twenty-four hours before the cows found a fence failure and a way off the property. My cattleman skills were woefully deficient. It took me hours and almost a dozen friends to get the cows back where they belonged. I was expressing my frustration by commiserating with a buddy who owns cattle. He told me I went at it all wrong. I was trying to herd them back onto the property. What I needed to do was let them smell some food and then walk back to the property with the food. He said they would follow the food all day long.

In some ways, people are like those cows. If there's something we like, something that makes life better, we will readily follow it. That principle is behind today's passage.

Zechariah wrote of a time when God's blessing would be on Israel in open and obvious ways. It would be apparent to the watching world. Seeing is believing, as the expression aptly says, and when the world got a good look at what God was doing, they would come and seek God. People from around the world will come to "entreat the favor" of the Lord, meaning they will ask God to show them grace and acceptance. They will do so because they become aware that God is present with his people.

This Scripture has an important application beyond the affirmation of a bright future for God's people. This passage reminds me of the importance of living a life that shines the love of God out of our own lives into a world of darkness. As we let God's light shine, people see it and want it. Like the cows that follow good food, people will want to know what makes our life different and how they too can find joy and peace. We can be beacons of light for God, causing others to entreat him and seek a relationship with the Divine One. This makes me live more deliberately today.

Lord, may your light shine through me so the world better sees you. In you, amen.

DECEMBER 15

Rejoice greatly, O daughter of Zion! Shout aloud, O daughter of Jerusalem! Behold, your king is coming to you; righteous and having salvation is he, humble and mounted on a donkey, on a colt, the foal of a donkey. (Zech. 9:9)

Russian nesting dolls are often my wife's inspiration for gifts. She will find a small gift and put it in a box. She puts that in a larger box, which then goes in a larger box. She layers one gift into another, and one peels away the boxes like an onion. I feel like Zechariah has done the same thing for the reader with today's passage. He has layers of important things to consider.

This one verse in Zechariah has so much packed into it that it alone could serve for almost a week of devotionals and teachings. Consider the start: the "daughter of Zion" is to "rejoice greatly!" Similarly, the "daughter of Jerusalem" is to "shout aloud!" This is in the context of warring passages and a city under siege. Wartime was especially difficult for women, who feared the deaths of their husbands and sons in battle as well as the brutal actions of conquering enemies. These most vulnerable are told to get very excited! God was coming to the rescue. When God rescues, all his people can shout and rejoice!

God's rescue was coming through a king. Kings were responsible for leading the people in battle. Leadership in battle was one of a king's most important jobs. God was sending in his king to take care of the people. This king was "righteous." He wasn't an evil king or an idol-worshiping king. Those were the kings that caused Israel to *lose* their battles and their homeland. This king was God's king, righteous and "having salvation." This means the king himself was saved but also denotes that he would bring salvation or deliverance to the people.

The verse adds that the king is "humble." The Hebrew is also translated as "poor" and "afflicted." The king isn't pompous and proud but comes in riding a young donkey. Warring kings came into conquered cities riding massive horses. This king comes in humility, riding a donkey. For Christians, this passage is cited as a prophecy of Jesus, who made his "triumphal entry" into Jerusalem on a baby donkey (see Matt. 21:5).

In all the layers of this Russian nesting doll, one sees the glory of God assured, taking care of his people in surprising ways. I find peace here.

Lord, come into my life and give me your peace. I rejoice and pray in you, amen.

DECEMBER 16

*Ask rain from the L*ORD *in the season of the spring rain, from the L*ORD *who makes the storm clouds, and he will give them showers of rain, to everyone the vegetation in the field.* (Zech. 10:1)

We celebrate Christmas in our house. We follow the same pattern that I grew up with in Mom and Dad's house. On Christmas Eve, we open family presents, then on Christmas Day, Santa Claus comes and leaves an array of gifts. (Yes, even to our now adult children!) One might believe that the gifts on Christmas Day mysteriously arrive, or one might believe that the gifts are put out by someone who cares enough to give them. Of course, it is the latter.

In the same way, today's passage gives a glimpse into life that reveals a spiritual truth, informing our prayers as we seek God. Look carefully at the passage.

God instructs the Jews to "ask rain from the LORD." Asking for rain from God shouldn't seem an unusual thing, especially in an agrarian society. But God says to do it "in the season of spring rain." Asking God to give rain in the season of rain seems a bit bizarre. After all, can't one expect rain to arrive in the spring with or without God? As an extreme example of what I mean, I'm in a season of breathing; does that mean I credit God with each breath?

Just like my Christmas illustration, this passage is teaching that life can be seen in two ways. Some think things happen randomly. Others see life through eyes of faith that God is behind good things, even if those good things are expected in their season. Zechariah's oracle is teaching that God is the giver of all good gifts, even the small ones that we expect will normally occur—like my breath.

This truth of God at work is also core to teaching us to pray. This passage instructs us to pray what we believe is God's will. In other words, we don't simply rely on God to rain in the rainy season; we ask God to do so. This prayer both directs our conscious thought to the truth that God is at work in everything but also reminds us that we are still responsible to pray for God's provision. God engages us in his work. It becomes a joint enterprise!

I need to thank God and pray for good things that align with his will. We need to trust God, even if those good things are normal or "expected."

Lord, bless me and those I love as we seek to bless you today. In your name, amen.

DECEMBER 17

"I will whistle for them and gather them in, for I have redeemed them, and they shall be as many as they were before." (Zech. 10:8)

My dad was a whistler. He could whistle any melody on key and with beautiful vibrato. I have rarely heard anyone who could whistle like Dad. He had one particular short whistle that was three notes. It was a high note that slid to a note two notes lower and then abruptly went back to the original high note. This whistle meant "Where are you?" It was to be answered by the listener coming to the whistler. So when we were separated in a store and it was time to check out, one might hear "the whistle." Similarly, growing up, when we were outside playing and it was time to come in, we would hear "the whistle." Dad is gone today, but the whistle lives on, as we have used it in our family with our children.

Dad didn't start the whistle. Families have used whistling to summon people and animals for millennia. God uses whistling as a metaphor for his call on his people. In today's passage, God says, "I will whistle and gather them in." God is going to give the call for his people to respond. It's a call that the people should hear and recognize. It comes from the God who has "redeemed" or "bought" or "ransomed" (the Hebrew *padah*—פדה—means all of the above) his people.

We didn't ignore Dad's whistle when we were young. Nor should we ignore God's whistle in our lives. God isn't the Wizard of Oz, where people have to work to find him and then try to convince him to help in their lives. Rather, God is seeking his people. God does the necessary work to redeem his people, and God is looking to gather his people to himself.

I would be a fool to run from God and his whistle, although I confess there are times in my life where I have done so. It makes no sense that any of us wouldn't readily respond to God in faith, yet how often we're so caught up in what we're doing that we put off the whistler for a bit.

My goal today is to hear the whistle of my God and respond. In the choices I make, in what I pursue, and in what I think and say, I want to be responsive and in alignment with the God who has redeemed me and even now is still seeking me and calling me to himself. I want to be there and nowhere else.

Lord, tune my ears to hear your whistle. Tune my mind to understand your redemption. I want to follow and be yours. In your holy name, amen.

DECEMBER 18

"I will make them strong in the Lord, *and they shall walk in his name," declares the* Lord. (Zech. 10:12)

I recently attended the funeral of a buddy who always kept an interesting perspective on life. He had set up a family foundation, and he had labels for the family groups who served on the foundation board. He was in a group he called G-1. His children were G-2, and his grandchildren were G-3. He had several great-grandchildren he termed G-4, but they weren't old enough to do much beyond sucking their thumbs. *G* was his abbreviation for *generation*. He was the first generation (G-1), his children the second, and so on. I like his terminology. He tied his family together tightly.

Today's passage is one that can tightly tie together generations. It's a passage I pray over my five children and their spouses, G-2, as well as my (as of now) ten grandchildren, G-3. I want them made strong in the Lord, and I want them walking in his name.

This desire is one reason I write these devotionals. I want to give them and others an aid to grow stronger in the Lord. I pray these direct our attention to these often-lesser-read books in God's word, the Minor Prophets, while also engaging our minds with a deeper understanding of God. This will hopefully grow our desires for him and his holiness. My hope is also to make these practical so that our walk with him will better reflect his character and nature. Or as the passage says, so that we will "walk in his name."

A very important part of this passage is that God is declaring *he* will make the people strong in the Lord. This is the work of God in our life. God's work isn't accomplished, however, by us sitting passively by and letting him do all the work. We work with God. God gives us instructions, motivates us, and gently moves us, but we are to be working with him. I can put all the words in the world on this page, but if they aren't read and followed, they will do no good.

With five children and, as of this writing, ten grandchildren, I have a lot to pray for. If I draw up a wish list of what I wish to see in the next generations, this passage rises to the top. But to get there, God will engage me and use me. I need to focus on how to be his tool for this noble purpose.

Lord, make my family and loved ones strong in you. In your name, amen.

DECEMBER 19

Open your doors, O Lebanon, that the fire may devour your cedars! Wail, O cypress, for the cedar has fallen, for the glorious trees are ruined! Wail, oaks of Bashan, for the thick forest has been felled! The sound of the wail of the shepherds, for their glory is ruined! The sound of the roar of the lions, for the thicket of the Jordan is ruined! (Zech. 11:1–3)

Harvey Weinstein was flying high. Some might even say he ran Hollywood. He started Miramax films with his brother in 1979, putting out award-winning movies like *The English Patient*, *Shakespeare in Love*, and *Pulp Fiction*. Selling his company for $80 million to Disney, he and his brother set up another company in the biz. Some believed him untouchable, a man who could make or destroy a career. Then in 2017, things began to unravel. He settled with eight women who accused him of unwanted physical touching and sexual harassment spanning three decades. Soon, his wife left him, his company fired him, and the Academy of Motion Pictures Arts and Sciences expelled him. He will spend the rest of his life behind bars for his horrendous crimes against women.

The rise and fall of Weinstein should instruct everyone. Pride, arrogance, and power are no one's friends. They are intoxicants that destroy others and ultimately one's self. It's no different in today's passage, save for the additional information that God is the one who sees to the ultimate justice.

Judah and Israel's condition was self-inflicted. Yet God was not going to let those who sat in judgment over his people escape from their own abuses and crimes. Foreign leaders are described in today's passage with typical ancient Hebrew metaphors. The trees (Lebanon's cedars and cypress, the oaks of Bashan), the shepherds and lions, and even the thicket of the Jordan represent the wealth, power, and pride of the nations. God is going to raze them and bring them down.

God did as he said, and it should come as a warning to everyone. Our lives need a godly focus on what we have, our place in this world, and our responsibilities in our lives. God gives everyone what they need to do God's work. He also expects them to then do his work. Our purpose in life isn't to build up our own accounts, garner our own prestige, or satisfy our own appetites. We are to recognize all we have is HIS to do HIS will in humility and love.

Lord, forgive my selfishness and pride. Let me live to your glory, to tell your story, and to praise your name with all that I have. I seek you today. In your name, amen.

DECEMBER 20

"On that day the LORD will protect the inhabitants of Jerusalem, so that the feeblest among them on that day shall be like David, and the house of David shall be like God, like the angel of the LORD, going before them." (Zech. 12:8)

Our twin granddaughters were twenty months old and had come for a visit. They were running, not walking, everywhere. They had a particular fascination with our stairs, and the moment no one was watching, they would beeline over and start climbing. We quickly realized we needed a temporary fence or gate to stop access to those under the age of two! The protection was for their own good.

I need protection too. Not only from myself but from this world. Tragedy befalls people daily; we see it every day in the news. Yet my earnest prayer is that God will keep safe those I love.

Today's passage brings this to mind. This passage is found in what most scholars agree is the most difficult chapter in Zechariah. Pinning down precisely what the prophet was foreseeing is really hard, and scholars are deeply divided on their meaning. Regardless of these various interpretations, today's passage clearly speaks one profound truth: when God protects someone, even the feeblest will be powerful, in ways reminiscent of King David.

Remember King David? He was the only Israelite who readily accepted the giant Goliath's taunting challenge. While the rest of God's people cowered in fear, David was stunned at the giant's audacity. David understood the giant wasn't challenging the army's soldiers to fight him. In the grand picture, Goliath was taunting and challenging God Almighty. Hence David's reply, "Who is this uncircumcised Philistine that he would defy the armies of the living God?" (1 Sam. 17:26). David didn't need the king's armor to battle Goliath; he needed only his sling and a few stones. As long as God was protecting David, he would be fine. The battle belonged to the Lord.

I live in a frail and fragile world. So do those I love. My prayer is that we in faith embrace God and his protection. We see our day's opportunities as God's opportunities. We are here to be used by God Almighty as he displays his power and will. In that way, we are protected and provided for. We can run with confidence!

Lord, protect me and those I love as we seek to follow you. In your name, amen.

DECEMBER 21

"And I will pour out on the house of David and the inhabitants of Jerusalem a spirit of grace and pleas for mercy, so that, when they look on me, on him whom they have pierced, they shall mourn for him, as one mourns for an only child, and weep bitterly over him, as one weeps over a firstborn." (Zech. 12:10)

Most people like order. We categorize naturally. Whether putting things in alphabetical order, in numerical order, in buckets, or whatever, we tend to like orderliness over chaos and randomness. We use expressions like "First things first" or "Don't put the cart before the horse." We teach short phrases that provide order like "Ready, aim, fire" or "Stop, look, and listen before you cross the street; use your eyes, use your ears, and then you use your feet."

Today's passage sets up an interesting and important order. First God says that he will pour out a "spirit of grace and pleas for mercy" on the house of David and inhabitants of Jerusalem. Most translations do not capitalize the word *spirit*, for scholars don't see this usage as referencing God's Holy Spirit. Rather, this is a common usage of the Hebrew *ruah* (רוּחַ), which denotes both desire and ability.

The first order of business, then, is God pouring out on everyone a desire and ability for "grace" and "pleas for mercy." Pleas for mercy could also be translated as "supplication." What is indicated by this is God will pour out on the people a desire and ability to seek God's help and forgiveness. The question then arises, What will the people do with this desire and ability?

In this passage, Zechariah foresees a repentance by the people. They will look at the damage they have done, see how they have offended and grieved God, and mourn, weeping bitterly. This movement of the people to recognize their sin and repent comes after God gives them a spirit of grace and supplication. Hence the importance of the ordering.

In this passage, I see God imparting a desire and ability for me to repent. This passage cries out for my response—a response of regret and seeking mercy. Some Christian scholars believe this passage references the cost of the death of Jesus to God as he was pierced on the cross and the way it should move God's people to repent. I see layers and layers of interpretation, all pointing me to my knees.

Lord, I repent for the ways I have flaunted your love and walked away from you. Forgive my sin, please Lord. In your holy name, amen.

DECEMBER 22

"And on that day, declares the LORD *of hosts, I will cut off the names of the idols from the land, so that they shall be remembered no more. And also I will remove from the land the prophets and the spirit of uncleanness. And if anyone again prophesies, his father and mother who bore him will say to him, 'You shall not live, for you speak lies in the name of the* LORD.*' . . . On that day every prophet will be ashamed of his vision when he prophesies. He will not put on a hairy cloak in order to deceive."* (Zech. 13:2–4)

I'm sitting at a hotel room desk, writing on this passage before I head to court. We were assigned a new judge in a case, and the judge has called a hearing. He wants to talk about the case's status and give us the dates for when we will go to trial. This judge is well known for not letting dates slide. When he assigns a date, he enforces it. The hearing should prove interesting.

Meanwhile, today's passage speaks of God as a judge and ultimate enforcer. God has repeatedly spoken in Zechariah of what he will do "on that day." In today's passage, I have selected twice where God promises to remove two different kinds of apostasy and sin "on that day." Like my judge today, God doesn't readily let his assigned dates slide. What will God do?

First, God says he's going to rid his people of their false idols. God's people will no longer worship fictional gods alongside the one true God. Their eyes will see God as the one true Lord of all. Second, God is going to shut the mouths of the false prophets. Israel and Judah had a problem with professional prophets who tended to say what those who paid them wanted to hear. A day was coming when God was going to put a stop to that as well.

I think we all have a tendency to want God to fix things immediately. At least, the important things we would like to see set aright as soon as they start straying. To use accounting terms, can't God balance the books moment by moment or at least day by day? But that isn't the way God works. Still, God does make certain that a day will come when he sets things right and balances the books. This was true in Zechariah's day, and it's true today. God is more precise on this than any earthly judge before whom I might appear. This means both that I can trust him and that I should walk carefully, seeking his goodness each day.

Lord, I trust you to set my days right in your insightful timing. But I ask for your help in living today in faith, trusting you for that day. In your name, amen.

DECEMBER 23

"And I will put this third into the fire, and refine them as one refines silver, and test them as gold is tested. They will call upon my name, and I will answer them. I will say, 'They are my people'; and they will say, 'The LORD is my God.'" (Zech. 13:9)

The process of refining silver isn't much different today from how it was in Zechariah's time. The contaminated silver ore is poured into a vessel and then heated to a melting point. The pollutants float to the top as dross and are skimmed off, leaving the purified silver to cool down and harden.

God uses the smelting process to describe his work among his people. God will put his people through fire to remove the impurities that mar their beauty and effectiveness. God purifies his people through trials. Today's passage then says that God will test these people in much the same way, for that is the testing of purity for gold as well.

God's people respond to the fires of life stronger and purer, for they survive by calling on the name of the LORD. This "calling" isn't a magic formula where one incants the name of God and receives a reward. "Name" was more than a label. The Hebrew idea behind the word *name* is a statement of one's character expressed through their actions. It is akin to the résumé that one presents today.

So to call on the name of the LORD is to seek God for who he is and what he's done. We call on God's name when we ask him to be consistent with his character and bring his almighty power to bear in our life. When we call on God in this way, he will answer. He will claim us as his people. He puts his stamp on our life, saying, "These are mine!" This links to the final clause as we, his people, proclaim to all that he, the LORD, is our God.

This is an amazing comfort when facing life's difficulties and trials. In faith, we can see God will work through those trials to make us better. We also know that we don't go through those trials alone. God is with us. We can call on his divine character and power to sustain us until he rescues us, knowing he will be faithful to do both. These experiences move us into a tight relationship with him. I might not like the fire, but I love the results!

Lord, I confess the fires in life can burn me deeply. I pray that you sustain me and work in those fires to make me a more fit vessel for you. In your holy name, amen.

DECEMBER 24

The oracle of the word of the LORD to Israel by Malachi. "I have loved you," says the LORD. But you say, "How have you loved us?" "Is not Esau Jacob's brother?" declares the LORD. "Yet I have loved Jacob but Esau I have hated." (Mal. 1:1–3)

Several of our grandchildren were at our home recently. These included our three-year-old grandson and his twin twenty-one-month-old sisters. Late in the day, our grandson hit his "pent-up energy" mode and began playing quite roughly. Our daughter stepped in and diverted his energy before he hurt his sisters through collateral damage. He wasn't happy with her stepping in and began to flail a bit. Our daughter put him in time-out. Meanwhile, the granddaughters took the moment to make a mad dash for the stairs, something they aren't old enough to maneuver safely. The off-limits stairs seem to have some appeal. Our daughter ran over and stopped them by step two. This was a great opportunity to watch some great parenting. It also informs me on today's passage.

Today starts the final of the "Minor Prophets," or "shorter prophets" as they might be termed. The oracle comes from Malachi, a word in Hebrew that means "my messenger." Malachi's message that underlies the entire book starts right here in the first verses. God declares to the Israelite audience, "I have loved you." The Hebrew verb tense doesn't mean God loved them only in the past. It means that God loved them in the past and loves them in the present. God wants his people to know that they are loved and implies they always will be loved. Full stop.

The audience of Malachi's message challenges God. "How have you loved us?" they retort. The book will make clear that their cynicism has grown from the seeming futility of following God. Life has never become the bed of roses they expected. It was tough and rocky, with no hope on the horizon.

Yet God loved them. He chose them from their beginning with Jacob. God didn't select the twin Esau, and that twin didn't receive God's special blessings. Does that mean all is roses? No! Just like my grandchildren, God has to stop us, at times put us in time-out, take us away from dangerous stairs we want to climb, and direct us in life. Being God's child is a daily, sometimes ordinary process of living a godly life. This message is important. God loves you and me. Life may not always seem to confirm that, but it is true!

Lord, help me appreciate your love. Grow your love in me. In your name, amen.

DECEMBER 25

"A son honors his father. . . . If then I am a father, where is my honor? . . . says the LORD of hosts to you, O priests, who despise my name. But you say, 'How have we despised your name?' By offering polluted food upon my altar. But you say, 'How have we polluted you?' By saying that the LORD's table may be despised. When you offer blind animals in sacrifice, is that not evil? And when you offer those that are lame or sick, is that not evil? Present that to your governor; will he accept you or show you favor? says the LORD of hosts." (Mal. 1:6–8)

Everyone has heard it. Character is most evident in how you behave when no one is watching. Think about it in your own life. Are there things you do or refrain from doing when someone is watching you versus when you're alone? Are there things that you should do but that don't get the full treatment when you're alone? Today's passage is a cousin to that principle.

God can't be seen. That truth is apparent to all. As a result, people have a tendency to act as though he isn't there or at least doesn't fully know what they're doing or thinking. Malachi's people had fallen into that state. Their excitement over finishing the temple rebuild had faded. Sacrifices were no longer a chance to show God great love and appreciation. They had become stale rituals. They were done at a cost, but the cost wasn't great. Although the people were supposed to sacrifice the purest and best from among their flocks, they had gotten to a point where they used the required sacrifices to cull their herds of sick or deformed animals. They acted as if God weren't truly there watching. Just because they couldn't see God, they weren't too concerned that he was seeing them.

God tells the people he is fully aware of their actions. As sons, they were to be honoring God the Father. Instead, they were giving him less than their best. This was, in fact, dishonoring God. For if their rulers came and asked for their share of sheep as a tax, they wouldn't pawn off on their rulers the worst of their sheep. They would give the ruler his proper due.

We don't see God, but does he see us? The answer is "Most definitely!" When we bring something of service to God, when we work for God, or when we seek to display him to the world, we should *always* bring him our best A game. We should seek to live godly lives and do what is right regardless of who is watching. After all, God always gives his best, even when we aren't looking.

Lord, forgive me, and help me give you my best efforts today. In your name, amen.

DECEMBER 26

"For from the rising of the sun to its setting my name will be great among the nations, and in every place incense will be offered to my name, and a pure offering. For my name will be great among the nations, says the LORD of hosts." (Mal. 1:11)

In youth group growing up, we used to sing a song based on this verse. We sang the simple refrain, "From the rising of the sun to the setting of the same, the name of the Lord is to be praised." We sang it enough that decades later, the melody and words play in my mind as I write today's devotional and teaching.

As I have mentioned in a few prior devotionals, the Hebrew idea of "name" becomes important in passages like this. In ancient Hebrew, a "name" isn't simply a label assigned at birth and registered in government documents. When one spoke of another's name, they spoke of the person's character as displayed in their actions. It's akin to their résumé or curriculum vitae.

So when called upon to praise the name of God, his people are called upon to recount his wondrous deeds and accord him the honor properly due him for those deeds—that is, the honor due his "name."

Think through the deeds of God. Maybe even say them out loud. We know God's biblical deeds. From creating a world to be habitable to humanity to creating humanity in ways that we can relate to him. From teaching people how to walk in fellowship with him to restoring that fellowship after humanity has betrayed and strayed from God. As Christians, we can celebrate the incarnation, life, death, and resurrection of Jesus our messiah. The list can go on and on.

But our praise of God's name should not be limited to his deeds in Scripture, for God is at work today. We should think about, proclaim, and give him due praise for his work today. From each breath I breathe to the opportunities to use my life for his service, from the depths of despair from which he raised me to the joy he has put in my heart, I should praise God. He has heard my cries for help. He has sustained me through dark nights. He has lifted me when I have fallen. Where would I be without this God?

We are right to praise him all day long! The song should never leave my mind!

Lord, I praise you for the wondrous God you are! WOW! In your NAME, amen!

DECEMBER 27

Have we not all one Father? Has not one God created us? Why then are we faithless to one another, profaning the covenant of our fathers? (Mal. 2:10)

I love America. As a country, we have many flaws, and much of our system is messed up, but we also have some amazing strengths. Interestingly, I find that many of our problems are tied to our strengths. It isn't always so simple as putting them into separate buckets. For example, America is a country of rugged individualism. Children are taught that it doesn't matter where their family is on the ladder of success; they can succeed. Any child born in America is allowed to become whatever they choose, within the scope of their abilities. No one is automatically stuck in some station in life simply because they were born into it.

Yet this same rugged individualism can be a source of problems. Because everyone has the freedom to be who they want to be and do what they want to do, we run certain risks. Within the bounds of the law, people are encouraged to *think* independently. While that is a good thing, it opens the door to people to *live* independently without regard to a true social obligation we have to one another as followers of God. This concern is delivered in today's passage.

Judah had reached a point where people weren't living up to their community obligations to one another. This was true on a larger scale, as the priests and leaders weren't properly fulfilling their roles to the detriment of the community. But it was also true on a more personal level where people were failing in their day-to-day living to the detriment of the greater community at large. Marriages were falling apart, families were divided, religion had become an empty ritual, and more. These were failings by individuals, but the target of today's passage is understanding the impact these personal failings had on the community.

Rugged individualism can be a good thing, but the idea of commitment to community must never be lost. We owe our neighbor the duty of loving them as we love ourselves. We should look to the interests of others as well as of those close and dear to us. That means we don't take advantage of the unwary, we help those who are downtrodden, and we give aid where helpful. As the community thrives, we thrive. But when the community suffers, we suffer. That is God's way.

Lord, help me live with a community consciousness, to your glory and name, amen.

DECEMBER 28

You have wearied the LORD *with your words. But you say, "How have we wearied him?" By saying, "Everyone who does evil is good in the sight of the* LORD, *and he delights in them." Or by asking, "Where is the God of justice?"* (Mal. 2:17)

I have a buddy, Bob, who figures God is good for a fixed number of his prayers. As Bob states it, he thinks God will listen for a bit, grant a few concerns, but then move on to another person's prayers. I have told Bob he has watched the movie *Aladdin* a bit too much. He has confused God with a genie. God no more tires of hearing the prayers of his children than I tire of getting phone calls from mine.

Yet here is a passage from Malachi where the prophet says, "You have wearied the LORD with your words." Does Malachi agree with Bob? Is it three wishes and you're out? Absolutely not! God's weariness in today's passage stems from the content of what the people are praying and saying, not the frequency or number of their requests. The people were mystified with the prosperity of the wicked. They wanted and thought God should smite those who were doing evil and getting away with it. Where was God's justice?

Even probing God with questions doesn't rile God up in Scripture, unless it's done in a certain way. Look more carefully at today's passage. The people weren't asking God why the evil prospered. They weren't seeking God's wisdom or revelation. They were indicting God. They were accusing him, trying him, and judging him. They had decided that God delighted in evil people doing evil things. They were denying that a God of justice existed.

This crossed a line. We are called to speak with God and even to question him. He wants us to understand him better. He wants us to challenge the evil in this world. But we do so with respect, remembering that he is God. We don't wrongfully accuse him and judge him. That's what made him weary, not the frequency of the prayers.

So for all the Bobs out there, talk to God incessantly, but remember who he is in the process. He's not your bellman, butler, or concierge to take your luggage to your room, get your laundry ready, or find you a dinner reservation. He's no genie in a bottle. He is the one true God. There is no other, and he delights in sincere dialogue with his children.

Lord, help me understand you better. Grow me closer to you. In your name, amen.

DECEMBER 29

"Then I will draw near to you for judgment. I will be a swift witness against the sorcerers, against the adulterers, against those who swear falsely, against those who oppress the hired worker in his wages, the widow and the fatherless, against those who thrust aside the sojourner, and do not fear me, says the LORD of hosts." (Mal. 3:5)

I had long been a Dylan fan when Bob released *Slow Train Coming* in 1979. The title song is an awesome recognition that God's accountability will arrive one day. We may not see it today, but it's coming down the tracks, most assuredly. It is Bob's slow train coming.

In the song, Bob begins by expressing his repulsion that people are oblivious to what the future holds: "Sometimes I feel so low-down and disgusted; can't help but wonder what's happenin' to my companions." Bob sings of people who are living as if judgment is never going to happen. In one verse, he explains, "Man's ego's inflated, his laws are outdated, they don't apply no more; you can't rely no more to be standin' around waitin'. In the home of the brave, Jefferson turnin' over in his grave. Fools glorifying themselves, trying to manipulate Satan." With each set of stanzas, Bob repeats, "And there's a slow, a slow train coming. Up around the bend." No one will stop the train of God's judgment.

Malachi could have footnoted Bob's song if Malachi were delivering today's passage in modern times. The passage is part of a section where the people are challenging God's justice. People saw blatant sinners prospering, and it made them wonder why God wasn't doing something about it. In Malachi's words, sorcerers, adulterers, liars, abusers, and manipulators were prospering. Or as Bob put it in modern terms, there were "big-time negotiators, false healers and woman haters, masters of the bluff and masters of the proposition, but the enemy I see wears a cloak of decency. All nonbelievers and men-stealers talkin' in the name of religion." Bob sang God's judgment was coming like a slow, powerful, unstoppable train. It was up around the bend. God said it in Malachi.

God will judge the evildoers of our world. Wrong may prosper temporarily but it won't eternally. God is going to bring judgment crashing down on all unrighteousness. Needless to say, the wise person will live accordingly, and the foolish person will suffer the consequences. I want to be wise!

Lord, forgive my foolish ways. Reclothe me in your righteousness. In you, amen.

DECEMBER 30

"Bring the full tithe into the storehouse, that there may be food in my house. And thereby put me to the test, says the LORD of hosts, if I will not open the windows of heaven for you and pour down for you a blessing until there is no more need." (Mal. 3:10)

Important life lesson on money: don't grocery shop on an empty stomach. I have done so. Repeatedly. Without exception, it leads to excess purchasing. I have bought food I don't even like because it seemed right in the moment.

Another important life lesson on money: don't rob God. "Well of course not!" you might exclaim. "No one sane would rob from someone who knows everything. You could never get away with it." Yet rob God we do. "How?" you might ask. See today's passage. These comments and questions are not mine; they are the people's response to God's declaration in verse 8 that they are robbing him. When God accuses the people of robbing him, the people recoil in horror. They say, "We never robbed you!" They were thinking about breaking into the temple and stealing something from God. That wasn't what God was talking about.

God had blessed the people. It may not have been as bountiful as the people wanted or even, at some times, needed. But God blessed them. So it is with us today. Every breath we take is a blessing from God. Every loved one is a blessing from God. These blessings are built into a system where, biblically speaking, they are entrusted to us by God. We acknowledge this by using the blessings from God to give back. Under Moses, God instructed his people to give a tenth of what they received.

The Old English had a word for "tenth"; it was *teoþa*. The letter that looks like an odd *p* is the Old English letter *thorne*, pronounced like a normal *th*. If we replace that letter with its sound (*th*), we can hear the Old English *teotha*, which evolved into the modern English word *tithe*. A *tithe* literally means a tenth.

The people failed to give God his tenth. Why? Were they uninformed? More likely, the text hints that they didn't think they could afford it. That was an insult to God. It was as if God couldn't give them enough for them to obey him. Mercy! God always gives enough for obedience. Hence he tells them, "Test me on this. You obey, and see if I don't rain down blessings!" I never need to doubt God.

Lord, give me faith to trust you with the blessings you provide. In you, amen.

DECEMBER 31

"But for you who fear my name, the sun of righteousness shall rise with healing in its wings. You shall go out leaping like calves from the stall. And you shall tread down the wicked, for they will be ashes under the soles of your feet, on the day when I act, says the LORD of hosts." (Mal. 4:2–3)

God is a communicator. He wants people to hear his message. God speaks truly, and he informs those who will listen about important things. God gives messages that instruct. His messages help people grow and mature. He offers insights that bring peace and joy. He explains life in ways that produce fulfillment and success. But these messages are both affirming and negating. God's messages include blessings as well as warnings of what brings misery, discontent, failure, and more.

In today's passage, God speaks through Malachi of what the future holds for those who follow God faithfully. Righteousness doesn't destroy the people of God; it brings them healing. Those who experience God in faithful love are like newborn calves bolting to life. The evil and wickedness of the world doesn't live in triumph over God's people. God will see that the wicked are destroyed at the right time.

God speaks these words as the twelve shorter prophetic books come to an end. He does so with a promise to speak further to his people and to send Elijah, which means "Jehovah is my God." He promises the coming Elijah will turn the hearts of the people toward one another and toward God. (This causes many in the days of John the Baptist to question whether he was the promised Elijah.)

As this year draws to a close and these devotional studies in the Minor Prophets finish, I ruminate on the lessons God's words have taught us over the year. God has spoken of the need for humble and faithful obedience. God has spoken of blessing over the faithful and destruction and judgment over the haughty, the abusers, and the disobedient.

God will always communicate; the question is, Will I listen and heed? Do I have enough sense to hear God's message, trust in it, and then respond in obedience? If I do, I will be blessed by God. Many in ancient Israel never really warmed up to God's message. But others lived and drank deeply from his promises. I want to live in the word of God and experience all that he offers in life.

Lord, forgive my sin as I seek to follow your word more deeply. In you is my amen.